Business B7

MW01519814

TABLE OF CONTENTS
& ACKNOWLEDGEMENTS

PAGE

Module 1

CREATING VALUE FROM SCIENCE AND TECHNOLOGY

John Medcof

1.1   INTRODUCTION

We live in a world imbued with technology. The hallmark of our age is the high standard of living brought to us through the harnessing of technology to human purposes. Modern medicine, automobile and aerospace transportation, refrigerators, electric lighting, heating devices, cell phones, televisions and access to the internet are all part of the technological cornucopia in which we live.

Remarkably, a very large proportion of these technologies have been brought to us by firms operating in markets with the intention of making profits. Although governments and individuals have done much to encourage the invention and dissemination of such technologies, private sector business firms and their founders have contributed greatly to the application of science and technology to practical purposes. Their business model is based upon the proposition that, if money is invested in the development of technology-based products that are useful to people, that money can be recouped by selling those products to those people. The success of this business approach is probably founded on two factors. First, those developing and selling the new products are motivated by the prospect of handsome profits to do the hard work and to take the risks necessary. That said, some of the great innovators have also been motivated by the opportunity to improve the lives of people with their inventions. The second factor in the business approach is that the market is an effective way to validate a new product. If people find that it is not worth their money, they stop buying. The market is a great discriminator in this respect but we can all think of cases in which it may not have made the best decision.

MINT (the Management of Innovation and New Technology) is the field of study which focuses upon firms and industries that prosper through the commercialization of science and technology. Although some science and technology can be found in almost any business, there are some industries which depend particularly upon the commercialization of science and technology. For example, in aerospace, billions of dollars are spent on developing new jetliners which are sold to airlines, governments and other businesses. Thousands of scientists and engineers are involved in such development efforts because a successful airliner uses the theories and principles of aerodynamics, electronics, materials and many other sciences. Similarly, the pharmaceuticals industry is built upon the discovery and creation of new drugs by thousands of scientists and medical practitioners who are experts in the medical sciences. These large up-front investments are made on the premise that they can be made back, with a profit, when the products are brought to market. As it happens, the commercialization of science and technology

- 1 -

has been for many years a very effective way to make money, as seen from the fortunes built in high technology industries such as aerospace, pharmaceuticals, biotechnology, automobiles, electronics, computers and software.

The study of the Management of Innovation and New Technology (MINT) focuses upon the management of innovation in high technology firms. Firms like IBM, GSK, Intel and Bombardier base their success on being able to out-innovate their competitors with products that embody high levels of technical sophistication. They come to market with original new products, and no sooner do competitors imitate them, than these firms launch yet another generation of even better products. For example, Microsoft brings new versions of its office suite to the market every few years. Although there are criticisms of each new generation, each is adopted and used by millions of organizations and individuals. If Microsoft did not constantly improve its office suite, competitors would soon take market share away from them. By constantly innovating Microsoft foils the efforts of competitors. Microsoft's software is a high tech product and Microsoft has legions of software engineers and people in related technical professions whose sole activity is to out-innovate competitors and prospective competitors.

Of course, innovation is not confined to high technology firms and can be pursued as a field of study outside of the context of high technology industries. In addition, high tech firms do many things very well in addition to innovation and their success is partly based upon those other capabilities. It remains true, however, that high technology and innovation have had a remarkably synergistic association over the last many years, and together they have driven the economic growth of firms (e.g. Intel), industries (e.g. consumer electronics), regions (e.g. Silicon Valley) and nations (e.g. Japan).

Management in innovative high technology firms is worthy of study because those firms are of great economic importance in the 21st century and because their methods of management are generally considered to be innovative, very effective, and appropriate models for other firms to imitate. But what do we mean by "high technology" and what do we mean by "innovation"?

1.1.1 What is High Technology?

Currently, there are three definitions of high technology in common use. All are widely used so we should be familiar with them to keep them clear in our writings and discussions.

The "Information Technology" Definition of High Technology

By one definition, firms and industries are said to be high tech if their products are used in information technology applications. By this definition firms like IBM, Dell, Compaq and Hewlett Packard are high tech because they make computers and related equipment; firms like Microsoft and Oracle are high tech because their product is software; firms like Intel, Texas Instruments and Solectron are high tech because they make electronic semiconductors; firms like Nortel, Lucent and Motorola are high tech because they make sophisticated telecommunications equipment. The primary high technology industries based in information technologies are: computers, software, electronics, and telecommunications equipment. Some firms are present in more than one of these industries. For example, IBM is big in computers and software. This information technology definition of high technology is widely used in the popular press, for instance, in newspapers and popular business magazines such as **Business Week**.

The "R&D Intensity" Definition of High technology

A second definition of high technology is based on the idea that any business that is highly dependent upon sophisticated science and engineering for its products is high tech, not just those in information technology industries. On the basis of this definition economists have invented a metric called "R&D Intensity" to measure dependence on high technology. Its premise is that the greater the proportion of income that is spent on science and technology, the greater the dependence on technology, and the more high tech a firm or industry is.

$$\text{R\&D Intensity} \;=\; \frac{\text{Total annual expenditure on R\&D}}{\text{Total annual sales income}}$$

Annual expenditure and income are the usual measures for R&D Intensity but five year or other time periods can also be used. Another variant is to divide the number of employees with technical backgrounds by the total number of employees. However, the usual measure is the annual expenditures and income as shown above.

On this second definition, the information technology industries (computers, software, electronics and telecommunications) are high tech and they are joined by the pharmaceutical and aerospace industries. Companies in the pharmaceuticals industry invest billions of dollars annually in the development of new drugs. A very high proportion of those expenditures are for the salaries of people with scientific and technical expertise who understand the science of drugs. The same holds in the aerospace industry. New airplanes, satellites and rockets involve investments of billions of dollars to develop the science that makes them possible. By this second broader definition of high tech firms such as Merck, Johnson & Johnson, Lilly and GSK are high tech because they make pharmaceuticals; and firms such as Boeing, Lockheed Martin, Bombardier and Airbus are high technology because they make aerospace products.

The "Total Expenditures Definition" of High Technology

The premise of this definition of high technology is that any firm or industry which spends a great deal of money on science and technology is high tech, even if the firm is not highly dependent on technology. For example, the automobile industry spends huge amounts of money on research and development every year but because its products are expensive and its annual sales so high the industry's R&D Intensity is not particularly remarkable. Yet, because the industry spends so much money on technology it is highly sophisticated in its business practices around those expenditures, and in the science and technology on which it is spent. Firms like GM, Toyota and BMW are high tech because they make automobiles full of the science of materials, electronics, emissions control and combustion.

– 3 –

In summary the MINT field of study focuses upon innovative high technology firms that tend to be found in industries such as aerospace, automobiles, computers, electronics, software, pharmaceuticals and telecommunications because those are the large industries which are highly dependent on technology and/or spend a great deal of money on technology. This is not to say that there are no innovative, high technology firms in other industries, only that these industries provide the most readily available examples. For example, many medical equipment firms develop and manufacture highly sophisticated equipment such as MRI's and artificial hearts. These others are high tech as well and will be used as examples from time to time.

1.1.2 What is Innovation?

Given that MINT focuses upon the management of innovation in high technology firms it is natural to ask what innovation is. Innovation is the creation of new products, processes or services which have economic value. Notice that for the purposes of MINT and the business perspective taken in this module, something new is not considered a true innovation unless it also has some economic value to the firm or other people.

The innovations of interest in the study of MINT are in both products and processes. **Product innovations** are changes in the things that firms sell to customers. For example, a new drug developed by a pharmaceutical firm is a product innovation. **Process innovations** are changes in how the firm does its business. For example, if a pharmaceutical firm develops a new way of manufacturing a drug which produces exactly the same drug but for half the cost, that is a process innovation. Henry Ford is famous for two innovations, a new product (the Model T car) and for a new way of manufacturing cars (the assembly line.)

Innovations can also vary in degree. **Radical innovations** make a fundamental change such as creating completely new product and/or way of making it. For example, the invention of the personal computer was a radical innovation since it lead to the creation of a completely new, multi-billion dollar industry. On a more modest scale, **incremental innovations** make small but economically significant changes. For example, the development of the rear-view mirror was an important contribution to the development of the automobile that has had economic impact but has not radically altered the industry or the automobile.

1.2   THE TECHNOLOGY COMMERCIALIZATION VALUE CHAIN

The fruits of science and technology are brought to market through the Technology Commercialization Value Chain. This value chain has three principal stages: **Invent, Create, Extract**; captured in the acronym **I♦C♦E.** You will notice that the letters in the acronym are separated by diamonds, the symbol for decision points in flow charts. Those diamonds represent extremely important decisions in the technology commercialization value chain which will be explained below. Figure 1.1 on the next page is a diagram of the technology commercialization value chain. Its parts will now be explained.

The essence of the technology commercialization value chain is the mobilization of technology to meet a market need in a way that constitutes a sound business proposition.

Consider **technology**. Millions of scientists and engineers around the globe are constantly working to increase our understanding of technology. Scientists focus on basic research which hopes to discover new scientific knowledge, such as the molecular structure of silicon or the metabolic processes of cancer cells. Engineers focus on the more practical applications of that scientific knowledge. For example, they design engines based on our scientific knowledge of metals and the processes of gasoline combustion. This great store of scientific knowledge has huge potential for meeting the needs of people; for transportation, medicine, entertainment, communication, to name just a few. In its raw state, though, this knowledge does not solve human problems. On the other side is the **market**. There are billions of people around the world with needs to be fulfilled. They have money which they are willing to spend to do that. The development of a technology to the point at which it can actually meet the needs of people, at a price they can afford, is the essence of the technology commercialization value chain. Further, the firms that develop, manufacture and market those products will do so only if it is a viable **business** proposition for them. The mobilization of technology to meet a market need in a sound business underlies all the stages of the technology commercialization value chain.

Figure 1.1
The Technology Commercialization Value Chain: I♦C♦E

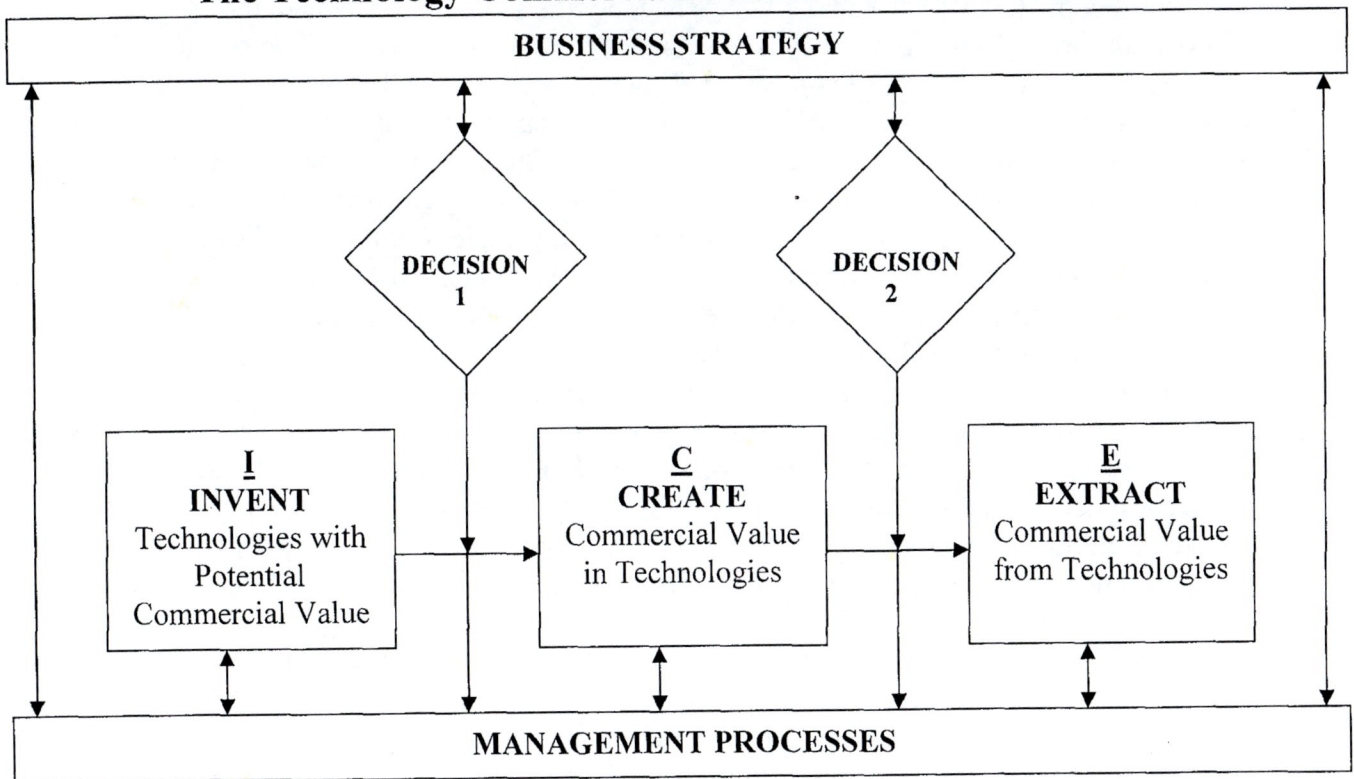

In the **Invent Stage** of the technology commercialization value chain organizations investigate technologies and markets looking for combinations of them which offer

module 1 (1) 2007 07 28.doc

5

business opportunities. **Technologies** are researched to find any that have the potential to meet identifiable market needs. For example, pharmaceutical firms look for molecules that have the potential to become drugs which can be sold to people with medical conditions. And firms do not necessarily confine themselves to scanning the potential technologies which they own themselves. They will scan scientific journals and visit universities and government laboratories to find any promising technologies that may be available. This increases their technology options immensely and can provide a very significant strategic advantage over competitors. Intellectual property protection through patents and other means is also investigated at this stage. Firms must ensure that there is sufficient protection to make the technology viable commercially. **Market** opportunities are also investigated to find any that might be pursued using available technology or a technology that could be developed. For example, by talking to customers in the 1970's IBM found that there was a growing demand for personal computers. They soon realized that they had technologies that could be developed to meet that growing market and set to work developing the IBM PC. Investigators must also be constantly asking if a technology/market match is a **viable business proposition**. There are two parts to this consideration. One is whether the proposition is financially viable. Will the income from the product cover the costs and provide some profit? The other is whether this proposition would be consistent with business strategy. For example, would the product that is being proposed be of high enough quality to be consistent with the quality image that the firm is trying to maintain for itself as part of its overall strategy? A particular market/technology/business opportunity that appears to have some promise is called an **MTB Proposition**. When a particular MTB Proposition is developed and then identified as very likely to be a viable business venture it is taken on to the next stage in the technology commercialization value chain, the Create Stage. However, at this point it is important to remember that the MTB Proposition still has only potential commercial value.

In the **Create Stage**, attention turns seriously to the implementation of a business proposition. There are three major tasks to be accomplished in this stage: technology development, market development, and development of a viable, detailed business plan. All these create value in the MTB Proposition which was not there before. **Technology Development** refers collectively to three activities. The first, **product development**, involves creating physical examples of the product as it would be used by customers. Several prototypes may be tried and intense technical work may be needed to give the product the characteristics which customers want. A second part of technology development, **process development**, creates the manufacturing technology that will be used to make the product. This may also require intense technical work and experimentation. The manufacturing process must be designed and costed. This can involve prototypes and trial runs with pilot manufacturing facilities. Process development helps confirm that the product can be manufactured at a cost that allows it to be sold to customers for a price they are willing to pay and with the product features that they want. A third facet of technology development is to develop more fully the level of **intellectual property protection** needed to protect the new product and process from imitation by competitors, through patenting for example. An appropriate level of protection must be agreed upon and implemented to make the MTB Proposition commercially viable. **Market development** is the second major facet of Value Creation. Thorough market research must be carried out to be sure that potential purchasers really do want the new product, how much they are willing to pay for it, and what changes to the original **product concept** will make it even more marketable. The **target market** must be identified with some precision for this to be done effectively. A **marketing strategy** must be developed. In high technology industries approval from **government regulatory bodies** is usually required in order to get legal access to the markets targeted. For example, in the pharmaceuticals and aerospace industries, government approvals for safety and other considerations typically take several years and tens of millions of dollars. In high technology industries ensuring **compatibility with standards** is also essential in market development. For example, a new computer must be compatible with existing networks and other computers and software if it is to be economically viable. The third major task in Value Creation is to develop a more complete and compelling **business plan** than was used at the end of the Identify Stage. Many more details are now necessary to make a complete case for the business viability of the proposed venture. As more specifics about the market, the product and the manufacturing process are developed, more specific income and cost projections can be developed to assess the viability of the venture. More details about how the venture will be managed can also be developed. When sufficient value creation has been carried out and it is clear that an MTB Proposition is promising as an implementable commercial venture (financially viable and consistent with business strategy), it will be moved on to the Extract Stage. Note that the Create Stage is, in essence, the continuation of the technology, market and business development which was begun in the Invent Stage.

Technology and market development, and the development of a business plan, all add value to the MTB proposition. As the Create Stage proceeds the MTB Proposition acquires more and more commercial value. Many writers use the terms "new product development" to refer to the entire Value Creation Stage. This term is widely used in this way because of historical precedent. However, it is not used here in this way because it does not reflect very well the wide range of activities involved in Value Creation.

In the **Extract Stage** the new product is **manufactured** and **marketed**. This is the stage at which the firm extracts the commercial value from the MTB Proposition that it had created in the two earlier stages. In the Extract Stage the MTB Proposition is put to the test in the real world and is no longer just a proposition. It is a **business**. As accounting and other information flows in, decision makers can assess the success of the business and the true commercial value of the MTB Proposition upon which it is based. Usually, incremental adjustments to marketing and manufacturing process are made as the realities of market and production are encountered. **Customer support** must also be provided to ensure they are able to use the technology-based product effectively and that repairs and service are provided appropriately. Business plans can be adjusted as experience with the new product accumulates. The cost of manufacturing, marketing, customer support and related activities must all be covered by the income from the business. In addition, that income must cover the costs incurred in the Invent and Create Stages. If all these costs are covered and a respectable profit is realized as well, the science and technology based venture will have been successful.

In addition to these three stages (Invent, Create, Extract); Figure 1.1 shows two diamonds labeled Decision 1 and Decision 2. These diamonds are also important for commercial success.

Decision 1

Decision 1 in the technology commercialization value chain occurs at the end of the Invent Stage before an MTB Proposition goes on to the Create Stage. The decision to be made concerns the next step in the fate of the MTB Proposition. The most fundamental question is whether the MTB Proposition is commercially viable or not. If not, it may be decided to stop work on the proposition altogether. It may not be worth any further investment. On the other hand, it may be decided that the MTB Proposition is not ready yet but with more investigation it probably will be. Plans may be made to send it back to the Invent Stage. If the proposition looks commercially viable, the decision may be made to move it on to the Create Stage and to invest more firm resources in it. The plan may be to do this immediately or at some future more appropriate time.

In large firms there are usually formally appointed committees which make these decisions. These committees usually consist of people representing several different functions in the firm including marketing, technology, strategy, finance, design and others, as deemed appropriate. All of these perspectives are important in making the complex, multifaceted decisions about next steps. Usually a document making the case for each MTB Proposition is prepared for the committee, with an oral presentation.

The fundamental question and the options just described are the traditional ones that have been addressed at Decision 1. In recent years, though, many of the most innovative firms have been developing more complex sets of options for themselves. These all arise from the question of how to maximize the returns from the investment in technology.

Some leading firms have developed a **portfolio approach** to Decision 1. These are typically large firms which make a point of always having a number of MTB Propositions in the Invent stage at any given time. They have regular meetings of the Decision 1 committee, perhaps quarterly or every six months. At those meetings they consider the several MTB Propositions that require decisions. So they are not considering a single MTB Proposition, they are considering a portfolio of propositions. They must decide next steps for all of them. Several of them may be judged ready to move on to the Create Stage. But the firm's development budget may not be big enough to support them all. Some must be chosen for immediate development and others set aside, at least for the time being. The question then becomes, "Which of these MTB Propositions will we move to next steps given that we have limited budgets and that we want to maximize the financial return for the firm?" A great many factors enter these decisions, such as firm strategy, the value creation budget, current and future market conditions, the uniqueness of the technology, the activities of competitors, other MTB Propositions in the Invent Stage which are not currently on the decision table, and MTB Propositions currently in the Create and Extract Stages.

Some of the most innovative firms have moved on to even more complex decisions by introducing **externalization options** into the mix. For example, when examining their portfolio of propositions they ask not just whether it is feasible for their own firm to take on a value creation task, but whether it can outsource some of the value creation work to move it along more quickly. Some of the technical work for product development might be contracted out to a university laboratory. Market research can also be outsourced. What will be the optimal mix of in-house work and outsourcing to get the best financial return from this MTB Proposition?

Thus, in recent years Decision 1 has become much more complex for some firms. It is no longer just a simple question of "go/no go" for a single proposition. It is a complex portfolio question with options available both inside and outside the firm. Successful firms have found that they can make these complex decisions effectively to increase their returns from their very significant investments in technology.

Decision 2

Decision 2 in the technology commercialization value chain occurs at the end of the Create Stage before an MTB Proposition goes on to the Extract Stage. As with Decision 1, it concerns the next steps in the fate of the MTB Proposition and is usually made by a formally appointed, multifunctional committee. The document making the case for the MTB Proposition is usually a complete, formal business plan.

The options before the committee are similar to those for Decision 1. Should the proposition be moved on to the next stage, Value Extraction, with the attendant further investment which that would involve? Should it be sent back to Value Creation for more work and investment? Should it be temporarily shelved until market conditions are more favourable? Perhaps the market is not as favourable for this MTB Proposition now as it was when Decision 1 was made, but is expected to improve in the mid-term. For larger firms these questions can all be asked in a portfolio context, as was the case with Decision 1. Externalization is also on the table. The manufacturing might be out-sourced and the marketing kept in house. Depending on the firm's strengths, manufacturing might be kept in-house and marketing outsourced. Or, the whole business might be spun off if the proposition as a whole is very promising but not very compatible with the firm's strategy. That spinoff would be a separate company, capitalized for the most part by external investors, whose primary business activity would be to commercialize this MTB Proposition. The company deciding to do the spinoff would have to plan how they would get a return from their original investment in the original MTB Proposition. One way is to take an equity position in the spinoff. Another is to license the technology to the spinoff. Newbridge Networks is famous for its spinoffs. Spinoffs were created for a number of MTB Propositions which the small firm could not afford to commercialize itself. Often, equity in the new firm was split three ways. One third would be held by Newbridge Networks, one third by the Newbridge employee who championed the proposition in the first place and who now went off to head the new firm and one third would be taken by the CEO of Newbridge who was an enthusiastic believer in spinoffs.

Management Processes

Across the bottom of Figure 1.1 are the management processes needed to ensure the coordinated operation of the technology commercialization value chain. Those processes must effectively coordinate the ICE stages and the decision points between them. The value chain must be operated within its budget and adhere to time-lines that ensure its effective contribution to the economic success of the firm. In some firms, particularly those in high technology industries, a Chief Technology Officer (CTO) is charged with the task of managing the technology commercialization value chain. CTOs usually have a technical background so that they understand the technical issues involved. But they must also be good managers because the technology commercialization value chain involves many uncertainties and requires the coordination of people from all across the organization with many different backgrounds and business objectives. In addition, the CTO must have an understanding of the business realities within which the value chain operates. The technology commercialization value chain is intended to support business success through the commercialization of technology.

Business Strategy

The final part of the technology commercialization value chain shown in Figure 1.1 is business strategy. It is stretched across the top to indicate that it should inform all the activities, stages and processes in the value chain. As the arrows indicate, Decisions 1 and 2 should be made in light of the business strategy of the firm so that the movement of MTB Propositions forwards though the chain, backwards in the chain, at a standstill in the chain, or out of the chain, are consistent with the overall vision and mission of the organization. Through its effect upon management processes business strategy will affect the activities in the Invent, Create and Extract Stages. As part of overseeing management processes CTOs are usually charged with ensuring that those processes operate consistently with business strategy. Given their technical expertise, CTOs may also be charged with ensuring that strategy reflects the technological uncertainties confronting the business.

This completes the description of the technology commercialization value chain, a process through which technologies are brought to market as sound business propositions. The technology commercialization value chain is a creative process which discovers ways to harness technology for human use within the constraints of economic viability. Many failures have come through the chain, showing that it is an imperfect process. However, it's many, many successes have contributed immeasurably to human welfare showing that it is fundamentally sound. The techniques for operating the technology commercialization value chain have been improved over the years by high technology firms working relentlessly to make it more economically efficient. Ever more innovative technology-based products have become available to us because of these refinements. We can expect those refinements to continue in the future with the consequent improvements to human welfare.

1.3   ORGANIZATIONAL FUNCTIONS

Most firms whose business model is based upon the commercialization of science and technology mobilize the ICE process through a fairly standardized set of activities. A fairly standardized set of terms has developed over the years to refer to those activities. Those terms and their interaction will now be explained for use in later modules. At this stage broad definitions will be provided to introduce the concepts. In later modules as more subtleties are introduced these definitions will be refined   Figure 1.2 is a Venn diagram which will be used as part of that explanation because it reflects the all-important integration of these activities which is found in the most successful high technology firms.

Figure 1.2
Interactions among Organizational Functions in Strategic Technology Management

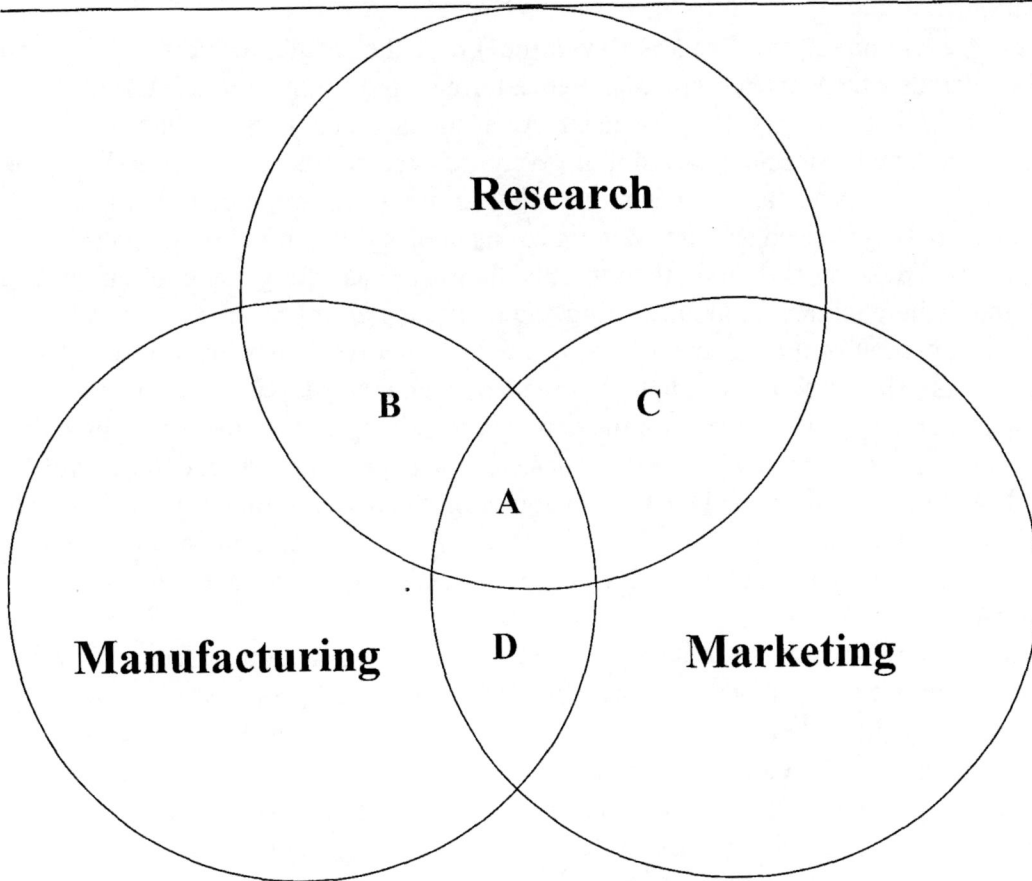

Each labeled circle in the Venn diagram represents a principal function, as follows.

Research is the discovery of new scientific knowledge which has the potential to act as a platform for the subsequent development of commercially viable products and services.

Manufacturing is the process of planning and executing the making of the physical products that are sold to customers.

Marketing is the process of planning and executing the conception, pricing, promotion and distribution of products.

- 11 -

All three of these functions have assigned tasks which they carry out more or less on their own. The day to day work of doing research is carried out by engineers and scientists in that function with very little consultation with manufacturing and marketing. Most manufacturing activities are carried out by the experts in that function without outside consultation. Similarly marketing is carried out for the most part by the people in that function. However, in high technology firms all of these functions have some role to play in commercializing technology and must have some access to technical expertise. Furthermore, many aspects of technology commercialization depend very heavily upon cooperative action between and among these principal functions.

Product Development and Process Development are the creation of new or improved products and processes which have commercial value, through the application of currently available scientific knowledge. Usually, the discovery of fundamentally new scientific knowledge is not involved. Since a successful new venture must be based upon sound science, a good manufacturing process and an understanding of customer wants, product and process development are usually practiced as joint activities of technology, manufacturing and marketing. Product and process development might, therefore, be thought of as taking place in region A of the Venn diagram, where research, manufacturing and marketing all intersect.

But the commercialization of science and technology involves other forms of cooperation among the functions. High tech firms usually house some technical people within the marketing function to support and help customers with the complex technologies they have bought and/or to help them adapt them to their particular needs. These technical people work in concert with marketing and sales and with technical specialists housed in the research function. This is called **Marketing Support** and since it involves the cooperation of technical and marketing people it can be thought of as taking place in Region C of the Venn diagram, where research and marketing intersect.

In high tech firms technical people are also housed in the manufacturing function where they apply their expertise to manufacturing problems. These technical people work with manufacturing experts and technical specialists housed in the research function. **Manufacturing Support** is the adaptation of already established process technology to some particular condition. Since manufacturing support often involves the cooperation of research and manufacturing people, it can be thought of as taking place in Region B of the Venn diagram.

At times, technical issues may arise which require minor adaptations of product and process, but do not require the high levels of expertise housed in the research function. In these cases technical people in marketing and manufacturing can resolve them together, through activities taking place in Region D of the Venn diagram. **Marketing/Manufacturing collaboration** is the resolving of low level technical issues through the collaboration of marketing and manufacturing without the participation of the technical function.

A very common way to refer generally to the technology activities of a firm is to call them **Research and Development** or **R&D**. This tends to be used as a blanket term which does not make the fine distinction between research and development activities that are made here. Expect to encounter the term but do not expect to hear it used with any precision of meaning.

1.4 THE ORGANIZATION OF THE MODULES THAT FOLLOW

The modules that follow in this course pack build out from the basic models presented in this the introductory module as shown in Figure 1.3. Modules 2, 3, 4 and 5 describe in more detail the stages of the ICE model. Modules 6 and 7 address the strategy and management issues. Module 6 provides an overview of the principal challenges currently facing high technology firms and the role of the technology commercialization value chain in meeting them. Module 7 addresses the management of the technology commercialization value chain with particular attention to technology leadership. Modules 8, 9 and 10 discuss in more detail three of the most important strategic issues currently facing high technology firms, open innovation, global technology management and green technology management.

Figure 1.3
Outline of Modules

1.0	Creating Value from Science and Technology (Introduction)	
2.0	Invent	
3.0	Create (Development)	**I♦C♦E**
4.0	Extract (Marketing)	
5.0	Extract (Manufacturing)	
6.0	Strategy: Firm and Technology	**Strategy**
7.0	Technology Leadership	
8.0	Open Innovation	**Strategic**
9.0	Global technology Management	**Issues**
10.0	Green Technology Management	

MINT is about competing through technical innovation.
MINT is about the management of innovation in high technology firms.

CHaOS BY DeSIGN

The inside story of
disorder, disarray, and
uncertainty at Google.
And why it's all part of the
plan.* BY ADAM LaSHINSKY

*They hope.

ILLUSTRATION BY EBOY

GOOGLE FOUNDERS
PAGE AND BRIN

Spend just a few minutes on

Google's sprawling campus in Mountain View, Calif., and you'll feel it right away: This is a company thriving on the edge of chaos. Google, age 8, is pulling in $10 billion a year in revenue and is worth about $125 billion, but the vibe is far more freshman mixer than profit-seeking firm whose every utterance is scrutinized for deeper meaning. The 1.3-million-square-foot headquarters is a mélange of two-story buildings full of

festive cafeterias (yes, they're all free), crammed conference rooms, and hallway bull sessions, all of it surrounded by sandy volleyball courts, youngsters whizzing by on motorized scooters, and—there's no better way to put this—an anything-goes spirit. It's a place where failure coexists with triumph, and ideas bubble up from lightly supervised engineers, none of whom worry too much about their projects ever making money.

Take the case of Sheryl Sandberg, a 37-year-old vice president whose fiefdom includes the company's automated advertising system. Sandberg recently committed an error that cost Google several million dollars—"Bad decision, moved too quickly, no controls in place, wasted some money," is all she'll say about it—and when she realized the magnitude of her mistake, she walked across the street to inform Larry Page, Google's co-founder and unofficial thought leader. "God, I feel really bad about this," Sandberg told Page, who accepted her apology. But as she turned to leave, Page said something that surprised her. "I'm so glad you made this mistake," he said. "Because I want to run a company where we are moving too quickly and doing too much, not being too cautious and doing too little. If we don't have any of these mistakes, we're just not taking enough risk."

When a million-dollar mistake earns a pat on the back, it's obvious this isn't your normal corporation. To figure the place out, I've repeatedly been told the person to see is Shona Brown, the 40-year-old ex-McKinsey consultant who is Google's senior vice president for business operations. That's what it says on her business card, anyway, but she might as well be Google's chief chaos officer. She literally wrote the book on the subject, a 1998 bestseller

called *Competing on the Edge: Strategy as Structured Chaos*. And fittingly, on the day I'm to see her at the Googleplex, my press escort and I get hopelessly lost. Finding anyone here requires precise navigation and the ability to read color-coded maps. We get so badly turned around—entering the wrong building's lobby, backtracking through shrubbery to another—that we arrive 17 minutes late. Even real estate at Google is chaotic.

Brown has made a career of arguing that anarchy isn't such a bad thing—which is why Page, co-founder Sergey Brin, and CEO Eric Schmidt hired her in 2003. A business theoretician in a company dominated by engineers, she considers Google the "ultimate petri dish" for her research, though her job is anything but theoretical. In addition to overseeing human resources (called "people operations"), Brown runs a SWAT team of 25 strategic consultants who are loaned out internally on ten or so projects at a time—restructuring a regional sales force here, guesstimating a market size there. The company's goal, says Brown, is to determine precisely the amount of management it needs—and then use a little bit less. It's an almost laughably Goldilocksian approach that Brown also advocates in her book, co-written with a Stanford business professor. The way to succeed in "fast-paced, ambiguous situations," she tells me, is to avoid creating too much structure, but not to add too little either. In other words, just make it not too hot and not too cold, and you're done. "If I ever come into the office and I feel comfortable,

DISORDERLY CONDUCT Page and Brin (wearing the goofball lab smocks in the right center picture; that's CEO Schmidt in the middle) never wanted Google to be like other companies. They succeeded.

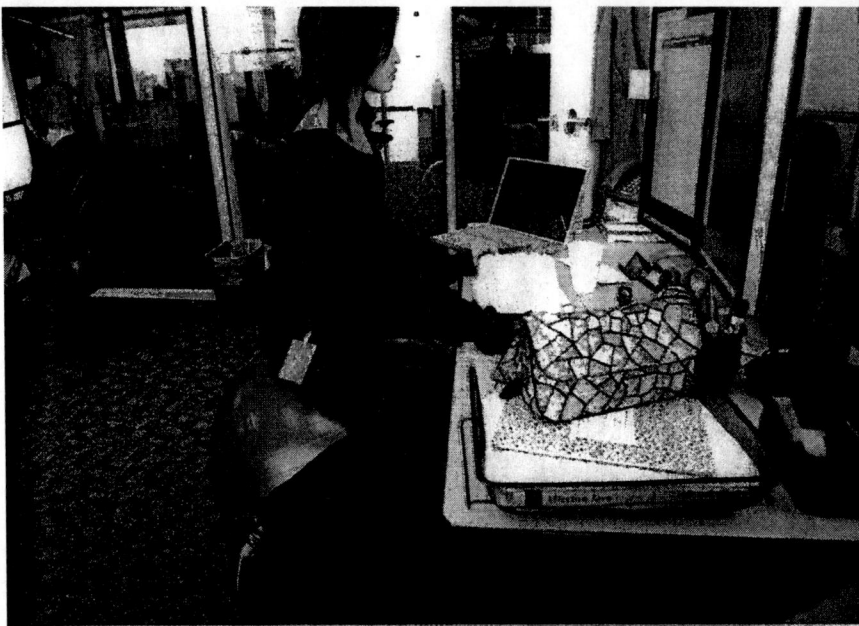

if I don't feel a little nervous about some crazy stuff going on, then we've taken it too far," she says.

Crazy definitely trumps comfy at Google. You have to keep your wits about you on campus just to avoid smashing into one of Google's 8,000-plus employees. Meetings typically start on the hour, and young Googlers tend to hover outside scarce conference rooms beforehand. They doodle on hallway whiteboards, contributing inside jokes, such as sinister new ways to expand the company's online advertising program. ("AdSense for Eyelids," reads one.) Celebrity sightings are ho-hum. A couple of years ago I was having lunch at Google's sunny outdoor courtyard when Page and Brin sat down at my table with their guest, comedian Chris Tucker. George Soros lectured at Google the day I met Brown. Google advisor Al Gore shows up often.

Nurturing such an off-the-wall culture is a luxury only a company that's performing stupendously well can afford, and Google is certainly doing that. Two years after going public, its stock is up more than fourfold, and it's so profitable that despite helter-skelter spending on everything from mammoth data centers to worldwide sales and engineering offices, Google is generating more than $800 million in cash each quarter. In the process, Google is thrashing the competition—in market share, deals won, buzz—notably Yahoo and Microsoft. It's also cozying up to a growing list of heavyweights you'd think would be warier, including News Corp., Viacom, and ad-agency giant WPP.

If Google's engine is running fast, then naturally it's also running hot. That sheds light on all kinds of blunders—many of them dwarfing Sandberg's—which Google likes to explain away as its Googley approach to business. (Googley being a cloying description these people actually say out loud. Frequently.) The company is figuring things out as it goes, and not quite as effectively as you'd expect from its stellar financial results. Its new products haven't made nearly the splash that its original search engine did. Critics have mocked its self-righteous "Don't be evil" motto when, for example, Google decided to scan copyrighted books for its book search index. Even Google's rocket-ship stock price has been grounded. After a run from $85 in August 2004 to $475 last January, it has puttered around $400 for most of the year. Says Benjamin Schachter, an analyst with UBS: "Investors are saying, 'Enough of what you're going to do. What does it do to the numbers?'"

What concerns investors is whether Google can come up with a second act. There's nothing to suggest that its growth engine—ad-supported search—is in trouble. But it's clear from Google's tentative lurches into new forms of advertising and its spaghetti method of product development (toss against wall, see if sticks) that the company is searching for ways to grow beyond that well-run core. It's

FEEDBACK *alashinsky@fortunemail.com*

BROWNIAN MOTION Google is Shona Brown's $125 billion "ultimate petri dish."

THE WORLD ACCORDING TO THE CHIEF CHAOS OFFICER

Shona Brown co-wrote *Competing on the Edge* in 1998, the year Google was founded. Four easier-said-than-done rules from the book that Google needs to master:

GET UNCOMFY That means never settle into an equilibrium (a.k.a. "rut"), but don't fall apart either (a.k.a. the "chaos trap").

PACE YOURSELF The goal should be creating an internal rhythm, not just moving fast for the sake of speed.

HANG LOOSE Encourage an innovative, adaptive culture, but avoid having too little structure. Still, too much structure—the "bureaucratic trap"—means death for a fast-moving company.

PLAY NICE A common cause of poor collaboration is the "star trap," when the company's big moneymaker doesn't share know-how or ideas with everyone else.

PHOTOGRAPHS BY NIGEL DICKSON

the reason, for example, that Google requires all engineers to spend 20% of their time pursuing their own ideas. Successful second acts are exceedingly rare in the technology business—or in any business, for that matter. Microsoft followed Windows with Office. Intel jettisoned its memory-chip line to rule microprocessors. Even Apple, which executed one of the most remarkable rebirths ever with the iPod, had to go through a painful decade to get there.

What emerges from months of interviews with employees ranging from fresh-out-of-college hires to the CEO is that Google firmly believes it has a framework for figuring out the future. It should come as no surprise that the plan is as irreverent, self-confident, and presumptuous as the company itself. Google's executives don't articulate it this way, but the framework can be found in the title of Shona Brown's book: structured chaos. Indeed, along with Googleyness, chaos is among the most important aspects of Google's self-image. Understanding how Google thinks about chaos—like Page's teachable moment after Sandberg's million-dollar mistake—is critical to divining where the company goes next. "Are lots of questions

WHO'S THE BOSS?

And who's the front man? What about the visionary? How Page, Brin, and Schmidt divvy up the responsibilities at Google.

EBOY

Google relishes being secretive and opaque—the better to confuse the competition—and one of the company's biggest mysteries is its leadership triumvirate. Figuring out what it is exactly that these three guys do is a Silicon Valley parlor game. Beyond the technology world, the trio's individual attributes are even murkier, with some having heard only a little about the middle-aged guy, Eric Schmidt, and not being able to distinguish at all between cofounders Larry Page and Sergey Brin, often called, even by those who know them well, "the twins."

The two co-founders are indeed often difficult to separate. They spend huge amounts of time together and have similar management quirks. Both, for instance, recently stopped using administrative assistants, choosing instead to keep their own calendars and answer their own messages, just like other 33-year-old businesspeople. It's unclear if the new approach will make them more respectful of

other people's time. They're both infamous for being unwilling to commit to appointments, often blowing them off altogether. And they have their differences, of course. Here's how they and their avuncular CEO divide their responsibilities.

ERIC SCHMIDT, chairman and CEO. Conventional wisdom is that Schmidt's job is to break ties between Page and Brin and to communicate with Wall Street and the news media. Insiders say that underplays his role. He sets the company's overall agenda, gives direction on workaday issues the co-founders don't care to address, and more than occasionally reminds Page and Brin to behave themselves. Schmidt is also becoming a power in his own right, having recently joined the board of Apple, the Valley's other buzziest company.

LARRY PAGE, president, products. Acknowledged as the thought leader of the company

and co-founder most likely to roll up his sleeves and make sure things get done. Page, who carries résumés home on the weekend so that he can review them before the week starts, is known for a short temper and great attention to detail—yes, the latter is a nice way of saying "micromanager." He was Google's CEO until Schmidt arrived in 2001, and many assume Page intends to be chief executive again someday.

SERGEY BRIN, president, technology. Mr. Outside to Page's Mr. Inside, Brin is responsible for advertising initiatives—the money-making part of Google—as well as overseeing business deals. He's considered more intuitive than Page and is more likely to scout the company's outside investments. Brin can chew up hours discussing which flat-panel TV he should buy. He's also been pushing hard for Google to streamline its product offerings, which officially is Page's purview.

GOLDEN Armstrong dismisses skeptics who say Google got taken in its $900 million ad deal with MySpace.

MEANWHILE IN PROFIT CENTRAL . . .

Three ways Tim Armstrong, Google's VP for advertising sales, is trying to expand the moneymaking part of Google.

GO BIG Google became a phenomenon by selling text ads a few dollars at a time. Armstrong's been calling on the likes of Dell, General Motors, and News Corp., asking for multimillion-dollar orders.

PRINT IT Newspapers and magazines view Google as the ultimate threat, which is why Armstrong wants to help them sell ads online. It's an 18-month-old experiment that's going slowly.

HIT THE AIRWAVES Google recently bought dMarc Broadcasting, which brokers radio ads. When dMarc morphs into Google Audio Ads this fall, Google will be pitching radio time to its advertisers. It's a mature business where Google's a mere toddler.

hanging out there in the market?" asks Sandberg. "Sure. Because we don't always have an answer. We're willing to tolerate that ambiguity and chaos because that's where the room is for innovation." Good strategy—if it actually works.

In *Competing on the Edge,* Brown describes a sizzling Silicon Valley software company from the 1990s that was confronting the joys and hardships of hypergrowth. She identifies it only with a pseudonym, Galaxy, and it bears a striking resemblance to Brown's current employer, which didn't exist yet. "Galaxy was populated by smart, hip twenty- and thirtysomethings who were chosen for their brains and their attitude," she wrote. "Tour Galaxy and you'll be struck by the college-like atmosphere. Landing a job at Galaxy is hard. The screening process is intense. Once hired, the Galaxy philosophy is to let people 'do their own thing.' " But Galaxy had one glaring weakness: "The firm was living off one set of unusually successful products, whereas the rest of the businesses were much more modest performers."

What vexed Galaxy is precisely Google's challenge today. For all its new products—depending on how you count, Google has released at least 83 full-fledged and test-stage products—none has altered the web landscape the way Google.com did. Additions like the photo site Picasa, Google Finance, and Google Blog Search belie Google's ardent claim that it doesn't do me-too products. Often new services lack a stunningly obvious feature. Users of Google's new online spreadsheet program, for instance, initially couldn't print their documents. The calendar product doesn't allow for synchronization with Microsoft Outlook, a necessity for corporate users. Other major initiatives like Gmail, instant-messaging, and online mapping, while nifty, haven't come close to dislodging the market leaders. Much-hyped projects like the comparison-shopping site Froogle (nearly four years in beta and counting) and Google's video-sharing site have been far less popular than the competition. One of Google's biggest misses is its social-networking site, Orkut, which is a hit only in Brazil and—as Marissa Mayer, Google's 31-year-old vice president of search products and user experience, says with an impressively straight face—is "very strong in Iran." Sometimes promising new products are buried so deep within Google's sites that users can't find them. "You can only keep so many things in your head," acknowledges CEO Schmidt. "Even if you're the No. 1 Google supporter, you cannot remember all the products we have."

This presents a conundrum: Impose order, and Google becomes just like everybody else; let chaos rule, and run the risk that Google's flailing about hurts its pristine brand and reputation for brilliance. Clarifying its intentions would be a start. "We need to do a better job of communicating which products we expect to be killer apps and which are experiments," Brin told a gathering of journalists in May. There's been progress. In June, Google released its online payment tool, Checkout, as a full-fledged product. Mayer, who has the final word (except for Page) on what appears on Google's home page, has established a war room to piece together a plan for better integrating Google's many products.

It's going to be a battle, though, simply because Googlers are adding features by the bushel—and more are coming. Niniane Wang, a young engineer who worked on Gmail, is now assigned to a confidential project believed to involve social networking. Louis Monier, a Digital Equipment veteran who launched its AltaVista search engine, recently left eBay to join Google in a top-secret capacity. Katie Jacobs Stanton runs Google Finance, Google Blog Search, and two other projects. This summer she temporarily moved with her husband and three children to Bangalore to get closer to the engineers who built the finance site. Since Google Finance doesn't run ads or any other revenue-generating features, I ask Stanton how long the site can ignore making money. Her response: "Theoretically, forever."

In fact, Google is making money slyly, if slowly, on some of the very products that seem like mere whiz-bang. Consider Google Earth, the ubiquitous cable-news prop and workplace time waster that lets users view incredibly detailed geographic photos from around the world. It started as a satellite-imaging software company called Keyhole. "Sergey [Brin] was playing around with it and got enamored with Keyhole," says John Hanke, Keyhole's original CEO (and now a Google employee) before Google bought it in 2004. "At a staff meeting, he put Keyhole up on one of the projectors and started showing people their houses and flying around." The startup, whose images were confined to the U.S., had been bringing in modest revenue from real estate companies, but that's not what interested Brin. "When we got to Google, one of the first questions Sergey asked was, 'Why can't you look at the whole world at once?'" says Hanke. Two years later the company is integrating ads into Google Earth. Search for "pizza" while hovering above your neighborhood, and you'll get the idea.

Neat toys are about more than creating web pages on which Google can slap ads. Google Earth has been downloaded more than 100 million times, and embedded in each download is a request

PROJECT MANAGEMENT FOR FUN AND (NO) PROFIT Stanton (left) runs Google Finance, a revenue-less unit. Sandberg says Google tolerates ambiguity to leave room for innovation.

nies like his. (Automated ad auctions entail less overhead than armies of schmoozing ad executives, goes the argument.) He titled a section of his latest annual report "Google: Friend or Foe?" In an interview, he suggests the short answer: "The bigger and more successful you get, the more people want to bring you down." But it's not that simple. WPP, Sorrell notes, is Google's third-largest customer, measured by the amount of advertising it purchases on Google for its clients. Sorrell says Google wants to improve its access to WPP's clients, and he's inclined to allow that—provided there's something in it for WPP. "We represent 20% of media revenue worldwide, and we're definitely not 20% of Google's revenue," he says. "We'll see how we can work together."

> **"I'm so glad you made this mistake," Page told Sandberg. "If we don't have any of these mistakes, we're just not TAKING ENOUGH RISK."**

Working with Google and grumbling about it is quite in fashion. Viacom's MTV recently signed a deal for Google to distribute its videos to the web publishers in Google's AdSense network, which lets the publishers run ads supplied by Google's advertisers. Comcast, which has been Google's ideological opponent in an acrimonious legislative battle over government regulation of Net access, is particularly pleased with the revenue it gets from having Google power the search results on its Comcast.net home page for broadband users. In both cases, the older companies profit from Google's superior Internet advertising network. Indeed, after initially scaring "old" media, Google has become the go-to partner for juicing Internet revenues.

from Google to place a toolbar, a web gadget that includes a search box, permanently on a user's web browser. That seemingly innocuous query is a gold mine for Google, because the ever present box increases the likelihood users will search on Google. The more people search on Google, the greater the chances someone will click on an advertiser's ads. "We know the lifetime value of a toolbar user," says Mayer, who offers the example to counter the notion that Google isn't trying to profit from its fancy doodads. "So we know how much value we're getting back out of somebody who downloads Google Earth and then subsequently downloads the toolbar."

This virtuous cycle of more users conducting more searches benefiting more advertisers is precisely what makes Google so irresistible to business partners—even those who feel threatened by it. Martin Sorrell, the chief executive of ad agency holding company WPP, has been outspoken in his fear that Google could obviate compa-

Chumminess with the establishment is in the air in mid-August when I meet with Schmidt, two days after Google's announcement of a landmark deal to provide search over numerous News Corp. properties, notably MySpace. (Google guarantees News Corp. $900 million over 3½ years in exchange for an unspecified share of ad revenue.) In our 90-minute interview, I remind Schmidt that at a lunch for journalists in March, he repeatedly mentioned MySpace almost wistfully, seeing how Google had been a bust in social networking. "We didn't know what to do about it," he says. "Now we know." He explains that Google's new social-networking effort has at least two prongs. The well-known part is the MySpace deal; the other is Google's technology to improve search on social-networking sites, which so far only MySpace has agreed to use. Schmidt's explanation is a bald attempt to declare victory after an obvious defeat, since MySpace trounced Google's Orkut (not including, of course, those triumphs in Brazil and Iran).

The MySpace deal reveals the Google leadership triumvirate's visceral style. The transaction might never have happened, says Schmidt, if Brin hadn't flown to meet with News Corp. executives in Pebble Beach, Calif., where Rupert Murdoch was hosting an A-list bull session on global issues. (Schmidt was vacationing in Europe; Page was in India.) "We sent Sergey because he's very intuitive," says Schmidt. "He goes down there and sort of hangs with them for a while and comes back and says, 'You know, I'm really sure we should do this.' And it's not a numbers argument. It's a feeling of commitment."

Winning MySpace kept the web's gem of the moment out of

> When asked how long Google Finance, like many other Google sites, can IGNORE MAKING MONEY, Stanton responds, "Theoretically, forever."

the hands of Microsoft and Yahoo, which both privately claim that Google overpaid by several hundred million dollars. Whether that's true won't be known for years. Tim Armstrong, Google's New York–based head of North American sales and the company's point man in the MySpace negotiations, pooh-poohs the notion that Google got taken. "What people aren't seeing is our ability to model deals," he says. "I would guess that Google was not offering to write the biggest check for this partnership." In any event, the deal created a fan in News Corp., which has steadfastly refused to place any of its Fox shows on Google's video site and yet is positively giddy about its budding advertising relationship. "I actually don't view them as overwhelmingly competitive with us," says Peter Chernin, News Corp.'s president and chief operating officer. "They are trying to sell advertising, and so are we. But at their core I view them as a technology company, and we are an entertainment company. It's a happy and convenient marriage."

It's great for Google that Murdoch & Co. love it so, but that doesn't change the impression that Google is winging it—after all, the deal only came together after Brin descended from the clouds to peer into News Corp.'s soul. When I ask Schmidt whether his company actually has a plan, he does what engineers tend to do in situations like this: He gets up and starts drawing on a whiteboard.

A billionaire at 51, Schmidt cuts the typical Silicon Valley figure of somebody's successful, but otherwise average, dad. His khakis-and-oxford uniform is standard, as are his wire-frame glasses and Supercuts-inspired hairdo. Schmidt's doodling, which he's also done

recently for the Google board of directors, tells the story of where he sees Google's money coming from for years to come. He draws a series of connected clouds representing the history of the computing industry, from mainframes to minicomputers to PCs to today's mobile devices. The gist of the illustration is that there's practically no money left to be made in computers, not in hardware or software. The money, instead, is all in web applications, a trend Schmidt had been predicting since his days as chief technology officer at Sun a decade ago. Users won't always be traveling to the web on the PC, which is why he scribbles lines for cellphones, cable set-top boxes, Treos, BlackBerrys, and so on. Schmidt's most compelling point—and the most visible glimmer of a method to Google's madness—is the power behind the not-so-secret data centers Google is building, particularly a 30-acre facility in Oregon whose existence he references without provocation. "That massive investment should translate into the ability to build applications that are impossible for our competitors to offer, just because we can handle the scale," says Schmidt. (Microsoft, Yahoo, and IBM, each of which is spending heavily on similar big iron, would beg to differ.) He's talking about processing-power-sucking Google applications like Gmail and Google Earth—and unannounced products on the drawing board.

Google has also begun to show how it plans to use that power for advertising services that go beyond search. Brokering video ads for MTV is new terrain, as are the graphical display ads Google plans to sell for MySpace. The company is engaged in an 18-month-old experiment to auction text and graphical ads for newspapers and magazines. It's also in the process of integrating its biggest acquisition to date, a radio-advertising company called dMarc Broadcasting, which Google bought in January for $102 million in cash plus a potential performance-based payout of more than $1 billion. dMarc automates the process for delivering radio ads to about 10% of the country's 10,000 stations. By merging dMarc into Google's AdWords, Google's online system for auctioning search terms, it will offer its advertisers—who so far hawk their wares in 75 words or less of written text—the ability to deploy radio ads as well.

It's a bold push. "We see very clear ways to improve advertising for all users," says Armstrong, the sales chief. It's the "all" in his aspirations that frightens anyone in Google's path. Or used to, anyway, before people started noticing that not everything Google does rocks the world. Nick Grouf, CEO of Spot Runner, a well-funded Los Angeles startup that does even more for television advertisers than dMarc does for radio, sees an Achilles' heel. "It's their incredible focus that got them this far," says Grouf. "But all these new initiatives suggest a dilution of that focus."

With so many moving parts, it's natural to wonder if Google is truly a company for the ages—or whether it's the next Galaxy, that fast-moving, arrogant, one-hit wonder in Shona Brown's book. To believe that Google will find its second act, you have to accept the hubris and the chaos, and that the brainiacs who got lucky once will do so again. Google desperately wants to believe its nonlinear approach is all part of the plan. But as the company's big thinkers are the first to admit, most of the questions about Google aren't answerable. Try as they may, no one can truly control chaos. ◼

500

COMPANY PROFILE

REVENUE:
$39 billion

PROFITS:
$1.5 billion

EMPLOYEES:
255,573

TOTAL RETURN TO SHAREHOLDERS:
−9.8%

RANK:

70

FedEx Chief Fred Smith on ... Everything: China, the U.S. Economy, the Value of a Good Name, and Why the Government Shouldn't Pay for a Liberal Arts Education.

Interview by Brian Dumaine

Photographs by WESLEY MANN

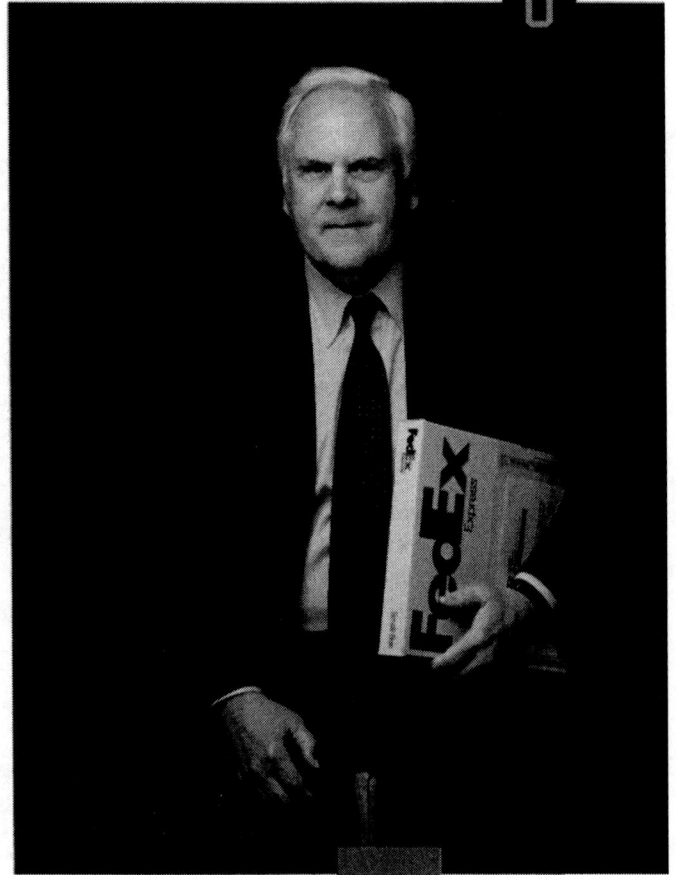

Fred Smith sees fast growth ahead in the developing world.

W

WHEN FRED SMITH *founded FedEx in 1971, he had just returned from the Vietnam War, where he had served as a Marine platoon leader and then a pilot, and he was casting around for something to do. As legend has it, a paper he had written at Yale—he doesn't remember the grade but is pretty sure it wasn't a good one—laid out the idea for a hub-and-spoke system for delivering time-sensitive items like computer parts. He borrowed money from his sisters, leased some jets, and started his service. Today FedEx, with headquarters in Memphis, has 255,000 employees, 688 planes, and more than 90,000 vehicles that operate in some 220 countries and regions. Here's the world according to Fred Smith. Edited excerpts:*

Q: In 2000 you started morphing from your traditional air express delivery business into ground and into freight. What was the thinking behind that strategy shift?

A: Well, in 2000 we were probably competing in a $50 billion annual [sales] market space. Today we're directly competing in about a $350 billion to $400 billion marketplace. Going into ground and freight opened up a market for us with the greatest growth potential over a sustained period of time: the developing world. Middle classes are emerging in various countries, including the BRIC nations [Brazil, Russia, India, and China]. And these middle-class populations are all knit together today for the first time in human history

"YOU HAVE TO PUT YOUR MONEY WHERE YOUR MOUTH IS. THERE ISN'T A YEAR THAT'S GONE BY WHERE WE HAVEN'T INVESTED AN ENORMOUS AMOUNT TO MAKE THE SERVICE BETTER."

FedEx is expanding its ground service in Beijing as well as other cities in China.

with a low-cost, standardized communication system that can intermediate language differences and show every product on the planet in visual format. And that of course is the Internet. Today if you want a component for an automobile—Volkswagen or Chrysler or whatever—you can look worldwide. And so that's the biggest opportunity. The growth of world trade and the growth of those emerging economies dwarfs the growth of GDP in the industrial countries.

What's one of your fastest-growing markets? We are now the biggest international transporter of goods by air in and out of China. We also have established a FedEx-branded domestic parcel service there. We use this business to move our international traffic to and from the major gateways.

In China, do they get the FedEx concept? Oh, yeah. You bet. One time Jiang Zemin [the former President of China] had our board of directors to his office, and he probably knew more about the company than a lot of them did, to tell you the truth.

I was surprised to learn about another new area of growth for you: a new service called FedEx Tech-Connect, where you will repair electronic items like the iPad and the Nook. It doesn't sound as if it's a core business to FedEx. First of all, we're probably one of the biggest repair shops for devices like that in the world for the very simple reason that FedEx basically invented the handheld, package-tracking device. Because a lot of that equipment is built into our DNA, we became very good at repairing it. And it was just a natural progression to tell a lot of our big customers that if you want us to also repair these devices, we can do it for you.

How big an opportunity is it? It's a $15 billion market, and it's also a very sticky application. In other words, nobody has the assets that we do. We have the retail network. We have thousands of people that stop in millions of locations every day, so if you want to send your electronic device to us to be repaired, we've got the transportation networks to get it to a centralized repair shop. We don't have to have 500 of these less efficient repair shops. So it's a niche market, but it's an important niche—although I don't think we're going to be

here in five years talking about that business overwhelming the transportation business.

I'd like to turn to leadership. You wrote a piece recently about reputational intelligence. Can you explain what that means? Well, what we call reputational intelligence is particularly important in our organization because at the end of the day we're essentially selling trust. People give us some of the most important things that they own. There's medical equipment that's going to a surgery this morning or a part that's going to determine whether the new 787 flies. So reputation is an integral part of the brand, but it's separate and distinct from the brand.

So how do you manage that? You have to put your money where your mouth is. There isn't a year that's gone by where we haven't invested an enormous amount into trying to make the service better. There have been some years when we could have taken the approach: "You know what? We're not going to try to make the service better. Let's just dial it back by 2%. Most people won't notice that, and we can put another 2% to the bottom line." We've never done that. But it's also directly related to the culture we've tried to create. Ask any FedEx team member anyplace what the Purple Promise is, and they'll tell you, "I will make every FedEx experience outstanding."

So I noticed in a recent letter to your employees that you talked about a video of a FedEx delivery man tossing a computer screen over a fence at someone's home. It got caught on a security camera, posted on YouTube, and it went crazy viral. Not exactly the Purple Promise. You know, what got into the mind of that young man I will never know. We went back, and the station he operated in was run by a great manager who communicated constantly about the importance of great service. And there's one thing pretty simple in our business: You don't throw or drop a package. That's pretty basic, right?

And of course what he did just made all of the other 255,000 of us just mad as hell because we work like hell and then there it was. We immediately had the head of our express delivery operations record his own YouTube video in which he said, "Look, this is not what we stand for. We apologize." That went viral too. Our quality-driven management says at its heart that you've got to use failures as an opportunity to improve. So that's why I mentioned it in my letter. It's not to hide it, but to make sure everybody looked at it and learned from it.

You're in a great position to see what's going on in the economy. Do you see U.S. growth slowing? Yeah, we took our projection down a little bit. Our forecast for calendar 2012 is now 2.1% GDP growth, compared with 1.7% for 2011. I think there are some good things, and I think there are some troubling things. We have the European crisis, and hopefully the financial contagion from that won't spill

over into the real economy in the U.S. Europe has definitely slowed down, but it's not the disaster a lot of people think that it is yet. Its economy is just not as robust as those in China and the United States.

Isn't part of the problem with the U.S. economy that it doesn't have the supply chains to compete with Asia? Over the next decade, we will benefit from a lot of manufacturing activities coming back to North America. It may not be all in the U.S. A lot of it may be in Mexico and Central America, but overall we will see stronger U.S. manufacturing aided by the rapidity with which supply chains can be replenished and orders can be fulfilled. And the reason for that is that the high price of oil is making it substantially more expensive to move things from China to the U.S., whether it's by air or ocean.

If you could wave your magic wand, what would you do to make the U.S. more competitive? The single biggest thing that the U.S. can do is to change the corporate tax system, because as it exists today, the system favors leveraged finance and financial services over industrial activities.

Such as interest payments being deductible? Absolutely. And in a capital-intensive business, you add leverage at your peril because when the inevitable downturn comes, we've seen what happens. So how do we get more competitive? First the corporate tax rate should be lowered to make it globally competitive. Just set the maximum rate at 20% or 25% across the board and eliminate all the other foolishness. Next, we should go to a territorial tax system so you don't get penalized for bringing money back into the United States. Put a different way, money that is made in China making baby food for Chinese babies should not be taxed if it's brought back into the United States. We want that money to come back in the United States so we can create jobs here.

FedEx technicians in Memphis now will repair your smartphone or tablet—for a price.

And then the third thing, depending on how the numbers come out, is to provide tax incentives for investment. Because the only thing that's correlated 100% with job creation—and particularly good job creation—is business investment. We strongly promote a 100% expensing of capital. Now, I don't think you could both lower the corporate tax rate and expense 100% of capital investment, because you'd add too much to the federal deficit. But being able to write off investment is preferable to a lower tax rate and the territorial thing.

But isn't it also a demand problem? U.S. corporations are sitting on a couple trillion dollars in cash, but they're not investing it because there's no demand. Based on my 40 years in business, I think the economy is driven mostly by entrepreneurs and the development of new products and services, which start to create demand that then creates a virtuous circle. When Steve Jobs invented the iPod and iPhone, that helped drive cloud computing and telecommunications systems, and so all of a sudden how many jobs have been created? The point is that if you talk to the people who are demand-side-oriented, they discount Steve Jobs or other entrepreneurs who create their own demand. The most important thing you can do is to incentivize private investment. And I don't think that Lord Keynes ever advocated taking money from one group of citizens and transferring it to another group of citizens. What he advocated was in periods of low demand that government invest—build roads, build dams, build ports, and so on.

You're a big advocate of rebuilding. Obama's budget includes billions for infrastructure. What do you think? The only way to produce well-paying blue-collar jobs is with public investment in infrastructure and education, and private investment in equipment. After going to China—oh, my God, it's embarrassing to fly into J.F.K. We need to pay to improve our infrastructure. One of the biggest opponents to this are the far right-wing Republicans—the Tea Party fiscal hawks who are against spending on anything. But infrastructure has a multiplier effect, as long as it's good infrastructure. I mean, not the bridge to nowhere.

You've started to buy electric vehicles. Do you think the government's going to put in the incentives to help electrify the transportation system? We're not seeing a positive return yet on our electric vehicles, so what we've

> **"I PERSONALLY THINK THAT THE FEDERAL GOVERNMENT—AND YOU'RE TALKING TO A LIBERAL ARTS MAJOR HERE—SHOULD RESTRICT ITS FUNDING OF HIGHER EDUCATION TO SCIENCE, MATH, AND ENGINEERING."**

been trying to do is to advocate policies that push down the cost of batteries by getting them built at scale. We advocated, for example, the reimposition of fuel-efficiency standards. Look, this is a national security and economic security matter, and you've got to look at these batteries as if they're an F-35 or a machine gun. Because what we've got to do is to get out of importing as much petroleum as we do from unstable and unfriendly parts of the world. Part of the problem is a political thing. I've watched this issue be pilloried by the right-wing media as an Obama thing. That's not true at all.

You mentioned earlier that investing in education is another key to creating more American jobs. I personally think that the federal government—and you're talking to a liberal arts major here—should restrict its funding of higher-education grants and loans to science, math, and engineering because that's where most of the value added comes. We put so much emphasis on "college degrees." Well, in Germany students at some point come to a fork in the road, and they either go on to university or they go on to a trade school. Say you're a FedEx airplane mechanic working on one of our Boeing Triple Sevens. That's a $100,000-plus job. You don't have to have a college degree to get that job. You don't have to know Chaucer and *The Canterbury Tales.* You can go right to West Memphis, Ark., where we have a relationship with the community college, and be trained to be a licensed mechanic. Then you can come to work at FedEx.

So, long term, you're bullish on America. Sure. But look, the U.S. political system is completely broken, and as a wise man once said, "What can't continue, won't." So we're either going to be stopped by the bond market at some point in time, or we're going to fix Washington. And I think we will be able to do it. ▪

Companies/ Industries

November 25 — December 1 2013

The Scariest Veggies of Them All

▶ Mutant crop developers take on Monsanto in the $34 billion seed market

▶ "Regulations are a huge incentive to go back and do things the old way"

Last July, when **Monsanto** withdrew its applications to sell genetically modified biotech seeds in the European Union, the move opened the way for competitors to challenge Monsanto's market share.

As opposition to genetically modified crops has spread across Europe and the world, leading chemical companies including **BASF** and **DuPont** have turned to mutagenesis—a technique that mimics the sun's irradiation of plants—to create herbicide-resistant crops. The process, which faces almost no regulation, creates opportunities for companies to grab a bigger share of the $34 billion global commercial seed market. But some scientists say mutant crops are more likely to pose health risks than genetically modified ones.

Mutagenesis isn't new: Breeders have relied on it for decades to produce thousands of varieties of lettuce, oats, rice, and other crops. BASF today licenses its technologies to 40 of the world's biggest seed companies, including DuPont and Switzerland's **Syngenta**, which in turn sell high volumes of mutant breeds, ranging from wheat to sunflowers, in markets that reject genetically engineered seeds.

Earnings at BASF's agriculture unit rose 27 percent in 2012 from the previous year, partly because of higher demand for mutant seeds in Eastern Europe, according to the company's latest annual report. "The flexibility is there to use this technology quite broadly," says Jonathan Bryant, vice president of the global strategic marketing group for herbicides at BASF. "Because it's a conventional breeding technique…it's very amenable for a wide range of seed companies."

How much of a challenge does this pose to Monsanto? The world's largest creator of genetically altered crops—it develops and sells seed produced by farmers it contracts with—accounts for a sizable chunk of the global seed market. It had $14.9 billion in sales in fiscal 2013; $10.3 billion of that was from the sale of seeds and genetic licenses. The St. Louis-based company doesn't break down sales figures, but it says most of its seed revenue comes from genetically modified organisms.

While earnings have grown at a rate of more than 20 percent the previous three years, Monsanto faces increased regulation and bans of its GMOs in ▶

31

◀ some countries as well as political hurdles that can delay product launches for years, or indefinitely.

The EU has approved planting only one of Monsanto's genetically modified crop varieties in two decades, prompting its decision to withdraw eight pending GMO requests last summer. It's not the only company confronting roadblocks with GMOs in Europe. BASF last year decided to move its plant science division, dedicated to engineered crops, to the U.S. from Germany. Even in the U.S., bills pending in 26 state legislatures and before Congress would, if passed, require labels on genetically modified foods. No such disclosures are required on ingredients derived from mutant crops.

All breeding techniques can create plants with increased levels of naturally occurring toxins or with proteins known to cause allergic reactions. Reports from the National Academy of Sciences, representing the consensus of experts in the field, say the risk of creating unintended health effects is greater from mutagenesis than any other technique, including genetic modification. Mutagenesis deletes and rearranges hundreds or thousands of genes randomly, spawning mutations that are less precise than GMOs. The academy has warned that regulating genetically modified crops while giving a pass to mutant products isn't scientifically justified.

BASF operating income growth

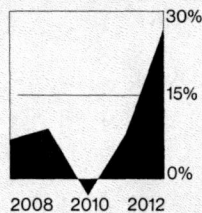

30%
15%
0%
2008 2010 2012

The risks associated with mutagenesis, the academy also says, are small relative to the incidence of foodborne illnesses such as salmonella. BASF maintains the crops are safe for consumers and the environment. "This has been a technique used for many decades without issue, without concern," Bryant says.

In addition to the regulatory-free environment they operate in, mutant crops are also gaining in popularity because they're cheaper to produce. Monsanto spends anywhere from $150 million to $200 million to launch a single genetically engineered product. Japan, by comparison, invested $69 million from 1959 to 2001 on mutant breeds that yielded $62 billion worth of products over that period, according to data from the United Nations' Nuclear Techniques in Food and Agriculture program.

"These difficulties in getting a GMO to the market, we don't have it in mutation breeding," says Pierre Lagoda, who heads up the UN program. That's spurred even more interest in the mutant varieties, he says. In 2013 alone, Lagoda's program has received requests to help irradiate a record 31 plant species ranging from sugar beets from Poland to potatoes from Kenya.

"The current regulations are a huge incentive to go back and do things the old way," including mutagenesis, says Wayne Parrott, a professor of crop science at the University of Georgia in Athens. Monsanto has also used mutation breeding, says the company's chief technology officer, Robb Fraley.

Industry experts say breeding and biotechnology are starting to converge. Over the past five years, breeders have increasingly used molecular markers and sequenced genomes of corn and other crops to improve crossbreeding, making conventional breeding more like genetic engineering. "There is not a black line between biotechnology and nonbiotechnology," says Paul Schickler, president of DuPont's Pioneer seed unit. "It's a continuum." —*Jack Kaskey*

Health

The cornstarch and sugar used in Cheerios will be GMO-free

MAYA KOVACHEVA—ALAMY

Hunger Games Cheerios has ditched GMOs. Does it matter?

BY BRYAN WALSH

NOT MUCH HAS CHANGED about the original Cheerios since General Mills shortened the name from Cheerioats four years after the cereal first appeared on breakfast tables in 1941. Which is why the company's announcement on Jan. 2 that the cereal would now be made without genetically modified ingredients is a sign that consumer tastes are shifting.

The whole-grain oats that are the main ingredient of Cheerios have always been GMO-free, but General Mills is now ensuring that the sugar and cornstarch used in the cereal come from non-GMO sources. It's not that the food giant thinks GMO ingredients pose a health risk. Quite the opposite. Rather, as Gen-

eral Mills VP Tom Forsythe wrote in announcing the change, "We did it because we think consumers might embrace it."

General Mills is probably right. According to a recent survey by the NPD Group, 20% of U.S. consumers—double the percentage in 2002—say they are "very" or "extremely" concerned about genetically modified food. And Cheerios could use the help: while sales of all cereals dropped 2.5% in the year ending Nov. 3, Cheerios sales fell by 7%.

But the GMO issue is bigger than one brand. Bills requiring all companies to label which foods contain GMO ingredients were introduced in 26 states last year. And although a similar bal-

lot initiative was narrowly voted down in Washington State—thanks in part to $22 million in funding from corporate food giants, including General Mills—some companies are labeling voluntarily. Whole Foods has pledged that by 2018 it will label all its products that contain GMO ingredients, and Chipotle is following suit.

Mass labeling will be a tall order, as 70% to 80% of the food consumed in the U.S. contains GMO ingredients. But that should tell you something: for all the angst over GMOs, studies overwhelmingly show that there have been no observed negative health effects from eating food with GMO ingredients and that GMO crops are easier on the environment than conventional ones. Then again, the food industry has never let science get in the way of capitalizing on health fads.

A Brief History Of 'Healthy' Food Fads

NO FAT
EARLY 1990s: The push to remove fat from foods still left a lot of calories and unhealthy additives like artificial sweeteners.

NO CARBS
EARLY 2000s: The suddenly popular Atkins diet said fat was fine but carbs were the devil. Bread sales plummeted.

NO TRANS FATS
MID-2000s: Trans fats are worse than saturated fats—but just because a bag of potato chips is trans fat–free doesn't make it healthy.

NO GLUTEN
PRESENT: Nearly a third of Americans want to cut down on gluten, a drive that has fueled a $4.2 billion market, though just 1 in 133 people has celiac disease.

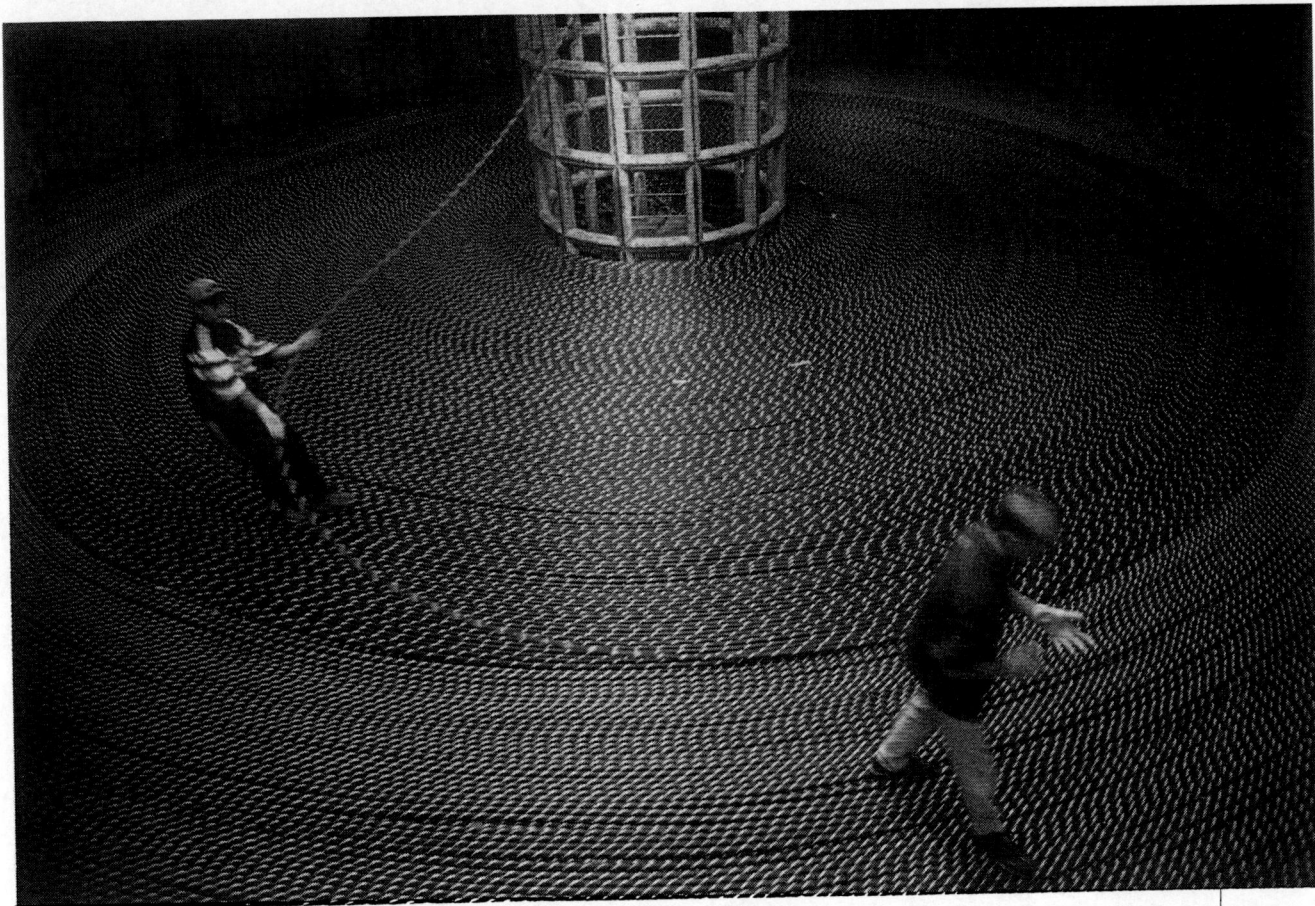

1

first

MAPPING THE INTERNET

Unspooling fiber-optic cable that will soon be laid on the bottom of the Atlantic Ocean

BY
ANDREW BLUM
GRAPHICS BY
NICOLAS RAPP

THE GLOBAL ECONOMY has arranged itself around a short list of dominant cities, the endpoints for movement of all kinds: goods, people, money, and, increasingly, packets of digital information. These packets—some trillion bytes a second—travel primarily as light through fiber-optic cable. E-mails, images, streaming movies, and money: millions and millions every millisecond.

We take it for granted that the Internet, as much as any city, has a physical reality. Tracing the movement of a packet of information throughout this geography of fiber-optic cables and data centers casts the global economy in a different light. In places, the packets piggyback on existing telecommunications systems, traveling through the same capitals of finance and trade that have long been at the center of things. Elsewhere, the Internet disrupts and reshapes the traditional endpoints of movement. By looking closely at our world's digital infrastructure, we can discern broader lessons about emerging economies. By understanding how information moves and how networks are constructed, we can see where the Internet is headed, and where the dominant cities of tomorrow might appear.

TURN THE PAGE FOR MORE ON THE GEOGRAPHY OF THE INTERNET →

BUILDING THE NET

A MORE CONNECTED NATION

Laying fiber-optic cable in Lac Qui Parle county in western Minnesota

THE INTERNET WAS born in the U.S., but we can hardly claim to have the greatest percentage of citizens online (in fact, we are 23rd, behind Slovakia). Why is that? We're accustomed to thinking the problem is the "last mile," meaning the connection between our phone or cable company's office and our homes. But that's only part of the story. Just as important is the "middle mile," meaning the connection between your Internet service provider (ISP) and the rest of the Internet. If you don't live in or near a city, the middle mile can be costly. The key indicator is the price of "Internet transit," the term for an ISP's wholesale access to the Internet's backbones.

The big commercial networks sell transit at competitive prices, but with a catch: Delivery isn't included. An ISP must physically connect its network to the wholesale providers in one of just a few dozen buildings around the country. As with hub airports, the path of least resistance isn't always the shortest or most efficient.

FAST AND SLOW: HOMES WITH ACCESS TO DOWNLOAD SPEEDS GREATER THAN 10 MEGABYTES PER SECOND

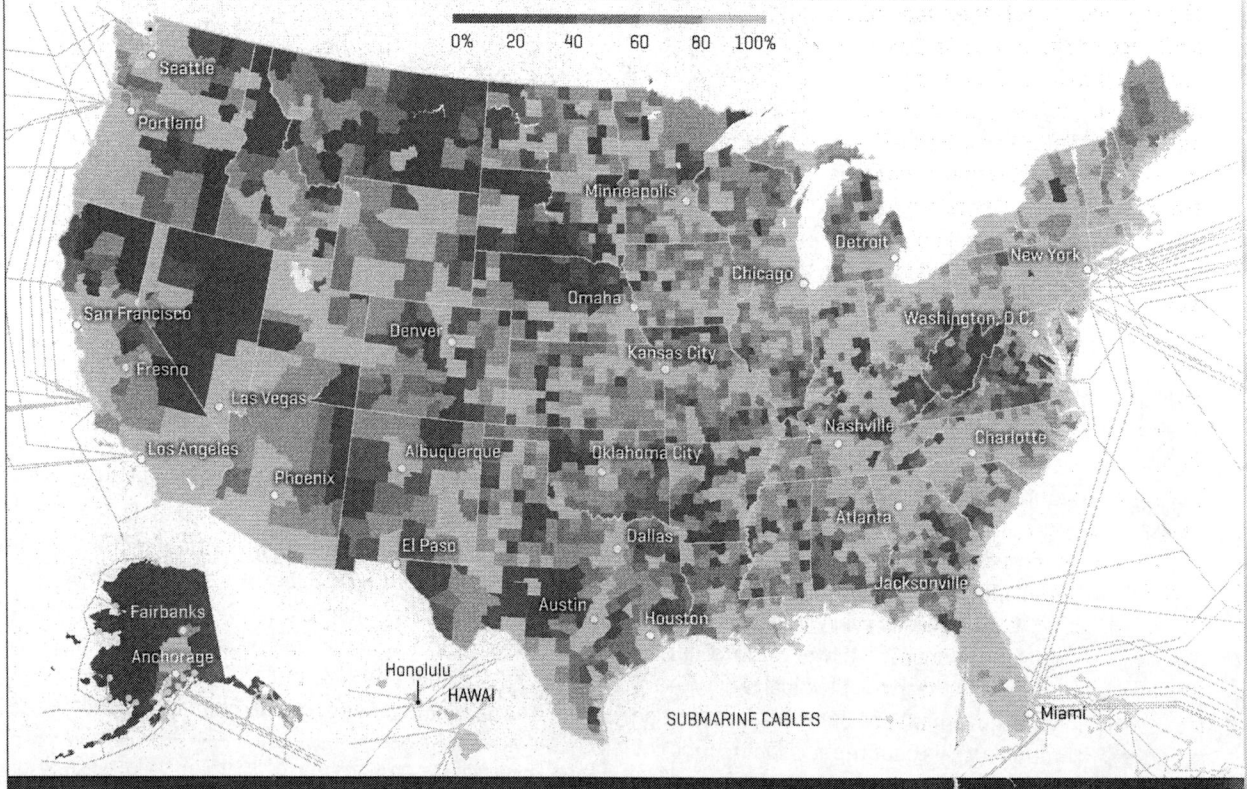

SUBMARINE CABLES

AVERAGE INTERNET SPEEDS [MAXIMUM ADVERTISED]

0   5   6   7   8   9   MEGABYTES PER SECOND

FIBER-OPTIC CABLES

NEW JERSEY

BRONX

HUDSON RIVER

MANHATTAN

QUEENS

EAST RIVER

NYSE

BROOKLYN

1 MILE

Sixty Hudson Street is one of the largest points of Internet traffic in the U.S.

FINANCIAL HUBS

JOSTLING FOR MILLISECONDS

WHEN, IN 1924, the Western Union Telegraph Co. went looking for land for a new headquarters in lower Manhattan, it had strict requirements: The building had to be close not only to the New York Stock Exchange and the commodities exchanges but also to the company's existing operations center, with its fixed cable links to the hinterlands. By the end of 1930, messenger boys were keeping the revolving doors of 60 Hudson Street spinning all day, shuttling messages to the trading firms piled up downtown.

Today's financial services companies—especially those in the business of high-speed algorithmic trading—are faced with exactly the same requirements. They, too, have clustered around 60 Hudson Street, where the majority of transatlantic undersea cables land, in a similar effort: to hear the news of faraway markets first, if only by a matter of milliseconds. The result has been the creation of a parallel Wall Street geography, based not on the location of bustling trading floors but on proximity to the darkened buildings that house today's automated trading platforms. The surrounding space is at a premium, as companies strive to literally shorten the wire that connects them to the hubs.

Andrew Blum is the author of Tubes: A Journey to the Center of the Internet *[Ecco, 2012, from which this is adapted].*

EMERGING MARKETS

WHERE THE NET WILL GO

IT'S ONE THING to bring fiber-optic cable to the coast of a landmass; it's quite another to then build that network into the interior of that landmass. Without much infrastructure already in place, the cost of new broadband cables is extremely high. The result is a bitter irony: Those who can afford it the least must pay the most to go online. In Africa seven undersea fiber-optic cables have made landfall in the past two years, and six more will arrive by 2013. But who will build this network into the continent, and what will it look like?

In Lagos, entrepreneur Muhammed Rudman grapples with these questions. Rudman runs Nigeria's sole Internet exchange point [IX]. An IX connects two networks, like a highway interchange, and reduces cost by aiding data flow. There is, however, a new path emerging, one that will minimize the reliance on such physical structures. If the traditional Internet is, literally, a series of tubes, this alternate structure is in the air. It's wireless. It's mobile. And its users are already those in emerging markets, who do more business on their phones, via SMS, than anyone else.

—*Benjamin Schenkel*

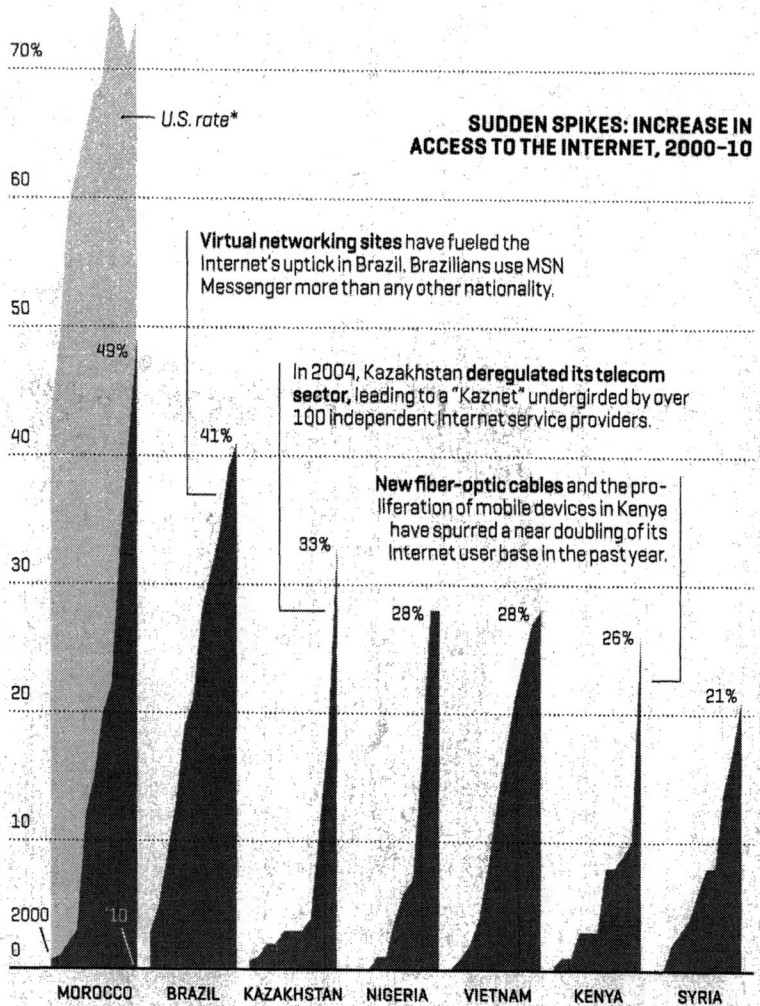

SUDDEN SPIKES: INCREASE IN ACCESS TO THE INTERNET, 2000–10

— U.S. rate*

Virtual networking sites have fueled the Internet's uptick in Brazil. Brazilians use MSN Messenger more than any other nationality.

In 2004, Kazakhstan **deregulated its telecom sector,** leading to a "Kaznet" undergirded by over 100 independent Internet service providers.

New fiber-optic cables and the proliferation of mobile devices in Kenya have spurred a near doubling of its Internet user base in the past year.

49%
41%
33%
28%
28%
26%
21%

MOROCCO   BRAZIL   KAZAKHSTAN   NIGERIA   VIETNAM   KENYA   SYRIA

An undersea fiber-optic cable hauled ashore in Mombasa, Kenya

*THE DIP IN 2008 IS THE RESULT OF AN FCC METHODOLOGY CHANGE.
SOURCES: (U.S. MAP) GEOTEL COMMUNICATIONS; (WORLD MAP) GEOTEL COMMUNICATIONS, WORLD BANK; (NEW YORK CITY MAP) GEOTEL COMMUNICATIONS, NATIONAL TELECOMMUNICATIONS AND INFORMATION ADMINISTRATION; (EMERGING MARKETS GRAPHIC) WORLD BANK

38

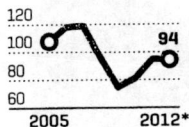

BANKING
Post-recession,
small-business
lending is
trending up.

120
100
80
60
94

2005   2012*

*FROM APRIL. SOURCE:
THOMSON REUTERS PAYNET
SMALL BUSINESS LENDING INDEX

VENTURE

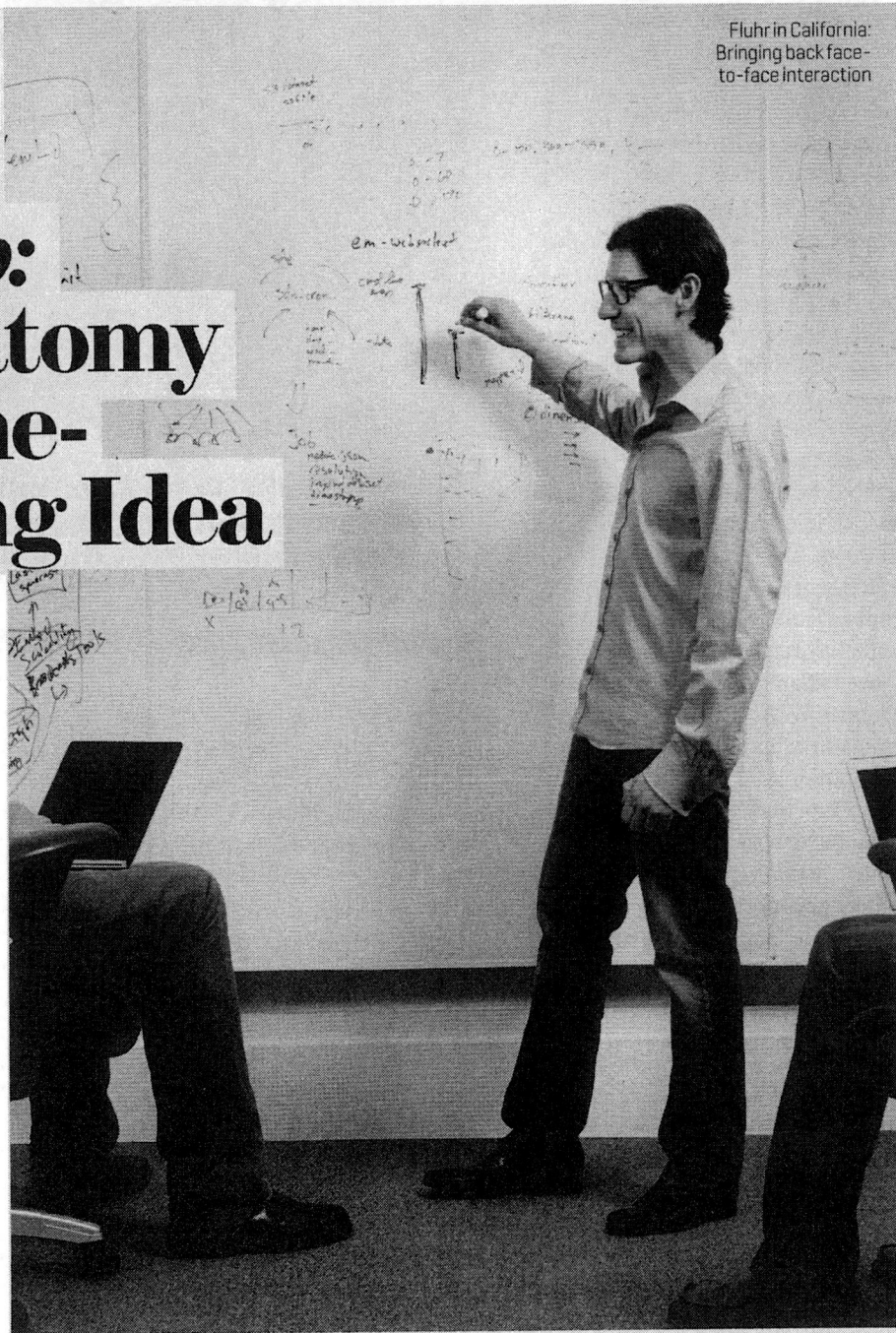

Fluhr in California:
Bringing back face-
to-face interaction

HOW I GOT STARTED

StubHub: The Anatomy of a Game-Changing Idea

JEFF FLUHR was looking for businesses that were "ripe for change." Scalpers were just the ticket.

Edited by Dinah Eng

MAKING MONEY THROUGH *technology is Jeff Fluhr's stock-in-trade. Fluhr, 38, was the co-founder of San Francisco's StubHub.com, an online ticket marketplace where fans buy and sell from each other. Fluhr sold it to eBay in 2007 for $310 million. Now he's trying for an encore with the launch of Spreecast.com, a social video platform designed to bring the intimacy of face-to-face conversations online. Here's his story:*

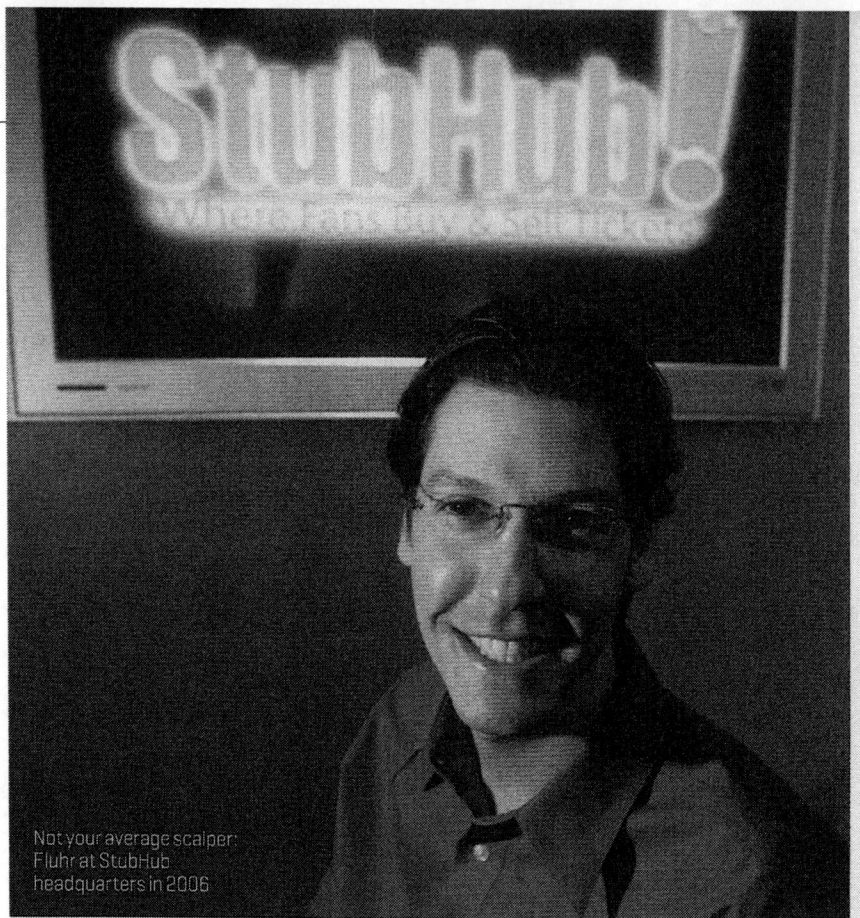

Not your average scalper: Fluhr at StubHub headquarters in 2006

MY FATHER [Zachary] was an electrical engineer for AT&T and my mother [Laura] worked at a women's designer-consignment shop in Manhattan owned by her dad [Michael Kosof]. She later took over the store. When my dad retired, he started a commercial real estate security business, so there's entrepreneurship in my family blood.

After I graduated from the University of Pennsylvania in 1996, my first job was at the Blackstone Group, a large financial services firm in New York. I decided that going into investment banking would be a great way to learn how to evaluate companies. Blackstone dealt with old-school manufacturing businesses, which were good for leveraged buyouts, but it wasn't interesting to me. I was an analyst and learned a lot, but decided to look for something that was more in the technology world.

In the late 1990s the Internet was coming into its own. Netscape, Yahoo, and eBay started, and I decided to move to San Francisco to work for Thomas Weisel Partners, a private equity firm that worked with tech companies. After a while, with my interest in business and technology, I decided to start a company of my own. I thought going to business school would be a great way to pivot, network with people, and have time to develop a business plan for a startup. So in 1999 I enrolled in Stanford's graduate school of business.

I wasn't sure what I wanted to do, but I met Eric Baker, another student who'd also worked at financial institutions. We talked about our mutual interest in starting a company and different ideas about industries that were ripe for change. Eric's dad was a season ticket holder for the Lakers, and my dad for the

> "I enjoy the intellectual challenge of building something. Entrepreneurs look at opportunities and seize them. They don't just talk about them."
> —*Jeff Fluhr, co-founder of StubHub.Com*

Yankees. We talked about the large quantity of tickets for sporting events, theater events, and concerts that weren't used, and the fragmented market of ticket brokers who resold those tickets.

It was a stigmatized business, with the perception that you'd get scammed if you bought a ticket from a scalper. But we thought there might be an opportunity for buying and selling tickets online. I wrote the idea up as a business plan for Stanford's business plan competition, and we were chosen as one of the six finalists. But we pulled out because we decided to start the company and didn't want competition before we got going.

We started networking, talked to executives in the music and sports industries, and found investors. By August 2000 we had raised $600,000 of seed capital for StubHub. It would

be an eBay for tickets. Sellers would set the price, more or less than a ticket's face value, depending on market demand. We'd take a percentage on every transaction—10% from the buyer and 15% from the seller. That first $600,000 was enough to get us to our beta product, get into the market, and learn and test different features. The seed money came from family and friends, but the next level was more difficult.

We had incorporated in March 2000, and right after that the dotcom bubble burst. As we went to raise our second round of funding, a lot of people said no. So we had to meet with more than 50 angel investors, venture capital firms, and others.

Eric stayed at Stanford to get his degree, but I left to become CEO and run the company. When he graduated in 2001, he joined as president.

My Advice

JEFF FLUHR
Co-founder, StubHub; founder, Spreecast

> **CHALLENGE THE STATUS QUO.** If you're disrupting the way businesses do things, you'll be told that's not how it works. But listen to your instincts. Spreecast wants to create a throwback to thousands of years before the Internet, when people had face-to-face interactions. Without face-to-face conversations, people are missing out on learning social skills.

CREATE A TEAM THAT WILL MESH WELL. The mistakes I made in hiring at StubHub have helped inform my decisions this time around. I'll be treading more carefully in bringing in senior people and look for different qualities. I'll focus less on experience and skill set and be more interested in personality, raw intelligence, and drive to make the person a better fit with the existing team.

ENCOURAGE YOUR TEAM TO SPEAK FREELY. When you're leading a company, if you work with people you trust, letting them speak their mind allows you to get good ideas on the table, even if they conflict with yours.

We had about 20 to 30 employees our second year, 60 people the next. By the time we sold to eBay in 2007, there were 350 to 400 employees.

In 2004, Eric and I had a difference in vision. He wanted to focus on partnerships with leagues, using their brands to build our brand. I felt we should concentrate on building our own brand, so both of us decided to part ways. He kept his share as co-founder and left the company. We got to cash flow positive in 2005, and revenue was about $50 million. We became a hot company growing rapidly, but there were still challenges.

Ten or 15 states had laws that restricted the amount you could charge to resell a ticket, either citing a fixed dollar amount over face value or a cap on the percentage over face value. We got letters from a few state attorneys general implying that we might not be in compliance. We argued that we weren't the sellers of the tickets, the users were. No attorney general ever filed a claim against the company. We actually hired some lobbyists and were successful in changing the laws in states like New York, Florida, and Pennsylvania.

Another challenge was Ticketmaster, which didn't like us or our business model. They said we were infringing on their contracts with venues or performing artists by reselling tickets. They never took legal action during my time but sent letters of complaint.

The one significant lawsuit we faced was with the New England Patriots, which filed suit when we were in discussions to sell to eBay in 2006. They said we were inducing their season ticket holders to violate their agreement with the team. We sold before the suit was decided, and eBay settled with them.

In 2006 the company was profitable, with $100 million in revenue. When eBay approached us, I had gotten to the point where I wanted to move on to the next thing. I had gotten married in 2005 while StubHub was rising, and my wife was pregnant. So we sold StubHub for $310 million in 2007 and closed the transaction two weeks before my first son was born. I took time off to travel with my family, and we went around the world. I played a lot of golf and tennis, started doing angel investing, and just enjoyed myself. I'm invested in 40 different companies now. Some are doing well, and some not. I stopped doing angel investing in 2010 and started Spreecast.com.

Over the last 10 years I noticed that with Facebook and Twitter and smartphones, people are spending a lot of time to stay connected. But there's something missing with the way we're communicating now with all this text-based, asynchronous communication. I wanted to bring back face-to-face interaction to the conversation, so I started Spreecast.

Spreecast is a social video platform where you can talk in a public forum about the same topics people are talking about on Facebook—whether it's the passing of Dick Clark or fashion—only it's in real time using a webcam and web browser.

In 2011 we raised $4 million start-up capital from people who invested in StubHub. That figure includes my own investment. The public beta launched in November 2011, and we're starting to see celebrities, politicians, journalists, and others who have a public persona experimenting with us to engage with their fans and followers. There's been nice growth, month over month.

I enjoy the intellectual challenge of building something from nothing and navigating through the challenges of starting a company. I think entrepreneurs look at opportunities and seize them. They don't just talk about them. ⏹

Technology
Coupon Deathmatch, Party of Two?

OpenTable seats 4 million people per month

Groupon splits revenue 50-50 with merchants

Gets up to $1 per head for every reservation

Groupon CEO Andrew Mason

Began a Groupon-like service in August

OpenTable CEO Jeff Jordan

17 million users and $173 million in funding

Credited with inventing online daily-deal coupons

▶ Restaurant booker OpenTable may be Groupon's most formidable competitor in online coupons

▶ "This is like the yellow pages business. They are going to need to cover hundreds of cities"

The Essex, on Manhattan's Lower East Side, offers creative cocktails, $1 oysters, and its signature Colorado lamb chops over ricotta gnocchi. On weekday nights and during off-peak hours, it also features lots of empty tables.

To fill his 150-seat restaurant in an economy that can spoil anyone's appetite, The Essex's owner, David Perlman, has turned to Internet coupons. Last spring, he used one of the hottest startups on the Web, **Groupon**, to sell $30 coupons at $15 each to about 1,500 people on the site's New York e-mail list. In August, Perlman went the discount route again, this time with the just-launched coupon service of **OpenTable**, the online restaurant-reservation booker. Slightly fewer than 1,000 people

purchased that deal, a $50 coupon for $25. Still, Perlman says he favors OpenTable's service because it brought in gourmet diners who were more likely to turn into repeat customers. "We had a positive, profitable experience with both, but I liked OpenTable better, just because it is more geared toward restaurants," he says. "The people we attracted with OpenTable are people we want to add to our customer base."

Daily deals are everywhere online. That has a lot to do with privately held Groupon, based in Chicago, which has emerged from nowhere to revolutionize local advertising and build a business recently valued at $1.35 billion, according to two people familiar with the company.

Groupon works like this: It sends a

daily e-mail to more than 17 million subscribers in over 230 cities, employing flowery prose ("A love of layers may even lead your archeological side through the house lasagna") to offer group discounts on everything from pastries and spa treatments to pilot lessons and restaurant meals. If enough people take the offer and pay in advance, the deal is activated and Groupon splits the resulting revenue 50-50 with the merchant. Subscribers get only one offer per day, which has left room for hundreds of copycats to offer their own variations on the formula. "We stuck a pin in something and now there's a giant eruption," says Andrew Mason, Groupon's 29-year-old founder. "The demand from business owners is much greater than

Technology

Botched
foreclosures,
longer slump
page 44 ▶

anything a single business like Groupon can meet."

Restaurants account for nearly half of Groupon's deals, making OpenTable the imitator best positioned to eat its lunch. OpenTable, started 12 years ago in San Francisco, has put its reservation-management system into more than 14,000 restaurants. (Restaurants either lease computers for a $600 installation fee plus a $199 monthly subscription or they use the cheaper, Web-only option.) It seats about 4 million diners each month. Restaurants pay OpenTable up to $1 dollar per head; diners make reservations for free. The company has the e-mail addresses of tens of millions of gourmands, as well as a sales force devoted to pitching additional marketing services to restaurants using Open-Table. And like Groupon, OpenTable has its own overcooked valuation: Its stock, valued at $1.56 billion, is trading at 72 times its estimated 2011 earnings—more than six times the S&P 500 average.

OpenTable unveiled its Spotlight coupon service in August and has rolled it out in Boston, New York, San Francisco, Chicago, Washington, and Philadelphia. Spotlight is Groupon-like right down to the verbiage. ("Their menus showcase artisanally grown, fresh fare that sings.") CEO Jeff Jordan says Groupon's deals aren't tailored to people's individual interests. "Groupon is sending me ads for hair removal. Nature is doing that for me," he jokes. That lack of focus, he says, has created an opening for him to hone in on foodies.

Groupon believes its size and some upcoming features meant to personalize pitches will keep the competition at bay. It has raised money at a ferocious pace. In April it received a $135 million infusion from two Facebook investors—the Russian-based investment group DST and venture capital firm Accel Partners—and others. Groupon has used the cash to enter new cities, buy competitors in Chile and Germany, and expand its 1,600-person sales force, which makes up about half its head count. The company is beginning to tailor deals to subscribers' location, gender, and any information they volunteer about their buying interests on Groupon's website. It aims to offer deals based on a subscriber's Groupon purchase history, Mason says. (And now it's planning to use that data to help its customers meet:

On Sept. 29 it announced the Groupon Date Assistant.)

Analysts are divided on how this coupon contest will play out. "What Groupon lacks in protective competitive moats, I think they get in the fact that this is a scale business," says Scot Wingo, CEO of e-commerce consulting firm ChannelAdvisor. He says the size of Groupon's sales staff is its best competitive advantage: "This is like the yellow pages business. They are going to need to cover hundreds of cities and have feet on the street in all of those places."

72

Ratio of OpenTable's stock price to estimated 2011 earnings

Mark Mahaney, an analyst at Citigroup, downgraded OpenTable's stock in June because he believed the shares were overvalued. He reversed course in September after the company sold 16,000 Spotlight offers in the program's first six weeks, bringing in an estimated $200,000 in revenue. "OpenTable can go right to its customers, all of whom are interested in restaurants," Mahaney says. Groupon and its other imitators acquire most customers either by word of mouth or by running targeted ads on Facebook and Google. Another formidable competitor is also joining the fray: Yelp, the local-business review site, is introducing a daily-deal service. With its 300-strong sales force focused on local ads, Yelp, too, has relationships with merchants.

One clear beneficiary of all this competition will be restaurants. As new entrants undercut each other on coupon commissions, rates could be driven below 50 percent. The coupons are already moving into the upper echelons of gastronomy. Metrazur, a high-end restaurant in New York's Grand Central Terminal, recently sold 1,200 $50 coupons for $25 using OpenTable; Rouge Tomate, another pricey New York eatery, just sold 385 $100 coupons for $50 on Yelp. Perlman, of The Essex, says discounting by the swankiest establishments helps him. "If anything, keeping such company on the deal sites actually enhanced our reputation," he says. —*Brad Stone*

The bottom line Groupon, which started the boom in daily-deal sites, faces tough competition from similar services offered by OpenTable, Yelp, and others.

Module 2

INVENT

Laila Bastedo

2.1 INTRODUCTION

Module 1 introduced the technology commercialization value chain the first stage of which is "I – Invent new technology with potential commercial value" (Figure 2.1).[1] The commercial value is only potential at this stage because a clear understanding of the ultimate product, its market and its business feasibility is still absent. During this stage opportunities for commercialization are first recognized and developed in a preliminary way. In the Invent Stage the organization is looking for MTB Propositions, combinations of market, technology and business that have commercial potential. This stage is sometimes called the "Fuzzy Front End" because it can be so unstructured, chaotic and unpredictable.[2] The interactions between people in the "I" stage can start informally with small teams or groups exploring various ideas and opportunities[3]. Part of this usually involves the investigation of, and speculation about, the technology or technologies that underlie the opportunity.[4] This involves both product and process technologies. As the opportunity is explored, the business marketing and technical feasibility of the opportunity becomes less ambiguous.

Figure 2.1
The ICE Model and the Technology Commercialization Value Chain

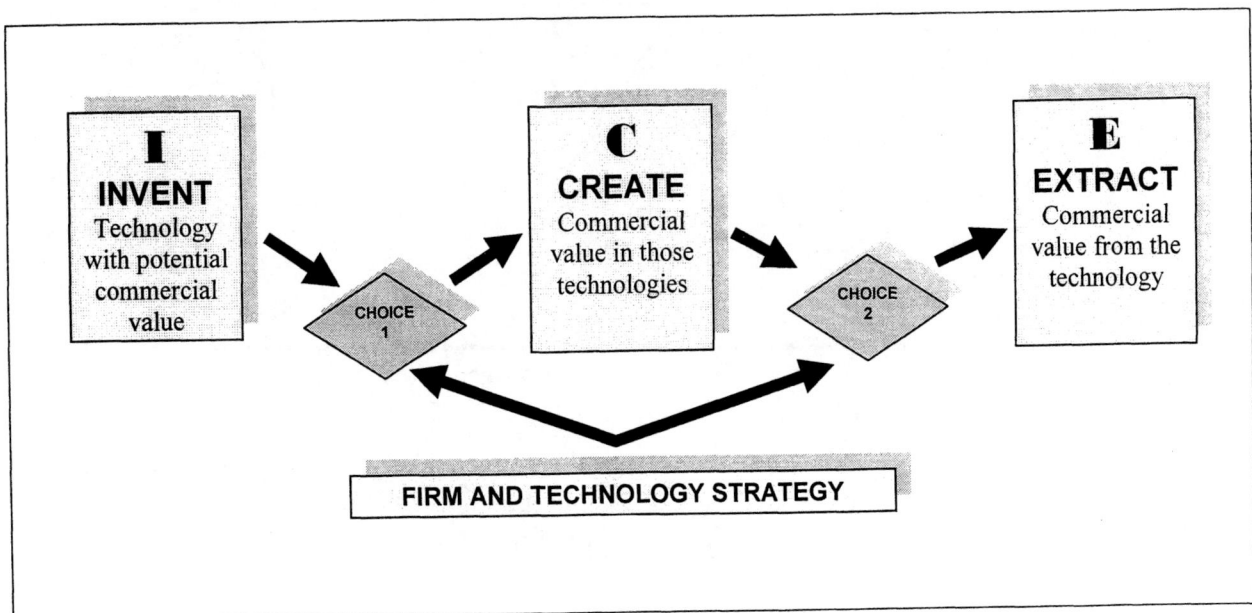

To call this the "Invent Stage" is a bit of a misnomer because it involves much more than just the invention of new technologies by scientists or other technical people. As just described it involves marketing, business issues and general opportunity scanning as well. One alternate

– 1 –

term for this stage would be "investigation" because it does involve the investigation of markets, technologies and business opportunities. But this misses the creative aspects of the process and the necessity to choose the best "inventions" to work with. Another term that might be used is "Identify" because this stage ends with the identification of the best opportunities. But this leaves out the investigation part and the creativity part. No term is entirely satisfactory and so "Invent" has been chosen as the most nearly satisfactory. It captures the idea of <u>new technology</u> with <u>potential value</u> found through that most human of attributes, <u>inventiveness</u>.

2.2 UNCERTAINTY

The invent stage involves high degrees of uncertainty around the technology, the market and business viability. Over time these uncertainties evolve. Vague ideas become possibilities for commercialization. These possibilities may evolve into perceived opportunities. Perceived opportunities may become MTB Propositions. But before the MTB Proposition can move from the Invent to the Create Stage uncertainty must be reduced to an acceptable level.

Figure 2.2
Reducing Uncertainty in the Invent Stage

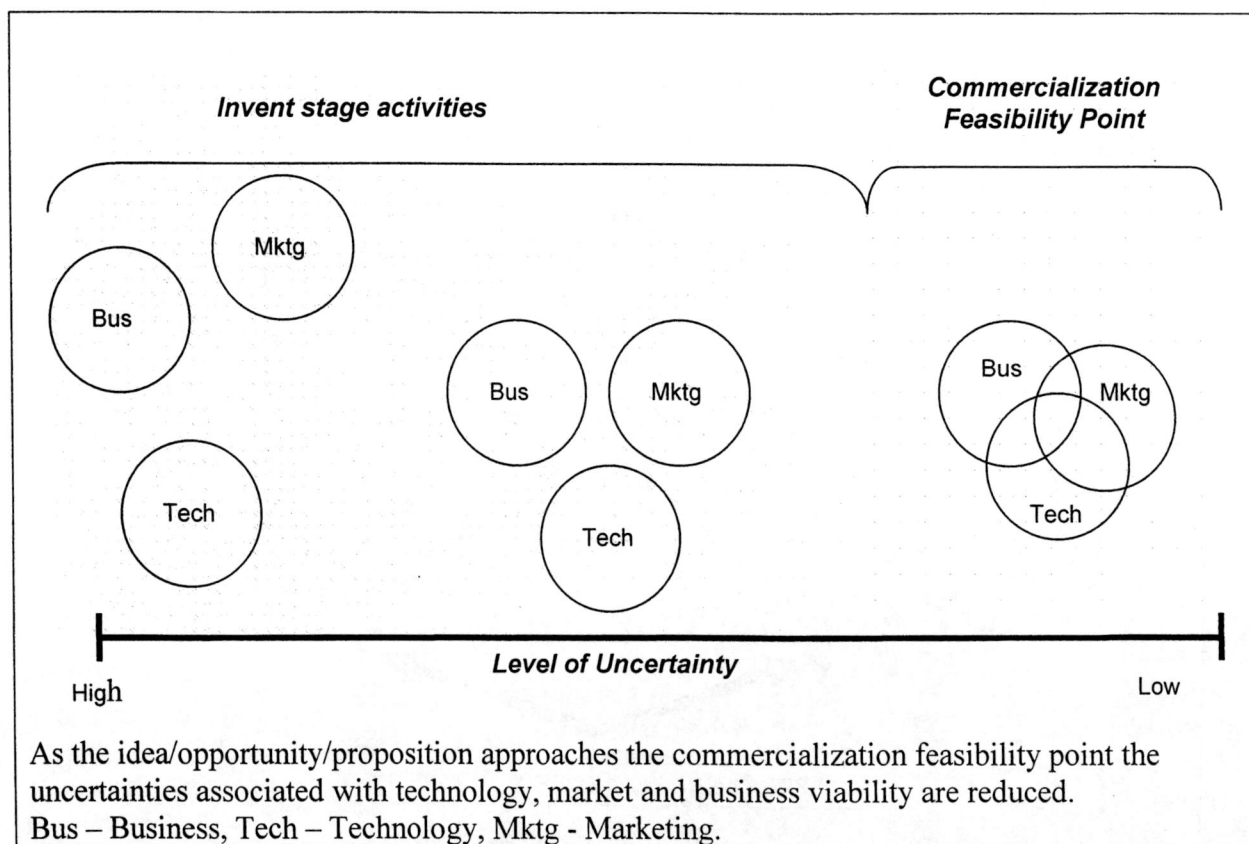

As the idea/opportunity/proposition approaches the commercialization feasibility point the uncertainties associated with technology, market and business viability are reduced.
Bus – Business, Tech – Technology, Mktg - Marketing.

As indicated, uncertainty is multifaceted. Technical uncertainty refers to the underlying technology or science. High degrees of uncertainty are particularly attached to technologies that have not yet been developed or tried. Uncertainties associated with both the product technology and manufacturing technology include the degree of task innovation. This includes, for example, the set of procedures for making a particular product using the available manufacturing technologies. Market uncertainties also increase the complexity. Complexities associated with the external environment include politics, financial support, resource allocation and socio-political climate. These can all add to the overall degree of uncertainty.

When the uncertainties are sufficiently reduced, the MTB Proposition reaches the **commercialization feasibility point**. It is here that the proposition looks like a true opportunity and a decision may be made to move it on to the Create Stage. This is shown in Figure 2.2. On the left there is high uncertainty so the circles are shown to be far apart. As uncertainty is reduced they move closer together until they intersect at the commercialization feasibility point. This indicates their convergence into a viable MTB Proposition. For example, a market need may be identified as a potential opportunity, but without the technology or the manufacturing ability, one cannot determine whether this opportunity will be commercially viable. Likewise, if a researcher discovers a novel chemical property, protein, or process, it does not mean that this new discovery is commercially feasible. The technology itself needs to be fine-tuned into something of value to a buyer. It must have manufacturing potential and there needs to be a defined market need. The level of uncertainty is high. As the technology opportunity is explored, the business and technical feasibility of the new product becomes less ambiguous.

The goal of the Invent Stage is to have the MTB Proposition reach the commercialization feasibility point. This implies that the **technology feasibility point, market feasibility point** and **business feasibility point** have all been reached. All these must come together in the MTB Proposition. Not all will necessarily arrive at feasibility at the same time although none is truly feasible until all are. For example, marketing might discover that there is high demand for a PC that costs $200.00 - $250.00 with basic functionality and that no other firm is currently filling that niche. This may be based on thorough market research so the market feasibility point has already been reached. The technology may still be highly uncertain though, so more research is needed to see if such a technology is at all feasible. That work may lead to a technology concept with a prototype which looks quite feasible. So the technology feasibility point is reached. Preliminary analysis may indicate, though, that the idea does not work as a business proposition. Further research might be done to figure out a better business model for the idea. When such a model is laid out the business feasibility point is reached. However, this may involve some adjustments to the technology and marketing plans. Now that all three are feasible it can be said that the commercialization feasibility point has been reached.

These feasibility "points" are rarely just points. Given the ambiguities at this early stage in the value chain it is difficult to tell exactly when feasibility is reached. It is subjective because the point depends on many factors including: i) the business culture, ii) prior experience with similar technologies, iii) internal and external pressures, iv) risk tolerance of management, v) core competencies of the technical or development personnel,[5] vi) logistics of any licensing, acquisitions, partnering. For example, if management's risk tolerance is high and if the current market opportunity is ripe, it is still possible for the project to be classified as reaching the commercial feasibility point even if the underlying technology has not met one-hundred percent of the initial performance criteria.[6] And, of course, the feasibility of one aspect depends upon the feasibility of the others. And, as just mentioned, some aspects reach feasibility before others. It might be more appropriate to label the "point" as a feasibility "window" or "region", reflecting a more ill-defined notion of when an MTB Proposition is ready.

In Module 1 the terms radical and incremental innovation were introduced and basic definitions provided. At this point we can add another layer of meaning to them.

A **radical innovation** is a product, process or service "with either unprecedented performance features or familiar features that offer significant improvements in performance or cost that transform existing markets or create new ones."[7] Radical innovations are usually new to the organization *and* new to the market.[8] There is a high degree of uncertainty associated with radical innovation. It can involve the use of untried technologies and may often involve technologies that do not exist and have yet to be developed. Other characteristics of radical innovation include processes and technologies that are unpredictable, non-linear, stochastic, and context dependent and with a high degree of resource and organizational uncertainty.[9] Radical innovations are often based upon basic scientific research of the kind that is often done in universities. Corporations are thus actively making an effort to partner with university research departments in hopes that their basic research will lead to radical innovations.[10]

In contrast, **incremental innovation** requires little product or process change. It often follows a liner process with fewer organizational and resource uncertainties. Incremental innovations are usually improvements to existing product lines or process. The repositioning of a product in the market or re-formulating the process so that costs are reduced, are also examples of incremental innovations.[11, 12] In other words, there are fewer uncertainties associated with what the underlying technologies are, what the product/service will do, how will the various aspects of technology, marketing and manufacturing work, and where the needed resources will come from. Ideas for incremental innovation are often determined from the organization's strategic plan. Some ideas can come from internal idea suggestion programs, as a cost-cutting measure, or from the needs of the market. Feasibility testing is technically easier because the various elements of the technology, manufacturing process and marketing are known and the incremental extension or innovation is a "tweak", or "modification" of what is already known. Reaching the commercialization feasibility point is quicker. The preliminary business case, market segmentation, product positioning, specifications, operational strategy and financial analysis are far more concrete for an incremental innovation than for a breakthrough.

Thus, incremental innovation enters the technology commercialization value chain closer to the commercialization feasibility point than does radical innovation (Figure 2.3). Incremental innovation therefore consumes fewer organizational resources in the evolution to the commercialization feasibility point and represents less of a commercial risk. This is why many firms gravitate to incremental innovations and shun the radical.

2.3 ACTIVITIES IN THE INVENT STAGE

To this point the Invent Stage has been described in general terms showing technology, marketing and business considerations in the movement of an opportunity/proposition towards the commercialization feasibility point. Now we will turn our attention specifically to the processes for managing technology during the Invent Stage.

2.3.1 Technology Planning

The goal of technology management is to proactively focus the research and development activities of an organization on those technology opportunities that can generate future corporate revenue. This is crucial for an organization to keep abreast of rapidly changing technology developments and market demands. A key process that underlies the management of technology is the organization's technology planning process which integrates the strategic business planning with technology opportunities.[13]

The technology planning process should run in parallel and be integrated with market and business planning processes. All are intricately tied to the corporate strategic goals so that innovative, cutting-edge, technology opportunities can be identified, prioritized, selected and developed for future commercialization. The result of a good technology planning process is a written actionable plan that contains the strategic goals of the organization, competitive position in the industry, internal technology position, technology opportunities, and tactical actions required to achieve the goals. In order to leverage new and existing technologies to meet changing consumer needs, to optimize resource allocation, and to meet the strategic and financial goals of the organization, the technology planning process must be continual, iterative, and collaborative across various cross-functional areas.[14]

Figure 2.3
Radical and Incremental Innovation

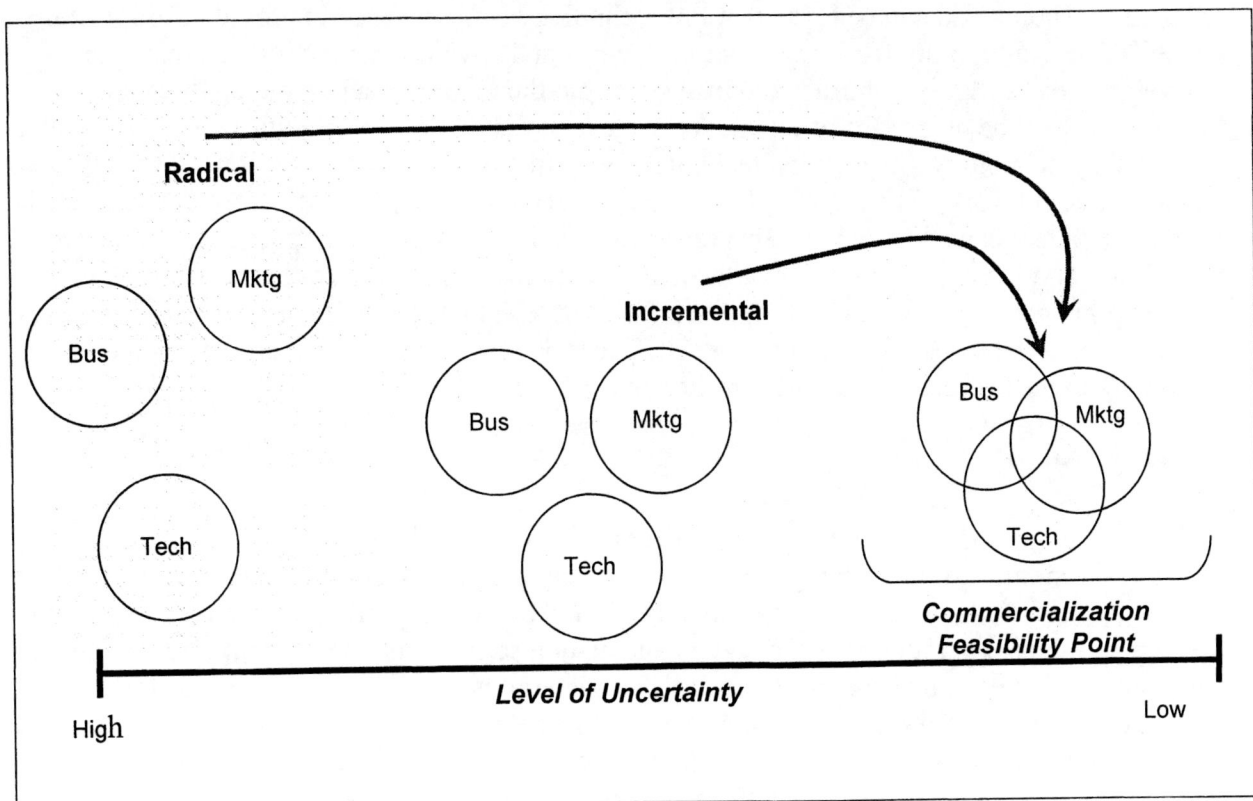

During its technology planning process the organization evaluates and considers its strengths and capabilities (competencies) and future directions. It is here that it probes the activities in the technology commercialization value chain and determines where current activities stand as well as future offerings. How and where will the needed technology be invented/discovered? What levels of uncertainty exist with different ventures and how will the organization support and facilitate their development? Which aspects will occur in-house and which will be contracted or acquired? What other technologies can be leveraged to new product lines or sold to competitors? What criteria will be used to shelf MTB Propositions that do not meet business needs? What management and organizational structures are required to support these various activities? Do they differ depending on the technology and business choices?

An idea or invention by itself does not have commercial value. An opportunity occurs when an invention is given potential commercial value. In other words, an idea or an invention needs an application and a market place for it to be called an "opportunity".[15] Opportunity recognition can occur through technology push or market pull, or some combination of the two. In **market pull** the needs of the market pull an organization to find an innovative technical solution to fill a market niche. For example, the catalytic converter was developed to fill the need for technologies that reduce cold-start emissions from automobiles.[16] That market demand arose from legislation, political pressure and the demands of the public. The pull was there so researchers set to work to find the technologies that fulfilled the need. In **technology push** a technology or application is discovered before the market need is identified. The technology triggers the idea for a market which is subsequently researched and then developed. For example, it was discovered in scientific laboratories that a thin wire will glow with light when enough electricity is passed through it and certain other conditions are present. The scientists who discovered this had no interest in electric lighting and probably did not even think of it at the time. Thomas Edison believed that this technology could be used to provide commercially viable electrical lighting for homes, factories, cities and a wide variety of other users. He developed the technology further and pushed it onto the market as a commercial venture.

One of the objectives of the Invent Stage is to reduce the uncertainties associated with a promising technology. A potential technology may just be an idea with no concrete plans of how it will or could work. The logistics of how the idea can be turned manufactured and marketed may not have received attention. This represents the left most side of Figure 2.3. As the idea incubates and the uncertainties are reduced it reaches the commercialization feasibility point. During the movement from left to right a number of technology specific activities are involved. These will now be described in more detail. These do not necessarily occur linearly but occur throughout the process and are often re-iterative.

2.3.2 Research

A major mechanism for the introduction of new technologies is research. Research can be classified into two main categories, basic and applied. **Basic research** seeks to advance the scientific knowledge base. It is often theoretical and exploratory. Basic research does not try to solve problems, but rather seeks to understand natural phenomena. For example, the study of the physical and chemical properties of radioactive material is basic research, so too is the characterization of the gene responsible for a specific type of cancer. **Applied research**, on the other hand, uses the knowledge gained from basic research to find solutions to problems. For example, the knowledge of the health hazards of radioactive materials may be used to develop materials that block the harmful effects of radiation. Alternatively, the characterization of the gene responsible for cancer can then be used to create diagnostic tests for those who may be pre-disposed to such cancers. Both basic and applied research can occur in the Research & Development units of organizations or in universities and government laboratories.

Running R&D departments that do research can be costly. The benefits, however, lie in that the organization has the greatest control of the technology and the greatest freedom in its use. The intellectual property of the discovery/development is retained by the organization which can then choose to license it, develop it further for any number of applications and products or to sell it. In other words, internal research offers a great deal of technology autonomy for the organization.[17]

One great value of basic research is the discovery of knowledge that can have practical use. The key is to recognize the opportunity that research results present.[18] Basic research, by itself, is thus quite uncertain. Research activities can occur at any stage in the technology value creation chain. Basic research can evolve into applied research as one proceeds to find solutions (develop commercialization value). This is where the "strong feeling" of a commercialization potential becomes more defined to include the general understanding of desired functions, features, and/or capabilities of the product.[19] Even when uncertainties of a proposed technology opportunity are approaching the technology feasibility point, an organization may find itself performing (or acquiring) more research to further refine the technology's potential. As one moves towards the technology feasibility point, the application of the research idea into something that can be marketed and manufactured becomes more and more clear.

2.3.3 Technology Mining

Although basic and applied research can play an important role in the discovery of new opportunities, organizations also actively search for opportunities within their existing portfolio of technologies. This is referred to as technology mining. Technology mining is an integral component of the technology planning process in many highly effective companies.[20] Technology mining is the process of looking at the technology used in current products or those not currently used which the organization has discovered or developed in the past.[21] This can uncover technologies that can be transferred from an existing product to another novel product application. The technology mining process focuses on answering the what, how, how much, and who of the technology as it relates to the company's business needs and culture.[22]

Many of a firm's discoveries may not be commercialized because other technologies appear to have more easily realized commercial value.[23,24] Companies generally use only five to twenty-five per cent of their patented technologies in their own products. The rest may remain unused and dormant.[25] For these technologies, technology mining can be used to identify those that might be sold or licensed to other firms, even competitors.[26] This is a particularly attractive prospect if the technologies do not appear to be related to the firm's core business. IBM has realized considerable income by licensing intellectual property and applications uncovered by mining their own internal patent archives. The revenue from this activity represents about one-ninth of their annual profits.[27]

Mining can also reduce the uncertainties associated with a market-driven opportunity. For example, an unmet market need may spur an idea on how to fulfill that need. The underlying technology to make a product to fill that need may at first be uncertain. Technology mining can uncover the needed technologies to move the idea and its associated technical, marketing and business uncertainties towards something that is more concrete and workable. Overall, technology mining can increase the overall innovativeness of the organization by enabling it to continuously identify opportunities and investigate their feasibility.

2.3.4 Technology Scanning

Technology scanning refers to scanning outside the firm to find new technologies the firm can use in its commercial activities. It represents an alternative to researching and developing the technologies in-house. Firms have turned to external scanning because internal R&D can be very costly and in many high-tech industries this cost is increasing. For example, in the pharmaceutical industry, the average cost to develop a single drug increased ten-fold in one decade to over $800 million.[28] In addition to the rising costs of technology development there is the ever-shortening life cycles of products. For example, in the pharmaceutical industry, the expected market life of new drugs has substantially shortened because of quicker entry into the market by generics and longer drug testing requirements.[29] Shorter product life cycles, rising development costs as well as market pressures for shorter lead times and reduced costs make it more and more difficult to justify large in-house technology investments.[30]

While these economic pressures on innovation are real, companies must innovate to stay competitive. For example, a company may run into technical hurdles that it cannot solve when trying to develop a specific application. They may find it too costly to continue research and technology investigation in-house. Or, an organization may want to strategically increase its product offerings, develop a radical new application, or venture into new technologies. It may not be financially feasible to invent and develop all the underlying technologies at home. Looking for and leveraging external research and development resources can address some of the economic pressures on innovation. Organizations can employ a number of strategies to scan the external environment for technology opportunities.

Industry Analysis. Analyzing industries and understanding their value chains can indicate where certain kinds of technologies are already used and suggest sources for those technologies. Some of those technologies may present opportunities for the scanning firm.

Patent Literature Searches. Most patents are never commercialized because the patent owners did not perceive commercial value or did not have the resources, or understanding to commercialize their invention. The U.S. Patent and Trademark Office's databases contain public domain patents that may contain commercialization potential for an organization.[31]

Customers and Suppliers. Customers and suppliers can be a good source of technologies for a firm.

Universities. Basic science researchers at universities often do not think about the commercialization potential of their discoveries. Collaboration with universities can uncover discoveries with potential, or can result in public/private partnerships for the creation of new products and knowledge.[32] Public universities short on funding have also recognized the prospects afforded by industry collaboration. A growing trend among universities is the formation of offices with the mandate to commercialize research activities and their products through relationship and alliance building with industry.

Government. Government agencies such as NASA (National Aeronautical and Space Administration), the Department of Defense, and NSERC (National Science and Engineering Research Council), offer grants and other programs for technology research.[33] Scanning government opportunities provides insight into trends and needs and also functions as a source of technology developers that an organization can support, partner with, or license from.

2.3.5 Sourcing Technology Externally

There are several strategies a company can employ to acquire new technologies externally once scanning and needs identification have been done. As discussed earlier, internal R&D offers the most autonomy for the organization. However, this autonomy is often weighed against other factors such as cost, time, and risk that external sources may alleviate.

Acquisition. An organization may choose to acquire another company that possesses the desired technology. This option is costly and can pose additional challenges of integrating the corporate cultures and research teams.[34] Alternately, a firm may just buy the specific technology to alleviate some of the problems associated with acquiring a company.

Joint Venture/Alliance. An organization may choose to form an alliance or joint venture with another company to share and develop needed technologies. Joint ventures can take some time to work out.[35]

External R&D Contracts. This involves subcontracting with external laboratories, research centers, and even universities for the development of a particular technology. The contracts can allow exclusive rights to the technology for the contracting organization. They can provide access to specialists and highly qualified research teams which would be too expensive to maintain in-house.[36]

Licenses. Organizations can license technology. License fees have to be paid to the license holder. However, licenses often have strict limits on how the technology can be used[37]. The licensee has to weigh this disadvantage with the benefit of accessing the technology. Licenses usually lead to the smallest amount of control of a technology for the licensee organization but if the technology is already developed and tested may provide quick access.

Private label. An organization can choose to purchase finished products or components of products for assembly. The product can be offered to the market under the organization's brand and trade mark.[38] For example, some products such as Swiffer Dusters, Crest SpinBrush, and Olay Regenerist are marketed as Procter & Gamble products but are licensed or acquired from other companies.

Education acquisitions. The provision of grants and affiliate programs with research universities allows organizations to stay abreast with new technologies.[39]

Venture capital. In this strategy, an organization invests in new and expanding companies. This equity holding allows some control over the technology development. If a technology development proves successful, the organization may choose to acquire the company, make a licensing arrangement or access the technology in some other way. General Electric and Dupont are two large US corporations that follow the venture capital approach.[40]

The use of external sources of technology can help an organization be innovative in a very cost effective way. Ideas from external sources can be used to develop products in-house. Genzyme licenses technology from the outside and develops it in-house to produce therapies that treat rare diseases. At the same time, intellectual property developed internally can be licensed to external parties.[41,42] In these examples, an idea can travel through invent, create and extract through two or more companies.[43]

Time and money can be saved by leveraging external resources. As discussed earlier, companies can stay innovative without spending large amounts of resources developing everything in-house. In the same way that they can obtain licenses for technologies, they can also enjoy increased revenue by licensing their own unused technologies and patents to others.[44,45] In Procter & Gamble's Pringle Print initiative, where every Pringle chip has words or printed pictures on it, the company did not solely develop the technology to print the chips. Instead, P&G adapted (not invented) an ink jet technology that was used to print messages on cookies in Bologna, Italy. [46]

For a venture such as this, the core idea may have merit but hold a lot of uncertainty in the technology used to achieve it and the manufacturing employed to produce the product efficiently. Should the technology be developed totally in-house? Is there a theoretical basis for the technology upon which the company can continue development? What are the current internal capabilities for a promising technology that would help achieve the vision of the idea (mining). The external environment may be scanned for potential technologies and processes (scanning). Does the technology exist in its entirety or do modifications have to be made? What are the logistics of acquiring the technology? The decisions here are a balancing act. There are no hard-and-fast rules to reduce the uncertainties associated with different decisions, nor are there any hard-and-fast rules that govern which decision will lead to a profitable outcome.

2.3.6 Testing and Feasibility Analysis

In the Invent Stage testing and analysis may be done to determine if a technology can meet the performance criteria needed to make a proposed product viable. For example, a growing need to rapidly detect specific kinds of DNA at very low concentrations has spurred the idea of using Polymerase Chain Reaction (PCR) to amplify small amounts of DNA so they can be detected. The application of PCR in a clinical diagnostic setting would have specific performance criteria with respect to target specificity and sensitivity.[47] A "litmus" test for the application of the PCR technology to assess if the basic performance criteria are met would be one of the many early tests conducted when considering the viability of the technology. Once feasibility testing shows that the basic performance criteria are met one more level of uncertainty is reduced and the technology feasibility point is one step closer. Unlike "product testing" which tests a prototype product this involves the testing of a base technology.[48] This kind of testing helps build the business case for the technology and its proposed product.[49] Feasibility testing usually requires some market and product intelligence.[50]

2.4 STRUCTURING ACTIVITIES IN THE INVENT STAGE

Practitioners and researchers have suggested structured processes which can be used to organize activities in the Invent Stage. The intention is to organize those activities to make them more efficient and effective at moving highly ambiguous ideas about technology potential through to the technology feasibility point. Two of them will be described here.

2.4.1 Technology Realization and Commercialization (TRAC)

Eldred and McGrath propose an integrated technology process termed Technology Realization And Commercialization (TRAC)[51]. They propose that organizations use a structured process from early in the Invent stage through to the technology feasibility point. The TRAC process includes a staged Technology Review Process with technical reviews at the end of each stage. The technical reviews are conducted by the Senior Review Committee composed of both scientific and business professionals. Technical reviews are evaluated for both scientific and business merits on the proposed technology/opportunity development. This model recognizes that outcomes of experiments can be uncertain, but requires a detailed plan only for the next upcoming stage. In the initial stage, a technology is evaluated against technical performance criteria. In the second stage, the model requires a technology strategy and approach as well as non-technical inclusions such as program team structure, experimental plan for the next stage, and resource requirements. In each of the subsequent stages, the technical reviews focus on the results of the experimentation from that stage as well as the detailed plans for the next upcoming

– 10 –

stage. Eventually, when the technical feasibility point is reached (when performance criteria are met), the MTB Proposition is ready for transfer to the Create Stage.

2.4.2 Technology Development Stage-Gate Model (TD Gate)

Cooper like many proponents of the traditional Stage-Gate model for the Create Stage has suggested that a structured gate process can also be useful in the Invent Stage. He suggests a three stage, four gate model that precedes the traditional new product development gate process of the Create Stage.[52] Like Eldred and McGrath's TRAC model[53] the TD Gate model has technical reviews at each stage conducted by senior representatives from both research and business. Unlike the TRAC model, which makes allowances for a flexible number of stages depending on the uncertainty level and scope of the initial idea, the TD Gate model has three set stages: project scoping, technical assessment, and detailed investigation.

2.4.3 Which Method?

The most effective method to move an idea through the Invent Stage to the technology feasibility point depends on many factors. In some cases, particularly with high ambiguity, a very unstructured process may be most effective as vague ideas and various suggestions are cycled though a number of attempts to bring a structured proposal to light. In other cases there may be more clarity present and so a structured process can be applied to move it ahead in a systematic way with controlled costs. In other cases an idea may begin in an unstructured process and move into a structured process as ambiguity is reduced. Firms adopt different systems depending on the levels of ambiguity in their Invent Stage and other considerations.

2.5   DECISION 1

2.6.3 Classification and Screening

As described in Module 1, Decision 1 takes place at the end of the Invent Stage before and MTB Proposition goes on to the Create Stage. As also described there, it may be decided to shelve or terminate an MTB Proposition, send it back to the Invent Stage for more work (perhaps with some of that work outsourced), move it on to the Create Stage for development in-house (perhaps with some aspects outsourced), or to find an external outlet for it through processes such as licensing and spin-offs. In many firms these decisions are made in a portfolio context. The fundamental question is, "How can the firm optimize the commercial potential of its portfolio of MTB Propositions that have reached the commercial feasibility point?" In more detail this involves determining which next step will be best for each MTB Proposition. The issues to be considered in these determinations concern the market, the technology and the business aspects of the proposition, as shown in Figure 2.4. At this stage these issues may have to be considered with only preliminary data and preliminary concepts of what the technology, product and market will be.

Figure 2.4
Issues/Criteria Commonly Considered in Decision 1

Business
>   Consistent with business strategy?
>   Able to generate a profit?
>   Sufficient return on investment?
>   Tangible and intangible benefits for the organization?
>   Workable collaboration with external partners?

Technology
>   Technical feasibility given organization's capabilities?
>   Is appropriate intellectual property protection feasible?
>   Feasible given the organization's manufacturing capabilities?
>   Workable collaboration with external partners?

Market
>   Product advantage in the marketplace?
>   Likely customer acceptance?
>   Safety, health and environmental considerations?
>   Likely competitors?
>   How large a market?
>   Workable collaboration with external partners?

2.6   MODULE KEY POINTS

- An idea, discovery or an invention, in itself, does not have commercial value. An opportunity, however, has potential commercial value. An idea, invention or discovery needs an application and a market place for it to be called an "opportunity".

- Opportunity recognition can occur through technology push or market pull. In the technology push the technology or application is discovered before the market need is identified. In market pull the needs of the market drive an organization to find an innovative technology solution.

- There are many uncertainties associated with development of technologies. The more radical an innovation, the more uncertainty is associated with the technology (product and process), market and business potential. The goal in the Invent stage is to reduce these various uncertainties. When the uncertainties are sufficiently reduced, the MTB Proposition reaches the commercialization feasibility point, which implies that technology, market and business feasibility have all been reached.

- Feasibility "points" are really "windows" or "regions" given the uncertainty surrounding the judgments about feasibility.

module 2 (2) 2007 07 29.doc

- A variety of activities take place during the Invent Stage including technology planning, research, technology mining, technology scanning, external sourcing and testing and feasibility analysis.

- Technology planning integrates business strategy with the discovery and development of technology opportunities.

- There are two main types of research: basic and applied. Basic research advances the scientific knowledge base of phenomena or behaviours. Applied research is the activity of finding solutions to problems using the knowledge and insights from basic research.

- Technology mining is the active search for technology and associated opportunities from within an organization's own portfolio. The mining process can reveal unused technologies or technologies that can be used in different ways for the development of novel product offerings. It can also mitigate some of the uncertainties associated with this stage by uncovering the needed technologies to move an idea and its associated technical and manufacturing uncertainties towards something that is more feasible.

- Technology scanning is the active search for technology opportunities external to the organization. Organizations can scan for technologies by conducting industry analysis, patent literature searches, gaining insight directly from customers and suppliers, building partnerships with universities, and keeping abreast of government activities.

- Instead of developing all technologies in-house, and organization can save considerable time and resources by acquiring technologies externally. Some mechanisms for this are: acquisition, joint venture/alliances, subcontracting with external R&D facilities, purchasing licenses for specific technologies, private label, provision of grants to research universities, and venture capital.

- Testing and feasibility analysis can occur continuously in the Invent Stage. It serves as the "litmus test" of whether the technology performs at a level necessary for proposed commercial products or processes.

- Radical innovations use untried technologies and are new to the market. Incremental innovations improve existing products or processes. Radical innovations have far more uncertainty associated with them and so have further to travel along the uncertainty reduction path of the Invent Stage than do incremental innovations.

- Decision 1 occurs when the MTB Proposition is brought to the commercial feasibility point. Decision 1 may or may not confirm that feasibility. Decision 1 decides how the firm can optimize the commercial potential of its portfolio of MTB Propositions.

- An organization must find the appropriate balance or internal and external solutions for the commercialization of MTB Propositions.

REFERENCES

[1] Medcof, J.W., "Creating Value from Science and Technology" In *Strategic Management of Technology, Commerce 4BK3 Custom Courseware*, ed. Medcof, J.W., 23-28. Hamilton: McMaster University, 2007.

[2] Koen, P.A., "The Fuzzy Front End for Incremental, Platform, and Breaktrhough Products", ", In *The PDMA Handbook of New Product Development*, ed. Kahn K.B., 81-65. US: John Wiley & Sons, 2005.

[3] Khurana, A., & Rosenthal, S. R., "Integrating the Fuzzy Front End of New Product Development," *IEEE Engineering Management Review* (1997): 35-49.

[4] Cooper, R.G., "Managing Technology Development Projects," Research Technology Management (2006): 49(6), 23-31.

[5] Eldred, E.W., & McGrath, M.E., "Commercializing New Technology – I", *Research Technology Management* (Jan – Feb 1997): 41 – 47.

[6] Eldred, E.W., & McGrath, M.E., "Commercializing New Technology – I", *Research Technology Management* (Jan – Feb 1997): 41 – 47.

[7] Leifer, R., O'Connor, G.C. and Rice, M., "Implementing Radical Innovation in Mature Firms: The role of hubs," *The Academy of Management Executive* (Aug 2001): 15 (3), 102-113.

[8] Koen, P.A., "The Fuzzy Front End for Incremental, Platform, and Breaktrhough Products", ", In *The PDMA Handbook of New Product Development*, ed. Kahn K.B., 81-65. US: John Wiley & Sons, 2005.

[9] Kenny, J., "Effective Project Management for Strategic Innovation and Change in an Organizational Context", *Project Management Journal* (Mar 2003): 34 (1), 43 –54.

[10] Allen, K. R., "Recognizing and Screening Technology Opportunities", In *Bringing New Technology to Market*, ed. Allen, K.R., 27-49. Prentice Hall, 2003.

[11] Allen, K. R., "Recognizing and Screening Technology Opportunities", In *Bringing New Technology to Market*, ed. Allen, K.R., 27-49. Prentice Hall, 2003.

[12] Leifer, R., O'Connor, G.C. and Rice, M., "Implementing Radical Innovation in Mature Firms: The role of hubs", *The Academy of Management Executive* (Aug 2001): 15 (3), 102-113.

[13] Evans, G., & Gausselin, P., "Technology Management", In *The PDMA Handbook of New Product Development*, ed. Kahn K.B., 319. US: John Wiley & Sons, 2005.

[14] Ibid., 320-321.

[15] Allen, K. R., "Recognizing and Screening Technology Opportunities", In *Bringing·New Technology to Market*, ed. Allen, K.R., 27-49. Prentice Hall, 2003.

[16] Allen, K. R., "Recognizing and Screening Technology Opportunities", In *Bringing New Technology to Market*, ed. Allen, K.R., 27-49. Prentice Hall, 2003.

[17] Dussauge, P., Hart, S., & Ramanantsoa, B., "Strategic Technology Management", 92 – 96. US: John Wiley & Sons, 1994.

[18] Allen, K. R., "Recognizing and Screening Technology Opportunities", In Bringing New Technology to Market, ed. Allen, K.R., 27-49. Prentice Hall, 2003.

[19] Eldred, E.W., & McGrath, M.E., "Commercializing New Technology – I", *Research Technology Management* (Jan – Feb 1997): 41 – 47.

[20] Evans, G., & Gausselin, P., "Technology Management", In *The PDMA Handbook of New Product Development*, ed. Kahn K.B., page. US: John Wiley & Sons, 2005.

[21] Evans, G., & Gausselin, P., "Technology Management", In *The PDMA Handbook of New Product Development*, ed. Kahn K.B., page. US: John Wiley & Sons, 2005.

[22] Evans, G., & Gausselin, P., "Technology Management", In *The PDMA Handbook of New Product Development*, ed. Kahn K.B., page. US: John Wiley & Sons, 2005.

[23] Chesborough, H. W., "Why Companies Should Have Open Business Models," *MIT Sloan Management Review* (2007): 48(2), 21 – 29.

[24] Evans, G., & Gausselin, P., "Technology Management", In *The PDMA Handbook of New Product Development*, ed. Kahn K.B., page. US: John Wiley & Sons, 2005

[25] Chesborough, H. W., "Why Companies Should Have Open Business Models," *MIT Sloan Management Review* (2007): 48(2), 21 – 29.

[26] Evans, G., & Gausselin, P., "Technology Management", In *The PDMA Handbook of New Product Development*, ed. Kahn K.B., page. US: John Wiley & Sons, 2005.

[27] Allen, K. R., "Recognizing and Screening Technology Opportunities", In *Bringing New Technology to Market*, ed. Allen, K.R., 27-49. Prentice Hall, 2003.

[28] Chesborough, H. W., "Why Companies Should Have Open Business Models," *MIT Sloan Management Review* (2007): 48(2), 21 – 29.

[29] Chesborough, H. W., "Why Companies Should Have Open Business Models," *MIT Sloan Management Review* (2007): 48(2), 21 – 29.

[30] Chesborough, H. W., "Why Companies Should Have Open Business Models," *MIT Sloan Management Review* (2007): 48(2), 21 – 29.

[31] Allen, K. R., "Recognizing and Screening Technology Opportunities", In *Bringing New Technology to Market*, ed. Allen, K.R., 27-49. Prentice Hall, 2003.

[32] Allen, K. R., "Recognizing and Screening Technology Opportunities", In *Bringing New Technology to Market*, ed. Allen, K.R., 27-49. Prentice Hall, 2003.

[33] Allen, K. R., "Recognizing and Screening Technology Opportunities", In *Bringing New Technology to Market*, ed. Allen, K.R., 27-49. Prentice Hall, 2003.

[34] Dussauge, P., Hart, S., & Ramanantsoa, B., "Strategic Technology Management", 92 – 96. US: John Wiley & Sons, 1994.

[35] Dussauge, P., Hart, S., & Ramanantsoa, B., "Strategic Technology Management", 92 – 96. US: John Wiley & Sons, 1994.

[36] Dussauge, P., Hart, S., & Ramanantsoa, B., "Strategic Technology Management", 92 – 96. US: John Wiley & Sons, 1994.

[37] Dussauge, P., Hart, S., & Ramanantsoa, B., "Strategic Technology Management", 92 – 96. US: John Wiley & Sons, 1994.

[38] Dussauge, P., Hart, S., & Ramanantsoa, B., "Strategic Technology Management", 92 – 96. US: John Wiley & Sons, 1994.

[39] Dussauge, P., Hart, S., & Ramanantsoa, B., "Strategic Technology Management", 92 – 96. US: John Wiley & Sons, 1994.

[40] Dussauge, P., Hart, S., & Ramanantsoa, B., "Strategic Technology Management", 92 – 96. US: John Wiley & Sons, 1994.

[41] Chesborough, H. W., "Why Companies Should Have Open Business Models," *MIT Sloan Management Review* (2007): 48(2), 21 – 29.

[42] Allen, K. R., "Recognizing and Screening Technology Opportunities", In *Bringing New Technology to Market*, ed. Allen, K.R., 27-49. Prentice Hall, 2003.

[43] Chesborough, H. W., "Why Companies Should Have Open Business Models," *MIT Sloan Management Review* (2007): 48(2), 21 – 29.

[44] Chesborough, H. W., "Why Companies Should Have Open Business Models," *MIT Sloan Management Review* (2007): 48(2), 21 – 29.

[45] Allen, K. R., "Recognizing and Screening Technology Opportunities", In *Bringing New Technology to Market*, ed. Allen, K.R., 27-49. Prentice Hall, 2003.

[46] Chesborough, H. W., "Why Companies Should Have Open Business Models," *MIT Sloan Management Review* (2007): 48(2), 21 – 29.

[47] Eldred, E.W., & McGrath, M.E., "Commercializing New Technology – I", *Research Technology Management* (Jan – Feb 1997): 41 – 47.

[48] Sheasley, D.W., "Leading the Technology Development Process," *Research Technology Management* (May – Jun 1999): 49 – 55.

[49] Evans, G., & Gausselin, P., "Technology Management", In *The PDMA Handbook of New Product Development*, ed. Kahn K.B., page. US: John Wiley & Sons, 2005.

[50] Evans, G., & Gausselin, P., "Technology Management", In *The PDMA Handbook of New Product Development*, ed. Kahn K.B., page. US: John Wiley & Sons, 2005.

[51] Eldred, E.W., & McGrath, M.E., "Commercializing New Technology – I", *Research Technology Management* (Jan – Feb 1997): 41 – 47.

[52] Cooper, R.G., "Managing Technology Development Projects," Research Technology Management (2006): 49(6), 23-31.

[53] Eldred, E.W., & McGrath, M.E., "Commercializing New Technology – I", *Research Technology Management* (Jan – Feb 1997): 41 – 47.

OPPORTUNITY RECOGNITION

Opportunity recognition happens when an entrepreneur sees a need in the marketplace and identifies a way to satisfy that need. Biotech scientists saw a way to apply genetics to the world of agriculture to increase yields and rid farmers of the problems associated with using pesticides. In contrast, opportunity creation occurs when an entrepreneur creates a demand for something that people did not previously know that they needed. How many people knew they needed personal computers in the late 1970s? Recall the discussion in Chapter 1 about incremental innovation and disruptive or radical technologies. Most new products are the result of incremental or evolutionary innovation—recognizing a need in the market that can be served by the incremental improvement of an existing technology. Disruptive or radical innovation creates an opportunity that never existed previously by making the preceding technology obsolete.

HOW OPPORTUNITY RECOGNITION HAPPENS

A growing body of research is providing an understanding of how entrepreneurs recognize opportunities. One thing is certain: The vast majority of people who find business opportunities find them in industries with which they are familiar or in a business for which they have worked.[18] Moreover, entrepreneurs who network in a variety of social circles tend to recognize more opportunities. In fact, the number of weak ties or connections outside immediate family and friends in the entrepreneur's network is positively correlated to the number of opportunities recognized.[19]

The literature is unclear as to whether opportunity recognition is a planned process. Some of the early research claimed that planning is not involved in opportunity recognition.[20] However, more recent research attributes opportunity recognition with active, well-planned searches for opportunities.[21] The reality is that both active searches and serendipity play significant roles in the ability of entrepreneurs to discover new opportunities.[22]

THE OPPORTUNITY RECOGNITION PROCESS

Hill, Schrader, and Lumpkin[23] created a five-step framework of the entrepreneurial opportunity recognition process. Note that their process is not linear. Instead, it is an iterative process with many feedback loops.

1. **Preparation.** Every entrepreneur brings prior knowledge and experience to the process, making the opportunity recognition process idiosyncratic to each entrepreneur.
2. **Incubation.** This is a period of time during which the entrepreneur contemplates the solution to the problem.
3. **Insight.** This is the moment when the entrepreneur sees the solution to the problem—the "eureka!" moment.
4. **Evaluation.** The process of defining a business concept and testing it in the marketplace to see if it is feasible.
5. **Elaboration.** The planning and the creation of a company to execute the business concept.

THE BOTTOM LINE

The real value of research lies in its ability to be applied in the real world. Unfortunately, for every characteristic, behavior, or process used to describe opportunity recognition, the reality is that it is a unique journey for each person. There are no formulas for success, and there are many uncontrollable variables: experience, social networks, knowledge, age, resources, and so forth. One graduate student used the analogy of a lightning strike, saying that although it cannot be predicted exactly where lightning will strike, what is known is that it will happen and there are some guidelines that suggest where it is likely to strike.* Similarly, entrepreneurs have a higher probability of recognizing an opportunity if they:

- Increase their knowledge and experience in an industry in which they are interested.
- Build a diverse network of strong and weak professional ties.
- Develop an opportunistic mindset.
- Exercise patience. The incubation period can sometimes take a long time.

SOURCES OF OPPORTUNITY

Chapter 1 explored the invention process. However, today, technology opportunities can come from many other sources. This section looks at how to find opportunity outside the realm of basic research, including capitalizing on the research of others.

STUDY AN INDUSTRY

Learning an industry is one of the most important first steps in finding opportunity, as most inventor/entrepreneurs discover their best opportunities in industries in which they have had experience. Trends, changes, and emerging needs in an industry present gaps or white spaces that can be turned into opportunities. A good place to start is by mapping the value chain in the industry to learn not only how the industry works, but also who the major players are. Once the industry has been mapped, consider the following questions:

- How are customer needs changing in this industry?
- What opportunities could arise from these changes?
- What are the industry drivers?
- How do businesses become profitable in this industry?
- What are some alternative scenarios to what is currently believed about the industry or seen occurring in the industry?

A good example of what not to do is what AT&T did in the late 1980s. The National Science Foundation (NSF) asked AT&T to take control of the Internet because it no longer wanted to administer it.[24] However, AT&T's view of the future was that its centrally switched telephony technology was going to dominate, and the

---

*Thanks to Ryan Vuletic, MBA 2000, Marshall School of Business, University of Southern California.

Internet had no place in that future. Of course, had AT&T considered any alternative scenarios—both best and worse case, it might have been in a better position to recognize changes occurring in the industry and position itself to respond quickly. For more information on how to analyze an industry, see Chapter 3.

SEARCH THE PATENT LITERATURE

The U.S. Patent and Trademark Office's database contains millions of U. S. and foreign patents. Searching their archives is an excellent way to spark an idea. In fact, searching the archives of patents now in the public domain could lead to an invention that was never commercialized. Most patents were never brought to market because they either had no inherent commercial value or their owners did not understand how to commercialize the invention they had developed.

TALK TO CUSTOMERS

More new product ideas have come from customers than probably any other source. Customers experience the pain of not having something they need, and they readily communicate that pain if someone is listening. The best way to understand customer needs is to use an anthropological approach to market research. What did Jane Goodall do when she wanted to understand the habits of chimpanzees? She moved in with them and lived with them for months on end. No one expects entrepreneurs to move in with their customers and devote months to understanding their needs, but they can spend a day in the life of their customer, shadowing what the customer does and listening carefully to that customer's pain. The cardiac device division of Hewlett-Packard needed to ensure that its measurement devices were thoroughly tested and worked the way their customers, the hospital staff, needed them to work, as it was literally a matter of life and death. The team spent weeks at the hospital observing and listening in order to create the best product.[25] Surveys, focus groups, and interviews are excellent ways to gather information, but nothing beats camping out with the customer.

LOOK INTO UNIVERSITY OPPORTUNITIES

For years the pharmaceutical industry has relied on university research laboratories for basic research leading to new drugs. The Human Genome Project is one example of how government, university, and public/private partners can work together to create new products and knowledge. In combinatory chemistry, companies such as Millennium Pharmaceuticals, Inc. have developed software models to build and analyze virtual chemicals that demonstrate biological effects. They can use these models to search for molecules that display similar effects and, using the capabilities of outside partners, test thousands of potential effects per day. With other partners, they can conduct animal and human testing.[26]

The basic research performed by university professors and researchers may result in the next major breakthrough in science and engineering. However, most researchers conduct their research without any thought of commercializing their discovery. A university's technology transfer office is a good place to look for ways to collaborate with university researchers to commercialize their technology.

INVESTIGATE GOVERNMENT SOURCES

Many government agencies regularly publish requests for proposals (RFPs) for technology that they would like to see researched and turned into inventions that can be commercialized. Agencies like NASA (National Aeronautical and Space Administration) own technology developed under government contracts that they will license to companies. Other federal agencies and laboratories that deal in technology transfer include the Department of Commerce, the Department of Defense, and the Department of Energy. See the end-of-chapter resources for Internet sources on licensing opportunities.

FIND NEW VALUE IN EXISTING TECHNOLOGY

Increasingly, companies are finding that some of their greatest opportunities lie with technologies whose patents have lain dormant because, for whatever reason, the company did not move forward with the transfer or commercialization of the technology. Intellectual property in the form of patents and trademarks is the new opportunity frontier. More and more companies are building growth strategies around finding new value in existing and oftentimes archived technologies. IBM was perhaps one of the earliest companies to reap the financial rewards of new royalty streams by licensing existing intellectual property. Through a judicious effort to mine its patent archives for new applications, it was able to boast its annual royalty stream from $30 million in 1990 to over $1 billion today. This revenue stream represents approximately one-ninth of its annual pretax profits, and it goes directly to its net profit. To achieve that same level of profit, IBM would have to sell about $20 billion in additional products each year, one-fourth of its worldwide sales.[27]

OTHER SOURCES

In addition to the sources already discussed, trade associations are a good source of technology-related information. Also consider trade publications, suppliers, and distributors. The Internet can play a role in finding opportunity. Patent exchange sites have sprung up that allow inventors to post their issued patents for licensing or sale (see the end-of-chapter resources for the URLs of some of these sites). Finally, some entrepreneurs have identified opportunities through direct mail solicitations to universities, corporations, government agencies, or trade associations.

SCREENING TECHNOLOGY OPPORTUNITIES

Idea generation and opportunity recognition are the starting points for technology commercialization. Ideas come easily; it is more difficult to generate opportunities from ideas. Therefore, it makes sense to have a process for screening opportunities. A small company or start-up venture may only have one product that is its raison d'etre—the reason it is in business. This company may not require a screening process. However, a larger company requires a more complex decision-making process because

```
                    ┌─────────────────┐
                    │    Determine    │
                    │ Compatibility with │
                    │      Goals      │
                    └─────────────────┘
                             │
                             ▼
                    ┌─────────────────┐
                    │   Categorize    │
                    │ Opportunity Type │
                    └─────────────────┘
```

Noncompetitive Product	Derivative Product	Stand-Alone Product
No Market	Goal Compatibility	Goal Compatibility
Insufficient Market	Project Impact	Technical Feasibility
No Capability	Technical Feasibility	Process Integration
Limited Capability	Benefits to Company	Benefits to Company
Technology Not Ready	Benefits to Licensee or Buyer	Benefits to Licensee or Buyer
	Economic Life	Economic Life
	Market Attractiveness	Market Attractiveness

```
                    ┌─────────────────┐
                    │   Classify the  │
                    │    Technology   │
                    └─────────────────┘
```

| Produce | License | Sell | Acquire |

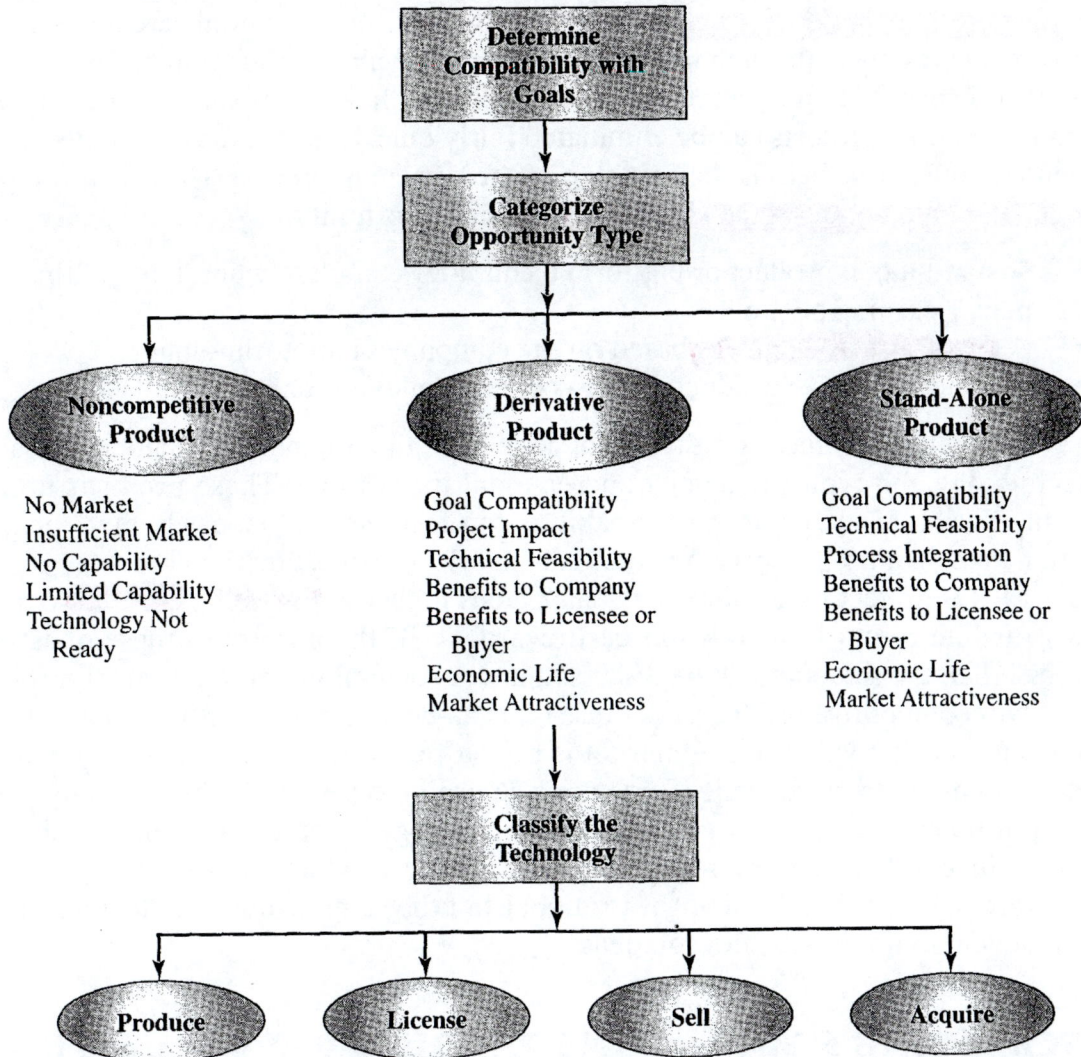

FIGURE 2-1   TECHNOLOGY SCREENING

it may already have a variety of products and processes that it has commercialized, thus the impact of a new opportunity may be more critical.

The phrase *Fuzzy Front End* (FFE) first began appearing in the product development literature in 1985. It refers to the portion of the product development cycle between when a new product project should start and when it actually does start, in other words, all the activities leading to the ultimate decision to proceed with a project into product development.[28] Today, this concept has taken on a more critical meaning as the window of opportunity for new products continues to shrink and anything that slows a company's ability to recognize an opportunity and act on it quickly can mean the difference between profits and no profits. The ability to quickly screen new product ideas becomes a vital organizational skill. Reinertsen has modeled the FFE in economic terms. Simply stated, the amount a person is willing to bet on a new product is a function of the probability of its success, the value of that success, and the cost of failure. Altering any one of these values will change the economics of the bet.[29]

In general, in a company with a technical/invention staff, 20 percent of that staff generates 80 percent of the development projects, and the initial screening of those projects takes place through informal discussions. Typically, the team has a good sense of what is possible and what is most compatible with the company's goals. Therefore, many potential projects can be eliminated fairly quickly as not feasible under the current circumstances. This is the first step of the screening process. The second step is to categorize the nature of the opportunity. Is the opportunity:

- A stand-alone product or platform technology completely unrelated to the company's existing portfolio?
- A derivative opportunity based on the company's core technology?
- A noncompetitive product with no commercial potential?

Derivative products are those that arise from the original stand-alone or platform technology and typically involve incremental innovations. These products normally easily fit within the company's capabilities; in fact, most fit so easily that companies often take on more projects than they can handle. The question then becomes, does this derivative product meet company goals? Does it have a big enough impact to make it worthwhile to put limited resources towards it? If the answer to these questions is "yes," then the screening filters discussed under stand-alone products are appropriate.

Noncompetitive products are those that can be determined rather quickly and that have no market value or the market is not sufficient to make the effort involved in developing them worthwhile. These are also products for which the company has limited or no capability for or for which the technology is years from being ready to use. When inventors and entrepreneurs brainstorm new product ideas, these types of products are the ones that stand out as irrational, but they are included in the brainstorming to prevent inhibiting the flow of ideas.

SCREENING STAND-ALONE PRODUCT OPPORTUNITIES

Stand-alone or platform technologies generally involve starting a new business to commercialize the technology or diversify the current product line. In either case, there are several issues that need to be addressed when deciding whether to go forward with initial product development and feasibility analysis.

QUANTIFY AND QUALIFY THE BENEFITS TO THE COMPANY

First and foremost, will taking on this project meet company goals? In general, development of a new technology opportunity should not be undertaken unless it is compatible with the strategic direction the company is taking. What is this technology opportunity going to do for the company? Will it allow the company to diversify its current offerings? Will it provide an opportunity to be a pioneer and capture a certain segment of the market? Is there a process that can be integrated with the product technology to strengthen the proprietary aspects of the technology? It is important to understand what the tangible and intangible benefits to the company will be. Are they worth the investment in time, money, and effort to develop and commercialize this technology?

QUANTIFY AND QUALIFY THE BENEFITS TO A POTENTIAL LICENSEE OR BUYER

Screening a technology opportunity for potential commercialization means looking at that technology from the customer's point of view. In this case, the customer is the potential licensee or buyer, most likely another company. Why would that customer want this technology, and why would they want to license or purchase it from this company? When the tangible and intangible benefits of the technology to the customer cannot be identified, the customer will not be convinced to go forward with the transaction.

CALCULATE THE ECONOMIC LIFE OF THE TECHNOLOGY

Although a patented technology has a legal life, that is, the length of time for which the patent is valid, it also has an economic life, the length of time during which it can generate revenue for the business. The earning period is affected by a number of factors:

- **The probability that the competition will be able to design around the patent and develop a competing product.** Competition could force the company to spend more marketing dollars to assure brand loyalty and expend more on research and development to continually improve on the product design and functionality.
- **The probability that the patent will be challenged.** Patents and patent infringement are covered in Chapters 5, 6, and 7, but suffice it to say here that one way that companies battle in the marketplace is to tie up their competitors in patent litigation.
- **Higher than estimated technology development costs.** It is difficult to predict with any degree of accuracy the total costs of developing a new technology from concept to production quality prototype; therefore, companies often estimate on the high side to keep from getting in the middle of R&D only to discover that they have run out of money. This means that many projects are not undertaken because the expected costs are too high and it would take too long to recoup them in the marketplace.
- **Potential impact of new laws.** Federal and state governments and their agencies regularly pass laws that affect the development of new technologies. Those laws can range from environmental protection regulations to regulations on stem cell research, all of which affect the kinds of technologies that can reach the marketplace. A new law passed while a technology is in the market can serve to shorten or cut off its economic life or, in some cases, breathe new life into a fading technology.
- **Escalation of supply pricing or actual loss of supply.** The prices of raw materials and components for technology development change over time. If those changes are significant, they can effectively reduce the economic life of the technology as competitors take advantage of alternate supplies with more cost-effective pricing. Likewise, the loss of access to raw materials can also cut off the economic life of a new technology.

DETERMINE THE ABILITY OF THE TECHNOLOGY TO BE TRANSFERRED

A technology needs to carry a strong form of intellectual property protection—usually a patent—to be able to be transferred without losing proprietary rights. It must also be capable of being produced or used in an environment other than the inventor's, that is, it must not be so tied to the company's in-house technology that it cannot be separated from it. Whether the technology is captive—essential to the company's core business—or nonessential, is important to determine so that transferring it is beneficial to the company, not detrimental.

IDENTIFY THE RESOURCE REQUIREMENTS TO TRANSFER THE TECHNOLOGY

Technology is rarely transferred without also providing some level of know-how to assist the licensee in using the technology appropriately. Some technologies depend so much on the know-how of the inventor or the invention team that it is difficult to transfer the technology to another firm to manufacture and distribute it or to develop additional applications. It is important to determine how the company's know-how will be transferred and if it will be necessary to put someone from the licensor's company inside the licensee's company for a time to help them through the process. Moreover, licensees will not learn of the technology without some marketing effort on the part of the inventing company. Both of these scenarios require money and human resources.

IDENTIFY THE RISKS ASSOCIATED WITH THE DEVELOPMENT

Product development is an inherently risky proposition, but it is made even more so by the requirements of today's dynamic environment. With everyone on the team moving as quickly as possible to get the product to market in as short a time as possible, there is no time to respond to things that go wrong. Moreover, routines that worked well previously fall apart under the pressure of fast-track development. With limited resources and short time frames, it is important to identify risks and determine how to deal with them in advance.

Every development project carries with it two basic types of risk: technical and market.[30] Technical risks arise when product developers are unable to build a product that meets the required specifications, whereas market risks occur when the company has misread the market or has failed to meet the needs of the customer. It is natural that engineers tend to focus on technical risks, but the reality is that most product failures are due to market risk. The work of Robert Cooper over 25 years studying 2,000 new products, has made it clear that new product success depends on six factors:[31]

- A superior product that is unique in the market
- A clearly defined product at the earliest stages of development
- Well-researched market and technical feasibility analyses
- A well-executed marketing plan
- A well-executed technology plan
- Cross-functional teams with representation from all the functional areas of the business

Note that the only factor that falls within the product development domain is the technology plan; the rest reside in market research.

Managing risk through the product development process is accomplished by continually looking for ways to reduce the probability that an identified risk will occur. Given that the amount of equity an entrepreneur has to give up to investors is directly related to the level of risk in the venture, this risk reduction strategy is the very one that entrepreneurs use to reduce the risk to potential investors, and thereby also reduce the amount of equity they need to give up to investors. For example, some of the technical risk is reduced at the prototype stage because there is a working model that can be tested. Market risk is reduced when the technology is proven with potential customers. Investors will make the decision to risk their capital on a new technology when the inventor has reduced the technical and market risk to the investors' level of comfort.

Potential risks are identified through creative brainstorming. The most effective risk brainstorming is performed in cross-functional teams, due to the fact that most risk crosses more than one functional area. By bringing together engineers and business people, it is more likely that both technical and market risks will be uncovered. The following are some ways to reduce risk during the product development process.

- **Use off-the-shelf or proven components whenever possible.** Where a particular component has worked well in a previous product, it should be used in the new product if possible.

- **Don't force a solution.** Sometimes two options appear workable, and the risk of choosing one and being wrong is more costly than producing both. For example, Black & Decker was attempting to determine the best handle size and shape for a battery-powered screwdriver. Certainly, this was a critical decision. Should it go with the thinner handle that held two cells and was more comfortable for smaller hands or with the thicker handle that held three cells and provided more power? Ultimately, Black & Decker decided to continue designing both until further market research could prove one more valuable than the other.[32]

- **Talk to the customer.** The best way to reduce risk in any technology screening and product development process is to get continual input from the customer. That means letting customers talk directly to design engineers. Pelco, Inc., a leader in video surveillance equipment, brings its customers to the manufacturing floor and creates rapid prototypes of their ideas on the spot. This saves design time and gives the customers a vested interest in Pelco's success.

- **Tackle the riskiest issues first.** When screening a technology idea, the natural tendency is to focus on the issues that carry the lowest risk and save the tougher issues for last. It is always more prudent to identify the highest risk with any development project first and make sure there is a way to reduce that risk. Otherwise, it could put the project in jeopardy after time and effort have been spent taking care of less critical risks.

The goal of risk management is to avoid failure. However, if a company is too concerned with avoiding failure, it may not take the appropriate risks necessary to achieve great successes. Invaluable information that may never have been learned otherwise is gained from failure. Product screening and development are inherently iterative processes that rely on trying one thing, testing another, and continually moving in a forward direction based on lessons learned.

CLASSIFYING TECHNOLOGIES AFTER THE INITIAL SCREENING

After the initial screening, opportunities should be classified as to how they might be commercialized or transferred. There are four major categories into which these technologies might be classified: produce the technology, acquire a technology, license the technology, or sell the technology. In some cases, a combination of these may be possible.

PRODUCE THE PRODUCT

Although the natural course of action would be to produce a product or technology that the company has invented, this is not always the best course of action. The company may not have the expertise or resources to properly produce the product; therefore, it may make more sense to use the capability of another company that does have those skills and resources. Alternatively, the inventing company may have the appropriate capability for a particular application of the technology, but not for other applications of the technology in other industries. In that case, it will seek companies that have those capabilities and give them the right to manufacture and distribute the product for that application. Companies that have the ability to produce the technology generally do so because they may be the only company with the capabilities to produce the product. In addition, they may produce the product in-house because they want to retain control of their intellectual property or they do not intend to patent the technology, keeping it as a captive application and trade secret for use in their business.

ACQUIRE THE TECHNOLOGY

Not all entrepreneurs are inventors, and not all inventors have the ability to take their inventions to market. Consequently, technology acquisition is a viable solution when an entrepreneur does not own the technology needed or does not have the resources to develop it. In many cases, acquiring the technology will speed the time to market with a new product because the entrepreneur will not have to spend time and resources in the typically lengthy R&D phase. Opportunities abound, not only in highly valued technologies, but also in those that have been undervalued or misapplied. Many of the sources of opportunity mentioned earlier in the chapter can be used to find needed technology. Before acquiring any technology, however, it is important to address some critical questions:

- What specifically is required in the way of technology?
- How much risk can the company incur?
- How much will it cost to acquire the technology versus developing and manufacturing it in-house?
- Is time a critical factor?
- What are the desired commercial features of the technology?
- Will the seller indemnify the company for patent infringement if it uses the technology?

LICENSE THE TECHNOLOGY

By licensing technology, a company has the opportunity to create multiple revenue streams and get the technology into more markets than it could probably achieve on its own. This is critically important when the company is trying to create the standard in a particular technology. It must get that technology adopted in as many markets as possible in order to create the momentum needed to establish it as the standard in the industry. Licensing is the subject of Chapter 6.

SELL THE TECHNOLOGY

Some inventors and entrepreneurs choose to sell outright the technologies they create. In some cases, they see their businesses as product development firms, not manufacturing, marketing, or distribution firms, and they would prefer to leave the commercialization task to someone else. There are other reasons that many new technologies are sold by the companies that create them. If the technology is not captive, that is, not tied to other company technologies or processes, and it has a patent position, it is a good candidate for a sale. This strategy is particularly useful if the product is in a different market than the company's core products and the buyer has a strong position in that market. Another reason to sell a technology is when the buyer has better access to needed raw materials, has underutilized manufacturing capacity in that area, or is already manufacturing the product but with a different, less advanced technology.

Once technology opportunities have been recognized and screened, it is time to turn those technology opportunities into business opportunities. Chapter 3 discusses how to develop and test a business concept.

❖ SUMMARY

Never before has creativity played such a vital role in the development of technology. Traditionally, creativity was applied to generating ideas for new products, but today it must also be applied to finding new ways of doing things—new marketing strategies, new distribution channels, and new organizational strategies. The creative process involves the connection of disparate ideas, discoveries, inventions, and applications. Natural creativity is often stifled by the barriers that people set up for themselves—not giving themselves time to be creative, fear of being criticized for being different, and the belief that they have no creative skills. These barriers can be overcome by developing an environment that inspires creativity and by making time for creative thought. Creative problem-solving skills such as restating the problem, asking why five times to get at the root of the problem, broadening or narrowing the scope of the problem, and working with the opposite of the problem can also be used. Creativity is the source of opportunity recognition, that is, an idea that has business potential. The ability to recognize opportunity can be enhanced by increasing knowledge and experience in an industry, building a diverse network of strong and weak ties, and developing an opportunistic mindset. Sources of opportunity include the patent literature, the industry of interest, customers, universities, government sources, online patent exchanges, and existing technologies in a company's archives. Technology opportunities need to be screened to determine whether they will result in a stand-alone product, a derivative opportunity based on core technology that the company already has, or a noncompetitive product with no commercial potential. With a stand-alone product, it will be important to determine what its economic life is, if it has transfer capability, and what it would take to transfer the technology. It will also be necessary to consider the risks associated with this technology opportunity. Once the technology has been classified, a decision to produce the technology, acquire it from someone else, sell it, or license it must be made.

❖ DISCUSSION QUESTIONS

1. Provide two examples that illustrate the difference between an idea and an opportunity.
2. What two challenges do you face in becoming more creative? How will you deal with those challenges?

MANAGING THE UNMANAGEABLE

Research into bootleg research concludes that managers should leave creative processes in the underground world and formal processes in the official world.

Peter Augsdorfer

OVERVIEW: *The lesson from this research into covert research—also known as "bootlegging"—is clear: do not even try to organize the early stages of innovation through formal processes. Interviews at 70 European companies reveal that organizing for creativity is impossible to tackle without contravening one or another organizational protocol. Consequently, it is recommended that managers abandon the arguments over control versus freedom to leave creativity and early innovation where it belongs: in the chaotic, messy and wild terrain of the corporate underground. Management should accept that innovative output emerges from the hidden life of corporations and, moreover, that it is more often than not in line with overall corporate strategy. The research shows that both organizational bureaucracy and the underground world co-exist and interact positively; hence, the long-running debate about how to integrate creativity into the formal organization becomes moot.*

KEY CONCEPTS: *R&D management, creativity, innovation strategy, bootlegging.*

After more than 40 years' research, debate continues to rage on how to manage for true creativity and early innovation (*1*). Some recommend more structure, more planning and more control while others advocate greater creative freedom and a "laissez-faire" management approach; still others again prefer a combination of leadership strategies.

A study of 70 European companies has revealed that, in spite of attempts at management control, many valuable

Peter Augsdorfer is professor at the Fachhochschule Ingolstadt in Germany and associate professor at the Grenoble École de Management in France. He teaches technology and innovation strategy, and has been involved in research about bootlegging since 1991 when he worked at the Science and Technology Policy Research Unit at Sussex University in the United Kingdom. He received his D.Phil. from Sussex University.
peter.augsdorfer@ggsb.com

innovations have emerged from extensive covert research in corporations. Often dismissed as a self-indulgent distraction, this underground research or "bootlegging" might just be the answer to the eternal paradox of organizing for front-end innovation. In other words, the answer may literally be under your nose. Consider the following example of BMW's 12-cylinder engine.

In 2004, BMW was awarded the "best innovators award" in Germany. B. Göschel, an R&D and purchasing executive, explained BMW's philosophy for basic innovations by noting that researchers need courage, creativity, uncontrolled space, and enthusiasm. He concluded with something extraordinary for a top manager: he actively encouraged researchers to by-pass management and carry out "bootlegging" and underground projects. Indeed, a couple of years earlier, the 12-cylinder engine machine had been developed over a period of five years by a bunch of motor aficionados without management approval. The engine, when unveiled to the public, was hailed as a success and contributed significantly to BMW's brand image of innovative automobile excellence. The BMW series 3 touring car emerged from a similar process and today contributes 40 percent of BMW's profit (*2*).

Most of us have heard similar stories. What they generally have in common is that the decision to invest corporate resources lies outside the formal organization and emerges from the hidden life of the corporation. It turns out that researchers decide at their own pace which research issues to take up. It is for the benefit of the company, but does not feature in the department's action plans nor have any formal resources allocated to it (*3*). This flies in the face of those who think that managers are in control of the processes of early innovation. Does this mean that creative corporate environments are essentially anarchic? It would seem so.

Consider for a moment what constitutes a corporate underground. Its definition would go beyond the informal relationship argument and concerns a firm's entire invisible infrastructure. It includes bootlegging, power struggles, making false declarations on punch

0895-6308/08/$5.00 © 2008 Industrial Research Institute, Inc.

cards to being off-site while in fact being present and continuing to work on-site, corruption, lending another project manager some of your own budget only to get it back at a later stage, and business-plan window dressing, to name but a few. Although they do not all apply at the same time, they do form part of the corporate underground eco-system.

What the Business Models Say

While research and the pursuit of innovation do involve rigorous discipline, at the heart of the early process lie creative feelings—a perception that is frequently hard to define. This stage is also called the "front end of innovation," which can be defined as "those activities that come before the more 'formal and well-structured' new product development" (4). Business models abound as to how to organize this creativity, always involving tighter or weaker management control mechanisms (5,6). There are many articles suggesting that deliberate organizational measures are possible but these get no closer to solving the conundrum (7,8). Most recognize that the organization of technological change and the translation of knowledge into artifacts remains an important but highly problematic area.

Those arguing for tighter control insist that if an organization is to act as an entity, it must have a "body of doctrine" that explains "what it is doing and what it ought to do." Becton Dickinson is one firm that successfully takes this approach. Innovation is set as a part of strategic planning. Management decides to invest in certain strategic objectives and establishes firm budgetary control. Thus, management takes on a watchdog role. They also practice open communication and expect their research staff to talk trustingly among themselves about new ideas.

Another case and probably the best-known example of formally organized freedom is 3M's "permitted bootlegging research." At 3M, privileged technical staff are allowed to spend up to 15 percent of their time on pet projects in the hope that they will come up with profitable innovations for the company.

Surprisingly, my research has shown that real bootleg entrepreneurs do not care whether bootlegging is permitted or not, or if the firm expects open communication. At Becton Dickinson, total transparency strikes them as an unrealistic demand and driven by wishful thinking on the part of management. At 3M, only few people make use of permitted bootleg time. It is generally only the divergent-thinking researcher who actually can make proper use of this time. This number is further decreased by another factor. When managers know about permitted bootleg projects, they will ask about them, thus affecting the researcher's sense of freedom. Some researchers interpret this scrutiny as a disturbance.

> # Real bootleg entrepreneurs don't care whether bootlegging is permitted or not.

Hence, in both firms underground activity is alive and well. What else do the findings reveal?

Research Design

The research into bootlegging and the early innovation process was carried out in the United Kingdom, France and Germany. The choice of companies interviewed was arbitrary, but they were selected with research activities in the following fields: software, telecommunications and computer science, electronics, chemicals, automobile and mechanical engineering, new materials science, and health care. The multidisciplinary and international make-up of the sample guaranteed that experience from a significant range of fields was captured. The methodology was based on the collection of qualitative primary data. The interviews were conducted at two levels in the management hierarchy: the head of a laboratory and one or more subordinate researchers. In total, 70 firms were visited and more than 170 interviews conducted and, where possible, backed up with case studies. Interviews started off with general questions about the organizational structure. When a certain level of confidence had been established inquiries were made as to the existence of bootlegging, the role of formal organization for innovation and the possibilities of carrying out a case study.

A typical series of questions would be, for example like this series asked of 3M:

Question (Q): Do you know anybody doing bootleg projects in your laboratory? Answer (A): Yes, I have one person in mind. He is very young and incredibly inventive. He is always late but has quite a few good ideas.

Q: Does your boss know about it? A: Yes, my boss knows that we have 5 to 10 percent of people working on other projects. But he doesn't want to know details. Anyway, he is not able to control it, because he has no time.

Q: What is the reason for doing bootlegging? A: If you bring a sample it goes down so much better. We made a mistake when we introduced a particular rubber valve to the boss. The answer of the boss was: "who told you to do it?" Once he asks this question, it is difficult to continue. We continued against orders on a much lower level. Provided we do the things we have to do, we can do it. On average, one bootleg product is developed per year. These are usually accepted.

Q: How can you by-pass the planning process? *A:* Everybody has to fill in time sheets. But as there are such a lot of categories, which can be anything, there is enough room to cheat. His boss looks at the total and not at individuals. Anyway, there is only 50 percent of the time spent on research, the rest is sickness, holidays. . .

Q: What is in it for the bootleg researcher? *A:* It is in them, I don't know. They are people who want to do it. They have a questioning mind.

Q: Are they more productive? *A:* You cannot say if they are better researchers—in terms of getting a product out of the door, NO; in terms of having new ideas, YES.

Most people interviewed could provide at least one example of bootlegging in the last five years. By and large, researchers were amused by the topic and talked freely. It was the first time in their experience that an attempt had been made to analyze the motivations for bootlegging and its role in the firm's innovative capacities. As these qualitative dynamics crystallized, an analysis was made of common themes among interviewees' responses. One common theme that emerged strongly was the role of creative individuals.

Organizing for Innovation Has Its Limits

A closer look at the main dilemmas faced by innovators and organizations throws light on some common themes:

• Creative people need an outlet for their creative energy and curiosity. Most formal organizations fail to provide sufficient space for people with ideas outside the mainstream.

• Decisions that concern innovations are important decisions but often have to be taken under conditions of high technical and market uncertainty. They must be based on careful analysis, with uncertainties reduced to a minimum. The researcher now finds himself in a chicken-and-egg situation. He must research his case well enough to get his idea accepted. However, how can he start on the research without a go-ahead? Unless he or she begins his research informally well in advance, there is no hope of formal approval.

• R&D budgets need to be planned. Usually this happens annually when objectives are linked to budgets. But ideas often occur between planning periods.

All these dilemmas can be overcome by resorting to underground activity. Over 80 percent of corporate orga-

Most bootleg projects were accepted by the firm after disclosure because they met its business needs.

nizations admit to its existence. Serendipity, spin-offs from current research, or other unforeseen events unleash creative ideas. Dissatisfaction with a manager's decision or rising personal interest in a current topic are further triggers.

It is common to spend some hours bootlegging on a regular basis. Friday afternoons or weekends are specially favored as they provide a quieter environment compared to the rest of the week. In most cases however, researchers bootleg over shorter but continuous periods of time. The longest bootleg project by two people was found to be three years. Their research was a genuine conspiracy, fostered by the head of department and embedded in the working schedule of the laboratory. Most bootleg projects were accepted by the firm after disclosure because they met the firm's business needs (*9*).

At its core, innovation depends on good ideas emerging from individual minds. Typically, these new ideas come from the same individuals in any organization (*10*). On average, only five to ten percent of R&D laboratory personnel can be described as being truly creative (*3*). One can call them creative because they think in a divergent way, opening up opportunities for the firm. Equipped with a very special personality, they are easily identified within the firm. They are often intellectually restless and stand out as "unconventional" and "nonconformist." Their behavior seems to be fueled by a basic need and intrinsic curiosity for studying interesting problems and discovering new solutions.

Often it is the case that one or two such creative minds provide the ideas for the whole research team. In a case at British Aerospace, one laboratory even survived on a single individual's ideas—only running out of steam five years after he left. Organizations that do not have such people working for them will have significantly fewer innovative ideas.

So, if we have the creative researchers providing all the ideas, how does one describe other laboratory personnel? They could be described as "reactively creative" or "responsive problem solvers." Their capabilities lie in finding the right algorithm for identified business projects. In general, such researchers prefer clear guidelines and a formal planning framework. Roussel christened them "engineer" types in comparison to more creative "scientist" types (5).

The relationship between these two types of researchers is easily explained—creative people provide new ideas that get developed or worked upon by others who flourish in a structured project environment. In the context of underground activity, this explains why projects initiated by a single individual can gradually develop into full-fledged conspiracies involving entire laboratories. It also demonstrates why variety among research staff is of utmost importance. Successful research requires both types of researcher.

The Cost of Bootlegging–Myths and Fears

While underground research requires financial resources, in most cases their lack appears to be a minor obstacle. Demonstrating feasibility does not need a huge budget and researchers show imagination in getting the resources they need. Typically, equipment and tools are already available in the laboratory. The expenses for materials are usually small, as bootleg researchers seem to be masters of improvisation. It is not unusual to find materials acquired by mutual favor from inside or outside the company. A typical case is that of the French company in which new alloy engine parts were produced alongside standard engine parts simply by adding another row to the assembly line. As one R&D manager from Shell confessed, "bootlegging is peanuts in comparison to the enormous money spent on R&D."

The most important resource is the time a researcher spends on bootlegging. Findings from this research indicate that underground creativity accounts for approximately 10 percent of creative individuals' working time. This seems to be sufficient to test out new ideas. Ideally management wants to see that time spent on formally approved projects. However, it is a hypothetical calculation that time saved on bootlegging is available for other projects. Creativity does not conform to a simple mathematical algorithm of addition and subtraction. Bootleg researchers seem to have a definite need for "intrinsic cross-fertilization" with several projects. Moreover, if formal projects are jeopardized, the bootleg project risks discovery, thus threatening his or her creative freedom and prime working motivation.

Last but not least, there is also the concern about use of covert activity for private purposes. The research did reveal staff members who repair their cars in corporate workshops in Germany, and French engineers designing

Only occasionally do underground ideas create radical breakthroughs.

decoders for private TV channels. However, it was found that "moonlighting" is far from being a large-scale phenomenon. Most managers tolerate little repair jobs and some see parallels with a famous story from Hewlett Packard (11): "One evening its founders found all tool cupboards locked. Deeply irritated, the next day they insisted that tool cupboards never be locked again. What is more, they encouraged their workforce to take tools home and experiment with them, thus extending their expertise at no cost to the company."

Breakthroughs and Boredom—Motivators of Research

Only occasionally do underground ideas create radical breakthroughs. Most companies interviewed characterized the usual bootleg idea as leading to a technological "improvement." The technology of existing products is improved either by adding functionality or replacing technological "imperfections" by brilliant specific refinements. "Researchers think all the time about things and how they could try to improve these . . .," said one researcher.

Most researchers seem to stop their covert research once they succeed in demonstrating the feasibility of their idea. Progressing beyond this point does not seem to motivate the researcher. Creative minds typically seem to enjoy the thrill of juggling with new ideas in the early stages. A secondary stage needing structured problem-solving skills, does not seem to interest them. Possibly this is because these researchers generally lack such skills and they are just bored once they have solved the problem—it probably feels too much like a day-to-day job.

A commonly expressed fear is that bootleg research is aimed at working up an idea so that an individual researcher can leave the company to set up his own venture. On the basis of this research, the fear is unfounded. Management need not fear losing creative people to self-employment once they have developed an idea. Again, self-employment implies more administrative and disciplined work than most maverick researchers like. Thus, entrepreneurship is not often an attractive option.

Researchers confirmed that in general they disclose their innovations "too early" rather than too late. But sometimes, underground researchers deliberately delay disclosure, largely for two very contrasting reasons—insecurity and heroism. Some need to be doubly sure about their work before disclosing it; others keep it a secret in order to be able to reveal the idea with a flourish, thus gaining the admiration of their colleagues.

The development of the 12-cylinder engine at BMW was presented to the management team as one such surprise. One GEC customer knew about a product earlier than the company's own management. At another firm, a product was sold 40 times before becoming an official product. And at HP in France, the bootleg innovation was even shown first at a trade fair. There are extreme cases of late disclosure that make good stories but in reality are rare.

The romance of underground activity is sometimes exaggerated. For example, in Nayak and Ketteringham's 1986 best-selling book *"Breakthroughs!,"* reference is made to Tagamet, the first billion-dollar drug in pharmaceutical history, developed at Smith Kline & French Laboratories (*12*). Tagamet is an anti-ulcer drug which made surgery for duodenal ulcers virtually redundant. The story is told of underground development of this drug over a period of 12 years by a group headed by the Nobel laureate Sir James Black. A lengthy interview with Sir James Black and a telephone call to William Duncan, his superior at the time, revealed in fact that this version was incorrect.

Why is Organizing Creativity So Difficult?

It is commonly recognized that creative ideas are unpredictable. Despite this widely held belief, all companies interviewed for this study employed a planning system in R&D whereby the budget was linked to objectives. The aim was to maximize output of R&D with limited resources. It is clear, however, that planning can only be applied to the structured part of the research process and not to the truly creative idea. What is more, most ideas emerge at unplanned moments, in-between funding periods. One solution to this could be to integrate these ideas into the next planning period. In most cases, however, once a researcher has an idea, there is usually a certain urgency in pursuing it. Delays or attempts to put it in a more convenient organizational structure result in a loss of curiosity and thus the loss of a potential new business idea.

The most obvious solution to managing non-programmed ideas is to leave some resources unallocated. The German firm, Krauss Maffei, has a small "war-kitty"; GSK gives "in-house grants." Even when such funds exist, they do not overcome the necessity to engage in covert research. The downside of the "war-kitty" approach is that the researcher has to apply for this grant and in the process disclose his or her idea. The

moment an idea is disclosed control is ceded to management. Should the researcher risk this? The case of permitted bootlegging is a similar dilemma. The moment a researcher seeks a grant or is given permission to undertake "permitted bootlegging," control and independence are relinquished.

Researchers often do not want to ask for permission, in order to avoid the psychological pressure of coming up with a result. Imagine being given "permitted bootleg time" and then not delivering a valuable innovation. Management phrases like this are no rarity: "If somebody wants to look around he can, but it is expected that he comes back with a good idea." Researchers, of course, feel uncomfortable about "coming back with nothing." In particular, if grant approval is linked to a cumbersome application procedure, it is easier for the bootlegger simply to disappear underground. This approach makes even more sense during periods of cost reduction and when there are pressures to deliver to the market.

Tight control, far from being beneficial, might in fact lead to less innovation. Observations in the course of this research revealed that whereas, in general, management seeks control over the researcher, the majority of researchers prefer uncontrolled space. Managers nevertheless need some method by which to evaluate ideas from a business perspective. Decisions are typically based on analytical methods such as predicted sales or returns. It goes without saying that the more information on hand, the more viable the proposal. Management always welcomes working prototypes that reduce technical uncertainty. "If you can present a working prototype, management finds it easy to accept it; otherwise you need a lot of saliva to convince them," said a researcher from the French company, Schneider Electric.

Management often asks for sales estimates to get a sense of the market potential and, more importantly, to protect themselves against the criticisms of their superiors. A written proposal serves as evidence and justification for their actions. Late disclosure of an idea gives it an advantage in the decision-making process.

Laboratories usually produce more ideas and proposals for research than the company can fund. As a result, researchers often hesitate to reveal their ideas at an early stage as lack of evidence makes it difficult to argue the case for investment. As an IBM R&D manager put it: "The quality of ideas can be divided into three groups: obviously good ideas, clearly bad ideas, and in-between are those ideas whose potential is unclear." He claimed that three quarters of the ideas are "somewhere in-between."

The most important quality of a new business idea is the minimum sales it is expected to generate upon implementation. If this is below a certain level, the idea is not economically justifiable. A British company with

6,000 employees and £1,700 million sales needs each new business idea to generate sales of £50 million. Not surprisingly therefore, over 50 percent of the researchers interviewed claimed that market results are the most difficult area to gauge.

These multiple requirements trap the researcher in a vicious circle, from which the only escape is to go underground. The company provides no time or resources for preparation, and unprepared proposals are likely to be rejected with comments like "think again and come back," commented a researcher from ICL (International Computers Ltd.). The backlog of ideas makes for a very competitive climate for proposals. This propels researchers into energetic collection of convincing material in the form of data and working prototypes, together with orchestration of extensive lobbying. The researcher's sole aim is to reduce the uncertainty of his proposal so that the risk of decision-making for managers is reduced in turn. Nearly all successful innovations have to overcome at some stage in their life the "brick walls" of formality or inadequate decision-making processes.

Digging Underground

In the light of these findings, should managers be concerned about the underground life of their companies? What if a deliberate strategy is put in place to leave creativity to itself? Does that not imply a total carte blanche? Surprisingly the answer is no! Imagine a researcher looking for new ideas. If he has any sense, he knows he cannot convince his company to commercialize a new type of washing machine if the firm is producing microchips. In fact, chances are slim that this will ever happen, because researchers working in a chip company are likely to be microchip experts and not washing machine specialists. In technical terms, historically accumulated knowledge about a technology defines a trajectory, which determines the range of ideas people come up with subsequently. Not surprisingly, almost all bootleg products researched were within the strategic research range as defined by the company.

Moreover, contemporary products and technology reach high degrees of complexity and can only be achieved with the combined skills of a large research team. For example, the development of a modern paint spray-gun requires expertise in electronics, mechanics, fluid mechanics, and pneumatics. Time and knowledge constraints make it impossible to develop the entire product or completely new technologies "single-handedly." That can make the secrecy of the underground a relative one. Often, everybody seems to know covert research is happening, but nobody admits to it. Although bootleg entrepreneurs work outside any formal procedures, they are in fact controlled by friends, colleagues and even, surprisingly, on occasion by customers. Criticism by others is useful for the "distillation" and refining the "quality of the idea," one researcher commented.

> **Contrary to perceived wisdom, bootlegging is the lifeblood of creative organizations.**

Formal Organization of Creativity is Pointless

Contrary to perceived wisdom, bootlegging is the lifeblood of creative organizations, rather than a self-indulgent activity happening "under the counter." Ideas typically emerge from a few creative individuals within an organization who often question mainstream approaches. Companies are, however, collectivist institutions and cannot offer special advantages to a handful of maverick employees among a group of researchers with similar seniority and privileges. At the same time, they would be ill-advised to grant permission for all staff to work as they wish. Not everybody has an outstandingly creative mind to come up with new ideas and make use of this time and freedom efficiently. In the event companies do favor individuals, the selection process could cause conflicts by provoking jealousy and resentment. On the other hand, if creative people never get time for their ideas, they will almost certainly leave the company.

Under these circumstances, bootlegging remains a safe option. Researchers were shown time and again to be making creative use of underground activity to channel their own creative energy. Without a researcher working away on how to eliminate air bubbles in cement, for instance, a company would not have been able to make its special cement more durable.

In one German company, a chemical was being sought to suppress pollen formation in plants. Only a chestnut tree from the banks of the Mississippi River was thought to have the required properties. A flight to Mississippi was ruled out. Nevertheless, the ingredients were acquired through covert channels.

In another German company, a new search algorithm was developed that far outstripped the contemporary world leader.

In this light, it is no surprise that this study reveals that most products with their origins in the corporate underground are commercially valuable for the firm. Underground R&D seems to be concomitant and inseparable from early innovation and is present in most companies. It reconciles corporate contradictions through researchers taking responsibility themselves for the development of new ideas and thus can be regarded as a corrective action for eternal organizational paradoxes. So, rather than looking at underground activity as a threat, why not accept it as the most fertile environment for innovation and learning? It seems that bootlegging in a research environment is not just inevitable, it is essential. A more fluid management approach is needed in response. Innovation cannot be turned on at the whim of management. The management lesson is to leave creative processes in the underground world and formal processes in the official world. Any attempt to mix the two worlds simply does not work. ⊛

References

1. Bessant, J. 2003. Speech at the conference *"What do we know about innovation?"* on the occasion of K. Pavitt's death at the University of Sussex, SPRU, Freeman Center, University of Sussex, Brighton, UK, 13–15 November.

2. Speech by BMW representative. 2006. *Workshop on Discontinuous Innovation,* The 2nd IET International Technology and Innovation Conference. The Institution of Engineering and Technology, Savoy Place, London. 5–6 July.

3. Augsdorfer, P. 1996. *Forbidden Fruit, An Analysis of Bootlegging, Uncertainty and Learning in Corporate R&D.* Avebury, Aldershot.

4. Koen, Peter. WWW.FRONTENDINNOVATION.COM

5. Roussel, P. A., Saad, K. N., and Erickson, T. J. 1991. *Third Generation R&D,* Arthur D. Little, Inc., USA.

6. Mintzberg, H. 1993. The Pitfalls of Strategic Planning. *California Management Review* Vol. 36, No. 1, pp. 32–47.

7. Amabile, T. et al. 2002. Creativity under the gun. *Harvard Business Review,* August, pp. 52–61.

8. Christensen, C. et al. 2001. Skate to where the money will be. *Harvard Business Review,* November, pp. 72–81.

9. Augsdorfer, P. 2005. Bootlegging and Path Dependency. *Research Policy* Vol 34, pp. 1–11.

10. Pinchot, G. 1988. Innovation Through Intrapreneuring, in Katz, R. (Ed.), *Managing Professionals in Innovative Organizations,* pp. 121–129, Ballinger, Cambridge, Mass.

11. On keeping storerooms open. *http://www.hp.com/retiree/history/founders/hewlett/quotes.html* (accessed April 13, 2008.)

12. Nayak, P. R. and Ketteringham, J. D. 1986. *Breakthroughs!,* Rawson Associates, N.Y.

▶ At W.L. Gore, the chemical company most famous for Gore-Tex, there are no management layers and there is no organizational chart. Few people have titles and no one has a boss. As at Whole Foods, the core operating units are small, self-managing teams, all of which share two common goals: "to make money and have fun."

Though there are no ranks or titles, some associates have earned the simple appellation "leader." Senior leaders do not appoint junior leaders. Rather, associates become leaders when their peers judge them to be such. A leader garners influence by demonstrating a capacity to get things done and excelling as a team builder. At Gore, those who make a disproportionate contribution to team success, and do it more than once, attract followers. "We vote with our feet," says Rich Buckingham, a manufacturing leader in Gore's technical-fabrics group. "If you call a meeting, and people show up, you're a leader."

The primary fuel for Gore's innovation machine is the discretionary time of its associates. All employees are granted a half day a week of "dabble time," which they can devote to an initiative of their own choosing—as long as they are fulfilling their primary commitments.

▶ Google once tried to impose the typical supervisory structure found in traditional software companies, where engineering managers have a relatively narrow span of control. It soon became obvious that an excess of oversight was putting a damper on innovation. Google's "I think I can" culture was in danger of becoming a "No, you can't" bureaucracy. Within weeks the new layer was ripped out and the recently appointed middle managers were reabsorbed into the engineering ranks. Today the average manager in Google's product-development group has more than 50 direct reports, and for some leaders the number tops 100.

Roughly half of Google's 10,000 employees—all those involved in product development—work in small teams, with an average of three engineers per team. Even a large project such as Gmail, which might occupy 30 people, is broken into teams of three or four, each of which works on a specific service enhancement, such as building spam filters or improving the forwarding feature. Each team has an "über-tech leader," a responsibility that rotates among team members depending on shifting project requirements. Most engineers work on more than one team, and no one needs the HR department's permission to switch teams. "If at all possible, we want people to commit to things rather

At W.L. Gore there are no management layers and there is no organizational chart. Few people have titles and no one has a boss.

DABBLE TIME Freedom to innovate leads Gore to new markets, like guitar strings.

than be assigned to things," says Shona Brown, Google's VP for operations. "If you see an opportunity, go for it."

How would you rate these companies in terms of the freedom they cede to their employees? Higher than your company? Probably. Higher than most companies? Without a doubt. Indeed, at first glance, one wonders how these loose-limbed organizations manage to meet budgets and delivery deadlines. First-line employees who set prices. People who take a day a week to work on whatever they like. Associates who can fire their leaders. A 50-to-1 span of control. All this sounds like a recipe for anarchy.

To understand how these companies manage to radically empower their employees and deliver consistent results, it's necessary to distinguish between the what and the how of discipline. Everyone can agree that discipline is a good thing—it's an essential what. The problem is with the how.

In most organizations, control is exercised via standard operating procedures, tight supervision, detailed role definitions, a minimum of self-directed time, and frequent reviews by higher-ups. These mechanisms certainly bring people to heel, but they also put a short leash on initiative, creativity, and passion. Luckily there are other ways of keeping things in check—other hows, if you will.

For example, while the in-store teams at Whole Foods have a significant degree of discretion over staffing, pricing, and product selection, they are also held accountable for the profitability of their various departments. Teams are assessed against monthly profitability targets, and when they meet those goals, team members receive a bonus in their next paycheck. Since the rewards are team-based, associates have little tolerance for colleagues who don't pull their weight. The fact that every team's performance is visible across the entire company is another incentive to work hard and stay focused. Turns out you don't need a lot of top-down discipline when four conditions are met:

1. First-line employees are responsible for results.
2. Team members have access to real-time performance data.
3. They have decision authority over the key variables that influence performance outcomes.
4. There's a tight coupling between results, compensation, and recognition.

Gore would also seem to suffer from a dangerous excess of freedom. Associates choose which teams to work on. They can say no to requests. And they allocate their dabble time as they see fit. But they also know they'll be reviewed by at least 20 of their peers at the end of each year—and that these assessments will determine their compensation. In addition, once a project moves beyond the dabble stage, a cross-functional review process periodically puts the development team through an exercise called "Real, Win, Worth." To attract resources, a product champion

Module 3

CREATE

Laila Bastedo

3.1 INTRODUCTION

Value creation is the second stage in the technology commercialization value chain as shown in Figure 3.1. In it the MTB Proposition is transformed into an implementable business venture. In the Create Stage technology development, market development and business development are carried out in parallel to create a compelling business plan for the proposition. If these value creation activities are successful then at the end of the Create Stage the MTB Proposition will move on to value extraction through commercialization in the marketplace.

Figure 3.1
The Technology Commercialization Value Chain: I♦C♦E

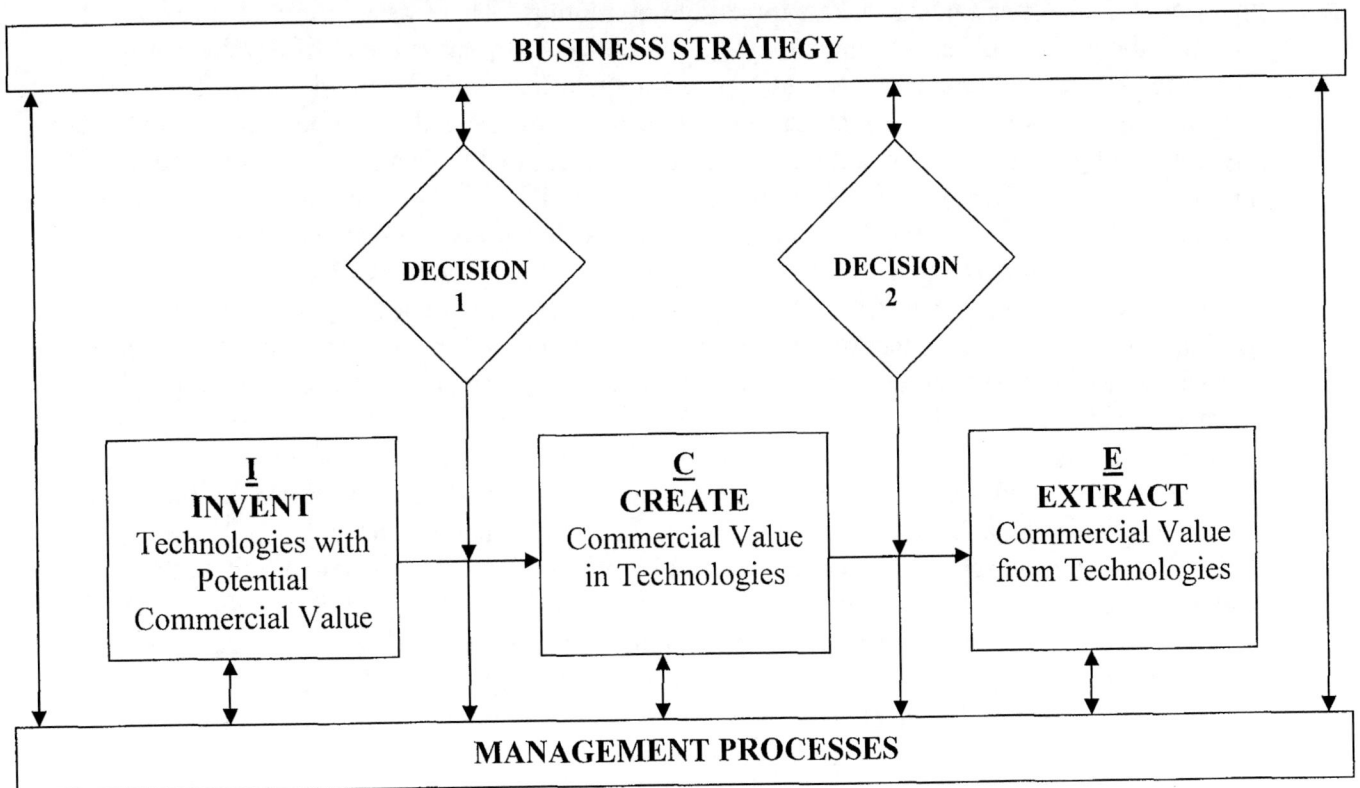

This module discusses the Create Stage under four main headings. First, some of the different kinds of processes that firms use to organize their value creation activities will be described and their relative merits discussed. Second, the increasing trend towards outsourcing value creation activities will be described. Third, the issues surrounding Decision 2, the decision point at the end of the Create Stage, will be covered. Finally, the management of value creating teams will be addressed. They present a unique set of management issues because of the

– 1 –

organizational role they play. Be reminded that the whole Create Stage is called "product development" by many writers. As explained in Module 1, this practice is not followed here. "Product development" is really just a part of value creation and so that term does not capture the multi-faceted nature of the Create Stage.

A key success factor in today's global economy is the ability of a company to meet customers' needs by producing a constant stream of innovative new products.[1] This is especially so in high technology industries such as biotechnology, computer software, pharmaceuticals and consumer and industrial electronics. Roughly 50% of annual sales in those industries come from products introduced within the last five years. Yet, up to two thirds of new products that reach the market fail to produce economic value for their organizations.[2] Another study estimates that 95% of new products fail to produce an economic return.[3] Hence, the Create Stage is critical to the economic health of organizations.

A number of studies have shown that the success of new products is correlated with the characteristics of the value creation process that produced them[4] so it is important for organizations to develop effective value creation methods.[5] This is partly because globalization has resulted in an increase in foreign competition which requires organizations to reduce product life cycles and provide differentiated products based on cost, quality and innovativeness.[6] For example, in the late 1980s, Japanese automakers took an average 30 months to move an MTB Proposition for a new automobile through the Invent and Create stages and into the market. At that time North American car makers took 48 to 60 months. This was a strong incentive to improve their ICE processes,[7] which they did. In the last 50 years product life cycles have decreased by over 400 percent.[8] Speedy, efficient and effective value creation provides a competitive advantage for an organization. A further pressure is the fragmentation of markets precipitated by manufacturing and technological advances that have allowed organizations to produce many variants of products for different market niches.[9] For example, Nike produces more than 250 variations of athletic shoes to serve a wide variety of niche markets.[10]

The reduction of cycle time (time to go through the Invent and Create Stages) is critical, particularly in high tech industries. A software firm that is slow to develop a new product may find that by the time its product reaches the market demand no longer exists. Instead, demand has shifted to the next generation of products mounted by a competitor using technological advances that occurred while the first company was developing its product.[11] Reducing cycle time also allows an organization to get to market first to establish its technology as the industry standard or dominant design.[12] For example, Intel established its microprocessor architecture as the dominant design and led the the resurgence of the US semiconductor industry.[13]

Studies have shown that a major cause of new product failure is new product attributes (features, quality, pricing) that do not meet customers' needs.[14] Thus, market analysis (including customer's wants, needs, and trends) is key to value creation. Preliminary market analyses are carried out in the Invent Stage as described in Module 2. As the MTB Proposition moves through value creation to launch, continuous market development is essential to ensuring that the end product can satisfy customer needs. The extent of market development as well as the extent and timing of customer interaction differ with different NPD processes, as described below.

3.2   PROCESSES FOR VALUE CREATION

Traditionally, value creation was done in a more or less *ad hoc* way by most firms. In the last 40 or 50 years, however, organizations have worked hard to develop better ways of

- 2 -

managing it. Improvements continue to be made as organizations compete relentlessly for faster and more efficient ways to create new products that delight customers. Both the Invent and Create Stages are difficult to manage using traditional management methods because both involve high levels of uncertainty, higher than those found in other activities such as production and accounting. Management methods for Invent and Create include higher levels of flexibility in order to deal with the unexpected contingencies that arise when creative new ideas are being brought to market. The high tech industries are famous for leading the development of the informal, flexible management methods that are increasingly used in all parts of our economy.

In this section two general approaches to value creation will be described. There are many variations on both, however, as management teams have modified them to meet their own unique value creation needs. One of these two general approaches is the "stage/gate" model which was originally pioneered by Professors Robert Cooper and Elko Kleinschmidt of McMaster University. [15] The second general approach, "customer collaboration" models, involves collaborating very closely with customers during the Create Stage.

3.2.1 Stage/Gate Models and their Derivatives

In the stage/gate approach value creation activities are broken down into a number of stages organized in a linear sequence. Each stage involves a set of related activities which must be accomplished before going on to the next stage, similar to an assembly line. After each stage is a gate. At each gate the progress of the project is evaluated and a decision made as to whether the project should i) proceed to the next stage, ii) be abandoned iii) be redirected back to the previous stage, or iv) redirected. [16,17] Similar to the technology commercialization value chain, stage/gate models are pictured as a sequence of boxes and diamonds with each box representing a set of activities (stage) and each diamond a decision point (gate). Typically stage/gate models involve more than the three stages in the ICE model, some having six or seven stages. The MTB Proposition moves from left to right along the sequence of stages and gates. In most stage gate models MTB Propositions are called projects. Unlike the technology commercialization value chain, stage/gate models are usually very specific about what needs to be done at each stage and which criteria are to be applied at each gate. This has been the hallmark of their success. By being clear and specific about what is being done and why, they have made value creation much more "business-like". Consequently, budgets are not over-spent nearly so often, time lines are much more likely to be met, and projects that have little hope of market success are terminated early before they eat up excessive amounts of organizational resources.

The gates or decision points enable management to consider whether the MTB Proposition is still consistent with the organization's strategic direction. Management can decide if external factors such as changing market needs, new technology, legal issues, or government policies require a shift in the proposition's direction (or in some cases more resources to help move it along more quickly). With this process, resources are not needlessly spent finishing value creation when a key issue for success is uncovered. For example, the development of pharmaceutical inhalants using CFC based pumps could be stopped at a gate if environmental regulations banned CFC pumps. With respect to the organization's technology management strategy, management has the opportunity at the gates to execute their role of setting strategic direction in light of the entire organization's MTB Proposition portfolio.

The number of stages in a given stage/gate process varies by product development project and organization. Typically, there are four to seven stages. The prototypical stage/gate process developed by Cooper and Kleinschmidt has five stages, as follow. [18] In this model there are five gates between these stages where progress is assessed and decisions made.

Stage 1 is **scoping** a product idea for its technical and market merits. The traditional model prescribes that the activities in this stage involve desk research or detective work with little or no primary research.

Stage 2 is **building the business case**. A market analysis, including customer specifications, competitive analysis, and concept testing is done. Detailed technical assessment also takes places. A detailed financial and business analysis is done to construct a business case for the product.

Stage 3 is **development** and design of the new product. This includes in-house testing and prototype development.

Stage 4 is **testing and validating** the new product (technical functionality) as well as verifying the marketing and production aspects of the project. Production runs may take place. A beta test or field trials help gauge customer acceptance. [19]

Stage 5 is the **launch** with full commercialization of the finished product. This is followed by a post launch review to assess the success of the new product.

This is the classic stage/gate model pioneered by Cooper and Kleinschmidt which has revolutionized technology commercialization and led to many variations and adaptations. As originally presented it was very rigorous about following the process and making stop/go decisions. Ettlie and Elsenbach[20] surveyed 72 automotive engineering managers representing 60 companies to discover how many were using this classic model, how many were using a modification of it, and how many were using neither. In their sample 48.6% used the traditional Stage/Gate model and 30% used a modified version of it. The most common modification was to allow for backtracking so that the gates can swing forward or backwards depending on the situation. Second, the traditional model was modified to allow for continuous improvement of the product or process during value creation, depending on the resources required and perceived changes in market opportunities. Last, collaborative virtual environments (due to internet and computer advances) have reduced the need for program reviews. Teams collaborate "anywhere, anytime" to identify and resolve issues making the gates redundant.

The classic stage/gate model is quite specific and prescriptive. For example, Cooper and Kleinschmidt emphasize the need to do market research thoroughly and early so that the product specifications can be very clearly stated very early in the process, preferably in Stage 2. Along with this, specific goals to be accomplished by each gate are also set early in the planning process. They based this on their study of companies using stage/gate models. As it happens, such early specification is not always possible and not always desirable.

3.2.2 Customer Collaboration Approaches

Customer collaboration approaches involve closer and more extended collaboration with the customer than does the classic stage/gate model. In the most extreme versions the selling organization and the customer organization become partners in creating the new product. This is usually because the customer is not really sure what it wants. The MTB Proposition under consideration is so new that there is no reliable way to assess accurately what is technically feasible, what is marketable, and what will be a good business proposition for the seller and the customer. They must work it out together to explore and discover what is commercially feasible.

module 3 (5) 2007 08 16.doc

Prototyping Models

In this approach a series of prototypes are provided to the customer beginning early in the process and continuing until the end of value creation. Although the classic stage/gate model recommends the use of prototypes the extent of use is not nearly so great. The creation of custom software systems for corporate clients is often done with a series of prototypes. This helps build a mutual understanding of what the customer really wants and what is technically possible within the cost parameters. [21] The earlier prototypes may be in the form of interface sketches or screen shots. They are often not working designs, but rather representations of the product. There are variations on this. In the *Spiral Model* a series of prototypes is provided to the customer with one goal being the identification of major risks associated with a value creation project. Often, once the risks are identified and the specifications defined, the design than progresses using a more structured stage/gate approach. [22] In the *Rapid-Prototyping Model* a disposable prototype is delivered to the customer early in the development process. This allows the customer to voice their preferences and allows the developers to solidify their specifications.

Advances in information technology have enabled the creation of virtual prototypes. The safety of automobile designs can be tested through virtual simulated crashes. Boeing developed the 767 jetliner using virtual computer generated prototypes. The financial industry also performs analysis of financial performance on computer generated simulations of markets. [23] The pharmaceutical industry uses complex databases and software to conduct pre-clinical trials using virtual patients. This helps avoid testing a drug on animals that is either highly toxic or does not have the intended therapeutic value. [24]

Evolutionary-Delivery Model (EDM)

In this approach versions of software are delivered to the customer in chunks with increasing functionality. With each succeeding chunk more is learned about additional specifications that are needed and can be delivered in later chunks. This allows at least some functionality to be delivered to the customer early on. [25] A fundamental assumption in EDM is that full customer specifications cannot be known up front. [26] For example, with a new electronic personal organizer some of the capabilities that customers will want do not become apparent until they have worked with the basic capabilities. Without this it is difficult to predict how customers would work with that technology.

A notable difference between the EDM and the classic stage/gate model is the flexibility the design team has with evolving the design. In the more structured approaches, the gate or phase reviews are based on whether the product has reached previously agreed upon goals based on the original product specifications. In EDM the product design evolves to meet the customer requirements based upon the evolving understandings developed earlier in the process. The development of the product is thus iterative so the team has the flexibility to alter the direction and re-focus development. A difference between EDM and prototyping models is that in EDM the early designs that customers test are actual working versions of the final product, and not disposable prototypes. Studies have shown that when customers test products early in development (when functionality and feature sets are small) the quality of the final product is usually higher than when customers test products later in development (when functionality and feature sets are larger). Product quality; defined as technical performance, breadth of functionality and reliability; is a function of the ability of customers to guide product development with on-going feedback.[27]

In 1995 Microsoft was severely lagging behind Yahoo! and Netscape with its internet browser technology. Time was crucial for Microsoft to provide a competitive product as both competitors were rapidly gaining market share. To meet this challenge the initial specifications for Internet Explorer 3.0 (IE3) were created early in the development process, but the details of the overall product architecture and final product features were left for later stages. In order to launch a working product quickly, many people had to work in parallel to evolve the product and architecture. While the first iteration of IE3 had about 30% functionality, it was enough to run tests and obtain performance feedback. Iterations of the product from that point occurred daily. New functionality based on customer input or internal testing was added daily and integrated into the design. This daily iteration is termed *rapid feedback cycle*. Within a month, Microsoft was able to distribute the first beta release of IE3 with contained 50 – 70% of the final functionality. Customers provided feedback and influenced the design of the final product.[28]

In the most extreme form of the customer collaboration models, the seller and customer work together on a series of versions of the intended product gradually refining them to be a product (technology) that the seller wants and can afford (market) and is a commercially viable proposition for the seller (business). It is more like a partnership than a buyer/seller relationship because both parties have the most to gain by cooperation.

3.3.2 Choosing a Value Creation Process

The preceding section has shown that there is a continuum in the degree of structure found in value creation processes. At one extreme is the classic stage/gate model which demands very early specification of product attributes, stage activities and gate criteria. In the classic model an MTB Proposition must meet all the gate criteria before it moves to the next stage. The various derivatives of the classic stage/gate model relax some of these requirements selectively so there is more flexibility in the process. For example, it may not be required that all criteria be met before a proposition passes a gate. Customer collaboration models allow even more flexibility. Product specifications are not finalized as early in the process and customer consultation can allow changes fairly late in the game. In the most flexible processes such as EDM, sellers and customers work as partners continually changing the specifications as they discover jointly what is technically and economically feasible for them both.

Firms have to choose from among these many models and variations. They must choose a process that is optimal for them and even then may have to make final adjustments for their own needs. There are several considerations in this choice and adjustment process.

One important consideration has to do with the costs associated with design changes at different stages in the value creation process. Changes made early in the process are usually less expensive than those made later.[29] For example, if a change is made late in the game after a pilot manufacturing plant has been build it may be very expensive to retool the plant. If that change had been made earlier the plant would have been built right in the first place and no changeover costs would have been incurred.

The consequences of this cost effect are different for incremental and radical innovation. The early setting of specifications is possible with incremental innovations because there is not much change from what is already being done and current practice is a good guide as to how to proceed. An incremental variation on a laundry detergent that is currently in the market is a

– 6 –

good example. It is likely that the current manufacturing process will have to be changed in only minor ways. The same will hold for the chemical composition of the detergent. The market for the new detergent will be pretty much the same as for the existing detergent and so will hold only minor uncertainties. With all these certainties it will be possible to establish at an early stage a set of steps and milestones for the value creation process that can be met on time and on budget. There will be a low likelihood of changes needed late in the process. Structured approaches can and do put a high premium on setting the product and process specifications early because it is possible to do so with few costly changes late in the process if the innovation is incremental.

But the more structured approaches tend to be more effective for incremental than for radical innovations. For more radical innovations current practice is not necessarily a good guide as to what should be done. Product and process specifications may need to change during value creation due to various factors such as unforeseen technical challenges, regulatory and legislative challenges, and customer needs. A very innovative product using new technologies cannot have a pre-defined set of performance criteria and specifications that the end customer desires. By its very nature, changes downstream will have to take place. In such cases the collaborative, flexible models are more appropriate. In addition, more innovative MTB Propositions are often delayed because the original time estimates do not take into account the learning required to accomplish tasks.[30] It is difficult to estimate time on tasks if the tasks themselves are new. Only through doing does one learn the details of how best to accomplish a task or construct an efficient process for it. For example, radical innovation propositions sometimes require new hardware-software systems to support them.[31] People have to learn how to configure and use these systems before being able to apply them to the value creation process.

The strict application of criteria in the structured approaches can also be problematic for radical innovations. If a highly structured approach is used the entire project can be delayed if one component is late. For example, if new legislation required an extended safety test on a component, an inflexible approach would require waiting for the test results before moving to the next stage. But this wait could delay a scheduled launch and may be riskier with respect to potential market penetration than to continue value creation while waiting for the test results.

3.3   OUTSOURCING IN VALUE CREATION

The process of value creation involves transforming technical, market and business knowledge into a viable MTB Proposition using available financial resources. But an organization, by itself, may not have all the knowledge and/or financial resources needed for that transformation. Confronted with this situation the organization can choose to develop the needed knowledge and resources internally or find collaborators to provide what is missing. For example, Microsoft, instead of deciding to develop online capabilities itself, established an alliance with America Online (AOL) to increase the market penetration of Internet Explorer 3 (IE3). The rapid adoption of IE3 was facilitated partly by using AOL's (the largest online service provider at the time) distribution channel. Choosing to build internal capability to provide online services would have taken valuable time and resulted in a lost opportunity to catch up with Netscape's market lead. [32]

Collaboration with suppliers can be a useful tactic because suppliers can contribute valuable ideas for product improvement and can help with technical solutions. Research has shown that higher quality products can be produced in less time and at a lower cost by incorporating suppliers into the value creation process.[33] For example, a supplier could suggest

- 7 -

an alternative material that could improve quality and/or lower cost – both of which customers may regard highly. [34,35] Supplier collaboration/integration can occur whether the process is highly structured or highly flexible. [36]

There can be varying degrees of supplier involvement. The supplier can act as a consultant to the value creation team on an *ad hoc* basis. Or, the supplier relationship can be deeper, more formal and enduring. For example, under a formal agreement the supplier can collaborate in the joint development of a prototype and in its testing. Alternately, the supplier might design and develop a complete component of a product based on the organization's specifications. Seating systems for automobiles is an example. Such outsourcing of entire modules is becoming more common.

The pharmaceutical industry provides a good illustration of the value of outsourcing in the value creation stage. The average cost of developing a drug so that it is ready for clinical trials on humans is more than $200 million. From that point it can take upwards of another $100 million to do those clinical trials and to get government approval for the market. This takes an average of seven years. Pharmaceutical companies are constantly working to find ways to reduce these enormous costs in time and money and are turning to outsourcing as a way to do that. The management of clinical trials is costly and complex. Some contract research organizations have developed specific skills to do that management in a resource efficient manner. For example, Quintiles Transnational (one of the largest contract research organizations in the world) saved Pfizer one year in the development of an anti-Alzheimer drug by doing the clinical trials for them. It is estimated that because Pfizer got into the market a year early they made an extra $580 million in income from the drug. The pharmaceutical companies that use contract research organizations have decided that they do not want to expend resources building the necessary internal capabilities that these contract organizations already have. These decisions are based in part on technology planning carried out as part of strategic planning.

The degree to which an organization collaborates in the Create Stage depends on strategic plans, internal capabilities and the nature of a particular MTB proposition. Options available for external sourcing include subcontracting with external laboratories, research centers, and universities for the delivery of particular technologies. Another approach is to acquire a technology by acquiring, aligning with, or investing in another organization. [37,38] Additionally, organizations can license technologies from other organizations. [39]

3.4   DECISION 2

Decision 2 is made at the end of the Create Stage before the MTB Proposition goes on to the Extract Stage (Figure 3.1). It is usually made by a formally appointed multi-functional committee. The document making the case for the proposition is usually a complete business plan. As discussed in Module 1, it may be decided to launch the new venture in the marketplace using the organization's own resources or to involve some outsourcing. In other cases the commercialization may be launched as a spin-off. Less promising propositions may be sent back to the Create Stage for more work, shelved for reconsideration when the business climate improves, or terminated. In the case of termination of an MTB Proposition there may be consideration of how value can be extracted from at least some of the various elements that made up the proposition. For example, although a proposition might be killed there might be an opportunity to license some of the technologies that were developed as part of it.

4.1 Decisions within the Create Stage

Decision 2 comes at the end of the Create Stage and is usually the last of several decision points in that Stage. The ICE model highlights the three major stages and two major decision points in the technology commercialization value chain but in practice most firms have more minor decision points within each stage. The number of such decisions varies by firm but most are intended to ensure that the MTB Proposition moves towards a commercially viable outcome in a more-or-less orderly way. These on-going assessments address the three major considerations discussed earlier, technology, market and business.

Technology

Testing and feasibility analysis of the product and the manufacturing process are on-going during the Create Stage. This allows the value creation team to identify and respond to technical problems in a timely way so that other aspects of development (e.g. product features) can also be modified earlier rather than later. Both the underlying technology for the product itself as well as the manufacturing process must be analyzed and problems addressed to increase the likelihood of product success. In other words, the final functionality of the product is a result of cumulative testing and analysis.

Market

A strong market orientation in value creation increases the likelihood of product success and can reduce time-to-market. Detailed market assessment is critical but is often an activity that is poorly executed and/or conducted only for product launch rather than throughout the value creation process.[40] Customer feedback at several points during the Create Stage improves the probability of success. Competitor analysis is also part of the market assessment. Additionally, market launch activities must be planned. The market plan (including launch) is part of a well-articulated business plan.[41]

Business

During the Create Stage the business case for an MTB Proposition must be fully developed, specifying how value will be extracted. Several major issues must be addressed.

Strategic Assessment. How well does the proposition align with business strategy? Does the product and process used to manufacture and distribute the product leverage the organization's core competencies? Should parts of the value creation stage be outsourced? Does the MTB Proposition move the organization in its intended direction?

Financial Assessment. The ultimate goal of value creation activities is to realize an economic return for the organization. Financial considerations such as the net present value (NPV), internal rate of return (IRR) and time to profit are ongoing considerations.[42] Financial projections will change over time as more detailed information is gathered and market conditions change. Unexpected developments such as delays in the target launch date or the need to retrofit equipment to handle new design changes also change the numbers so the financial prospects for each proposition need continuous evaluation.

Risk Assessment. As with the other considerations, risk assessments are a continuing activity. If development is delayed, what are the financial risks and market risks? Will a competitor realize first mover advantage or establish a dominant design? What are the risks of collaborating with another organization for product distribution or sub-assembly? Will the suppliers be able to mass produce and deliver the component parts to the required specifications? Does the organization have enough people and dollar resources to create a successful product? In addition to the risks directly associated with the product, the organization must assess the external environment for changes that may risk delay or make the product obsolete or redundant. For example, the external environment includes regulatory and legislative bodies that impact the industry and market conditions.

Whether an organization uses a relatively structured or a more flexible value creation process, periodic progress reviews need to take place. In the structured approaches gate reviews are the formal mechanisms for assessing the progress and risks. Some organizations explicitly use these as a funneling process to kill those propositions that are doing poorly, have high risk, or show no future economic potential for the organization.[43] In more flexible systems informal meetings of teams charged with particular parts of proposition development make the assessments and make recommendations.

3.4.2 Decision 2 and the Business Plan

Decision 2 is the culmination decision for all the decision making that has taken place during the Create Stage. When the serious issues surrounding an MTB Proposition have been identified, analyzed, and for the most part solved, a decision must be made about whether extraction should be launched and what form it should take.

At this point, as with some of the earlier decision points, tough decisions sometimes have to be made. The toughest are those to kill an MTB Proposition. The challenge for the decision making team is to actually make a decision given political pressures and organizational climate. For example, if management is viewed as "failing" if a project is killed, then killing a project when it is no longer relevant for the organization will be difficult.[44] Such decisions are more likely to occur if the decision makers are provided with a clear set of decision criteria and process guidelines.[45,46] If the process does not have clear criteria for killing projects, or the decision making team does not have clear support from senior management, it becomes easier to let a project continue despite the analyzed risks.[47] Studies have shown that better performing organizations have clear processes and criteria for culling weak MTB Propositions.[48]

Decision 2 is a weighty one because it can have very significant financial and reputational consequences. The decision to move a proposition to the Extract Stage usually involves a very significant further investment by the firm and a failed market launch can negatively impact the reputation of the firm with customers.

Because of the seriousness of Decision 2 many firms create thorough business plans for the propositions being assessed. This helps ensure a thorough and comprehensive evaluation of the risks and opportunities. A business plan is a comprehensive description of the business and its economic viability based on the MTB Proposition.[49] Many authors have presented their detailed versions of what a business plan should include and although they differ in detail they usually address the same fundamentals. Figure 3.2 lists the sections that are usually included in a business plan. Such templates are not usually followed religiously because each MTB Proposition is unique and requires a unique statement of its business plan. Different sections will

- 10 –

have different levels of importance for different MTB Propositions. This example shows, however, the comprehensiveness of such plans.

Figure 3.2
Example of the Sections of a Business Plan

---

1. Executive Summary
2. Industry, Company, Products, Services
    This is an overview of the proposed business, the industry niche into which it will fit and its value proposition for customers
3. Market Research and Analysis
    The detailed market analysis for the product
4. Detailed Marketing Plan
    This describes how the marketing will be carried out, how to reach the customers identified in section 3.
5. The Economics of the Business
    Describes the key economic drivers of the business and how money will be made and includes spreadsheets of projected incomes and expenses over several years.
6. Financial Plan
    Explanation of how capital will be raised and how it merges with the economics of the business.
7. Operations and Management Plan
    Explains how manufacturing and other operations will be carried out including a description of organizational structures and processes. May include names of the principal individuals who will be involved and their role. Schedule of principal activities over the next several years.
8. Risks, Problems, and Assumptions
    Explains the primary risks in the venture and how they will be dealt with if they materialize. Principal assumptions being made, sensitivity analyses of them and actions to be taken if they do not materialize.
9. Appendices

Typically, the body of a business plan is 25 to 30 pages long. The appendices are usually much longer as they provide detailed material supporting the narrative in the body of the plan.

3.5 MANAGING VALUE CREATION TEAMS

As indicated earlier in this module and in preceding modules, value creation will be most effective if it is carried out by cross-functional teams. Cross-functional teams include individuals from the different functional areas within the organization which can make a contribution to the value creation process. Usually, marketing, manufacturing, research and engineering are the principal participants as they have the most important contributions to make. But value creation teams often include representatives from finance, design, sales and other

module 3 (5) 2007 08 16.doc

functions, if not permanently, at least on a consultative basis to ensure that all facets of the MTB Proposition are effectively developed. As seen in the discussion above, the value creation process can also include customers, suppliers, and other organizations that are outsourced to or partnered with, to create and market the final product. Cross-functional collaboration increases the likelihood of success by i) bringing together the expertise to maximize the fit between the product's functionality and the customer requirements and ii) accelerating the development time by allowing all functions to respond immediately to a change in one function thereby reducing time delays and extra costs. Successful collaboration reduces overall costs and thus increases the economic return for a project. Empirical work shows that a large contributor to value adding failure is the result of mis- (or no) communication between different functional areas.[50]

In a study by Jassawalla and Sashittal (1999), cross-functional teams introduced into the value creation process transformed a sequential value creation process to a more parallel one. As discussed earlier, concurrent activities help reduce value creation times.[51] Jenkins *et al* studied companies using cross functional teams of eight to ten full-time members to manage the value creation phase.[52] One advantage of this was that all members of the team were aware of the effect of the project on their functional areas. Cross-functional collaboration also allowed teams to plan activities in parallel thus enabling concurrent engineering.[53] Furthermore, it was found that the cross-functional teams helped decision makers assess risks associated with moving projects forward when all the deliverables have not been met at a particular gate. A cross-functional team thus has the expertise to "predict the chances of delivering the incomplete task within an acceptable time scale".[54] Other studies have shown that a large percentage of project slippage (going over schedule) is due to a lack of communication between functional areas, and using sequential problem solving when parallel cross-functional problem solving was required.[55] Last, studies in the automotive industry has shown that those projects that incorporated both manufacturing personnel and process engineers in the value creation process performed better with respect to cycle time and engineering productivity and quality.[56]

From an organizational behaviour standpoint, effective cross-functional teams display a high degree of participation in their value creation activities. Team members contribute equally to team decisions and demonstrate high levels of enthusiasm and energy. Successful cross-functional teams also engender a high degree of transparency among different functional areas. This is important in that it helps reduce the likelihood that a functional area will work on its part in a silo. Important too is the level of synergy in effective cross-functional teams. The diversity of views and experiences from different functional areas increases creativity and results in outcomes that are better than the sum of members' individual abilities. Value creation processes with little collaboration are often associated with hidden political agendas and turf protection which can increase overall costs and time-to-market.[57]

While cross-functional collaboration is a prerequisite to effective value creation it does not magically happen by itself. Strong team leadership and access to appropriate resources and training is essential.[58,59] Poorly implemented cross-functional teams and collaboration result in low morale and exacerbate divisiveness among members.

The most effective strategy for managing cross-functional teams depends, in part, on the degree of uncertainty involved in the team's task. Different degrees of uncertainty require different management strategies.[60] The degree of uncertainty in a project can be thought of as arising from two sources, the project environment and the degree of innovation in the product. The project environment includes such factors as market pressures to gain first mover advantage (or not lag severely behind the competition), possible changes to legislation and compliance

- 12 -

requirements, mergers and acquisitions that the organization is currently involved with, and outsourcing activities. Degree of product or technical innovation was discussed above in Module 2. The total uncertainty of a value creation project is the sum of these two as shown in Figure 3.3, based on the work of Rondinelli, Middleton and Verspoor.[61]

Figure 3.3
Levels of Project Uncertainty

	Incremental	Radical
High	Open-Mechanistic	Adaptive
Low	Mechanistic	Professional – Adaptive

Environmental Uncertainty (vertical axis, High to Low)

Product Innovativeness (horizontal axis)

There are four main management strategies depicted in Figure 3.3, depending on the overall level of uncertainty. The two extremes are **Mechanistic** (low levels of both environmental uncertainty and innovativeness) and **Adaptive** (high levels of environmental uncertainty and innovativeness). Between the two extremes are strategies with mixed characteristics: **Open-Mechanistic** and **Professional-Adaptive**. Different management strategies are appropriate for these different uncertainty types, as shown in Figure 3.4.

3.6   Module Key Points

- Creating Value involves a series of activities that take the MTB Proposition from the Commercialization Feasibility Point through to the Extract Stage.

- Successful organizations are those that can produce a steady stream of innovative products that meet customer needs and provide an economic return for the organization.

- The majority of MTB Propositions fail to find market success. Successful MTB Propositions tend to come from organizations that have high quality Invent and Create processes.

- There are many ways to structure value creation processes. These vary from highly structured approaches like the classic stage/gate model to more flexible customer collaborative processes such as the evolutionary delivery model.

– 13 –

Figure 3.4
Management Strategies for Different Levels of Project Uncertainty

Mechanistic

1. The product is well defined and project work is done in a relatively certain environment
2. Tasks require little change from existing practices
3. Centralized decision making with top-down hierarchies in communication and command
4. Functional classification of jobs
5. Control by adherence to rules and regulations
6. Motivation by monetary rewards and punishment
7. Functional organization structures are well suited for this.

Open Mechanistic

1. Development work is routine, but occurs in a highly uncertain environment (e.g. the process to produce the product is certain, but the technology is awaiting acquisition)
2. May involve search for solutions and alternatives when "performance gaps" appear
3. Requires close monitoring of the environment while maintaining bureaucratic control
4. Functional and matrix structures work well here

Professional Adaptive

1. The product is innovative requiring flexible development but the environment is relatively certain (e.g. development projects performed by groups of professionals in a research or special project management unit)
2. Technical issues are often dealt with experimentally
3. Management monitors inputs and results rather then supervising detailed activities
4. Best suited organizational structures are balanced matrix, project matrix, project team

Adaptive

1. Development tasks are innovative and carried out in uncertain environments
2. Management must periodically adjust strategies based on organizational/project learning and economic conditions
3. Coordination of project teams and other strategic alliances through negotiation and mutual adjustment
4. Jobs organized around objectives rather than tasks
5. Control is based on meeting objectives and professional judgment not conformance to rules and regulations
6. Motivation by participation, job satisfaction and professional achievement.
7. Best suited organizational structures: balanced matrix, project matrix, project team

- The choice of which value creation process to adopt depends on a number of factors including the innovativeness of the product and process (incremental *vs.* radical), the degree of technical and market uncertainty, the complexity and scope of the project, and the risks associated with costs and time-to-market.

- Concurrent product and process design (parallel processes) requires a flexible process and results in shorter product cycle times. Parallel processes also have a built in early warning system that signals problems for manufacturing and marketing downstream.

- Organizations that lack the entire complement of knowledge and resources necessary to successfully develop and launch a promising MTB Proposition may outsource some of those requirements, including significant portions of the value creation process. In the extreme case the whole proposition may be spun-off for value extraction.

- A key success factor in the Create Stage is to maximize the fit of the new product with the customer's requirements. This involves working with the customer to define the functionality (features, performance) they require and the marketing environment that the product is presented in (e.g. price and distribution)

- Benefits are realized by minimizing value creation cycle time. Reduction of cycle time allows an organization to launch a new product before their competitors. This allows them to gain first mover advantage, leverage the dominant design, encourage other organizations to develop complementary products, and reduce costs associated with longer value creation times. Thus the likelihood of a positive economic return for the organization is higher with reduced cycle times.

- Development teams and senior management must continually perform assessments on the market, technology and business viability of any MTB Proposition. Decisions may be made throughout value creation on whether to continue, go back and rework, redirect focus, outsource or to completely abandon the proposition.

- A business plan can be an important guide for value creation activities and a good basis for assessment at decision points. The business plan must be updated periodically to reflect any changes made in market, technical and/or business plans.

- Cross-functional teams enhance the value creation process and increase the likelihood of success by i) bringing together the expertise to maximize the fit among all parts of the MTB Proposition (market, technology, business) and ii) reducing cycle time.

- Effective cross-functional teams have a high degree of participation by team members and a high degree of transparency among functional groups. They reduce functional turf protection issues.

- The more uncertainty associated with a project, the greater the need for a flexible, autonomous management strategy.

Refernces

[1] Jenkins, S., Forbes, S., Durrani, T.S. & Banerjee, S.K., "Managing the Product Development Process – (Part I: An Assessment)," *Int. J. Technology Management* (1997): 13(4), 359 - 378.

[2] Schilling, M.A. & Hill, C.W.L, "Managing the New Product Development Process: Strategic Imperatives," *IEEE Engineering Management Review* (1998): Winter: 55 – 68.

[3] Shilling, "Managing the New Product Development Process" article with "Chapter 11".

[4] Jenkins, S., Forbes, S., Durrani, T.S. & Banerjee, S.K., "Managing the Product Development Process – (Part I: An Assessment)," *Int. J. Technology Management* (1997): 13(4), 359 - 378.

[5] Jenkins, S., Forbes, S., Durrani, T.S. & Banerjee, S.K., "Managing the Product Development Process – (Part I: An Assessment)," *Int. J. Technology Management* (1997): 13(4), 359 - 378.

[6] Schilling, M.A. & Hill, C.W.L, "Managing the New Product Development Process: Strategic Imperatives," *IEEE Engineering Management Review* (1998): Winter: 55 – 68.

[7] "Customer/Supplier Integration into New Product Development" – in folder of articles, but don't know the reference.

[8] Cooper, R.G., "New Products – What Separates the Winners from the Losers and What Drives Success," In *The PDMA Handbook of New Product Development*, ed. Kahn K.B., 3 - 29. US: John Wiley & Sons, 2005.

[9] Schilling, M.A. & Hill, C.W.L, "Managing the New Product Development Process: Strategic Imperatives," *IEEE Engineering Management Review* (1998): Winter: 55 – 68.

[10] Schilling, M.A. & Hill, C.W.L, "Managing the New Product Development Process: Strategic Imperatives," *IEEE Engineering Management Review* (1998): Winter: 55 – 68.

[11] Schilling, M.A. & Hill, C.W.L, "Managing the New Product Development Process: Strategic Imperatives," *IEEE Engineering Management Review* (1998): Winter: 55 – 68.

[12] Schilling, M.A. & Hill, C.W.L, "Managing the New Product Development Process: Strategic Imperatives," *IEEE Engineering Management Review* (1998): Winter: 55 – 68.

[13] Afuah, A., "Strategies to Turn Adversity into Profits," Sloan Management Review (1999): Winter: 99 – 109.

[14] Schilling, M.A. & Hill, C.W.L, "Managing the New Product Development Process: Strategic Imperatives," *IEEE Engineering Management Review* (1998): Winter: 55 – 68.

[15] Cooper, R.G., "New Products – What Separates the Winners from the Losers and What Drives Success," In *The PDMA Handbook of New Product Development*, ed. Kahn K.B., 3 - 29. US: John Wiley & Sons, 2005.

[16] Jenkins, S., Forbes, S., Durrani, T.S. & Banerjee, S.K., "Managing the Product Development Process – (Part I: An Assessment)," *Int. J. Technology Management* (1997): 13(4), 359 - 378.

[17] Cooper, R.G., "New Products – What Separates the Winners from the Losers and What Drives Success," In *The PDMA Handbook of New Product Development*, ed. Kahn K.B., 3 - 29. US: John Wiley & Sons, 2005.

[18] Cooper, R.G., "New Products – What Separates the Winners from the Losers and What Drives Success," In *The PDMA Handbook of New Product Development*, ed. Kahn K.B., 3 - 29. US: John Wiley & Sons, 2005.

[19] Cooper, R.G., "New Products – What Separates the Winners from the Losers and What Drives Success," In *The PDMA Handbook of New Product Development*, ed. Kahn K.B., 3 - 29. US: John Wiley & Sons, 2005.

[20] Ettlie, J.E. & Elsenbach, J.M., "Modified Stage-Gate Regimes in New Product Development," *Journal of Product Innovation Management* (2007): 24: 20 – 33.

[21] McCormack, A., "Product-Development Practices that Work: How Internet Companies Build Software," *MIT Sloan Management Review* (2001): Winter: 75 – 84.

[22] McCormack, A., "Product-Development Practices that Work: How Internet Companies Build Software," *MIT Sloan Management Review* (2001): Winter: 75 – 84.

[23] Hayes, R., et al., "Creating and Edge Through New Process Development," In, *Operations, Strategy and Technology*, ed. Hayes, R. et al., 195 – 218. US: John Wiley & Sons, 2005.

[24] Carr, G., "A Survey of the Pharmaceutical Industry: The Alchemists", *The Economist* (1998): February, 2-18.

[25] McCormack, A., "Product-Development Practices that Work: How Internet Companies Build Software," *MIT Sloan Management Review* (2001): Winter: 75 – 84.

[26] McCormack, A., "Product-Development Practices that Work: How Internet Companies Build Software," *MIT Sloan Management Review* (2001): Winter: 75 – 84.

[27] McCormack, A., "Product-Development Practices that Work: How Internet Companies Build Software," *MIT Sloan Management Review* (2001): Winter: 75 – 84.

module 3 (5) 2007 08 16.doc

98

[28] McCormack, A., "Product-Development Practices that Work: How Internet Companies Build Software," *MIT Sloan Management Review* (2001): Winter: 75 – 84.

[29] Jenkins, S., Forbes, S., Durrani, T.S. & Banerjee, S.K., "Managing the Product Development Process – (Part II: Case Studies)," *Int. J. Technology Management* (1997): 13(4), 379 - 393.

[30] Ettlie, J.E. & Elsenbach, J.M., "Modified Stage-Gate Regimes in New Product Development," *Journal of Product Innovation Management* (2007): 24: 20 – 33.

[31] Ettlie, J.E. & Elsenbach, J.M., "Modified Stage-Gate Regimes in New Product Development," *Journal of Product Innovation Management* (2007): 24: 20 – 33.

[32] Schilling, M.A. & Hill, C.W.L, "Managing the New Product Development Process: Strategic Imperatives," *IEEE Engineering Management Review* (1998): Winter: 55 – 68.

[33] Shilling, "Managing the New Product Development Process" article with "Chapter 11".

[34] Schilling, M.A. & Hill, C.W.L, "Managing the New Product Development Process: Strategic Imperatives," *IEEE Engineering Management Review* (1998): Winter: 55 – 68.

[35] "Customer/Supplier Integration into New Product Development" – in folder of articles, but don't know the reference.

[36] "Customer/Supplier Integration into New Product Development" – in folder of articles, but don't know the reference.

[37] "Customer/Supplier Integration into New Product Development" – in folder of articles, but don't know the reference.

[38] Shilling, "Managing the New Product Development Process" article with "Chapter 11".

[39] Dussauge, P., Hart, S., & Ramanantsoa, B., "Strategic Technology Management", 92 – 96. US: John Wiley & Sons, 1994.

[40] Cooper, R.G., "New Products – What Separates the Winners from the Losers and What Drives Success," In *The PDMA Handbook of New Product Development*, ed. Kahn K.B., 3 - 29. US: John Wiley & Sons, 2005.

[41] Cooper, R.G., "New Products – What Separates the Winners from the Losers and What Drives Success," In *The PDMA Handbook of New Product Development*, ed. Kahn K.B., 3 - 29. US: John Wiley & Sons, 2005.

[42] Cooper, R.G., "New Products – What Separates the Winners from the Losers and What Drives Success," In *The PDMA Handbook of New Product Development*, ed. Kahn K.B., 3 - 29. US: John Wiley & Sons, 2005

[43] Cooper, R.G., "New Products – What Separates the Winners from the Losers and What Drives Success," In *The PDMA Handbook of New Product Development*, ed. Kahn K.B., 3 - 29. US: John Wiley & Sons, 2005

[44] Jenkins, S., Forbes, S., Durrani, T.S. & Banerjee, S.K., "Managing the Product Development Process – (Part II: Case Studies)," *Int. J. Technology Management* (1997): 13(4), 379 - 393.

[45] Lester, D.H., "Critical Success Factors for New Product Development," *Research Technology Management* (1998): January-February, 36 – 43.

[46] Cooper, R.G., & Kleinschmidt, E.J., "Winning Businesses in Product Development: The Critical Success Factors, *Research Technology Management* (1996): July-August, 18 – 29.

[47] Ettlie, J.E. & Elsenbach, J.M., "Modified Stage-Gate Regimes in New Product Development," *Journal of Product Innovation Management* (2007): 24, 20 – 33.

[48] Cooper, R.G., & Kleinschmidt, E.J., "Winning Businesses in Product Development: The Critical Success Factors, *Research Technology Management* (1996): July-August, 18 – 29.

[49] Allen, K.R., "Developing a business Plan for Sustained Innovation," In, *Bringing New technology to Market,* ed. Allen, K.R., 335 -351, Prentice Hall Inc., 2003..

[50] Cooper, R.G., "New Products – What Separates the Winners from the Losers and What Drives Success," In *The PDMA Handbook of New Product Development*, ed. Kahn K.B., 3 - 29. US: John Wiley & Sons, 2005.

[51] Jassawalla, A.R. & Sashittaal, H.C., "Building Collaborative Cross-Functional New Product Teams," *Academy of Managemetn Executive* (1999): 13(3): 50 – 62.

[52] Jenkins, S., Forbes, S., Durrani, T.S. & Banerjee, S.K., "Managing the Product Development Process – (Part II: Case Studies)," *Int. J. Technology Management* (1997): 13(4), 379 - 393.

[53] Jenkins, S., Forbes, S., Durrani, T.S. & Banerjee, S.K., "Managing the Product Development Process – (Part II: Case Studies)," *Int. J. Technology Management* (1997): 13(4), 379 - 393.

[54] Jenkins, S., Forbes, S., Durrani, T.S. & Banerjee, S.K., "Managing the Product Development Process – (Part II: Case Studies)," *Int. J. Technology Management* (1997): 13(4), 379 - 393.

[55] Cooper, R.G., "New Products – What Separates the Winners from the Losers and What Drives Success," In *The PDMA Handbook of New Product Development*, ed. Kahn K.B., 3 - 29. US: John Wiley & Sons, 2005.

[56] Hayes, R., et al., "Creating and Edge Through New Process Development," In, *Operations, Strategy and Technology*, ed. Hayes, R. et al., 195 – 218. US: John Wiley & Sons, 2005.

[57] Jassawalla, A.R. & Sashittaal, H.C., "Building Collaborative Cross-Functional New Product Teams," *Academy of Managemetn Executive* (1999): 13(3): 50 – 62.

[58] Jassawalla, A.R. & Sashittaal, H.C., "Building Collaborative Cross-Functional New Product Teams," *Academy of Managemetn Executive* (1999): 13(3): 50 – 62.

[59] Hayes, R., et al., "Creating and Edge Through New Process Development," In, *Operations, Strategy and Technology*, ed. Hayes, R. et al., 195 – 218. US: John Wiley & Sons, 2005.

[60] Rondinelli, D.A., Middleton J. and Verspoor, A.M., "Contingency planning for innovative projects", American Planning Association - Journal of the American Planning Association (Winter 1989), pp. 45-56.

[61] Rondinelli, D.A., Middleton J. and Verspoor, A.M., "Contingency planning for innovative projects", American Planning Association - Journal of the American Planning Association (Winter 1989), pp. 45-56.

HOW COMPANIES ARE REINVENTING THEIR IDEA—TO—LAUNCH METHODOLOGIES

Next-generation Stage-Gate systems are proving more flexible, adaptive and scalable.

Robert G. Cooper

OVERVIEW: *The Stage-Gate® system introduced in the mid-1980s has helped many firms drive new products to market. But leaders have adjusted and modified the original model considerably and built in many new best practices. They have made the system more flexible, adaptive and scalable; they have built in better governance; integrated it with portfolio management; incorporated accountability and continuous improvement; automated the system; bolted on a proactive front-end or discovery stage; and finally, adapted the system to include "open innovation." All of these improvements have rendered the system faster, more focused, more agile and leaner, and far better suited to today's rapid pace of product innovation.*

KEY CONCEPTS: *Stage-Gate, next-generation Stage-Gate, idea-to-launch process, best practices.*

The Stage-Gate® process has been widely adopted as a guide to drive new products to market (*1,2*). The original Stage-Gate model, introduced in the mid-1980s, was based on research that focused on what successful project teams and businesses did when they developed winning new products. Using the analogy of North American

Robert Cooper is emeritus professor at the DeGroote School of Business, McMaster University, Hamilton, Ontario, Canada. He is also ISBM Distinguished Research Scholar at Penn State's Smeal College of Business Administration and president of the Product Development Institute. He has won two Maurice Holland awards for the best paper published in Research-Technology Management *("New Products: What Distinguishes the Winners," in 1990, and "Debunking the Myths of New Product Development," in 1994) and has published over 100 articles and six books. A thought leader in the field of innovation management, he is a Fellow of the Product Development Management Association, and creator of the Stage-Gate new product process used by many firms. He received his Ph.D. in business administration from the University of Western Ontario.*
robertcooper@cogeco.ca; www.stage-gate.com

football, Stage-Gate is the playbook that the team uses to drive the ball down the field to a touchdown; the stages are the plays, and the gates are the huddles. The typical Stage-Gate system is shown in Figure 1 for major product development projects.

With so many companies using the system, invariably some firms began to develop derivatives and improved approaches; indeed, many leading firms have built in dozens of new best practices, so that today's stage-and-gate processes are a far cry from the original model of 20 years ago. Here are some of the ways that companies have modified and improved their idea-to-launch methods as they have evolved to the next-generation Stage-Gate system (*3*).

Focus on Effective Governance

Making the gates work

Perhaps the greatest challenge that users of a stage-and-gate process face is making the gates work. "As go the gates, so goes the process," declared one executive, noting that the gates in her company's process were ineffectual. In a robust gating system, poor projects are spotted early and killed; projects in trouble are also detected and sent back for rework or redirect—put back on course. But as quality control check points, the gates aren't effective in too many companies; gates are rated one of the weakest areas in product development with only 33 percent of firms having tough, rigorous gates throughout the idea-to-launch process (*4*).

Gates with teeth

A recurring problem is that gates are either non-existent or lack teeth. The result is that, once underway, projects are rarely killed at gates. Rather, as one senior manager exclaimed, "Projects are like express trains, speeding down the track, slowing down at the occasional station [gate], but never stopping until they reach their ultimate destination, the marketplace."

0895-6308/09/$5.00 © 2009 Industrial Research Institute, Inc.

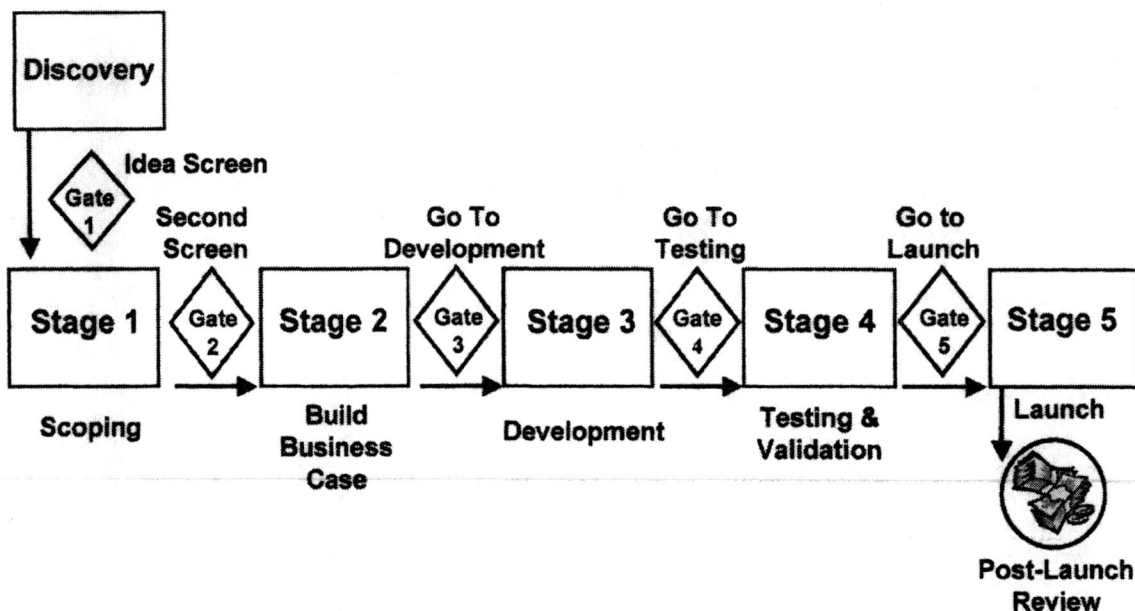

Figure 1.—Many firms use a Stage-Gate® system to drive development projects to commercialization. Shown here is a five-stage, five-gate process typically used for major new product projects. Such a model provides a guide to project teams, suggesting best-practice activities within stages, and defining essential information or deliverables for each gate. Gatekeepers meet at gates to make the vital Go/Kill and resource commitment decisions.

Example: In one major high-tech communications equipment manufacturer, once a project passes Gate 1 (the idea screen), it is placed into the business's product roadmap. This means that the estimated sales and profits from the new project are now integrated into the business unit's financial forecast and plans. Once into the financial plan of the business, of course, the project is locked-in: there is no way that the project can be removed from the roadmap or killed. In effect, all gates after Gate 1 are merely rubber stamps.

Management in this firm missed the point that the idea-to-launch process is a *funnel, not a tunnel,* and that gates after Gate 1 are also Go/Kill points; this should *not* be a one-gate, five-stage process! In too many firms, like this example, after the initial Go decision, the gates amount to little more than a project update meeting or a milestone check-point. As one executive declared: "We never kill projects, we just wound them!" Thus, instead of the well-defined funnel that is so often used to shape the new product process, one ends up with a tunnel where everything that enters comes out the other end, good projects and bad. Yet management is deluded into believing they have a functioning Stage-Gate process.

In still other companies, the gate review meeting is held and a Go decision is made, but resources are not committed. Somehow management fails to understand that approval decisions are rather meaningless *unless a check is cut* and the project leader and team leave the gate meeting with the resources they need to advance their project. Instead, projects are approved, but resources are not—*a hollow Go decision,* and one that usually leads to too many projects in the pipeline and projects taking forever to get to market.

If "gates without teeth" and "hollow gates" describe your company's gates, then it's time for a rethink. Gates are not merely project review meetings or milestone checks! Rather, they are Go/Kill and resource allocation meetings: Gates are where senior management meets to decide whether the company should continue to invest in the project based on latest information, or to cut one's losses and bail out of a bad project. And gates are a *resource commitment meeting* where, in the event of a Go decision, the project leader and team receive a commitment of resources to move their project forward.

Example (5): Cooper Standard Automotive (no relation to the author) converted its gates into "decision factories." Previously management had failed to make many Kill decisions, with most gates merely automatic Go's. The result was a gridlocked pipeline with over 50 major projects, an almost-infinite time-to-market, and no or few launches. By toughening the gate meetings—making them rigorous senior management reviews with solid data available—and forcing more kills, management dramatically reduced the number of projects passing each gate. The result was a reduction today to eight major, high-value projects, time-to-market down to 1.6 years, and five major launches annually.

Leaner and simpler gates

Most companies' new product processes suffer from far too much paperwork delivered to the gatekeepers at each gate. *Deliverables overkill* is often the result of a project team that, because they are not certain what information is required, prepare an overly comprehensive report, and in so doing, attempt to *bullet-proof* themselves. The fault can also be the design of the company's idea-to-launch system itself, which often includes elaborate templates that must be filled out for every gate.

While some of the information that gating systems demand may be interesting, often much of it is not essential to the gate decision. Detailed explanations of how the market research was done or sketches of what the new molecule looks like, add no value to the decision. Restrict the deliverables and their templates to the essential information needed to make the gate decisions:

Example (6): "*Lean gates*" is a positive feature of Johnson & Johnson Ethicon Division's Stage-Gate process. Previously, the gate deliverables package was a 30-to-90-page presentation, and a lot of work for any project team to prepare. Today, it's down to the bare essentials: one page with three back-up slides. The expectation is that gatekeepers arrive at the gate meeting knowing the project, having read and understood the deliverables package prepared by the project team (the gate meeting is not an educational session to bring a poorly prepared gatekeeping group up to speed). Senior management is simply informed at the gate review about the risks and the commitments required. Finally, there is a standardized presentation format. The result is that weeks of preparation work have been saved.

Example (7): One of the compelling features of Procter & Gamble's latest release of SIMPL (its Stage-Gate process) is much leaner gates—a "simpler SIMPL." Previously, project teams had decided which deliverables they would prepare for gatekeepers. Desirous of showcasing their projects and themselves, the resulting deliverables package was often very impressive but far too voluminous. As one astute observer remarked, it was "the corporate equivalent of publish or perish." The deliverables package included up to a dozen detailed attachments, plus the main report.

In the new model, the approach is to view the gates *from the decision-makers' perspective*. In short, what do the gatekeepers need to know in order to make the Go/Kill decision? The gatekeepers' requests boiled down to three key items:

> # The greatest challenge stage-and-gate users face is making the gates work.

- Have you done what you should have—are the data presented based on solid work?

- What are the risks in moving forward?

- What are you asking for?

Now the main gate report is no more than two pages, and there are four required attachments, most kept to a limit of one page.

The emphasis in lean gates is on making expectations clear to project teams and leaders—that they are not required to prepare an "information dump" for the gatekeepers. The principles are that:

- Information has a value only to the extent it improves a decision; and

- The deliverables package should provide the decision-makers only that information they need to make an effective and timely decision.

Page restrictions, templates with text and field limits, and solid guides are the answer favored by progressive firms.

Who are the gatekeepers?

Many companies also have trouble defining who the gatekeepers are. Every senior manager feels he or she should be a gatekeeper, and so the result is too many gatekeepers—more of a herd than a tightly-defined decision group—and a lack of crisp Go/Kill decisions. Defining governance roles and responsibilities is an important facet of Stage-Gate. At gates, the rule is simple: The gatekeepers are the senior people in the business who *own the resources* required by the project leader and team to move forward.

For major new product projects, the gatekeepers should be a cross-functional senior group—the heads of Technical, Marketing, Sales, Operations and Finance (as opposed to just one function, such as Marketing or R&D, making the call). Because resources are required from many departments, the gatekeeper group must involve executives from these resource-providing areas so that alignment is achieved and the necessary resources are in place. Besides, a multi-faceted view of the project leads to better decisions than a single-functional view. And because senior people's time is limited, consider beginning with mid-management at Gate 1, and for major projects, ending up with the leadership team of the business at Gates 3, 4 and 5 in Figure 1. For smaller, lower-risk projects, a lower-level gatekeeping group and fewer gates usually suffices.

Fostering the right behavior

A recurring complaint concerns the behavior of senior management when in the role of gatekeepers. Some of the bad gatekeeping behaviors consistently seen include:

• Executive "pet projects" receiving special treatment and by-passing the gates (perhaps because no one had the courage to stand up to the wishes of a senior person—a case of the "emperor wearing no clothes").

• Gate meetings cancelled at the last minute because the gatekeepers are unavailable (yet they complain the loudest when projects miss milestones).

• Gate meetings held, but decisions not made and resources not committed.

• Key gatekeepers missing the meeting and not delegating their authority to anyone.

• Gate meeting decisions by "executive edict"—the assumption that one person knows all.

• Using personal Go/Kill criteria (rather than robust and transparent decision-making criteria).

Gatekeepers are members of *a decision-making team.* And decision teams need "rules of engagement." Senior people often implement Stage-Gate in the naïve belief that it will shake up the troops and lead to much different

The new approach is to view gates from the decision-makers' perspective.

behavior in the ranks. But quite the opposite is true: *the greatest change in behavior takes place at the top!* The leadership team of the business must take a close look at their own behaviors—often far from ideal—and then craft a set of *gatekeeper rules of engagement* and commit to live by these. Table 1 lists a typical set.

Portfolio Management Built In

Portfolio management should dovetail with your Stage-Gate system (*8*). Both decision processes are designed to make Go/Kill and resource allocation decisions, and hence ideally should be integrated into a unified system. There are subtle differences between portfolio management and Stage-Gate, however:

• Gates are an evaluation of *individual projects* in depth and one-at-a-time. Gatekeepers meet to make Go/Kill and resource allocation decisions on an on-going basis (in real time) and from beginning to end of a project (Gate 1 to Gate 5 in Figure 1).

• By contrast, portfolio reviews are more holistic, looking at the *entire set of projects,* but obviously less in-depth per project than gates do. Portfolio reviews two to four times per year are the norm (*9*). They deal with such issues as achieving the right mix and balance

---

Table 1.—Rules of the Game: Sample Set from a Major Flooring-Products Manufacturer.

• All projects must pass through the gates. There is no special treatment or bypassing of gates for pet projects.
• Once a gate meeting date is agreed (calendars checked), gatekeepers must make every effort to be there. If the team cannot provide deliverables in time for the scheduled gate, the gate may be postponed and rescheduled, but timely advance notice must be given.
• If a gatekeeper cannot attend, s/he can send a designate who is empowered to vote and act on behalf of that gatekeeper (including committing resources). Gatekeepers can attend electronically (phone or video conference call).
• Pre-gate decision meetings should be avoided by gatekeepers—don't prejudge the project. There will be new data presented and a Q&A at the gate meeting.
• Gatekeepers should base their decisions on the information presented and use the scoring criteria. Decisions must be based on facts, not emotion and gut feel!
• A decision must be made the day of the gate meeting (Go/Kill/Hold/Recycle). The project team must be informed of the decision—face to face, and reasons why.
• When resource commitments are made by gatekeepers (people, time or money), every effort must be made to ensure that these commitments are kept.
• Gatekeepers must accept and agree to abide by these *Rules of the Game.*

of projects in the portfolio, project prioritization, and whether the portfolio is aligned with the business's strategy.

Besides relying on traditional financial criteria, here are methods that companies use to improve portfolio management within Stage-Gate (*10*);

1. Strategic buckets to achieve the right balance and mix of projects

The business's product innovation and technology strategy drives the decision process and helps to decide resource allocation and strategic buckets. Using the strategic buckets method, senior management makes *a priori* strategic choices about how they wish to spend their R&D resources. The method is based on the premise that *strategy becomes real when you start spending money.* So make those spending decisions!

Most often, resource splits are made across project types (new products, improvements, cost reductions, technology developments, etc.), by market or business area, by technology (base, pacing, embryonic) or by geography. Once these splits are decided each year, projects and resources are tracked. Pie charts reveal the actual split in resource (year to date) versus the target split based on the strategic choices made. These pie charts are reviewed at portfolio reviews to ensure that resource allocation does indeed mirror the strategic priorities of the business. The method has proven to be an effective way to ensure that the right balance and mix of projects is achieved in the development pipeline—that the pipeline is not overloaded with small, short-term and low-risk projects.

2. Scorecards to make better Go/Kill and prioritization decisions

Scorecards are based on the premise that qualitative criteria or factors are often better predictors of success than financial projections. The one thing we are sure of in product development is that *the numbers are always wrong,* especially for more innovative and step-out projects. In use, management develops a list of about 6–8 key criteria, known predictors of success (Table 2). Projects are then scored on these criteria right at the gate meeting by senior management. The total score becomes a key input into the Go/Kill gate decision and, along with other factors, is used to rank or prioritize projects at portfolio review meetings. A number of firms (for example, divisions at J&J, P&G, Emerson Electric and ITT Industries) use scorecards for early-stage screening (for Gates 1, 2 and 3 in Figure 1). Note that different scorecards and criteria are used for different types of projects.

3. Success criteria at gates

Another project selection method for use at gates, and one employed with considerable success at firms such as P&G, is the use of *success criteria*: "Specific success criteria for each gate relevant to that stage are defined for each project. Examples include: expected profitability, launch date, expected sales, and even interim metrics, such as test results expected in a subsequent stage. These criteria, and targets to be achieved on them, are agreed to by the project team and management at each gate. These success criteria are then used to evaluate the project at successive gates"(*11*). For example, if the project's estimates fail on any agreed-to criteria at successive gates, the project could be killed.

Table 2.—A Typical Scorecard for Gate 3, Go to Development: An Effective Tool for Rating Projects (10).

Factor 1: Strategic Fit and Importance
- Alignment of project with our business's strategy.
- Importance of project to the strategy.
- Impact on the business.

Factor 2: Product and Competitive Advantage
- Product delivers unique customer or user benefits.
- Product offers customer/user excellent value for money (compelling value proposition).
- Differentiated product in eyes of customer/user.
- Positive customer/user feedback on product concept (concept test results).

Factor 3: Market Attractiveness
- Market size.
- Market growth and future potential.
- Margins earned by players in this market.
- Competitiveness - how tough and intense competition is (negative).

Factor 4: Core Competencies Leverage
- Project leverages our core competencies and strengths in:
  - technology
  - production/operations
  - marketing
  - distribution/sales force.

Factor 5: Technical Feasibility
- Size of technical gap (straightforward to do).
- Technical complexity (few barriers, solution envisioned).
- Familiarity of technology to our business.
- Technical results to date (proof of concept).

Factor 6: Financial Reward versus Risk
- Size of financial opportunity.
- Financial return (NPV, ECV, IRR).
- Productivity Index (PI).
- Certainty of financial estimates.
- Level of risk and ability to address risks.

Projects are scored by the gatekeepers (senior management) at the gate meeting, using these six factors on a scorecard (0–10 scales). The scores are tallied and displayed electronically for discussion. The Project Attractiveness Score is the weighted or unweighted addition of the six factor scores (averaged across gatekeepers), and taken out of 100. A score of 60/100 is usually required for a Go decision.

105

4. The Productivity Index helps prioritize projects and allocate resources

This is a powerful extension of the NPV (net present value) method and is most useful at portfolio reviews to prioritize projects when resources are constrained. The Productivity Index is a financial approach based on the *theory of constraints* (*12*): in order to maximize the value of your portfolio subject to a constraining resource, take the factor that you are trying to maximize—e.g., the NPV—and divide it by your constraining resource, for example the person-days (or costs) required to complete the project:

$$\text{Productivity Index} = \frac{\text{Forecasted NPV}}{\text{Person-Days to Complete Project}} \quad \text{or}$$

$$PI = \frac{\text{Forecasted NPV}}{\text{Cost to Complete Project}}$$

Then rank your projects according to this index until you run out of resources. Those projects at the top of the list are Go projects, are resourced, and are accelerated to market. Those projects beyond the resource limit are placed on hold or killed. The method is designed to maximize the value of your development portfolio while staying within your resource limits.

Make the System Lean, Adaptive, Flexible and Scalable

A leaner process

Over time, most companies' product development processes have become too bulky, cumbersome and bureaucratic. Thus, smart companies have borrowed the concept of *value stream analysis* from lean manufacturing, and have applied it to their new product process in order to remove waste and inefficiency. A value stream is simply the connection of all the process steps with the goal of maximizing customer value (*13*). In NPD, a value stream represents the linkage of all value-added and non-value-added activities associated with the creation of a new product. The *value stream map* is used to portray the value stream or product development process, and helps to identify both value-added and non-value-added activities; hence, it is a useful tool for improving your process (*14*).

In employing value stream analysis, a task force creates a map of the value stream—your current idea-to-launch process for typical development projects in your business. All the stages, decision points and key activities are mapped out, with time ranges for each activity and decision indicated.

Once the value stream is mapped, the task force lowers the microscope on the process and dissects it. All procedures, activities and tasks, required deliverables, docu-

> # Most companies' product development processes have become too bulky and bureaucratic.

ments and templates, committees and decision processes are examined, looking for problems, time-wasters and non-value-added activities. Once these are spotted, the task force works to remove them.

Example: In one B2B company, field trials were found to be a huge time waster, taking as much as 18 months and often having to be repeated because they failed. A value stream analysis revealed this unacceptable situation, and a subsequent root cause analysis showed that there were huge delays largely because field trials could be done only when the customer undertook a scheduled plant shut-down—in this case a paper machine, costing in excess of $100 million—and further there was little incentive for the customer to agree to a field trial, especially one that did not work. The lack of early involvement of technical people (the first phases of the project were handled largely by sales and business development people) meant that technical issues were often not understood until too late in the project and after commitments had been made to the customer. Solutions were sought and included: first field trials on a pilot paper machine (several universities rented time on these in their pulp and paper institutes); involving technical people from the beginning of the project; and offering the customer incentives such as limited exclusivity and preferential pricing.

Value stream analysis can result in *leaner gates,* a topic mentioned earlier, but it goes well beyond gates and looks for efficiency improvements in *all facets of the process* as noted in the example. The result of a solid value stream analysis invariably is a much more streamlined, less bulky idea-to-launch system.

An adaptable, agile process

Stage-Gate has also become a much more adaptable innovation process, one that adjusts to changing conditions and fluid, unstable information. The concept of *spiral or agile development* is built in, allowing project teams to move rapidly to a final product design through a series of "build–test–feedback–and–revise" iterations (*15*). Spiral development bridges the gap between the need for sharp, early and fact-based product definition before development begins versus the need to be flexible and to adjust the product's design to new information and fluid market conditions as development proceeds. Spiral development allows developers to continue to incorporate valuable customer feedback into the design even after the product definition is locked-in before going into Stage 3. Spiral development also deals with the need to get mock-ups in front of customers earlier in the process (in Stage 2 rather than waiting until Stage 3).

A flexible process

Stage-Gate is a flexible guide that *suggests* best practices, recommended activities and likely deliverables. *No activity or deliverable is mandatory.* The project team has considerable discretion over which activities they execute and which they choose not to do. The project team presents its proposed "go-forward plan"—what needs to be done to make the project a success—at each gate. At these gates, the gatekeepers commit the necessary resources, and in so doing, approve the go-forward plan. But note that it is the *project team's plan,* not simply a mechanistic implementation of a standardized process.

Another facet of flexibility is *simultaneous execution.* Here, key activities and even entire stages overlap, not waiting for perfect information before moving forward. For example, it is acceptable to move activities from one stage to an earlier one and, in effect, overlap stages.

Example: At Toyota, the rule is to synchronize processes for simultaneous execution (*16*). Truly effective concurrent engineering requires that each subsequent function maximizes the utility of the stable information available from the previous function as it becomes available. That is, development teams must do the most they can with only that portion of the design data that is not likely to change. Each function's processes are designed to move forward simultaneously, building on stable data as they become available.

Simultaneous execution usually adds risk to a project. For example, the decision to purchase production equipment before field trials are completed, thereby avoiding a long order lead-time, may be a good application of simultaneous execution. But there is risk too—that the project may be cancelled after dedicated production equipment is purchased. Thus, the decision to overlap activities and stages is a *calculated risk,* but it must be calculated. That is, the cost of delay must be weighed against the cost and probability of being wrong.

Scaled to suit different risks

Stage-Gate has become a *scalable process,* scaled to suit very different types and risk levels of projects—from very risky and complex platform developments through to lower-risk extensions and modifications, and even to handle simple sales force requests (*17*).

When first implemented, there was only one version of Stage-Gate in a company, typically a five-stage, five-gate model. But some projects were too small to put through the full five-stage model, and so circumvented it. The problem was that these smaller projects—line extensions, modifications, sales-force requests—while individually small, collectively consumed the bulk of resources. Thus, a contradictory situation existed whereby projects that represented the majority of development resources were "outside the system."

Each of these projects—big and small—has risk, consumes resources, and thus must be managed, but not all need to go through the full five-stage process. The process has thus *morphed into multiple versions* to fit business needs and to accelerate projects. Figure 2 shows some examples: Stage-Gate *XPress* for projects of moderate risk, such as improvements, modifications and extensions; and Stage-Gate *Lite* for very small projects, such as simple customer requests.

Multiple versions for platform/technology development projects

There is no longer just Stage-Gate for new product projects. Other types of projects—platform developments, process developments, or exploratory research projects—compete for the same resources, need to be managed, and thus also merit their own version of a stage-and-gate process. For example, ExxonMobil Chemical has designed a three-stage, three-gate version of its Stage-Gate process to handle upstream research projects (*18*); while numerous other organizations have adopted a four-stage, four-gate system to handle fundamental research, technology development or platform projects (more on this topic later).

Add a Robust Post-Launch Review

Next-generation Stage-Gate systems build-in a rigorous post-launch review in order to instill *accountability for results,* and at the same time, foster a culture of *continuous improvement.* Continuous improvement is one of the main tenets of lean manufacturing and lends itself readily to application in the field of product innovation.

Continuous improvement in NPD has three major elements (*19*):

• *Having performance metrics in place* that measure how well a specific new product project performed. For example, were the product's profits on target? Was it launched on time?

• *Establishing team accountability for results,* with all members of the project team fully responsible for performance results when measured against these metrics.

• *Building-in learning and improvement*, namely, when the project team misses the target, focus on fixing the cause rather than putting a band-aid on the symptom, or worse yet, punishing the team.

Example (20): At Emerson Electric, the traditional post-launch reviews were absent in most divisions' new product efforts. But in the new release of Emerson's idea-to-launch process (NPD 2.0), a post-launch review is very evident. Here, project teams are held accountable for key financial and time metrics that were established and agreed to much earlier in the project. When gaps or deficiencies between forecasts and reality are identified, root causes for these variances are sought and continuous improvement takes place.

Emerson benefits in three way. First, estimates of sales, profits and time-to-market are much more realistic now that project teams are held accountable for their attainment. Second, with clear objectives, the project team can focus and work diligently to achieve them—expectations are clear. Finally, if the team misses the target, causes are sought and improvements to the process are made so as to prevent a recurrence of the cause—*closed loop feedback and learning*.

It works much the same way at Procter & Gamble *(21)*: "Winning in the marketplace is the goal. In many firms, too much emphasis is on getting through the process, that

> ## Next-generation Stage-Gate systems build-in a rigorous post-launch review.

is, getting one's project approved or preparing deliverables for the next gate. In the past, P&G was no different. By contrast, this principle emphasizes winning in the marketplace as the goal, not merely going through the process. Specific success criteria for each project are defined and agreed to by the project team and management at the gates; these success criteria are then used to evaluate the project at the post-launch review, and the project team is held accountable for achieving results when measured against these success criteria."

The post-launch review is the final *point of accountability* for the project team. The project's results are gauged, for example: the first year's sales, the launch date achieved, and the NPV based on latest results. These numbers are then compared to the projections—to the original success criteria. Accountability issues are high on the

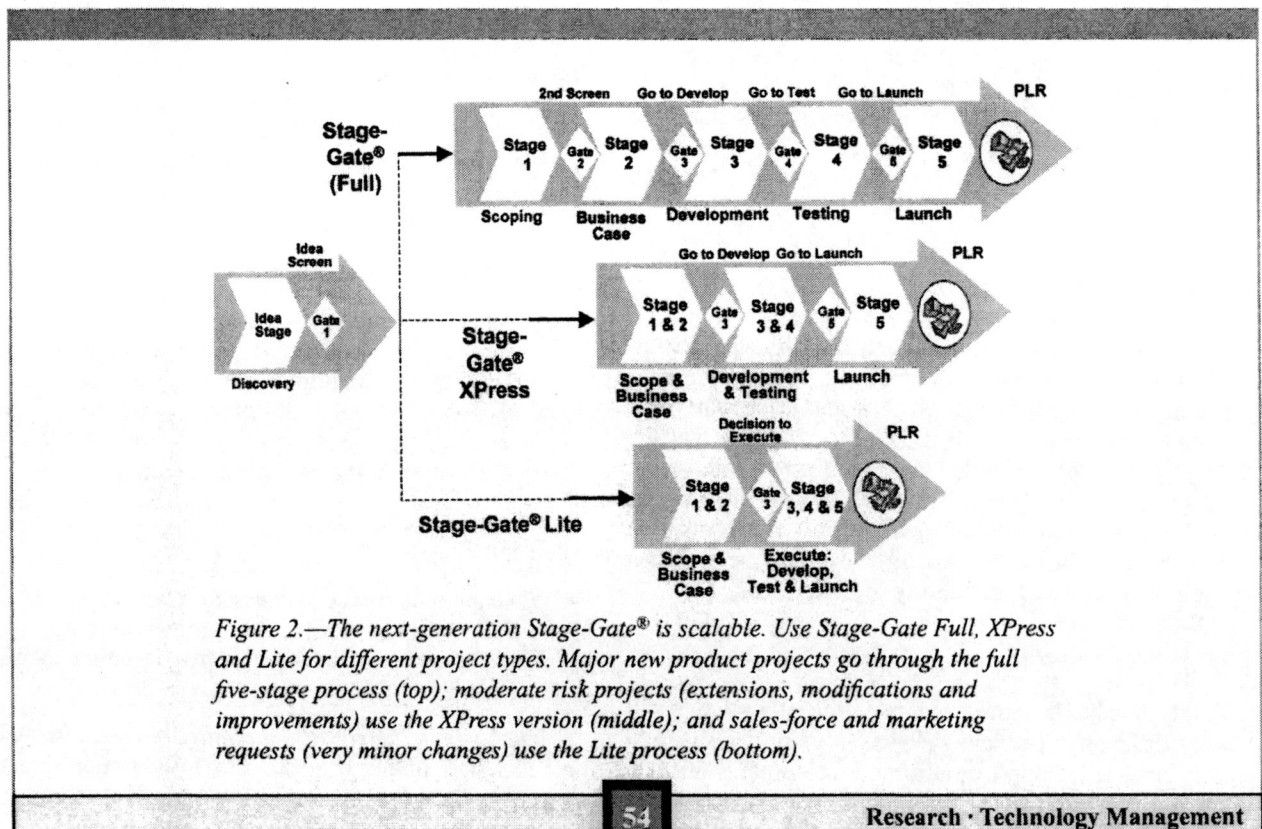

Figure 2.—The next-generation Stage-Gate® is scalable. Use Stage-Gate Full, XPress and Lite for different project types. Major new product projects go through the full five-stage process (top); moderate risk projects (extensions, modifications and improvements) use the XPress version (middle); and sales-force and marketing requests (very minor changes) use the Lite process (bottom).

108

agenda of this vital best-practice review: Did the team achieve what was promised when measured against the success criteria?

The continuous learning and improvement facet must be in place too; if results are measured and deficiencies are identified but no action is taken, there's no improvement and one keeps repeating the same mistakes. Thus, at the post-launch review, when a project team misses the target, a *root cause analysis* ensues to determine the cause of the deficiency and to prevent its recurrence. The focus is on continuous improvement—a learning organization—rather than on blaming the team and creating a culture of fear and retribution.

Example (*22*): EXFO Engineering boasts a solid Stage-Gate system coupled with a strong portfolio management process. EXFO has added an additional gate in its process—Gate 5—whose purpose is to ensure the proper closing of the project (Launch is Gate 4.1 in this company's numbering scheme). At this final gate meeting, management ascertains that all the outstanding issues (manufacturing, quality, sales ramp-up, and project) have been addressed and closed. Feedback is presented based on a survey of initial customers; the project post-mortem is reviewed, which highlights the project's good and bad points; and the recommendations for improvement from the team are examined. Typically, Gate 5 occurs about three months after initial product delivery to customers. Additionally, sales performance and profitability (ROI) of the project are monitored for the first two years of the product's life.

Build-In a Discovery Stage To Feed Innovation Funnel

Feeding the innovation funnel with a steady stream of a new product ideas and opportunities has become the quest in many companies as they search for the next blockbuster new product. Traditionally, the "idea" has been shown as a light-bulb at the beginning of the new product process, with ideas assumed to happen magically or serendipitously. No longer. Now, progressive firms such as P&G, Swarovski AG, ITT Industries, and Emerson Electric, have replaced the light-bulb with a new and proactive Stage 0 called Discovery (see Figure 1). Discovery encompasses some of the following activities:

Fundamental research and technology development

Organizations like ExxonMobil Chemical, Timex, Donaldson, and Sandia Labs recognize that technology development projects—where the deliverable is new knowledge, a new technical capability, or even a technology platform—are quite different in terms of risk, uncertainty, scope, and cost from the typical new product project found in the Stage-Gate model of Figure 1.

Moreover, these technology development projects are often the platform that spawns a number of new product (or new process) development projects and hence acts as a trigger or feed to the new product process. Thus, such organizations have modified the front end of their Stage-Gate process and in effect "bolted on" a *technology development process* that then feeds the new product process, as shown in Figure 3 (*23*). The "Stage-Gate TD process" is technologically driven and features quite different stages with more opportunity for experimentation and iterating back, and the system relies on less financial and more strategic Go/Kill criteria at the gates.

Other Discovery stage elements

In addition to technology development projects, progressive firms have redefined Discovery to include many other ideation activities, including:

• *Voice-of-customer* methods, such as ethnographic research (*24*), site visits with depth interviews, customer focus groups to identify customer "points of pain," and lead-user analysis (*25*).

• *Strategically driven ideation*, including crafting a product innovation strategy for the business in order to delineate the "search fields" for ideation, exploiting disruptive technologies (*26*), peripheral visioning (*27*), competitive analysis, and patent mining.

• *Stimulating internal ideation*, such as installing elaborate systems to capture, incubate and enhance internal ideas from employees, much as Swarovski has done (*28*).

• *Open innovation* as a source of external ideas, outlined next.

Make Your Process an "Open System"

Stage-Gate now accommodates *open innovation,* handling the flow of ideas, IP, technology, and even fully developed products into the company from external sources, and also the flow outward (*29*). Kimberly–Clark, Air Products & Chemicals, P&G, and others have modified their Stage-Gate processes—built in the necessary flexibility capability and systems—in order to enable this network of partners, alliances and vendors from idea generation right through to launch. For example, P&G's SIMPL 3.0 version of its system is designed to handle externally-derived ideas, IP, technologies, and even fully developed products.

Innovation via partnering with external firms and people has been around for decades—joint ventures, venture groups, licensing arrangements and even venture nurturing. Open innovation is simply a broader concept that includes not only these traditional partnering models, but all types of collaborative or partnering activities, and with a wider range of partners than in the past.

109

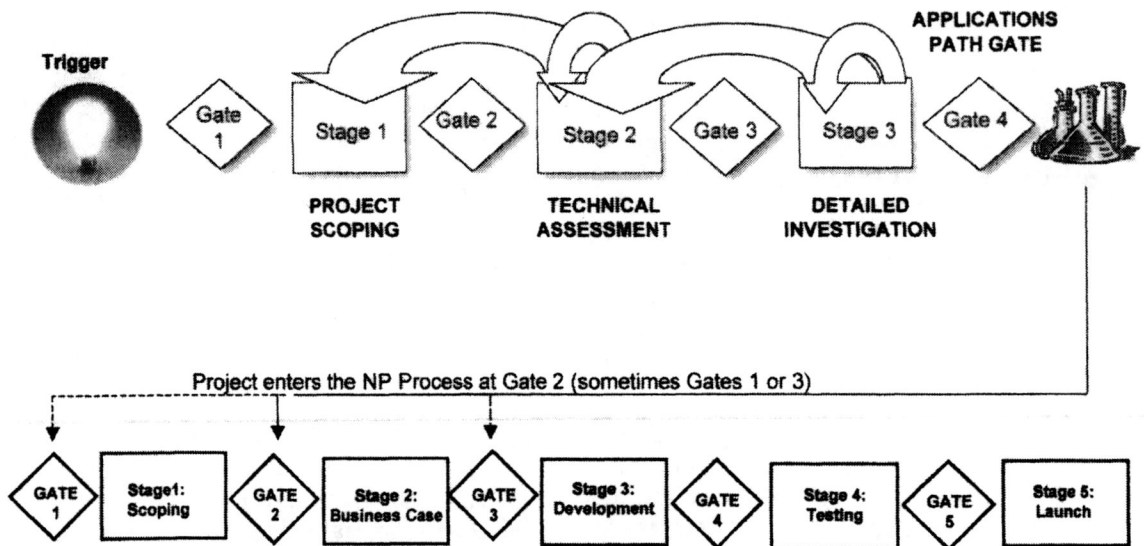

The 3-Stage Technology Development Process

The Standard 5-Stage, 5-Gate Stage-Gate® New Product Process

Figure 3.—The Technology Development Process handles fundamental science, technology development, and technology platform projects. It typically spawns multiple commercial projects which feed the new product process at Gates 1, 2 or 3. Note that the TD Process (top) is very flexible: it is iterative and features loops within stages and potentially to previous stages. Gates rely less on financial criteria and more on strategic criteria (23).

In the traditional or *closed innovation model,* inputs come from internal and some external sources—customer inputs, marketing ideas, marketplace information, or strategic planning inputs. Then, the R&D organization proceeds with the task of inventing, evolving and perfecting technologies for further development, immediately or at a later date (*30*).

By contrast, in open innovation, companies look inside-out and outside-in, across all three aspects of the innovation process, including ideation, development and commercialization. In doing so, much more value is created and realized throughout the process (see Figure 1):

• *Discovery stage:* Here, not only do companies look externally for customer problems to be solved or unmet needs to be satisfied, but to inventors, start-ups, small entrepreneurial firms, partners, and other sources of available technologies that can be used as a basis for internal or joint development.

• *Development stage:* Established companies seek help in solving technology problems from scientists outside the corporation, or they acquire external innovations that have already been productized. They also out-license internally-developed intellectual property that is not being utilized.

• *Launch or commercialization stage:* Companies sell or out-license already-developed products where more

value can be realized elsewhere; or they in-license—they acquire already commercialized products that provide immediate sources of new growth for the company.

Automate Your Stage-Gate System

Progressive companies recognize that automation greatly increases the effectiveness of their new product processes. With automation, everyone from project leaders to executives finds the process much easier to use, thereby enhancing buy-in. Another benefit is information management: the key participants have access to effective displays of relevant information—what they need to advance the project, cooperate globally with other team members on vital tasks, help make the Go/Kill decision, or stay on top of a portfolio of projects. Examples of certified automation software for Stage-Gate are found in Ref. *31*.

The Path Forward

This article has outlined new approaches that firms have built into their next-generation Stage-Gate® systems. If your idea-to-launch system is more than five years old, if it's burdened with too much "make work" and bureaucracy, or if it's getting a bit creaky and cumbersome, the time is ripe for a serious overhaul. Design your innovation process for today's innovation requirements—a faster, leaner, more agile, and more focused system. Reinvent your process to build-in the latest thinking, approaches and methods outlined above and move to the next-generation Stage-Gate system. Ⓐ

References and Notes

1. Stage-Gate® is a registered trademark of the Product Development Institute Inc (*www.prod-dev.com*), and the term was coined by the author.

2. PDMA and APQC studies show that about 70 percent of product developers in North America use a Stage-Gate or similar system. See: *The PDMA Foundation's 2004 Comparative Performance Assessment Study* (CPAS), Product Development & Management Association, Chicago, IL. Also: Cooper, R.G., S.J. Edgett and E.J. Kleinschmidt, *New Product Development Best Practices Study: What Distinguishes the Top Performers*. Houston: APQC (American Productivity & Quality Center), 2002.

3. Parts of this article are based on previous publications by the author. See: Cooper, R.G. and S.J. Edgett, *Lean, Rapid and Profitable New Product Development*, Product Development Institute, *www.stage-gate.com*, 2005; Cooper, R.G., The Stage-Gate Idea-to-Launch Process—Update, What's New and NexGen Systems, *J. Product Innovation Managements* 25, 3, May 2008, pp. 213-232; and: Cooper, R.G., NexGen Stage-Gate®—What Leading Companies Are Doing to Re-Invent Their NPD Processes, *PDMA Visions*, XXXII, No 3, Sept. 2008, pp. 6-10.

4. See APQC study ref. 2; also: Cooper, R.G., S.J. Edgett and E.J. Kleinschmidt, Benchmarking Best NPD Practices-2: Strategy, Resources and Portfolio Management Practices, *Research-Technology Management* 47, 3, May-June 2004, pp. 50-60.

5. Osborne, S. Make More and Better Product Decisions For Greater Impact. *Proceedings, Product Development and Management Association Annual International Conference*, Atlanta, GA, Oct. 2006.

6. Belair, G. Beyond Gates: Building the Right NPD Organization. *Proceedings, First International Stage-Gate Conference*, St. Petersburg Beach, FL, Feb. 2007.

7. Private discussions with M. Mills at P&G; used with permission.

8. Cooper, R.G., S.J. Edgett and E.J. Kleinschmidt. Optimizing the Stage-Gate® Process: What Best Practice Companies Do—Part II. *Research-Technology Management* 45, 6, Nov.-Dec. 2002., pp. 43-49.

9. Edgett, S. (subject matter expert). *Portfolio Management: Optimizing for Success*, Houston: APQC (American Productivity & Quality Center), 2007.

10. These portfolio tools are explained in: Cooper, R.G. and S.J. Edgett, Ten Ways to Make Better Portfolio and Project Selection Decisions, *PDMA Visions*, XXX, 3, June 2006, pp. 11-15; also Cooper, R.G., S.J. Edgett and E.J. Kleinschmidt, *Portfolio Management for New Products*, 2nd edition. New York, NY: Perseus Publishing, 2002.

11. Cooper, R.G. and M. Mills. Succeeding at New Products the P&G Way: A Key Element is Using the 'Innovation Diamond'. *PDMA Visions*, XXIX, 4, Oct. 2005, pp. 9-13.

12. The Productivity Index method is proposed by the Strategic Decisions Group (SDG). For more information, refer to Matheson, D., Matheson, J.E. and Menke, M.M., Making Excellent R&D Decisions, *Research-Technology Management*, Nov.-Dec. pp. 21-24, 1994; and Evans, P., Streamlining Formal Portfolio Management, *Scrip Magazine*, February, 1996.

13. Fiore, C. *Accelerated Product Development*. New York, NY: Productivity Production Press, 2005, p 24.

14. For more information on value stream mapping, plus examples, see: Cooper & Edgett, ref. 3, ch 6.

15. Spiral development is described in Cooper, R.G. and S.J. Edgett. Maximizing Productivity in Product Innovation. *Research-Technology Management*, March-April 2008, pp. 47-58.

16. Morgan, J. *Applying Lean Principles to Product Development*. Report from SAE International Society of Mechanical Engineers, 2005. *www.shop.sae.org*.

17. Cooper, R.G. Formula for Success. *Marketing Management Magazine* (American Marketing Association), March-April 2006, pp. 21-24; see also Cooper & Edgett ref. 3.

18. Cohen, L.Y., P.W. Kamienski and R.L. Espino. Gate System Focuses Industrial Basic Research. *Research-Technology Management*, July-August 1998, pp. 34-37.

19. See Cooper & Edgett *RTM* article in ref. 15.

20. Ledford, R.D. NPD 2.0, *Innovation*, St. Louis: Emerson Electric, 2006, p. 2: and NPD 2.0: Raising Emerson's NPD Process to the Next Level, *Innovation*, St. Louis: Emerson Electric, 2006, pp. 4-7.

21. Cooper and Mills, ref. 11.

22. Bull, S. Innovating for Success: How EXFO's NPDS Delivers Winning New Product. *Proceedings, First International Stage-Gate Conference*, St. Petersburg Beach, FL, Feb. 2007.

23. Cooper, R.G. Managing Technology Development Projects - Different Than Traditional Development Projects, *Research-Technology Management*, Nov.-Dec. 2006, pp. 23-31.

24. R.G. Cooper and S.J. Edgett. Ideation for Product Innovation: What Are the Best Sources? *PDMA Visions*, XXXII, 1, March 2008, pp. 12-17.

25. More on lead user analysis in Von Hippel, E. *Democratizing Innovation*. MIT Press, Cambridge MA, 2005; and Thomke, S. and E. Von Hippel. Customers As Innovators: A New Way to Create Value, *Harvard Business Review*, April 2002, pp. 74-81.

26. Christensen, C.M. *The Innovator's Dilemma*. New York: Harper Collins, 2000.

27. Day, G. and P. Shoemaker. Scanning the Periphery. *Harvard Business Review*, Nov. 2005, pp. 135-148.

28. Erler, H. *A Brilliant New Product Idea Generation Program: Swarovski's I-Lab Story*, Second International Stage-Gate Conference, Clearwater Beach, FL, Feb. 2008.

29. Chesbrough, H. *Open Innovation: The New Imperative for Creating and Profiting from Technology*. Cambridge, MA: Harvard Business School Press, 2003. This section is based on material in Cooper and Edgett, ref. 3, ch 5.

30. Docherty, M. Primer on 'Open Innovation': Principles and Practice, *PDMA Visions*, XXX, No. 2, April 2006.

31. A number of software products have been certified for use with Stage-Gate. See *www.stage-gate.com*.

Crafting a Deployment Strategy

Deployment Tactics in the U.S. Video Game Industry

In the U.S. video game industry, the introduction of each generation of console has ushered in a new battle for market dominance. New entrants have made startling entrances and toppled seemingly invincible incumbents. Games developers, distributors, and customers have had to watch the battle closely in order to place their bets about which console would emerge as the generation's victor. Each generation has also revealed which deployment strategies have paid off—or proven fatal—for the contenders.[1]

Pong: The Beginning of an Era

In 1972, Nolan Bushnell founded a company called Atari and introduced Pong, a Ping-Pong-like game that was played on a user's television set with the aid of the Atari console. In its first year, Pong earned more than $1 million in revenues. Pong and over 60 similar knockoffs soon flooded the market. In these early years of the video game industry, swift advances in integrated circuits enabled a rapid proliferation of new consoles and games. By 1984, video game console and games sales had reached $3 billion in the United States alone. However, console makers in this era did not utilize strict security measures to ensure that only authorized games could be played on their consoles, leading to explosive growth in the production of unauthorized games (games produced for a console without authorization of that console's producer). As a result, the market was soon saturated with games of dubious quality, and many unhappy retailers were stuck with video game inventories they were unable to move. Profits began to spiral downward, and by 1985, many industry observers were declaring the video game industry dead.

The Emergence of 8-Bit Systems

Much to everyone's surprise, however, two new companies from Japan entered the U.S. video game market: Nintendo, with its 8-bit Nintendo Entertainment System (NES) introduced in 1985, and Sega, which launched its 8-bit Master System in the

United States in 1986. Unlike Atari, which had spent only a few hundred thousand dollars on advertising, Sega and Nintendo spent $15 million promoting their systems. Both systems offered technological advantages over the previous generation of video game consoles. Sega's Master System appeared to be slightly superior to Nintendo's, but Nintendo spent much more on the development of quality games and characters and had more game titles available than Sega. The NES sold over 1 million units in the first year, sold 19 million units by 1990, and could be found in more than a third of the households in America and Japan.[2]

From 1985 to 1989, Nintendo held a near monopoly of the U.S. video game industry. The company sold its consoles for a price very close to production costs, while earning the bulk of its profits from games. Nintendo both made games for its system in-house and licensed third-party developers to produce games through very strict licensing policies that (a) limited the number of titles a developer could produce each year, (b) required the developer to preorder a minimum number of cartridges from Nintendo (which had its own contract manufacturers produce the games), and (c) restricted the developers from making similar games for other consoles. Nintendo also restricted the volume and pricing of consoles sold through distributors, ensuring that no single distributor acquired significant bargaining power.[3] Nintendo's restrictive policies were very profitable; however, they also incurred sanctions by the Federal Trade Commission, and they alienated distributors and developers, potentially leaving the company more vulnerable to a competitor.

The 16-Bit Video Game Systems

In September 1989, Sega introduced the 16-bit Genesis to the U.S. video game market. The Genesis offered dramatic performance enhancement over 8-bit systems. Further, Sega leveraged its popular arcade games to the Genesis and made it backward compatible with its 8-bit Master System games. There were 20 Genesis game titles available by December 1989. NES also introduced a 16-bit system, the TurboGrafx-16, in the fall of 1989 and had 12 game titles by December 1989. Though Nintendo had its own 16-bit system in the works, it delayed introducing it to the United States for fear of cannibalizing its 8-bit system sales.

By the end of 1989, Sega had already sold 600,000 consoles in the United States, and NES had sold 200,000. In 1990 and 1991, both Sega and NES added game titles to their lists, bringing their totals to 130 and 80, respectively. By the end of 1991, Sega had sold 2 million consoles in the United States, and NES had sold 1 million. Unlike Sega, which produced a major portion of its games in-house, NES relied completely on external games developers, who found the system to have only a small technological advantage over 8-bit systems.[4] Developers began to abandon the NES platform, and NES exited the market in 1991. Nintendo finally introduced its own 16-bit Super Nintendo Entertainment System (SNES) in 1991, but it was too late to quell Sega's momentum. In 1992 Nintendo controlled 80 percent of the video game market (based on combined 8-bit and 16-bit sales), but by 1994, Sega was the market leader.

Like Nintendo, Sega made little profit on the consoles and focused instead on increasing unit sales to drive game sales and software developer royalties. Sega, however, used less restrictive licensing arrangements than Nintendo and rapidly lured a large number of developers to make Sega game titles. Further, though Nintendo could have made its 16-bit system backward compatible, thus linking the value consumers possessed in their 8-bit game libraries to the new system, Nintendo chose to make the system incompatible with the 8-bit games. By the end of 1991, the SNES had 25 game titles compared to the 130 available for Genesis. Nintendo had given Sega two years of installed base lead on a system that offered a significant technological advantage, and then entered the market at a ground-zero position with respect to the availability of complementary goods. The consequence of Nintendo's late move is aptly captured in a review of video game players published in *Fortune:* "To tell the truth, Nintendo just isn't cool anymore. This one is 16 bits, so it's better than the original Nintendo. But the company only made it to compete with Sega, and most kids already have that. So they don't need Super Nintendo, unless they're jerks and have to have everything. That's just idiotic."[5] Over time, sales of the Nintendo SNES accelerated, and it would ultimately prove to be one of the more successful game systems ever introduced, but Nintendo's near-monopoly position had been broken; Sega had successfully leapfrogged Nintendo.

32/64-Bit Systems

The late 1980s and early 1990s also attracted other competitors to the video game market. In 1989, Philips announced its 32-bit Compact Disc Interactive (CD-i), an interactive multimedia compact disc system that would serve as a game player, teaching tool, and music system. However, the CD-i was very complex, requiring a 30-minute demonstration. Furthermore, it was expensive—introduced at $799 and later reduced to a below-cost $500 (more than twice the cost of Nintendo or Sega systems).[6] While the product was actually much more than a video game console, customers compared it to the popular Nintendo and Sega systems and were dismayed by its price and complexity. Making matters worse, Philips was reluctant to disclose the technical specifications, greatly limiting the software development for the system. The Philips CD-i never attained more than a 2 percent market share.[7] Other companies also introduced 32-bit systems, including Turbo Technologies' Duo and 3DO's Interactive Multiplayer, but the cost of the systems ($600 to $700) was prohibitive. Turbo Tech's Duo was very short-lived and received little attention. But 3DO's system received considerable attention. The company was founded in October 1993 by Trip Hawkins, formerly of video games developer Electronic Arts. However, 3DO's unique strategy of licensing out all game and hardware production made it impossible to achieve the low console prices of Sega and Nintendo by subsidizing console production with game royalties. The hardware producers (Matsushita and Panasonic) for 3DO did not sell games and were unwilling to sell the consoles without a margin. Sales of the machine never took off, and 3DO exited the market. Atari also made a surprising return to the video game market in 1993 with the technologically advanced Jaguar. However, Atari's long struggle had not inspired great confidence in either developers or distributors, and several of the large retail chains chose not to carry the product.[8]

In 1995, two 32-bit systems arrived on the scene that would survive: Sega's Saturn and Sony's PlayStation. Both systems were introduced with great fanfare and considerable developer support. Although only Sega had experience and brand image in the video game market, Sony entered with tremendous brand image in consumer electronics and access to (and leverage in) extensive distribution channels in electronics and media. To rapidly gain insight into the toy industry, Sony hired experienced toy industry veteran Bruce Stein to head the video game unit. Sony's size and previous success in several electronics markets (including the development and control of the compact disc format) also enabled it to persuade several games developers (including Electronic Arts, the largest game developer in the United States at that time) to produce only PlayStation titles for the first six months after its introduction. There were 50 PlayStation titles by the end of 1995, and this number had grown to 800 by the end of 2000.

Though Sega's Saturn had beaten Sony's PlayStation to market by several months, it was shipped to only four retailers due to limited supply: Toys "R" Us, Babbage's, Software Etc., and Electronics Boutique. This aggravated retailers such as Best Buy and Wal-Mart, which had long supported Sega.[9] Developers also felt that it was easier to program for the PlayStation than the Saturn, causing it to lose crucial developer support.[10] By the end of 1996, the installed base of Sony PlayStation in the United States (2.9 million units) was more than double that of the Sega Saturn (1.2 million units).

In 1996, after more than 2 years of announcements, Nintendo finally introduced its 64-bit game system called Nintendo 64. Though only two software titles were available at the console's release (one being Super Mario), the game units were sold out within weeks of their release. Though Nintendo's 64-bit system gained rapid consumer acceptance, neither Nintendo nor Sega was able to reclaim dominance over the video game industry. Though several new entrants (and one returning entrant, Atari) had tried to break into the video game industry through technological leapfrogging, only Sony had the successful combination of a product with a technological advantage, strategies, and resources that enabled it to rapidly build installed base and availability of complementary goods, and a reputation that signaled the market that this was a fight it could win.

128-Bit Systems

In September 1999, Sega launched its 128-bit Dreamcast console, a $199 gaming system that enabled access to the Internet. Before the Dreamcast release, Sega was suffering from its lowest market share in years at 12 percent. The Dreamcast was the first 128-bit system to market, and 514,000 units were sold in the first two weeks. An installed base of 5 million was achieved by October 2000. Sega's success turned out to be short-lived, however. In March 2000, Sony launched its 128-bit PlayStation2 (PS2) in Japan and introduced the system to the United States in October. Despite price cuts on the Dreamcast and a promotion rebate that would make the console essentially free (in exchange for a 2-year contract for Sega's SegaNet Internet service), the Dreamcast was crushed in the holiday sales season. In early 2001, Sega announced it would cease making consoles and transform itself into a third-party developer of games for other consoles.

Sony's PS2 was an unprecedented success. Not only did it offer a significant technological advantage over the 32-bit systems, but it was also backward compatible, enabling gamers to play their PlayStation games on the console until they amassed new game libraries.[11] During the opening sales weekend of March 4, 2000, PlayStation2 sales reached about 1 million units, a figure that eclipsed by 10 times the amount of original PlayStation units sold during the 3-day release period in 1994. Demand for the new unit was so high that on the opening day of pre-orders on Sony's Web site, more than 100,000 hits in 1 minute were received, and Sony was forced to briefly shut down the Web site.

At the time of the PlayStation2 release, Nintendo had just postponed the launch of its new 128-bit system, the GameCube, to a release date in the first half of 2001. Unlike the PS2, the GameCube did not offer backward compatibility with Nintendo 64 games. The GameCube was also targeted toward a younger market (8- to 18-year-olds) than Sony's 16- to 24-year-old demographic. The real threat to Sony's PlayStation2 came in the form of a new entrant to the video console industry: Microsoft's Xbox. The Xbox, launched in November 2001, was targeted at the 18- to 34-year-old male, positioning it directly against the PS2.

Microsoft had previously produced PC-based computer games (such as Flight Simulator and the Age of Empires series) and operated an online gaming service (Microsoft Gaming Zone), and thus had some familiarity with the industry. However, it did not have either the arcade experience of Sega or Nintendo or the consumer electronics experience of Sony. By the time the Xbox hit the market, PlayStation2 already had a significant lead in installed base and availability of games (more than 300 PS2 game titles were available at the end of 2001), but Microsoft was counting on the technological advantages offered by the Xbox to tip consumer preferences. The Xbox offered a faster processor and more memory than the PlayStation2. Furthermore, customers did not have to trade off technological advantages against price: The Xbox launched at a retail price of $299, significantly less than its production costs (it is estimated that Microsoft lost between $100 and $125 per unit).[12]

To rapidly deploy the console and build installed base, Microsoft leveraged its existing relationships with distributors that carried its software, though it was now forced to seek much greater penetration into distributors such as Toys "R" Us, Babbages, and Circuit City. Microsoft also faced the challenge of cultivating a radically different brand image in the game console market than the one that it had achieved in the software market, and to make much greater use of marketing channels such as television advertising and gaming magazines. To that end, Microsoft budgeted $500 million to be spent over 18 months to market the Xbox—more than any other marketing campaign in the company's history.[13] Microsoft planned to produce 30 to 40 percent of its games in-house and gave away $10,000 game development kits to attract third-party games developers.

Both the Xbox and Nintendo's GameCube were launched just in time for the extremely important 2001 Christmas season and sold briskly. By the year's end, it was estimated that 1.3 million GameCube units had been sold, and 1.5 million Xbox units had been sold.[14] However, both of the new consoles were outrun by PS2, which sold 2 million units in the month of December alone. This market share pattern remained remarkably consistent over the next few years. By the end of fiscal year 2005, Microsoft reported it had shipped a total of 22 million

Xbox consoles, which was slightly more than Nintendo's 20.6 million GameCube shipments, and far behind the Sony PS2's 100 million consoles shipped.[15]

An Unfolding Battle . . .

In late 2005, Microsoft was first to introduce the next generation console: Xbox 360. Though severe manufacturing shortages resulted in only 600,000 units being sold in the 2005 Christmas season, Microsoft was hoping its head start over Sony and Nintendo (both of which would not debut their next generation consoles until late 2006) would enable it to attain a dominant position.

The console was designed around a custom IBM processor that had three Power PC processors on a single chip, and a custom graphics processor from ATI. The result was a powerful console that generated high-definition video with stunning graphics. The Xbox 360 was also backward compatible with a portion of the Xbox game library (though not with all Xbox games). At launch, buyers could get a basic model for $299 or a premium model for $399.[16] More importantly (from Microsoft's perspective at least), the console was supposed to be for more than just games—it was Microsoft's next attempt to secure control over the digital living room. Users could download music, movies, TV shows, and purchase premium content. With an optional high-definition DVD drive users could also watch high-definition movies (or at least they could have if Microsoft's bet on Toshiba's HD-DVD standard had not gone awry—in early 2008, Toshiba conceded defeat to Sony in the high-definition DVD format war, and announced that it would stop making the drives). By early 2006 Microsoft had sold 3.2 million Xbox 360s. The number would have been higher but the company could not keep up with demand.[17]

Sony launched its Playstation 3 in November of 2006. The console had a powerful IBM cell processor, it included Sony's Blu-ray disc player (for playing high-definition DVDs), and launched with a price tag of $599 for a 60-gigabyte model, or $499 for a 20-gigabyte model. Estimates put the cost of the components used to produce the consoles at $840 and $805, respectively, meaning that Sony lost more than $200 on every unit.[18] Sony claimed that the Playstation 3 was backward compatible with all games written for the Playstation and PS2, but it turned out that not all of the older games would play on the new system. Though the console sold out within minutes of its launch, by early 2007 Sony had sold only 3.5 million Playstation 3s worldwide—significantly less than it had forecasted.

Instead of joining Sony and Microsoft in a technological arms race, Nintendo changed the rules of the game with its Wii console. Instead of a controller with buttons or a joystick that players had to vigorously manipulate, it offered an innovative wireless motion-sensing remote that enabled users to simulate real play, such as swinging a tennis racket in a tennis match or punching an opponent in a boxing match. The console was also launched at a price of $250—significantly cheaper than the Xbox 360 or Playstation 3. It was fully compatible with Game Cube games, and because it was much cheaper to develop a Wii game (as little as $5 million compared to the $20 million for a Playstation 3 game, for example), it attracted third-party developers in droves. The net result was dramatic—the console attracted casual gamers in unprecedented numbers, and from a remarkably wide range of demographics. Wiis were being used in nursing homes, for Wii bowling leagues, and on cruise ships.[19] Instead of simply being purchased by soccer moms for their children, they were being played by the soccer moms themselves. By mid-2007, the Wii was selling twice as fast as the Xbox 360 and four times as fast as the Playstation 3. While Microsoft and Sony lost money on every console in hopes of profiting on future game sales, Nintendo was estimated to make $50 on every unit of the Wii sold.

In Fall of 2008, Microsoft slashed the price of the Xbox 360 to $199, making it the cheapest console of the generation. However, even Don Mattrick, senior vice president of Microsoft's Interactive Entertainment Business admitted that the Xbox 360 was unlikely to overtake the Wii, noting: "I'm not at a point where I can say we're going to beat Nintendo . . . we will sell more consoles this generation than Sony."[20] Sony followed suit by lowering the price of its starter model to $399. According to NPD Group, by February of 2009, over 19 million Wiis had been sold worldwide, compared to 14.2 million Xbox 360s, and 7 million Playstation 3s.

Discussion Questions

1. What factors do you think enabled Sega to break Nintendo's near monopoly of the U.S. video game console market in the late 1980s?

2. Why did Nintendo choose not to make its early video game consoles backward compatible? What were the advantages and disadvantages of this strategy?

3. What strengths and weaknesses did Sony have when it entered the video game market in 1995?

4. What strengths and weaknesses did Microsoft have when it entered the video game market in 2001?

5. Comparing the deployment strategies used by the firms in each of the generations, can you identify any timing, licensing, pricing, marketing, or distribution strategies that appear to have influenced firms' success and failure in the video game industry?

OVERVIEW

The value of any technological innovation is only partly determined by what the technology can *do*. A large part of the value of an innovation is determined by the degree to which people can understand it, access it, and integrate it within their lives. Deployment is not just a way for the firm to earn revenues from its innovations; deployment is a core part of the innovation process itself.

Deployment strategies can influence the receptivity of customers, distributors, and complementary goods providers. Effective deployment strategies can reduce uncertainty about the product, lower resistance to switching from competing or substitute goods, and accelerate adoption. Ineffective deployment strategies can cause even brilliant technological innovations to fail. As shown in the opening vignette, 3DO's Interactive Multiplayer and Philips' Compact Disk Interactive were two of the first 32-bit video game systems introduced to the market and offered significant technological advantages over previous generations of consoles. However, both were priced so high and introduced with so few games that neither was able to attract a significant share of the market. When Sega introduced its 32-bit system to the market—beating Sony's PlayStation by several months—the price was low and some popular games were available, but weak distribution ultimately hobbled the console's deployment. On the other hand, despite being a newcomer to the video game industry, Sony's exceptionally executed deployment strategies for the PlayStation made the console a nearly overnight success. Sony used a combination of intense marketing, low prices, strong games availability, and aggressive distribution to ensure that the product launched with unmistakable impact.

We will cover five key elements of the deployment process in this chapter: launch timing, licensing and compatibility, pricing, distribution, and marketing. Several of these topics warrant entire courses and textbooks in their own right; only an introduction to the issues most central to the deployment of a new technological innovation will be covered here.

LAUNCH TIMING

As illustrated by the video game industry, the timing of the product launch can be a significant part of a company's deployment strategy. For example, even though Nintendo had a 16-bit video game system in development when Sega's 16-bit Genesis was introduced, Nintendo delayed introducing a 16-bit system for fear of cannibalizing its 8-bit system sales. The advantages and disadvantages of being a first, early-but-not-first, or late mover were discussed in Chapter Five; the focus here is on how a firm can use timing as a deployment strategy.

Strategic Launch Timing

Generally, firms try to decrease their development cycles in order to decrease their costs and to increase their timing of entry options, but this does not imply that firms should always be racing to launch their products as early as possible. A firm can strategically use launch timing to take advantage of business cycle or seasonal effects, to position its product with respect to previous generations of related technologies, and to ensure that production capacity and complementary goods or services are in place. The role of each of these tactics is illustrated in the video game industry.

Nintendo, Sony, and Microsoft all took advantage of seasonal effects by introducing their consoles shortly before Christmas so that the hype of the consoles' launch would coincide with the Christmas buying season. The majority of video game consoles are sold in December. By launching their consoles close to December, firms could target their advertising for this time and leverage the free publicity that surrounded a console's launch such as press releases announcing the introduction and external product reviews.

Because the video game industry is characterized by distinct generations of technology, the timing of a console's launch also plays a key role in its positioning within a technological generation and with respect to competing consoles. If a console is introduced too early, it is likely to receive a tepid welcome because customers who recently purchased the previous-generation console are reluctant to spend money on a new console so soon. For example, though the Xbox offered a processor that was double the speed of the PlayStation2, its introductory timing positioned it as being in the same generation as the PlayStation2. Many customers saw it as a competitor to a product they already had, rather than as a next generation technology. If the console is introduced too late, the company can lose its image as a technological leader and may have already conceded a considerable installed base lead to earlier entrants. This is aptly illustrated in the quote about Nintendo's late introduction of the SNES in the opening vignette: "To tell the truth, Nintendo just isn't cool anymore. This one is 16 bits, so it's better than the original Nintendo. But the company only made it to compete with Sega, and most kids already have that. So they don't need Super Nintendo . . . ."

Finally, timing the introduction of a console to coincide with production capacity and games availability has proven very important in the video game console industry. For example, in Sega's rush to ensure that the Saturn beat Sony's PlayStation to market, it introduced the product before it had built adequate production capacity. Sega was subsequently unable to stock many important distributors, and it alienated companies that had supported Sega in previous generations. Similarly, the importance of having games available at the time of launch is also clearly demonstrated: Every video game console producer that has been successful in at least one generation (e.g., Atari, Nintendo, Sega, Sony, Microsoft) has ensured that games would be available at the console's launch, even if that meant buying games development companies to force them to produce compatible games! Games availability was also encouraged through licensing strategies, as discussed later in the chapter.

Optimizing Cash Flow versus Embracing Cannibalization

cannibalization
When a firm's sales of one product (or at one location) diminish its sales of another of its products (or at another of its locations).

A second key point about timing of entry is also illustrated in the video game industry. For firms introducing a next generation technology into a market in which they already compete, entry timing can become a decision about whether and to what degree to embrace **cannibalization**. Traditionally, research on product life cycles has emphasized the importance of timing new product introduction so as to optimize cash flows or profits from each generation and minimize cannibalization. If a firm's current product is very profitable, the firm will often delay introduction of a next generation product until profits have begun to significantly decrease for the current product. This strategy is intended to maximize the firm's return on investment in developing each generation of the product. However, in industries driven by technological innovation, delaying the introduction of a next generation product can enable competitors to achieve a significant technological gap. If competitors introduce products that have a large technological advantage over the firm's current products, customers might begin abandoning the firm's technology.

Instead, if the firm invests in continuous innovation and willingly cannibalizes its existing products with more advanced products, the firm can make it very difficult for other firms to achieve a technological lead large enough to prove persuasive to customers. By providing incentives for existing customers to upgrade to its newest models, the firm can further remove any incentive customers have to switch to another company's products when they purchase next generation technology. Many would argue that this is where Nintendo made a key mistake. In the late 1980s, Nintendo was deriving significant profits from its 8-bit system and thus was reluctant to cannibalize those sales with a 16-bit system. However, by not embracing cannibalization, Nintendo enabled Sega to steal customers away by offering a product with a significant technological advantage.

LICENSING AND COMPATIBILITY

Chapter Nine revealed how making a technology more open (i.e., not protecting it vigorously or partially opening the technology through licensing) could speed its adoption by enabling more producers to improve and promote the technology and allowing complementary goods developers to more easily support the technology. However, the chapter also pointed out that making a technology completely open poses several risks. First, if a firm completely opens its technology, other producers may drive the price of the technology down to a point at which the firm is unable to recoup its development expense. If competition drives the price down so no producer earns significant margins on the technology, no producer will have much incentive to further develop the technology. Finally, opening a technology completely may cause its underlying platform to become fragmented as different producers alter it to their needs, resulting in loss of compatibility across producers and the possible erosion of product quality.

Each of these effects was demonstrated in the opening vignette. By not protecting their technologies enough, video game console producers in the first generation relinquished their ability to control game production quantity and quality. The resulting market glut of poor-quality games decimated the video game industry. But Nintendo's highly restrictive licensing policies for its 8-bit system made games developers eager to give their support to the first rival that appeared viable. In the 16-bit, 32/64-bit, and 128-bit generations, the console makers sought to achieve a delicate balance of making licensing open enough to attract developer support while making licensing strict enough to control game quantities and quality.

In deploying a technological innovation, often a firm must decide how compatible (or incompatible) to make its technology with that provided by others or with previous generations of its own technology. If there is an existing technology with a large installed base or availability of complementary goods, the firm can sometimes leverage the value of that installed base and complementary goods by making its technology compatible with current products. For instance, producers of IBM-compatible computers (as detailed in Chapter Nine) were able to tap IBM's installed base and complementary goods advantages by offering computers that operated identically to those made by IBM. Users of IBM compatibles reaped the same installed base advantages and had access to all the same software as they would have with an IBM computer.

backward compatible
When products of a technological generation can work with products of a previous generation. For example, a computer is backward compatible if it can run the same software as a previous generation of the computer.

If the firm wishes to avoid giving away its own installed base or complementary goods advantages to others, it may protect them by ensuring its products are incompatible with those of future entrants. Most competitors in the U.S. video game industry (with the exception of Atari) have been fairly successful at this strategy. Nintendo, for example, uses a security chip to ensure that only licensed Nintendo games may be played in its consoles, and only Nintendo consoles may be used to play Nintendo games.

Firms must also decide whether or not to make their products **backward compatible** with their own previous generations of technology. Nintendo repeatedly opted not to make its consoles backward compatible, believing it would be more profitable to require customers to purchase new games. This is understandable given that the consoles were sold at cost and profits were made through game sales; however, it also meant that Nintendo forfeited a significant potential source of advantage over Sega. In contrast, Sega made its 16-bit Genesis compatible with its 8-bit Master System games—though this may not have proven terribly persuasive to customers given the limited success of the Master System. More significantly, Sony made its PlayStation2 console backward compatible with PlayStation games, thereby not only ensuring a tremendous existing library of compatible games at its launch but also providing a significant incentive to PlayStation owners who were considering upgrading to a 128-bit system to choose the PlayStation2 as opposed to Sega's Dreamcast, or waiting for the Xbox or GameCube.

Some firms use a particularly powerful strategy that combines continuous innovation with backward compatibility. A firm that both innovates to prevent a competitor from creating a technological gap and utilizes backward compatibility so that its new platform or models are compatible with previous generations of complementary goods can leverage the existing value yielded by a large range of complementary goods to its new platforms. While such a strategy may cause the firm to forfeit some sales of complementary goods for the new platform (at least initially), it can also effectively link the generations through time and can successfully transition customers through product generations while preventing competitors from having a window to enter the market. Microsoft has utilized this strategy deftly with Windows—though the operating system is regularly updated, each successive generation provides backward compatibility with most of the major software applications developed for previous generations. Thus, customers can upgrade without having to replace their entire libraries of software applications.

PRICING

Pricing is a crucial element in the firm's deployment strategy. Price simultaneously influences the product's positioning in the marketplace, its rate of adoption, and the firm's cash flow. Before a firm can determine its pricing strategy, it must determine the objectives it has for its pricing model. For example, if a firm is in an industry plagued with overcapacity or intense price competition, the firm's objective may be simply *survival*. A survival price strategy prices goods to cover variable costs and some fixed costs. It is a short-run strategy, however; in the long run, the firm will want to find a way to create additional value. One common pricing objective is to *maximize current profits*. Under this pricing strategy, the firm first estimates costs and demand and then sets the price to maximize cash flow or rate of return on investment. This strategy emphasizes current performance, but may sacrifice long-term performance.

For new technological innovations, firms often emphasize either a *maximum market skimming* objective or a *maximum market share* objective. To skim the market, firms will initially set prices high on new products. The high price may signal the market that the new product is a significant innovation that offers a substantial performance improvement over previously available products. The high price can also help the firm recoup initial development expenses, assuming there is also high initial demand. However, high initial prices may also attract competitors to the market and can slow adoption of the product. If costs are expected to decline rapidly with the volume of units produced, a skimming strategy can actually prove less profitable than a pricing strategy that stimulates more rapid customer adoption.

When achieving high volume is important, firms will often emphasize a maximum market share objective. To maximize market share, firms often use **penetration pricing**.

penetration pricing
When the price of a good is set very low (or free) to maximize the good's market share.

The firm will set the lowest price possible hoping to rapidly attract customers, driving volume up and production costs down. Effective utilization of penetration pricing often requires that the firm builds large production capacity in advance of demand. In the short run, the firm may bear significant risk from this capital investment, and it may lose money on each unit if the price is less than its initial variable costs. However, if its volume increases and drives its production costs down, the firm can achieve a very powerful position: It can have a low-cost position that enables it to earn profits despite a low price, and it can have a substantial share of the market.

Firms in industries characterized by increasing returns (strong learning-curve effects and/or network externalities) will often use the objective of maximizing market share and a penetration pricing strategy. In such industries, there is strong pressure for the industry to adopt a single dominant design (as discussed in Chapter Four). It is in the firm's best interest to accelerate adoption of its technology, building its installed base, attracting developers of complementary goods, and riding down the learning curve for its production costs.

For example, Honda's hybrid electric vehicle, the Insight, was introduced at a price ($20,000) that actually caused Honda to lose money on each Insight it sold. However, Honda believed the hybrid technology would become profitable in the long term, and that the experience it would gain by working with hybrid technology and the continuance of its "green" car company image were strong enough motivations to sell the Insight at a loss for the first few years.[21]

Sometimes firms price below cost because the losses are expected to be recouped through profits on complementary goods or services. In the video game industry, this has proven to be a very important strategy. Nintendo, Sega, Sony, and Microsoft have each sold their video game consoles at a price very close to (or below) production costs while profiting from subsequent game sales and licensing royalties. Similarly, when Microsoft launched its Internet Explorer Web browser, it gave the product away so it could quickly catch up to Netscape's Web browser, which had been introduced to the market almost a year earlier. Though consumers paid nothing for the Internet Explorer browser, Microsoft earned profits selling other compatible software products to businesses.

Firms can also influence cash flow and the customers' perception of costs through manipulating the timing of when the price of a good is paid. For instance, while the most typical pricing model requires the customer to pay the full price before taking ownership, other pricing models enable the customer to delay paying the purchase price by offering a free trial for a fixed time. This permits the customer to become familiar with the benefits of the product before paying the price, and it can be very useful when customers face great uncertainty about a new product or service. Another pricing model enables customers to pay as they go, such as through leasing programs, or a pricing model whereby the initial product is free (or available at a low price) but the customer pays for service. For example, when cable television subscribers order cable service, they typically pay little or no fee for the equipment and instead pay a significant amount (often between $20 and $90 depending on the package) for monthly service that may include some portion for the equipment expense. By contrast, when users subscribe to XM Radio's satellite radio service, they must buy the equipment from one of the many manufacturers (e.g., Sony, Pioneer) for a price that might range from \$150 to \$1,000 and then pay a very low monthly fee (about \$10) for the service.

When it is unclear how customers will respond to a particular price point, firms often use introductory pricing that indicates the pricing is for a stipulated time. This allows the company to test the market's response to a product without committing to a long-term pricing structure.

DISTRIBUTION

Selling Direct versus Using Intermediaries

manufacturers' representatives
Independent agents that promote and sell the product lines of one or a few manufacturers. They are often used when direct selling is appropriate but the manufacturer does not have a sufficiently large direct sales force to reach all appropriate market segments.

wholesalers
Companies that buy manufacturer's products in bulk, and then resell them (often in smaller or more diverse bundles) to other supply channel members such as retailers.

retailers
Companies that sell goods to the public.

Firms can sell their products directly to users through their direct sales force or an online ordering system or mail-order catalog. Alternatively, firms can use intermediaries such as **manufacturers' representatives, wholesalers,** and **retailers**. Selling direct gives the firm more control over the selling process, pricing, and service. It also can enable the firm to capture more information about customers and can facilitate the customization of products for customers. However, in many situations selling direct can be impractical or overly expensive. Intermediaries provide a number of important services that can make distribution more efficient. First, wholesalers and retailers *break bulk*. In general, manufacturers prefer to sell large quantities of a limited number of items, while customers prefer to buy limited quantities of a large number of items. Wholesalers and retailers can pool large orders from a large number of manufacturers and sell a wider range of goods in small quantities to customers.

For example, a typical book publisher produces a limited range of book titles, but desires to sell them in high volume. The average final consumer may wish to purchase only one copy of a particular book title, but often wants a wide range of book titles to choose from. Both wholesalers and retailers provide valuable bulk-breaking services in this channel. A wholesaler such as Ingram will purchase pallets of books from many different publishers such as McGraw-Hill, Simon & Schuster, and Prentice Hall. It then breaks apart the pallets and reassembles bundles of books that include titles from multiple publishers but have fewer copies of any particular book title. These bundles are then sold to retailers such as Barnes & Noble or Borders, which offer a wide range of titles sold on an individual basis. Though publishers could sell directly to final consumers using the Internet or a mail-order catalog, customers would have to examine the offerings of many different publishers to be able to consider the same range of books offered by a retailer.

Intermediaries also provide a number of other services such as transporting goods, carrying inventory, providing selling services, and handling transactions with customers. Many intermediaries also offer greater convenience for customers by offering geographically dispersed retail sites. Location convenience can be particularly important if customers are geographically dispersed and they are likely to want to examine or try different product options or to need on-site service. By contrast, if the product is primarily sold to a few industrial customers or if the product can be routinely ordered without close examination, trial, or service, geographic dispersion may be less important.

original equipment manufacturer (or value-added reseller)
A company that buys products (or components of products) from other manufacturers and assembles them or customizes them into a product that is then sold under the OEM's own name.

disintermediation
When the number of intermediaries in a supply channel is reduced; for example, when manufacturers bypass wholesalers and/or retailers to sell directly to end users.

Original equipment manufacturers (OEMs) (also called **value-added resellers, or VARs**) provide an even more crucial role in the distribution process. An OEM buys products (or components of products) from other manufacturers and assembles them into a product that is customized to meet user needs. The OEM then sells this customized product under its own name and often provides marketing and service support for the product. OEMs are very common in the computer and electronics industries where manufacturers are often specialized in the production of individual components but users prefer to purchase whole, assembled products. Dell Computer, for example, is a very successful OEM in the computer industry. OEMs can provide a very valuable coordinating function in an industry by aggregating components and providing a single contact point for the customer.

In some industries, advances in information technology (such as the Internet) have enabled **disintermediation** or a reconfiguration in the types of intermediaries used. For example, online investing services such as E-trade or Ameritrade caused some disintermediation in the investment market by enabling customers to bypass brokers and place their own stock or bond orders online. In industries where the product is information that can be conveyed digitally, such as newspapers, software, and music, the Internet can deliver the product from the manufacturer straight to the consumer. In most industries, however, information technology has simply shifted the roles of intermediaries or expanded the services they provide. For example, online stores such as Dell.com or Amazon.com enable customers to bypass traditional retail outlets such as computer stores or bookstores. However, in most cases this has not shortened the supply chain by which goods are delivered to customers—it has just rerouted it. In other instances, moving commerce online has required creating additional intermediaries (such as companies specialized in delivering the goods of others) or enhanced the services that intermediaries provide. For example, while grocers traditionally required customers to provide their own distribution for "the last mile" (the distance between the store and the customer's home), online grocery shopping shifts the responsibility of moving goods "the last mile" to the stores, requiring them either to develop their own delivery services or to purchase delivery services from other providers. Barnes & Noble uses online sales to complement its bricks-and-mortar retail outlets: Customers can come into the stores to see and physically handle books (an option many book shoppers express a strong preference for), but they can also order books online—from home or from within a Barnes & Noble store—if they are looking for a book that is not stocked at a convenient location.

To determine whether to use intermediaries and what type of intermediaries would be appropriate, the firm should answer the following questions:

1. *How does the new product fit with the distribution requirements of the firm's existing product lines?* Whether the firm already has an existing sales channel that would suit the product will be a primary consideration in how the product should be distributed. For example, if the firm already has a large direct sales force and the new product would fit well with this direct sales system, there may be no need to consider other distribution options. On the other hand, if the firm does not have an existing direct sales force, it will have to determine whether the new product warrants the cost and time of building a direct sales force.

2. *How numerous and dispersed are customers, and how much product education or service will customers require? Is prepurchase trial necessary or desirable? Is*

installation or customization required? If customers are dispersed but require little product education or service, mail order or online ordering may suffice. On the other hand, if customers are dispersed and require moderate amounts of education, service, or prepurchase trial, using intermediaries is often a good option because they can provide some on-site education and service and/or trial. If customers are not dispersed, or will require *extensive* education and service, it may be necessary for the firm to provide the education and service directly. Furthermore, if the product will require installation or customization, the firm will often need to employ either a direct sales force or an intermediary capable of providing extensive service.

3. *How are competing products or substitutes sold?* The firm must consider how competing or substitute products are sold, because this both determines the nature of the existing distribution channel options and shapes customer expectations about how products will be purchased. For example, if customers are used to purchasing the product in a retail environment where the product can be viewed and handled and where customers can receive personal sales assistance, they may be reluctant to switch to a sales channel with less contact, such as online purchasing or mail order. How the product is sold may also affect the product's positioning from the perspective of the customer. For example, if competing products are primarily sold in a high-contact mode such as specialty stores or via a direct sales force, selling the new product in a lower-contact channel such as mass discounters or through mail order might cause the customer to perceive the product as being of lower quality or more economical. Market research can assess how the sales channel influences the customer's perception of the product.

Strategies for Accelerating Distribution

When the industry is likely to select a single technology as the dominant design, it can be very important to deploy the technology rapidly. Rapid deployment enables the technology to build a large installed base and encourages the developers of complementary goods to support the technology platform. As the technology is adopted, producer and user experience can be used to improve the technology, and producer costs should also decrease due to learning effects and economies of scale. The firm can use a variety of strategies to accelerate distribution, such as forging alliances with distributors, creating bundling relationships, sponsoring or contracting with large customer groups, and providing sales guarantees.[22]

Alliances with Distributors

Firms introducing a technological innovation can use strategic alliances or exclusivity contracts to encourage distributors to carry and promote their goods. By providing a distributor a stake in the success of the new technology, the firm may be able to persuade the distributor to carry and promote the new technology aggressively. Firms that already have relationships with distributors for other goods are at an advantage in pursuing this strategy; firms without such relationships may need to cultivate them, or even consider forward vertical integration to ensure that their product is widely available.

Lack of distribution may have contributed significantly to the failure of the Sega Saturn to gain installed base. Sega had very limited distribution for its Saturn launch, which may have slowed the building of its installed base both directly (because customers had limited access to the product) and indirectly (because distributors that were initially denied product may have been reluctant to promote the product after the limitations were lifted). Nintendo, by contrast, had unlimited distribution for its Nintendo 64 launch, and Sony not only had unlimited distribution, but also had extensive experience negotiating with retailing giants such as Wal-Mart for its consumer electronics products. Consequently, Sony PlayStation had better distribution on its first day of business than the Sega Saturn, despite Sega's decade of experience in the market.[23]

Bundling Relationships

Firms can also accelerate distribution of a new technology by bundling it with another product that is already in wide use. Bundling enables the new technology to piggyback on the success of another product that already has a large installed base. Once customers acquire the new product in tandem with something else that they already use, switching costs may prevent customers from changing to a different product, even if the different product might have initially been preferred. As customers become familiar with the product, their ties to the technology (for instance, through the cost of training) increase and their likelihood of choosing this technology in future purchase decisions may also increase. Bundling arrangements have proven to be a very successful way for firms to build their installed base and ensure provision of complementary goods. Consider, for example, Conner Peripherals (whose disk drives were bundled with Compaq's personal computers), Microsoft's MS-DOS (whose initial bundling with IBM led to bundling arrangements with almost all PC clone makers and also facilitated the later bundling of Windows with PCs), and Microsoft's Internet Explorer (which gained a larger installed base through a bundling arrangement with America Online, one of the largest Internet providers in the United States).

Contracts and Sponsorship

Firms can also set up contractual arrangements with distributors, complementary goods providers, and even large end users (such as universities or government agencies) to ensure that the technology is used in exchange for price discounts, special service contracts, advertising assistance, or other inducements. For example, when medical equipment manufacturers introduce significantly new medical devices such as new ultrasound equipment or magnetic resonance imaging machines, they will often donate or lend a number of these machines to large teaching hospitals. As the new equipment's benefits become clear to the doctors and hospital administration, their likelihood of purchasing additional machines increases. Because large teaching hospitals train medical staff that may ultimately work for other hospitals and are often influential leaders in the medical community, providing these hospitals with free equipment can be an effective way of encouraging the rest of the medical community to adopt the product.

Guarantees and Consignment

If there is considerable market uncertainty about the new product or service, the firm can encourage distributors to carry the product by offering them guarantees (such as promising to take back unsold stock) or agreeing to sell the product on consignment. For example, when Nintendo introduced the Nintendo Entertainment System to the U.S. market, distributors were reluctant to carry the console or games because many had been stuck with worthless inventory after the crash of the video game market in the mid-1980s. Nintendo agreed to sell the Nintendo Entertainment System to distributors on consignment: Nintendo would be paid only for consoles that were sold, rather than requiring distributors to buy consoles up front. Retailers bore little risk in distributing the good because unsold units could be returned to Nintendo, and the video game industry was reborn.

A similar argument can be made for offering guarantees to complementary goods producers. If complementary goods producers are reluctant to support the technology, the firm can guarantee particular quantities of complementary goods will be purchased, or it can provide the capital for production, thus bearing the bulk of the risk of producing complementary goods for the technology. The complementary goods producer may still have forfeited time or effort in producing goods that may not have a long-term market, but its direct costs will be less at risk.

MARKETING

The marketing strategy for a technological innovation must consider both the nature of the target market and the nature of the innovation. For example, is the target market composed primarily of large industrial users or individual consumers? Is the innovation likely to appeal only to technophiles or to the mass market? Are the benefits of the technology readily apparent, or will they require considerable customer education? Will customers respond more to detailed technical content or eye-catching brand images? Can the marketer alleviate customer uncertainty about the innovation? Major marketing methods are briefly reviewed next, along with how marketing can be tailored to particular adopter categories. Also explored is how marketing can shape perceptions and expectations about the innovation's installed base and availability of complementary goods.

Major Marketing Methods

The three most commonly used marketing methods include advertising, promotions, and publicity/public relations.

Advertising

Many firms use advertising to build public awareness of their technological innovation. Doing so requires that the firm craft an effective advertising message and choose advertising media that can convey this message to the appropriate target market.

In crafting an advertising message, firms often attempt to strike a balance between achieving an entertaining and memorable message versus providing a significant quantity of informative content. Too much focus on one or the other can result in advertisements that are memorable but convey little about the product, or advertisements that are informative but quickly lose the audience's attention. Many firms hire an advertising agency to develop and test an advertising message.

The media used are generally chosen based on their match to the target audience, the richness of information or sensory detail they can convey, their reach (the number of people exposed), and their cost per exposure. Some of the advantages and disadvantages of various advertising media are provided in Figure 13.1.

FIGURE 13.1
Advantages and Disadvantages of Major Advertising Media

Source: From Philip Kotler, *Marketing Management,* 11th edition, Copyright © 2003. Adapted by permission of Pearson Education, Inc., Upper Saddle River, NJ.

Medium	Advantages	Disadvantages
Newspapers	Timeliness; good local market coverage; broad acceptance; high believability	Short life; poor reproduction quality; small "pass-along" audience
Television	High sensory richness that combines sight, sound, and motion; high attention; wide reach	High absolute cost; fleeting exposure; less audience selectivity
Direct mail	High audience selectivity; no ad competition within the same medium; personalization; enables communication of significant technical content; may be passed along to others	Relatively high cost; "junk mail" image
Radio	High geographic and demographic selectivity; medium reach; low cost	Audio presentation only; nonstandardized rate structures, fleeting exposure
Magazines	High geographic and demographic selectivity; high-quality reproduction; long life; can enable significant technical content; good pass-along readership	Long ad purchase lead time; some waste circulation
Outdoor (e.g., billboards)	High repeat exposure; low cost; low competition	Limited audience selectivity; creative limitations
Yellow Pages	Excellent local coverage; high believability; wide reach; low cost	High competition; long ad purchase lead time; creative limitations
Newsletters	Very high selectivity; full control; enables communication of significant technical content; interactive opportunities	Narrow reach; potential for high costs
Telephone	Interactive; can give personalized message	Relative high cost; can be perceived as annoyance
Internet	High selectivity; interactive possibilities; relatively low cost	Relatively new medium with low number of users in some countries; high clutter

Promotions

Firms can also use promotions at the distributor or customer level to stimulate purchase or trial. Promotions are usually temporary selling tactics that might include:

- Offering samples or free trial.
- Offering cash rebates after purchase.
- Including an additional product (a "premium") with purchase.
- Offering incentives for repeat purchase.
- Offering sales bonuses to distributor or retailer sales representatives.
- Using cross-promotions between two or more noncompeting products to increase pulling power.
- Using point-of-purchase displays to demonstrate the product's features.

Publicity and Public Relations

Many firms use free publicity (such as articles that appear in a newspaper or magazine about the company or its product) to effectively generate word of mouth. For example, Pfizer's drug Viagra got an enormous amount of free exposure from unofficial celebrity endorsements and humorous coverage on TV shows such as *The Tonight Show* and *Late Show with David Letterman.* Other firms rely on internally generated publications (e.g., annual reports, press releases, articles written by employees for trade magazines or other media) to reach and influence target markets. Firms may also sponsor special events (e.g., sporting events, competitions, conferences), contribute to good causes (e.g., charities), or exhibit at trade associations to generate public awareness and goodwill.[24] Farmos even involved potential customers in the testing process of its drug Domosedan to generate awareness, as described in the accompanying Theory in Action.

Tailoring the Marketing Plan to Intended Adopters

As described in Chapter Three, innovations tend to diffuse through the population in an s-shape pattern whereby adoption is initially slow because the technology is unfamiliar, it then accelerates as the technology becomes better understood and utilized by the mass market, and eventually the market is saturated so the rate of new adoptions declines. These stages of adoption have been related to the adopter categories of *innovators* (in the very early stages); followed by *early adopters,* which cause adoption to accelerate; then the *early majority* and *late majority* as the innovation penetrates the mass market; and finally the *laggards* as the innovation approaches saturation.[25] The characteristics of these groups make them responsive to different marketing strategies.

Innovators and early adopters are typically looking for very advanced technologies that offer a significant advantage over previous generations. They are willing to take risks and to pay high prices, and they will accept some incompleteness in the product, but they may also demand considerable customization and technical support.[26] They are more likely to respond to marketing that offers a significant amount of technical content and that emphasizes the leading-edge nature of the innovation. Marketing channels that enable high content and selective reach are appropriate for this market. To market to the early majority, on the other hand, requires that the company communicate the product's completeness, its ease of use, its consistency with the customer's way of life, and its legitimacy. For this market segment, detailed technical information is not as important as using market channels with high reach and high credibility.

Firms often find it is difficult to make the transition between successfully selling to early adopters versus the early majority. While early adopters may be enthusiastic about the innovation's technological features, the early majority may find the product too complex, expensive, or uncertain. This can result in a chasm in the product's diffusion curve: Sales drop off because the early adopter market is saturated and the early majority market is not yet ready to buy (see Figure 13.2).[27] The company must simultaneously weather a period of diminished sales while scaling up its production capacity and improving efficiency to target the mass market.

To target the late majority and laggards, firms will often use similar channels as those used to target the early majority, although emphasizing reducing the cost per exposure. The marketing message at this stage must stress reliability, simplicity, and

When the Finnish company Farmos Group Limited introduced its veterinary drug Domosedan, executives knew that building awareness of the drug among known opinion leaders would be crucial. Domosedan represented a disruptive innovation in painkillers for horses and cattle; it would significantly alter the way veterinarians performed their examinations and treatments. Unlike previous sedatives and painkillers used in the treatment of large animals, Domosedan enabled veterinarians to conduct clinical and surgical examinations without tying up or anesthetizing their patients. Animals could be treated while standing, and in most instances they would not have to be transported to the veterinarian's clinic.

Farmos knew that university professors and advanced practitioners were important opinion leaders in veterinary medicine. To educate this group and encourage them to support the product, Farmos asked them to help with the testing process required for the drug's approval and sales permit. University professors were involved in the preclinical testing, and visionary practitioners were utilized for clinical testing. By proactively involving these influential potential adopters, the testing simultaneously acted as a premarketing tool while establishing the drug's efficacy and safety. This enabled opinion leaders to acquire advanced knowledge of and experience with the product before it was released. By the time the drug was launched, many of these influential users were already enthusiastic supporters of the product.

Because the drug represented a scientific breakthrough, it was featured in presentations at scientific conferences and was investigated in numerous dissertations, generating further awareness and excitement about the drug. When it was launched in Finland, the company hosted a large dinner party for all practicing veterinarians to attend, creating a celebratory atmosphere for the drug's introduction. Farmos' tactics were successful—Domosedan was adopted rapidly, spreading quickly around the world, and became a significant commercial success.

Source: Adapted from Birgitta Sandberg, "Creating the Market for Disruptive Innovation: Market Proactiveness at the Launch Stage," *Journal of Targeting, Measurement and Analysis for Marketing* 11, no. 2 (2002), pp. 184–96.

cost-effectiveness. The marketing channel need not enable high content, but it must have high credibility and not be so expensive as to drive product costs up significantly.

Recently, marketers have begun to tap the contagion-like spread of information by targeting individuals most likely to rapidly spread information. This is described in detail in the accompanying Research Brief.

FIGURE 13.2
The Chasm between Early Adopters and Early Majority Customers

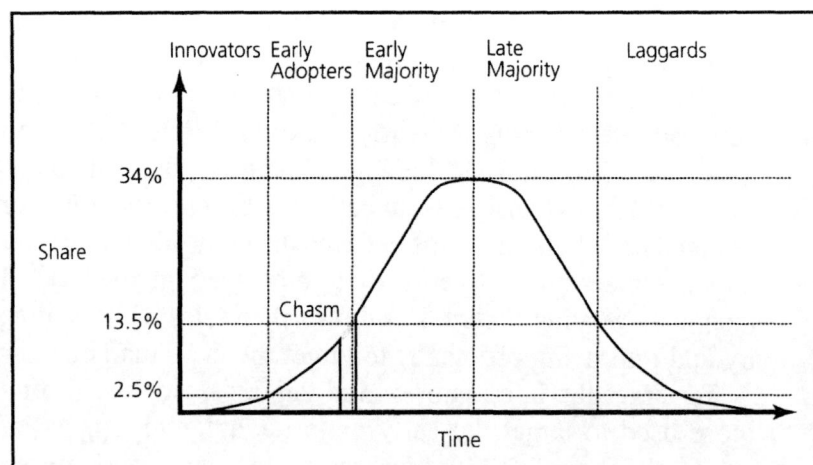

300

Using Marketing to Shape Perceptions and Expectations

As described in Chapter Four, when distributors and customers are assessing the value of a technological innovation, they are swayed not only by evidence of the innovation's actual value, but also by their perception of the innovation's value and their expectations for its value in the future. Advertising, promotions, and publicity can play a key role in influencing the market's perceptions and expectations about the size of the installed base and the availability of complementary goods. Preannouncements can generate excitement about a product before its release, while press releases extolling forecasted sales can convince customers and distributors that the product's installed base will increase rapidly. The firm can also shape expectations about the future of the technology by signaling the market (including distributors, end users, manufacturers of complementary goods, and perhaps even other potential contenders for the new standard) that this is a battle it intends to win and is capable of winning. The firm's reputation may create a signal about its likelihood of success. Firms may also use credible commitments such as major fixed capital investments and guarantees to convince stakeholders that the firm has what it takes to challenge the incumbents.

Preannouncements and Press Releases

A firm that aggressively promotes its products can increase both its actual installed base and its perceived installed base. Even products that have relatively small installed bases can obtain relatively large mind-shares through heavy advertising. Since perceived installed base may drive subsequent adoptions, a large perceived installed base can lead to a large actual installed base. Such a tactic underlies the use of "vaporware"—preadvertised products that are not actually on the market yet and may not even exist—by many software vendors. By building the impression among customers that a product is ubiquitous, firms can prompt rapid adoption of the product when it actually is available. Vaporware may also buy a firm valuable time in bringing its product to market. If other vendors beat the firm to market and the firm fears that customers may select a dominant design before its offering is introduced, it can use vaporware to attempt to persuade customers to delay purchase until the firm's product is available.

The Nintendo 64 provides an excellent example. In an effort to forestall consumer purchases of 32-bit systems, Nintendo began aggressively promoting its development of a 64-bit system (originally named Project Reality) in 1994, though the product would not actually reach the market until September 1996. The project underwent so many delays that some industry observers dubbed it "Project Unreality." Another interesting vaporware example was Nintendo's rewritable 64M disk drive. Though the product was much hyped, it was never introduced.

Major video game producers also go to great lengths to manage impressions of their installed base and market share, often to the point of exaggeration or deception. For example, at the end of 1991, Nintendo claimed it had sold 2 million units of the SNES to the U.S. market, while Sega disagreed, arguing that Nintendo had sold 1 million units at most. Nintendo also forecast that it would sell an additional 6 million units by the end of 1992 (actual installed base of Super Nintendo systems in the United States reached just over 4 million units in 1992). By May 1992, Nintendo was claiming a 60 percent share of the 16-bit market, and Sega was claiming a 63 percent share. Similar tactics were deployed in the battle for the 32/64-bit market. For example, in

Research Brief   Creating an Information Epidemic

Some individuals, by virtue of their natural proclivities and talents, can initiate a cascade of information that travels with startling momentum through a population. Such individuals can have a remarkable effect on marketplace behavior. Gladwell identifies three distinct types of individuals who have such a disproportionate amount of influence: connectors, mavens, and salespersons.[28]

Connectors are individuals who tend to form an exceptionally large circle of acquaintances. Sociologists have found that if a random sample of people is asked to identify the individuals they know on a first-name basis, connectors will identify many times the number of people an average person identifies.[29] These people may have an exceptionally high social drive; they also tend to have a knack for remembering people's names and keeping track of social details such as birthdays. However, it is not just the quantity of acquaintances that distinguishes connectors. Connectors also tend to have a diverse array of affiliations. They may belong to a number of different kinds of clubs, associations, or other social institutions. They belong to multiple social worlds. Thus, connectors can bring together people who would otherwise be unlikely to meet.

Mavens are individuals who are driven to obtain and disseminate knowledge about one or more of their interests. Economists have widely studied "market mavens," otherwise known as "price vigilantes." These individuals will closely track the prices charged by various retailers (or other market outlets) and will vociferously complain if they find something inappropriate, such as a promotion that is misleading.[30] Other mavens may take great pride in always knowing the best restaurants or hotels, or they may be avid readers of *Consumer Reports*. Mavens not only collect information, but they are also keenly interested in educating others. They will frequently volunteer information and derive great pleasure out of helping other consumers.

Finally, *salespersons* are those individuals who are naturally talented persuaders. Such individuals are gifted at providing verbal responses that their listener is likely to find compelling. They may also have an acute ability to send and respond to nonverbal cues, enabling them to influence other people's emotional response to something. These individuals can infect others with their mood![31]

Any of these individuals is capable of sparking an information epidemic. While a connector with a valuable piece of information is likely to expose a great number and diversity of people, the maven is likely to convey the information to fewer people but in more detail, making it more convincing. The salesperson may not expose as many people as the connector and may not be driven to acquire and disseminate the volumes of information that the maven transmits, but the people the salesperson does transmit information to are likely to find it irresistible. Some individuals possess more than one of these traits simultaneously, making them a veritable typhoon of influence in the marketplace.

October 1995, Sony announced to the press that it had presold 100,000 consoles in the United States, to which Mike Ribero, Sega's executive vice president for marketing and sales, countered that Sony's figures were deceptive, arguing that many preorders would never materialize into actual purchases.[32]

Reputation

When a firm is poised to introduce a new technological innovation, its reputation for both technological and commercial competence will critically influence the market's expectation about its likelihood of success.[33] Customers, distributors, and complementary goods producers will use the firm's track record for technological innovation as an indicator of the new product's functionality and value. The firm's prior commercial success acts as an indicator of the firm's ability to build and manage the necessary support network around the new technology (distribution, advertising, alliances) to create the necessary momentum in the installed base–complementary goods cycle.

When Sega entered the video game market, it had the benefit of having several highly successful arcade games to its credit (both Atari and Nintendo had also been arcade game producers before developing home video games). The company had a reputation for developing exciting games, and this reputation may have facilitated customer acceptance of its 16-bit challenge to Nintendo's 8-bit dominance. By contrast, when Sony entered the video game market, it did not have the arcade background that underscored the other primary competitors. However, it did have a wealth of technological expertise as a consumer electronics manufacturer and exceptional brand equity in electronic products. Furthermore, Sony had demonstrated its ability to win a format war through its successful introduction of the CD format (with Philips) that supplanted vinyl records and analog cassettes.

Similarly, reputation was probably Microsoft's greatest strength in the battle for dominance over 128-bit video game systems. Microsoft's near monopoly in the personal computer operating system market was achieved through its unrivaled skill in using network externalities to its advantage. Microsoft had skillfully leveraged its controlling share in PC operating systems into domination over many categories of the software market, obliterating many would-be competitors. Microsoft's reputation sent a strong signal to distributors, developers, and customers that would shape their expectations for its future installed base and availability of complementary goods. Microsoft's success was not assured, but it was a powerful force to be reckoned with.

Credible Commitments

A firm can also signal its commitment to an industry by making substantial investments that would be difficult to reverse. For example, it was well publicized that Sony spent more than $500 million developing the PlayStation, in addition to manufacturing the system and establishing an in-house games development unit. By contrast, 3DO's cumulative research and development costs at the launch of its multiplayer were less than $37 million, and the company utilized a strategy whereby all console and game production was performed by third parties. Thus, 3DO may not have signaled the market that it had enough confidence in the platform to bear the brunt of the capital risk.

Summary of Chapter

1. A firm can use its launch timing strategy to take advantage of business cycle or seasonal effects, to influence its positioning vis-à-vis competitors, and to ensure that production capacity and complementary goods are sufficiently available at time of launch.

2. The launch timing decision must also consider the need to harvest cash flows from existing product generations versus the advantages of willingly cannibalizing existing products to preempt competitors.

3. Successful deployment requires striking a careful balance between making a system open enough to attract complementary goods providers (and/or other

producers if that is desirable) and protected enough to ensure that product quality, margins, and compatibility can be sustained.

4. Common pricing strategies for technological innovations include market skimming and penetration pricing. While the first attempts to maximize margins earned on early sales of the product, the second attempts to maximize market share. Pricing strategies should consider the firm's ability to earn profits from sales of complementary goods or services—if profits from complements are expected to be high, lower prices on the platform technology may be warranted.

5. Firms can manipulate the customer's perception of the product's price (and the timing of cash flows) through the timing of when the price is paid.

6. Intermediaries provide a number of valuable roles in the supply chain, including breaking bulk, transporting, carrying inventory, providing selling services, and managing customer transactions.

7. Sometimes a firm can accelerate distribution of its innovation by forging relationships with distributors, bundling the good with others that have a wider installed base, sponsoring large customer groups, or providing sales guarantees to distributors or complements producers.

8. Marketing methods vary in attributes such as cost, reach, information content, duration of exposure, flexibility of message, and ability to target particular segments of the market. When designing the marketing plan, the firm must take into account both the nature of the innovation (e.g., Is it complex? Are benefits easy to observe?) and the nature of the customer (e.g., Does the customer require in-depth technical detail? Is the customer likely to be influenced by brand images and/or reputation? How much uncertainty is the customer likely to tolerate?)

9. Marketing strategies can influence the market's perception of how widely used the product is or will be, and thus can influence the behavior of customers, distributors, and complementary goods producers. Preannouncements, the firm's reputation, and credible commitments can all influence the market's assessment of the product's likelihood of success.

Discussion Questions

1. Identify one or more circumstances when a company might wish to delay introducing its product.

2. What factors will (or should) influence a firm's pricing strategy?

3. Pick a product you know well. What intermediaries do you think are used in bringing this product to market? What valuable services do you think these intermediaries provide?

4. What marketing strategies are used by the producers of the product you identified for Question 3? What are the advantages and disadvantages of these marketing strategies?

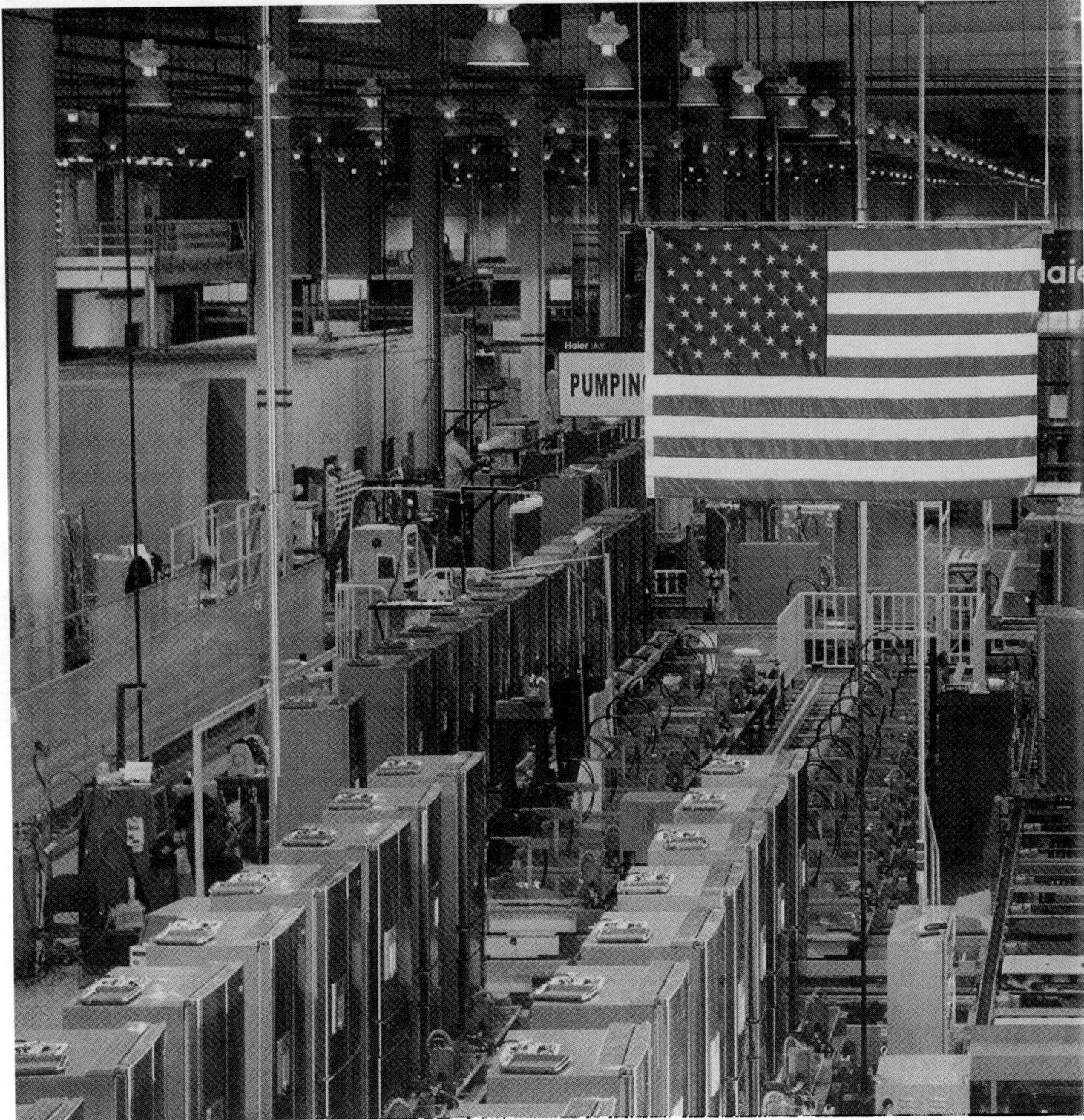

American made...

Companies from CHINA are spending billions to build factories in the U.S.—

HAIER'S REFRIGERATOR FACTORY IN CAMDEN, S.C., NOW EMPLOYS 250 AMERICANS.

...*Chinese owned*

and creating new JOBS FOR AMERICAN WORKERS.

by Sheridan Prasso
photographs by Gregg Segal

A BOUT A MILE PAST the Bountiful Blessings Church on the outskirts of Spartanburg, S.C., make a right turn. There, tucked into an industrial court behind a row of sapling cherry trees not much taller than I am, past a company that makes rubber stamps and another that stitches logos onto caps and bags, is a brand-new factory: the state-of-the-art American Yuncheng Gravure Cylinder plant. Due to open any day now, it will make cylinders used to print labels like the ones around plastic soda bottles. But unlike its neighbors in Spartanburg, Yuncheng is a Chinese company. It has come to South Carolina because by Chinese standards, America is darn cheap.

Yes, you read that right. The land Yuncheng purchased in Spartanburg, at $350,000 for 6.5 acres, cost one-fourth the price of land back in Shanghai or Dongguan, a gritty city near Hong Kong where the company already runs three plants. Electricity is cheaper too: Yungcheng pays up to 14¢ per kilowatt-hour in China at peak usage, and just 4¢ in South Carolina. And no brownouts either, a sporadic problem in China. It's true that American workers are much more expensive, of course, and the overall cost of making a widget in China remains lower, and perhaps always will.

But for hundreds of Chinese companies like Yuncheng, the U.S. has become a better, less expensive place to set up shop. It could be the biggest role reversal since, well … when Nixon went to China. "The gap between manufacturing costs in the U.S. and China is shrinking," explains John Ling, a naturalized American from China who runs the South Carolina Department of Commerce's business recruitment office in Shanghai. Ling recruited Yuncheng to Spartanburg, and others too: Chinese companies have invested $280 million and created more than 1,200 jobs in South Carolina alone.

Today some 33 American states, ports, and municipalities have sent representatives like Ling to China to lure jobs once lost to China back to the U.S.: Besides affordable land and reliable power, states and cities are offering tax credits and other incentives to woo Chinese manufacturers. Beijing, meanwhile, which has mandated that Chinese companies globalize by expanding to key markets around the world, is chipping in by offering to finance up to 30% of the initial investment costs, according to Chinese business sources.

The enticements are working. Chinese companies announced new direct investments in the U.S. of close to $5 billion in 2009 alone, according to New York City–based economic consultancy the Rhodium Group, which tallied the numbers for *Fortune*. That's well below Japanese investment in the U.S., which peaked at $148 billion in 1991, but a big jump from China's previous investments, which had been averaging around $500 million a year. Chinese firms last year acquired or announced they were starting more than 50 U.S. companies. And when China finally allows the value of its currency, the yuan, to appreciate—and it's just a question of when—Americans can expect to see Chinese projects, small today, really take off and have an impact on the U.S. economy. This could be a good thing for relations between the two countries. "It will take many years to balance out the flow of U.S. investment into China," says Dan Rosen, a principal at the Rhodium Group. But, he says, China's aggressive interest in U.S. investment suddenly gives Washington some leverage as it seeks to negotiate with Beijing on tariffs, trade issues, and economic policy.

None of that matters much in Spartanburg. Skilled workers at American Yuncheng will earn $25 to $30 an hour, line operators $10 to $12. That's a lot more than the $2 an hour that unskilled labor costs in China, but the company can qualify for a state payroll tax credit of $1,500 per worker (for any company creating more than 10 jobs). And by being closer to companies like Coca-Cola, Yuncheng can respond more quickly when they need new labels designed to show that a product has reduced its fat content or added more flavor. If business goes well, company president Li Wenchun

expects to double the size of his operation, maybe in five to 10 years, and employ up to 120 Americans. "I'd like it to be next month, but it depends on how fast we develop the market here," he tells me through a Mandarin interpreter.

So far there's little sign of anti-Chinese sentiment among South Carolinians, who watched their state lose its cotton-based textile-manufacturing industry to low-cost countries like China. *Fortune* asked Sen. Jim DeMint, a Republican torchbearer for conservative causes, what he thinks of communists creating work in his home state. "South Carolina is one of the best places in the world to do business, and that's why so many international companies are moving jobs into our state" is his only reply.

Brenda Missouri, a 43-year-old leaks tester who works for appliance maker Haier, speaks about her employer in glowing terms. Haier was the first Chinese company to build a factory in the U.S.—a refrigerator plant in Camden, S.C., in 2000. "They're good business folks; they get the job done," she says. As for communism? "Doesn't matter," she shrugs. "It's money that makes the difference."

LAST DECEMBER the National Committee on U.S.-China Relations dispatched me to Corpus Christi to give a speech about the Chinese and their economy. Why? Because, they told me, the region is about to become home to the largest-ever Chinese-built factory in the U.S., a $1 billion plant by Tianjin Pipe Group to manufacture seamless pipe for oil drilling. If everything proceeds as planned—the company received its air-quality permit on April 14 and hopes to break ground by fall—Tianjin Pipe expects to employ 600 Texans by 2012 and to provide an estimated $2.7 billion to the local economy over the next decade. Corpus Christians, it turned out, wanted to know more about their new neighbors,

Here to Stay?

Chinese investment in the U.S., from new factory construction to acquisitions, picked up momentum during the recession.

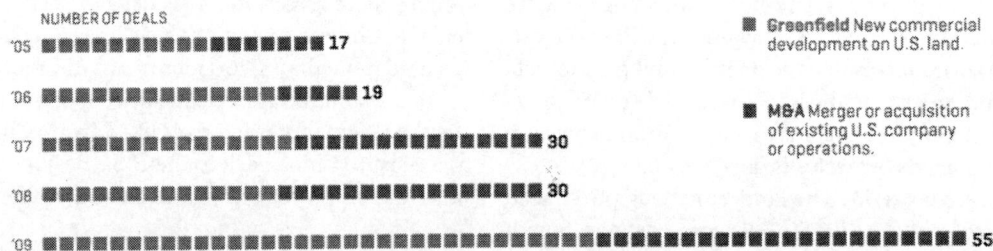

NUMBER OF DEALS

'05 ████████████████ 17

'06 ██████████████████ 19

'07 █████████████████████████████ 30

'08 █████████████████████████████ 30

'09 ██ 55

■ **Greenfield** New commercial development on U.S. land.

■ **M&A** Merger or acquisition of existing U.S. company or operations.

M&A DEALS VALUED AT $5 MILLION TO $500 MILLION. SOURCES: DELOITTE, FDI MARKETS, THOMSON M&A

who are expected to relocate 40 to 50 families to Texas.

Upon arrival, I find it impossible not to notice the resemblance of Corpus Christi's long, curving coastline on the Gulf of Mexico to the one near Tianjin on the Bohai Sea between northern China and Korea. Some 75 U.S. locales competed for the factory, but when Chinese delegations from Tianjin Pipe visited Corpus Christi, the townspeople made them feel at home by welcoming the visitors to backyard barbecues. They even enlisted the Taiwan-born former owner of the local Chinese restaurant, Yalee Shih—perhaps the only woman in town who could speak Mandarin—to help them navigate cultural nuances. Shih, who also sits on the board of the Texas State Museum of Asian Cultures, delicately helped prevent a multimillion-dollar translation error over building costs that might have cost Corpus Christi the project, and also quashed what would have been an impolitic gift of clocks—which to the Chinese symbolize death or the end of a relationship—from a local retailer. She and others in the region's business community plan to help guide their new residents through life in America, like how to buy a car, how to rent a house, as well as where to go to buy fragrant rice instead of Uncle Ben's.

In the end, while feeling at home helps, it does come down to business, says J.J. Johnston, executive vice president and chief business development officer of the Corpus Christi Regional Economic Development Corp. "They like the strategic location of our region, the convenient access to materials coming in—mostly scrap metal and pig iron—and the ability to export to North and South America through the port of Corpus Christi," he says.

There are other incentives. On April 9 the U.S. Commerce Department imposed import duties of up to 99% on the type of seamless pipe that is to be manufactured by Tianjin Pipe—a reprisal prompted by the United Steelworkers union. The Chinese company, the world's largest maker of steel pipe, had said it could not afford to export to the U.S. if tariffs were over 20%. Now its pipe will be made in America. "It's just another reason they have to have a U.S.-based production facility," says Johnston.

Even without tariffs, Tianjin had been looking to expand— as are many Chinese companies once they reach about $100 million in annual sales. "Chinese companies, as they get bigger, have to start thinking about their global positioning," says Clarence Kwan, who runs the Chinese Services Group

AT GREENFIELD INDUSTRIES, PURCHASING MANAGER WENDY WEN, A U.S. PERMANENT RESIDENT FROM CHINA, CONFERS WITH MACHINE OPERATOR MARVIN EARLE.

at Deloitte, which advises Chinese companies on doing business in the U.S. Officially the Chinese government has given approval to over 1,200 Chinese investments in the U.S., but that number is considered low because it doesn't count those made via Hong Kong—where many Chinese companies earn equity capital from being publicly traded—or tax havens like the Virgin Islands, where Chinese investment may stop first before flowing to the U.S. Plus, investments below $100 million don't need Beijing's nod and may be approved at the local level.

Chinese companies see America as more than a manufacturing center. So far this year they have announced plans to build a wind-energy turbine plant and wind farm in Nevada that will create 1,000 American jobs; purchased the 400-employee Los Angeles Marriott Downtown out of foreclosure; and acquired a shuttered shopping center in Milwaukee, with plans to turn it into a mega-mall for 200 Chinese retailers. In some cases Chinese companies are resuscitating American outfits that had been left for dead. About 70 miles west of Spartanburg, near the Georgia border, past signs reading "24-hour fried chicken," another Chinese company is hiring engineers—metallurgical and mechanical, some from nearby Clemson University. In June 2009, Top-Eastern Group, a tool manufacturer based in China's coastal city of Dalian, acquired a factory here along with three other facilities from Kennametal, one of America's largest machine-tool makers, after the U.S. company, based in Latrobe, Pa., reported a $137 million loss (citing a slowdown in industrial activity) in the quarter before the sale.

This plant, in Seneca, S.C., makes drill bits. And in the months since his purchase of it for $29 million, Top-Eastern founder Jeff Chee has invested another $10 million to upgrade machinery, built a $3 million logistics center, brought back Kennametal's furloughed workers, hired 120 more, and now has his 260-employee plant working overtime filling orders for the Cleveland Twist Drills, Chicago Latrobe, Putnam, and Bassett brands he acquired. He brought back the company's old name, which was Greenfield Industries before Kennametal acquired it in 1997, and emblazoned it on a sign out front.

General Electric's former CEO, Jack Welch, he volunteers, is his inspiration. "I've read a lot of books, and I learned a lot from him," Chee says in broken English amid the sharp smell of grinding steel. "One person can change a lot." As one of China's self-made entrepreneurs, who started Top-Eastern in 1994 with just $500, Chee now has worldwide sales of more than $120 million, 4,000 employees, and factories in Germany and Brazil. He visits the South Carolina plant monthly to make sure all is proceeding as planned, and employs American managers to run it in his absence rather than bring over Chinese. "There's good, experienced people and good know-how already here," he says.

How can he make a drill bit factory profitable where Kennametal had struggled? By increasing productivity with new equipment and cutting costs, he says. Plus, Chee forges his own steel, and he owns the mines back in China for two of its more expensive components, tungsten and molybdenum. The fact that he can source from himself means he keeps the margins—and now his tools are officially made in the U.S. The cost of making those products is much higher than in China, he says, "but the problem is customers just accept 'made in U.S.A.' products, so I have no choice. Lots of customers here have government contracts that have 'made in U.S.A.' requirements."

And how do the employees feel about having a Chinese entrepreneur come to their rescue? "Just because it's a Chinese owner, they don't really care," says Scott Henderson, a 47-year-old manufacturing manager who had been furloughed one week a month along with his workers before Chee bought the factory. "They're all happy to be working 40 hours a week." They also have the opportunity for overtime, and a third, graveyard shift has been added to serve a nearly 40% rise in orders. "I feel great about it," says Sam Marcengill, a 24-year-old technician at the plant. Last year he was laid off for six

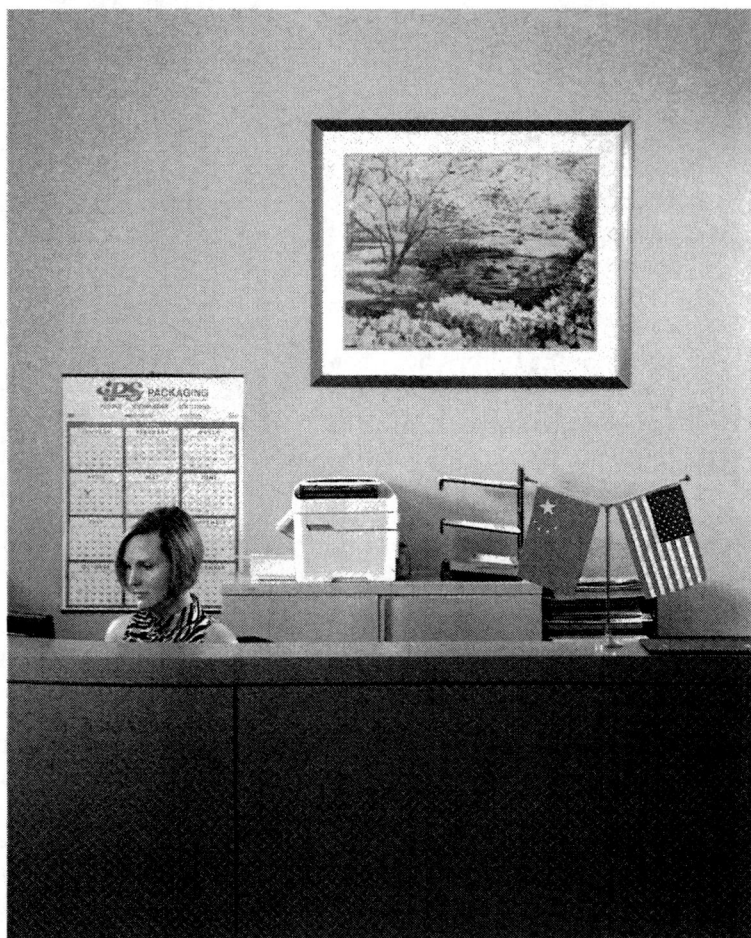

WORKING FOR THE CHINESE: EMPLOYEE TERESA JUSTICE IN HAIER'S CAMDEN LOBBY

months before Chee's purchase gave him his job back. Now he's on overtime, 48 hours a week. "The work's a lot more steady. It's better. Personally I'm a lot better off. It's a great thing."

NEVER MIND THE HICCUPS Chinese companies experienced when they tried to enter the U.S. before. In 2005, Washington famously blocked China's National Offshore Oil Corp. (CNOOC) from buying Unocal, and Chinese appliance maker Haier failed to acquire Maytag. Now, like the Japanese in the 1980s—when U.S. trade frictions combined with Japan's boom blossomed into Honda and Toyota manufacturing plants—the Chinese are here to stay. Their presence initially made some folks uneasy. A few years ago a caller to *The Rush Limbaugh Show* complained that as he was driving past the

> Rather than retool its factories in China, appliance maker Haier makes high-end refrigerators at its Camden, S.C., factory and ships them home to China for a small but growing number of wealthy consumers.

Haier plant in Camden, the Chinese flag was flying higher than the American flag and the South Carolina state flag out front. It was an easy mistake to make by anyone looking at the three equal-height flagpoles from an angle.

Conservative media joined in and called for protests, and the public rang the factory to complain. The Chinese executives at Haier had no idea flags were such a big deal, and it became their bugaboo. The complaints continued until about a year and a half ago when Haier America factory president Joseph Sexton, who was new to the job, decided to fix it. He had two of the poles lowered so that the U.S. flag looks highest from all angles.

It took Haier some time to work through the issues of being a Chinese employer in a small, historic Southern town (pop. 6,682) lined with stately antebellum houses and home to two Revolutionary War battlefields. "Having a Chinese manager didn't work. That's why they took all the Chinese managers out of here," says Haier's human resources director, Gerald Reeves, who was one of the first hired by Haier and guided the Chinese through the realities of American-style personnel management—including convincing them that they needed to offer health insurance. He once even asked John Ling, South Carolina's man in Shanghai, to fly home from China to talk to a manager who was arousing employee resentment by publicly embarrassing the workers, Chinese-style, for their mistakes.

Now the only way to know you're in a Chinese factory is by looking up at the large Chinese flag hanging from the rafters—alongside an American one, of course—and by the very Chinese motivational slogans on the walls: SPIRIT OF ENTREPRENEURSHIP—STRIVE FOR A CLEARLY DEFINED OBJECTIVE AND MAKE THE IMPOSSIBLE POSSIBLE WITHOUT AN EXCUSE reads the banner over the refrigerator testing line. And if you come in February, Sexton organizes a Chinese New Year party with food and outdoor firecrackers.

What is perhaps most startling about the Haier factory is that it is actually shipping goods back to China. Best known for its mini-fridges for dorm rooms and studio apartments, Haier's U.S. plant also makes large units, good for supersized American McMansions but too large for a typical Chinese household. Now a growing number of wealthy people in China want to supersize too, so Haier has realized it can ship a small number, maybe 4,000 a year, of its highest-end refrigerators home and sell them for $2,600 apiece—more than China's average annual income of around $2,000. (Haier also ships U.S.-made refrigerators to India, Australia, Mexico, and Canada.) There aren't enough wealthy customers yet to make it worthwhile retooling any of the 29 Haier factories in China, but the nearby deepwater port in Charleston, S.C., makes export easy enough. "There are folks in China who want high-end products," says Haier America factory president Joseph Sexton. "China is a much different place than people think."

CHINESE NEWCOMERS would do well to learn from Haier's missteps as well as its great strides. "They're coming with little experience into a highly sophisticated market, and they are bound to make mistakes," says Karl Sauvant, executive director of the Vale Columbia Center on Sustainable International Investment at Columbia University and a law lecturer there, who in February published an edited volume titled *Investing in the United States: Is the U.S. Ready for FDI From China?*

"This is the thing the Japanese did fairly successfully: You have to be a good corporate citizen, source locally, contribute to causes and charities in the local community, and be familiar with how to navigate the corridors of Washington," says Sauvant. "And in key managerial positions you should have Americans." Legal questions, such as whether Chinese companies operating in America would be subject in U.S. courts to the Foreign Corrupt Practices Act for business practices in, say, India or elsewhere have yet to be tested, he says. And then there's the issue of the local sensitivities exhibited in the Haier flag-flying incident.

Unlike Japan, China is no U.S. military ally—despite President Obama's naming China a "strategic partner," instead of the "strategic competitor" label it had under the Bush administration. Politically it remains a communist country, despite its capitalist economy. There's obviously more to overcome.

Chinese investors say they don't care too much about politics, but hope their entry into the U.S. can be a positive force. "This will definitely help U.S.-China relations," remarks Li, the manager of the print-cylinder factory Yuncheng, as he guides me on a tour. "Increasing communication makes the two sides closer." Even if it doesn't, business is business. "Good products are borderless," he notes. And there's always a Chinese proverb to cite: "It takes 10 years to make a sword," says Li. In other words, keep at it till you get it right, and the outcome will be strong and lasting. And perhaps transform into the plowshare that sows a mutually beneficial harvest for America and China both. ◼

LightSaver says
it's cheaper to produce
in San Diego

Pigtronix's cash flow has
improved since
it returned to New York

Made in China?
Not Worth the Trouble

▶ Put off by piracy and quality problems, small companies are returning to U.S. factories

▶ "People are trying to come back. Everyone knows they're miserable"

When Sonja Zozula and Jerry Anderson founded **LightSaver Technologies** in 2009, everyone told them they should make their emergency lights for homeowners in China. After two years of outsourcing to factories there, last winter they shifted production to Carlsbad, Calif., about 30 miles from their home in San Clemente. "It's probably 30 percent cheaper to manufacture in China," Anderson says. "But factor in shipping and all the other B.S. that you have to endure. It's a question of, 'How do I value my time at three in the morning when I have to talk to China?' "

As costs in China rise and owners look closely at the hassles of using factories 12,000 miles and 12 time zones away, many small companies have decided manufacturing overseas isn't worth the trouble. American production is "increasingly competitive," says Harry Moser, founder of the Reshoring Initiative, a group of companies and trade associations trying to bring factory jobs back to the U.S. "In the last two years there's been a dramatic increase" in the amount of work returning.

An April poll of 259 U.S. contract manufacturers—which make goods for other companies—showed 40 percent of respondents benefited this year from work previously done abroad. And nearly 80 percent were optimistic about 2012 sales and profits, according to the survey by MFG.com, a website that helps companies find manufacturers. "A decade ago you just went to China. You didn't even look locally," says Ted Fogliani,

"A decade ago you just went to China. You didn't even look locally"
——Ted Fogliani, CEO, Outsource Manufacturing

ⓕ Enterprise

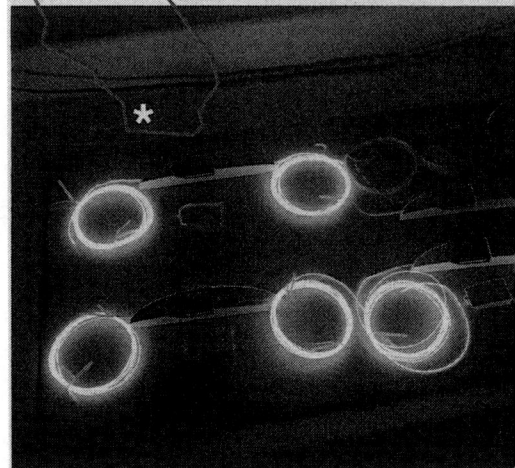

chief executive officer of **Outsource Manufacturing**, the San Diego company working with LightSaver. "Now people are trying to come back. Everyone knows they're miserable."

For LightSaver, the decision was simple. Neither of the founders has ever been to China, which made communicating with manufacturers difficult. Components that were shipped from the U.S. sometimes got stuck in customs for weeks. And Anderson had to spend hours on the phone to explain tweaks in the product. "If we have an issue in manufacturing, in America we can walk down to the plant floor," Anderson says. "We can't do that in China." Anderson says manufacturing in the U.S. is probably 2 percent to 5 percent cheaper once he takes into account the time and trouble of outsourcing production overseas.

Dana Olson makes a living convincing small manufacturers that it pays to produce domestically. About 10 percent of the roughly 60 companies that his Minneapolis firm, **Ecodev**, has worked with have moved manufacturing to the U.S. or decided not to send it overseas, and another half-dozen are considering similar moves. "There's a growing sense, with the economy doing what it's doing, of U.S. companies wanting to produce in the United States," says Olson. "It's very important to them to have 'Made in the U.S.A.' on their label again."

Since 2008, **Ultra Green Packaging**, one of Olson's clients, has used manufacturers in China to make compostable plates and containers from wheat straw and other organic materials. By yearend, Ultra Green expects to start producing the bulk of its wares at a plant in North Dakota to cut freight costs and protect its intellectual property. "They're infamous over there for knocking [products] off," says Phil Levin, chairman of the 10-employee company. "All anybody needs to do is find a different factory and make a mold."

For **Unilife**, moving production to the U.S. helped it win regulatory approval for an important product: pre-filled syringes with retractable needles that make it almost impossible for medical personnel to accidentally stick themselves. Although the company used Chinese manufacturers for earlier offerings, syringes preloaded with medications are subject to stringent U.S. Food and Drug Administration rules. So in March 2011, Unilife began making its syringes at a $32 million, 165,000-square-foot plant it built in York, Pa. "The very thing in the U.S.A. that oftentimes we complain about—the complexity of the rules and the regulations—works for us," says CEO Alan Shortall. "FDA compliance is the main reason we're here."

Even with strong Mandarin skills, Brian Bethke grew frustrated with manufacturing in China. The co-founder of **Pigtronix**, which makes pedals that create electric guitar sound effects, discovered that he couldn't adequately monitor quality at Chinese factories. The original idea for the company was to develop products in the U.S. and make them in China, where Bethke was living. But after several years of finding technical glitches in as many as 30 percent of pedals, the company decided to move production to Port Jefferson, N.Y. At its small factory in a Long Island office park, the company can run multiple tests on its products and even has a guitarist play each of the 500 to 1,000 pedals it sells monthly before they're packed and shipped.

Pigtronix's move back, completed three years ago, has helped improve cash flow. While manufacturing pedals in the U.S. can cost anywhere from three to six times as much as it does in China, Bethke says Pigtronix benefits from not having capital tied up in products that spend weeks in transit and then pile up in inventory. "In China, you have high minimum quantities you have to order, so you're building a couple thousand of every guitar pedal," Bethke says. "Your carrying costs start to get huge." Today the company only makes those pedals it's confident it can sell quickly.

While goods for U.S. consumers are less likely to be made in China these days, overseas production may still make sense for companies that plan to target foreign markets. "What we're seeing is regionalization, buying stuff from manufacturers in the region where you're going to sell it," says Michael Degen, CEO of **Nortech Systems**, a contract manufacturer based in Wayzata, Minn., that has eight factories in the U.S. and one in Mexico. "It's very noticeable. ... We've seen movement in terms of manufacturing in country for country." —*David Rocks and Nick Leiber*

The bottom line *Although manufacturing in China can cost a third what it does in American factories, small companies are bringing production back to the U.S.*

> "In China you have high minimum quantities ... so you're building a couple thousand of every guitar pedal"
> —Brian Bethke

U.S. production lets Pigtronix more extensively test its guitar pedals

50

MADE IN CHINA

MADE IN ETHIOPIA

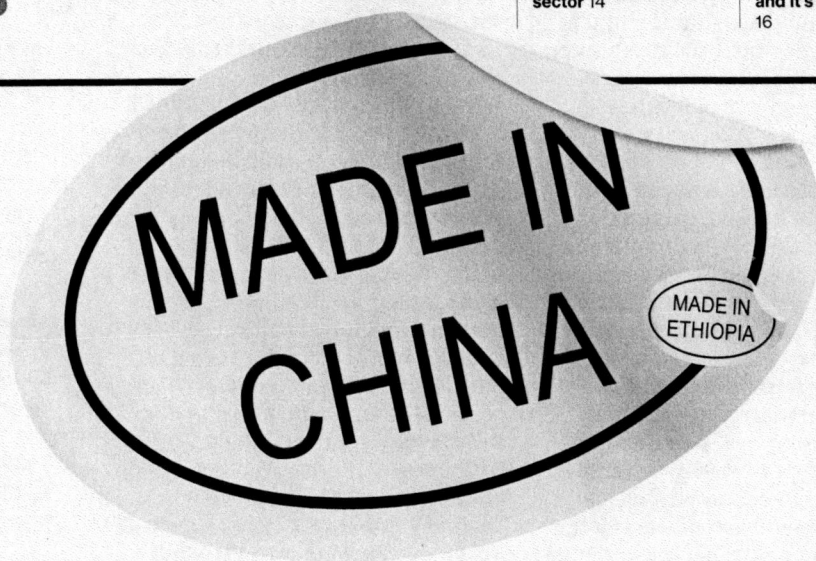

Turning Ethiopia Into China's China

▶ Ethiopians make $40 a month stitching shoes. Their Chinese counterparts make more than $400

▶ "I pay my rent and I can look after myself. It's transformed my life"

Ethiopian workers walking through the parking lot of **Huajian Shoes'** factory outside Addis Ababa in June chose the wrong day to leave their shirts untucked. The company's president, just arrived from China, spotted them through the window, sprang up, and ran outside. Zhang Huarong, a former People's Liberation Army soldier, harangued them in Chinese, tugging at one man's polo shirt and forcing another worker's into his pants. Amazed, the workers stood silent until the eruption subsided.

Zhang's factory is part of the next wave of China's investment in Africa. It started with infrastructure, especially the kind that helped the Chinese extract African oil, copper, and other raw materials to fuel China's industrial complex. Now China is getting too expensive to do the low-tech work it's known for. African nations such as Ethiopia, Kenya, Lesotho,

Rwanda, Senegal, and Tanzania want their share of the 80 million manufacturing jobs that China is expected to export, according to Justin Lin Yifu, a former World Bank chief economist who teaches economics at Peking University. Weaker consumer spending in the U.S. and Europe has prompted global retailers to speed up their search for lower-cost producers.

Shaping up employees is one part of Zhang's quest to squeeze more profit out of Huajian's factory, where wages of about $40 a month are less than 10 percent of what comparable Chinese workers may make. Just as companies discovered with China when they began manufacturing there in the 1980s, Ethiopia's workforce is untrained, its power supply is intermittent, and its roads are so bad that trips can take six times as long as they should. "Ethiopia is exactly like China 30 years ago," says Zhang, 55, who quit the military in 1982

to make shoes from his home in Jiangxi province with three sewing machines. He now supplies such well-known brands as **Nine West** and **Guess**.

Almost three years after Zhang began his Ethiopian adventure at the invitation of the late Prime Minister Meles Zenawi, he says he's unhappy with profits at the plant, frustrated by "widespread inefficiency" in the local bureaucracy, and struggling to raise productivity from a level that he says is about a third of China's. Transportation and logistics that cost as much as four times what they do in China are prompting Huajian to set up its own trucking company, according to Zhang. That will free Huajian from using the inefficient local haulers, but it can't fix the roads. It takes two hours to drive 30 kilometers (18 miles) to the Huajian factory from the capital along the main artery. Oil tankers and trucks stream along the bumpy, potholed, and at ▶

11

147

times unpaved road. Goats, donkeys, and cows wander along, occasionally straying into bumper-to-bumper traffic. Minibuses and dented taxis, mostly blue Ladas from Ethiopia's past as a Soviet ally, weave through oncoming traffic, coughing exhaust.

In a country where 80 percent of the labor force is in agriculture, manufacturers don't have to worry about finding new workers. The population of about 96 million is Africa's second-largest after Nigeria's. Cheap labor and electricity and a government striving to draw foreign investment make Ethiopia more attractive than many other African nations, says Deborah Brautigam, author of *The Dragon's Gift: The Real Story of China in Africa* and a professor of international development and comparative politics at Johns Hopkins University. "They are trying to establish conditions for a transformation," Brautigam says. "It could become the China of Africa." Foreign direct investment in Ethiopia jumped 3.4 times to $953 million last year from the year before, according to estimates by the United Nations Conference on Trade and Development.

Huajian's 3,500 Ethiopian workers produced 2 million pairs of shoes last year. Located in one of the country's first industrial zones—which offer better infrastructure and tax exemptions—the factory began operating in January 2012. It became profitable its first year and now makes $100,000 to $200,000 a month, Zhang says—an insufficient return that he claims will rise as workers become better trained. Beneath bright fluorescent lights and amid the drone of machines, workers cut, glue, stitch, and sew **Marc Fisher**

leather boots destined for the U.S. market. Supervisors monitor quotas on whiteboards, giving small cash rewards to winning teams and criticizing those who fall short.

Zhang spends about half his time in Ethiopia, he says. During his June visit to the Huajian plant he spoke to about 200 uniformed supervisors, a mixture of Ethiopians and Chinese, assembled in the parking lot. He berated supervisors for their inefficiency, then praised them for their loyalty, his words translated into Amharic, Ethiopia's national language, and Oromo, the local language. He ordered staff to march on the spot as they all chanted together in Chinese. Then they recited slogans: "Unite as one." "Improvement together." "Civilized and efficient." They sang the *Song of Huajian*, which urged "we Huajian people" to move forward, hold the banner of Huajian high, and "keep our business forever." Chinese supervisors led the song, while their Ethiopian colleagues stumbled over some words.

Later, Zhang explained why he can't be as tough as he'd like. "Here the management cannot be too strong as there will be a problem with the culture," he said through a translator. "On one hand we have to have strict requirements, on the other hand we have to take care of them. They may be poor, but we have to respect their dignity."

Five workers interviewed at the factory describe strict standards, with rewards for good work and pay docked for ruined shoes. Taddelech Teshome, 24, says her day starts at 7:20 a.m. after her Chinese employers provide workers with a breakfast of bread and tea. When her morning

Frontier Manufacturing
Cheap labor makes Ethiopia attractive for offshoring, but poor infrastructure is a drawback

Foreign direct investment in Ethiopia

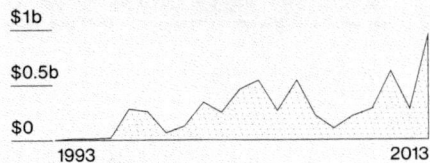

2013 labor cost per hour, shoe manufacturing

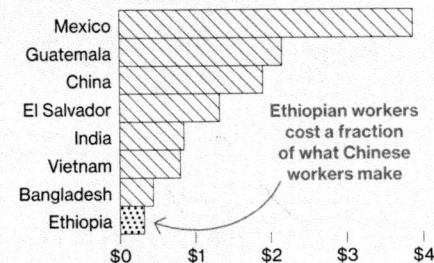

Ethiopian workers cost a fraction of what Chinese workers make

Ethiopia's percentile rank, World Bank Ease of Doing Business Index

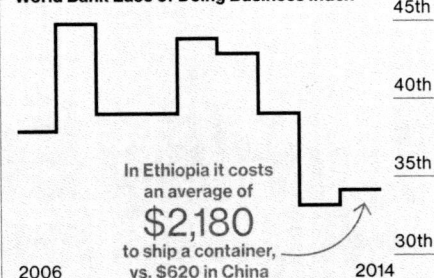

In Ethiopia it costs an average of
$2,180
to ship a container, vs. $620 in China

shift ferrying shoes from the factory floor to the warehouse is over, she gets fed the national staple sour bread for lunch, then resumes work until 5:15. After that a Huajian bus takes her to nearby Debre Zeit, where she rents a room with her sister for $18 a month. Taddelech came to work at Huajian just over a year ago from her home 165 kilometers away in the Arsi region after her sister started work at the factory. "The work is good because I pay my rent and I can look after myself," she says. "It's transformed my life."

Huajian's Zhang wants to increase its workforce in Ethiopia to as many as 50,000 within eight years. A model of a planned new plant at the edge of Addis Ababa is displayed at the factory. It shows a 341-acre complex, partly financed by more than $300 million from Huajian, that will include apartments for workers, a wooded area, and a technical university.

In the parking lot, after supervisors had sung the company song, Zhang dismissed the Ethiopians but continued to rail against the Chinese

A banner reads "100% cooperation"

Winning teams get cash awards for beating goals

Addis Ababa

2m
pairs of shoes a year

managers. To make his points he thrust a broomstick toward them repeatedly. He finally left the stage, laughing and raising his fist in triumph.
—*Kevin Hamlin, Ilya Gridneff, and William Davison*

The bottom line Ethiopians and other Africans want to attract the low-cost manufacturing that's becoming too expensive to do in China.

Factory Jobs Are Gone. Get Over It

▶ Politicians think creating millions of high-tech manufacturing jobs is the answer. It isn't

▶ "What's with the political fetish for manufacturing? Are factories really so awesome?"

In the runup to this year's State of the Union address, President Obama has been busy trying to fulfill pledges from last year's. He went to Raleigh, N.C., to announce it would become a high-tech manufacturing hub to ensure that the U.S. attracts "the good, high-tech manufacturing jobs that a growing middle class requires."

The president is one of many politicians of both parties as well as pundits who think manufacturing deserves special treatment. But this factory obsession is based on flawed economics. As the Brookings Institute economist Justin Wolfers asked recently, "What's with the political fetish for manufacturing? Are factories really so awesome?"

Not really—at least not for the U.S. in 2014. Any attempt to draw lessons from the 1950s, when many a high school-educated (white, male) person got a job in a factory and joined the middle class, doesn't account for the changes in the U.S. and global economy since the middle of the last century. While it's smart to focus on creating more stable, remunerative jobs, few of them are likely to come from manufacturing.

In 1953 manufacturing accounted for 28 percent of U.S. gross domestic product, according to the U.S. Bureau of Economic Analysis. By 1980 that had dropped to 20 percent, and it reached 12 percent in 2012. Over that time, U.S. GDP increased from $2.6 trillion to $15.5 trillion, which means that absolute manufacturing output more than tripled in 60 years. Those goods were produced by fewer people. According to the Bureau of Labor Statistics, the number of employees in manufacturing was 16 million in 1953 (about a third of total nonfarm employment), 19 million in 1980 (about a fifth of nonfarm employment), and 12 million in 2012 (about a tenth of nonfarm employment).

Service industries—hotels, hospitals,

151

media, and accounting—have taken up the slack. Even much of the value generated by U.S. manufacturing involves service work—about a third of the total. More than half of all people still employed in the U.S. manufacturing sector work in such services as management, technical support, and sales.

Over the past 30 years, manufacturers have spent more on labor-saving machinery and hired fewer but more skilled workers to run it. From 1980 to 2012 across the whole economy, output per hour worked increased 85 percent. In manufacturing output per hour climbed 189 percent. The proportion of manufacturing workers with some college education has increased from one-fifth to one-half since 1969.

Across richer countries, growth has been accompanied by a decline in the number of manufacturing jobs and the rise of service jobs. Some of the richer countries, such as France, that have seen the slowest decline in manufacturing's share of employment have actually suffered some of the most sluggish growth. In the U.S., Eric Fisher of the Federal Reserve Bank of Cleveland suggests that those states where the shift from manufacturing employment has been the most rapid are those where wages have climbed the fastest.

Developing countries have taken over much of the low-skilled, low-capital production once done in the U.S.: Consider the garment industry or tire manufacturing. Such low-tech work is even more mind-numbing and poorly paid than it was when the work was done in the U.S. through the 1970s. Many of the workers killed in the recent Rana Plaza garment factory collapse in Bangladesh earned just $3 a day. Some politicians have regretted the loss of similar jobs in the U.S. The question is: Do we want such jobs here now?

Shutting the borders to low-cost imports in the hope of reviving low-skilled manufacturing employment at home would likely kill jobs, not save them. When Obama in 2009 slapped tariffs on Chinese tire imports that had flooded the U.S. market, he temporarily preserved 1,200 jobs in the tire industry as supplies tightened and U.S. tiremakers helped make up the difference. But the impact on the U.S. labor force as a whole was negative. Gary Hufbauer

of the Peterson Institute estimates that the cost to U.S. consumers was more than $1 billion. As tires got more expensive, tire buyers had less money to spend on other goods. The effect of that drop in demand on retail employment was a loss of 3,731 jobs, three times the number preserved in the tire industry.

Champions of reindustrialization often cite the cluster effect as a reason to back manufacturing. If a company builds a factory, then other factories will pop up in the same place to benefit from the industry knowledge and experienced workforce found there. If that theory were strongly supported by the facts, that might be a reason for governments to subsidize early investors in building the first plant somewhere. But work by economists Glenn Ellison of Massachusetts Institute of Technology and Ed Glaeser of Harvard suggests that while "slight concentration is widespread" among industries, "extreme concentration" is the exception. High levels of concentration aren't a particularly common or unique feature of high-tech manufacturers (although high-tech service industries cluster in Silicon Valley). In manufacturing, the two economists suggest clustering is most evident in fur, wines, hosiery, oil and gas, carpets and rugs, sawmills, and costume jewelry.

189%

Gain in manufacturing output per hour from 1980 to 2012 in the U.S.

Obama should foster high-tech manufacturing. But a state-of-the-art chipmaker is not a major job creator. That leaves the service industries to generate jobs and the government to retrain workers. According to MIT's David Autor, for every dollar spent by the federal government on retraining workers and helping them find jobs after they lost theirs to trade competition, the U.S. spends about $400 on Social Security and disability payments for those who exit the workforce rather than seek new work. Retraining programs have a mixed record, but improvement is possible. The German government has had considerable success in this area.

Germany also embraces stronger

union rights and collective bargaining, which help raise wages across industries. In the U.S., minimum-wage hikes are one obvious tool to increase the number of people earning middle-class incomes. Another approach might be rebalancing taxes on employers, wages, and investment. Income taxes are higher than capital gains taxes that favor investors.

The crisis of unemployment and inequality demands a serious response. It is not a problem that a few high-tech manufacturing jobs can fix—however fancy the hubs are. —*Charles Kenny*

The bottom line Manufacturing makes up 12 percent of the U.S. economy and employs only 10 percent of the nonfarm workforce.

13

Big Enough to Drive a Government Contract Through

▶ Companies that register abroad to avoid taxes get federal dollars

▶ "There is no reason the U.S....should reward tax runaways"

Ingersoll-Rand is a great American success story. Founded 143 years ago by a Connecticut farmer who invented a steam-powered rock drill, the company made tools that carved out the Panama Canal and shaped Mt. Rushmore. More recently it's become a leader in energy-efficient air conditioners: Ingersoll-Rand's Trane unit has won more than $350 million worth of federal contracts to retrofit government buildings and military facilities as part of a U.S. Department of Energy conservation program. When President Obama announced an expansion of the initiative in May, Chief Executive Officer Michael Lamach was a guest. Obama offered "thanks to all the companies who are doing the great work."

What Obama didn't mention is that Ingersoll-Rand is no longer a U.S. company, at least not on paper. In 2001, amid a wave of corporate expatriations, it shifted its legal address to Bermuda, cutting its tax bill in half. Other companies that did business with the U.S. government, including **Tyco International** and **Accenture**, had also adopted Bermuda addresses, prompting members of Congress to say they'd punish corporations that pull up stakes. "There is no reason the U.S. government should reward tax runaways with lucrative government contracts," fumed Democratic Senator Harry Reid of Nevada, whose father wielded an Ingersoll-Rand jackhammer as a hard-rock miner. Republican Charles Grassley of Iowa called for an end to "fat government contracts" for such companies.

In the years since, Congress has passed several pieces of legislation to limit or ban these contracts. Yet the law is riddled with exemptions that allow the offshore companies to legally bid for government work. A company that avoids domestic taxes by shifting its address abroad can still be eligible for federal contracts if it has "substantial business" in its new home–thus nominally demonstrating its move wasn't solely for tax reasons. The rules also don't cover U.S. companies that acquire foreign addresses, and tax benefits, through takeovers of overseas competitors.

More than 40 U.S. companies have reincorporated in tax havens, a strategy known as inversion, 11 of them since 2012. Seven more are in the process ▶

25

153

Medtronic

Seeking Greener Pastures
Since 1982 more than 40 companies have moved abroad

□ = one company

McDermott Intl. adopts the address of a Panamanian subsidiary as its legal headquarters

Chicago Bridge & Iron reincorporates in The Hague

Ingersoll-Rand joins a wave of corporate inversions

Medtronic announces plans to become Irish

CBI

IR Ingersoll-Rand

1982　1985　　1990　　1995　　2000　　2005　　2010　　2014

◄ of doing so. Last month, **Medtronic**, a Minnesota medical device maker whose customers include the Veterans Affairs Department, announced plans to become Irish. The government awards more than a dozen companies that have left the U.S. contracts worth more than $1 billion a year.

The law defining inverted companies doesn't cover Accenture, a company with Chicago roots that incorporated in Bermuda in 2001. The same is true for **Chicago Bridge & Iron**, a Texas-run corporation with a Dutch address. According to public records, Accenture earned $960 million from federal contracts in 2013, and CB&I made $734 million. A spokesman for CB&I says the company complies with the law. Accenture spokesman James McAvoy says the company is eligible for government contracts because it was never incorporated in the U.S. When it first separated from Chicago-based Arthur Andersen in 1989, it was set up as a network of separate partnerships around the world overseen by a Swiss entity. For that reason the U.S. General Accounting Office concluded in 2002 that Accenture wasn't an inverted company. McAvoy says a 2012 review by the U.S. Department of Homeland Security confirmed that Accenture, now based in Ireland, isn't subject to the ban.

In its brochures, Ingersoll-Rand touts its projects for the Army and Navy. Yet for years it told shareholders and cus-

$1ᵇ

Amount U.S. companies with overseas addresses earn from federal contracts annually

tomers in public filings that it might be subject to the law. Recently the company conducted an "exhaustive legal analysis" and decided it's not covered, says spokeswoman Misty Zelent. The government relies on contractors to police themselves. Zelent says the company works closely with government contracting officials to ensure compliance with a "complex area of the law." Its contracts show just how complex it is and how many legal ways there are around the rules.

For the most part, Ingersoll-Rand has been able to sidestep the question of whether it's inverted. Three separate gaps have allowed the company to continue doing business with the U.S. government. First, the ban applies only to contracts funded by annual congressional appropriations. Ingersoll-Rand sought contracts paid for with other money, including a contract to maintain equipment at military-base supermarkets. Signed in March 2010, it's funded with a 5 percent surcharge on purchases at the stores.

Second, Ingersoll-Rand was awarded contracts during periods when the rules had lapsed. Congress's first government-wide contracting ban expired in September 2008 and didn't go back into effect until the following March, when Congress passed a funding bill for the 2009 fiscal year. In the interim, Energy Department officials added the company to a list of contractors authorized to pursue up to $5 billion in government work over as many as 10 years. Ingersoll-Rand has been awarded two projects under authority of the DOE deal.

Third, some contracts allow Ingersoll-Rand to bid on new projects under what spokeswoman Zelent calls a "grandfather clause," without running afoul of the law. Thus Ingersoll-Rand has bid for and won energy-saving projects under the authority of Energy Department contracts signed years earlier.

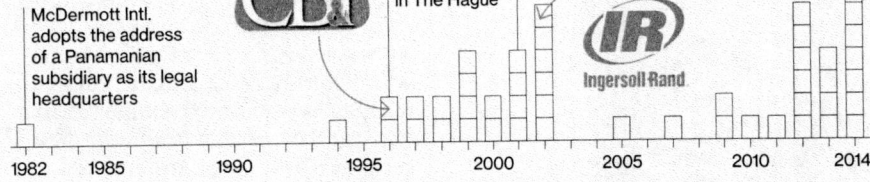

The biggest was a $124 million project at Naval Air Station Oceana in Virginia Beach, Va., the East Coast home of the Navy's fighter jets. In August 2009, Ingersoll-Rand's Trane unit was hired to replace an old steam plant with a more efficient heating system, with the cost covered by the Navy's energy savings. It was Trane's third such job at the base. The project came under the authority of a Trane contract from 1999. "The Navy had no legal basis for not considering Trane's proposal, which the Navy found to be the best value to the government," a Navy spokesman said in an e-mail.

Democratic Representative Rosa DeLauro of Connecticut, who was instrumental in passing the first federal contracting ban in 2002, says she's working on a bill to expand the prohibition to cover more corporate runaways, including most of the current crop. "We should not be rewarding them," DeLauro says. "Let's give it to the companies that stay here, employ people here, and pay their taxes here." —*Zachary R. Mider*

The bottom line U.S. companies that head overseas to avoid taxes are still able to win lucrative government contracts.

How to Stop Companies From Deserting America Before It's Too Late

CORPORATE INVERSIONS HEAT UP U.S. companies are heading offshore to save taxes. This year, which is barely half over, is likely to set a record for inversions.

12 companies ... *Number of companies heading offshore* ... 2010 2011 2012 2013 2014 ... 14*

By
Allan Sloan

asloan@fortunemail.com

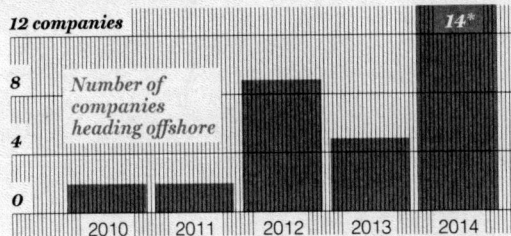

SOMETIMES EVEN JOURNALISTS GET IT RIGHT. My essay about companies incorporating overseas to dodge taxes, "Positively Un-American," featured in our last issue, clearly struck a nerve. Since its publication, these corporate "inversions"—a euphemism for "desertions"—have taken on a life of their own.

Barely a day seems to pass without a corporation announcing that it plans to leave the U.S. to save taxes but wants to continue having its business, its employees, its directors, and especially its top executives benefit from our rule of law, democratic system, and the other great things that make America America. It just doesn't want to pay its fair share for those things. This makes me angry. Judging from the reaction I've gotten from readers, it makes a lot of other people angry too.

What to do? In an ideal world I would slap serious penalties on inverters that do business with the federal government, and require them to underbid genuinely U.S. competitors in order to get federal business. Medtronic and Walgreen, that means you.

But we have to deal with what we have, not with what I would like to have. So what should we do? For starters, we shouldn't make this political, because this is an American problem, not a Democratic or Republican problem.

Unfortunately, instead of using its influence quietly behind the scenes, the Obama administration has publicly entered the fray, via a July 15 letter from Treasury Secretary Jack Lew that invoked "economic patriotism" and urged Congress to do something about inversions. Pardon my skepticism, but the letter felt as if it was designed more to give President Obama populist talking points than to influence Congress to fix the problem.

Is there a solution? Glad you asked. The conventional wisdom is that we can't solve the inversion problem without reforming the corporate income tax, which is a mess on multiple levels: a high rate, a million loopholes, mind-boggling complexity.

But I think the conventional wisdom is wrong. We have an emergency, folks, with inversions begetting inversions. As I was writing this column, another one hit: Drugmaker AbbVie announced it would buy Britain's Shire for $54 billion. There's a critical mass of hedge funds, corporate raiders, consultants, investment bankers, and others who benefit from inversions, and you can bet they're all trying to make sure that nothing changes.

So I think we need to deal with the symptom—inversions—immediately. And with the cause—the tax system—later. The quick fix is legislation sponsored by Sen. Carl Levin (D-Mich.) and his brother, Rep. Sandy Levin (D-Mich.), that would stop inversions dead, at least for now. It would require companies that invert after May 8 of this year to do deals in which the foreign firm's shareholders own at least 50% of the combined company (current threshold: 20%). In addition, managers of the inverting firm would have to step down. Opponents say that this is futile: Despite two previous fixes, we're still awash in inversions, and stopping inversions will reduce any pressure to fix the tax system. There's something to those arguments—but I still think we need to stop inversions cold right now to keep our tax base from eroding beyond repair.

We need more than just lower rates to solve our problem. There will always be some place—Ireland, a Swiss canton like Zug, some other revenue-hungry country—that will undercut the U.S. rate, even if we slice it to 20% or 25% from the current 35%. So we have to be clever. Many of the proposals made by the unfortunately dead-on-arrival Tax Reform Act of 2014, pushed by Ways and Means Committee chair Rep. Dave Camp (R-Mich.), would have tightened loopholes, reduced rates, and made staying in the U.S. more attractive and deserting less so.

Let's not demonize each other, and let's not quibble about whether we need temporary or permanent fixes. We need both. First, Levin, with a two-year limit to keep the pressure on. Second, we need some modified Camp. Thanks to our toxic political environment, it won't be easy. But it can be done. With luck, in a few years I'll be writing a new essay: "Positively American."

Go to the tablet to hear Allan Sloan's most recent interview on the Marketplace Morning Report.

The New Trend? Reducing Stress in the Workplace— by Order of Management INSIGHTS

Causes of workplace stress

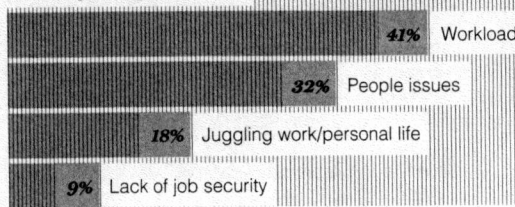

41%	Workload
32%	People issues
18%	Juggling work/personal life
9%	Lack of job security

OCCUPATIONAL HAZARDS Today's employees are much more likely to feel anxiety about having too much work than about the prospect of being out of a job.

By
Geoff Colvin

geoffrey_colvin@fortunemail.com

ELLNESS IS THE NEW GREEN," says Kirsten Ritchie, and as director of sustainable design at the big Gensler architecture and design firm, she would know. I had asked her about important trends in workplaces. For years employers and employees have been insisting on eco-friendly buildings, and they still do—it's just that now that's all taken for granted. People assume their building is good for the environment; now they want a building that's good for them. And that shift is part of a larger trend.

The wellness-at-work movement is accelerating in the U.S. at a time when employers generally are desperate to cut costs, and you have to wonder why. Employers on average will spend 15% more per employee on wellness programs this year than last, says a recent survey. More companies are offering free massages, gym memberships, nutrition counseling, meditation courses, and cash incentives to exercise. In addition, when they renovate an office building, the changes can be radical, says Ritchie—lots more natural light, high-rate air exchange, generous communal spaces.

Again, why all this now? Here's what seems to be happening. As work becomes increasingly cognitive, fast-changing, and uncertain, we're wearing people out in new ways. These are unforeseen effects of the friction-free economy. Back in the 1960s economists predicted that today's typical worker would be so astoundingly productive that he'd have a low-worry occupation and get to spend 13 weeks a year on vacation. Instead, if you're like most Americans, you're not even taking all the vacation leave you've been granted. And when you do go on vacation, are you really recharging your batteries or just draining them at a slightly slower rate by checking email a bit less frequently?

The government workweek statistics mean less every year. They're from the era when work was more sharply defined and the job stressors were largely physical. Today Cleveland Clinic offers wellness programs to employers and finds that physical issues—tobacco use, inactivity, poor nutrition—aren't the biggest problem. Rather, "stress support is our clients' No. 1 request," says Joe Sweet, an executive at Cleveland Clinic Wellness. "The workforce is experiencing increased stress, anxiety, and depression at all levels. Nobody is immune to the rapid technology advances, and all feel the pressure to stay ahead of them or lose."

A couple of high-profile suicides last year—of Zurich Insurance's CFO and Swisscom's CEO—raised the issue's visibility, especially because of hints that high stress played a role in both cases. The two incidents are more emotionally than statistically significant. But Wall Street firms have responded with a spate of new policies, for example, urging employees to take all their vacation and forbidding them to come to the office on Saturdays; "exceptions should be rare and defensible," says Citigroup's policy, and if you really want to come in on Saturday, you need a manager's approval.

Friction made the economy less efficient, but it protected people; sometimes it was simply not possible for you to be reached or to get information or participate in a meeting. In today's friction-free economy the old protections are gone, and employers and employees are struggling more than ever to figure out the new ones. "Some organizations are ramping up the promotion of their employee-assistance programs," reports Cleveland Clinic's Sweet, "in an effort to extinguish the supposed stigma of meeting with a clinical counselor to discuss anxiety, burnout, or depression."

My advice? Take all your vacation this year, though I know you probably won't. Don't check work email more than once a day on vacation, though I realize that's also impossible. Sign up for the mindfulness course at work. I know you don't have time, but remember that people who meditate have a saying that if you don't have time for a half-hour of meditation a day, you need an hour.

We've been replacing the physical stressors of work with mental and emotional stressors for many years. What's new is that we're hitting a resistance point. Many people seem to be reaching a limit. In an increasingly friction-free economy, mental and emotional health is the new wellness. ⬛

GRAPHIC SOURCE: COMPSYCH CORP.

Module 7

TECHNOLOGY LEADERSHIP

Kim Atkinson and John Medcof

7.1 INTRODUCTION

Leadership Is Essential in Technology Management. The business environment in which technology is managed is undergoing accelerating change driven by the forces of globalization, advances in information and communication technologies, rapidly evolving product and process technologies, the economic acceleration of some emerging economies (e.g. the BRIC countries) and world-wide cultural evolution. To meet these challenges firms with business models based upon technological innovation are developing, implementing and experimenting with new approaches to doing business such as open innovation, global technology networks, and venture capital financing. Although we are developing an improved understanding of how these new approaches work none of them can be successfully implemented without good leadership. Leadership is essential to developing a vision of where the organization is going and how innovations can contribute to that mission. Leadership is essential to communicating that vision to all the relevant stakeholders, including: employees, the organization's board, alliance partners, customers, suppliers, the financial community and governments; to name just some. Leadership is essential to engaging those stakeholders in activities intended to accomplish the mission so that all necessary contributions come to the table; be they the work of employees, financial backing, effective partner collaboration or a supportive regulatory climate. Without leadership there is no effective implementation. This module provides an overview of leadership in the effective management of technology.

A Definition of Leadership. There are many, many definitions of leadership and a very long book could be written about which is best[1]. However, the definition proposed by Elenkov and her colleagues has been found to be particularly useful for discussing the management of innovation and technology in a dynamic and uncertain business environment. Elenkov and her colleagues propose a three part definition of leadership as follows[2]:

> **Leadership is the process of:**
> **1. Forming a vision of the future**
> **2. Communicating it to others**
> **3. Engaging them in activities intended to achieve that vision**

The Importance of Vision and Non-subordinate "Followers". This definition has two distinguishing characteristics that make it particularly suitable for the discussion of technology and innovation management. First, most theories of leadership address only parts 2 and 3 of this definition; communication with others and the engagement of their efforts. These are essential to leadership but they will be futile efforts if they are directed towards accomplishing the wrong vision. A very crucial role for the leader is to find the right vision. Vision forming is a difficult and risky task, particularly when the business environment is highly dynamic and uncertain, as is

1

the case for many technology-driven businesses. Such firms do not have the luxury of an enduring vision that can be honed and adhered to over long years, as may have been the case for some businesses in the past. Leaders must always be adjusting the vision and communicating it to others, and they had better get it right. The second distinguishing characteristic of this definition is that it refers to the leadership of "others". It does not refer to "subordinates" or "followers" as many definitions do. As suggested above and explained more fully below, leadership in current technology management often involves people from outside the home department and even outside the home organization. Most such people cannot be considered subordinates in the conventional sense and might well resent being called followers.

7.1.1 Leadership and Management Distinguished

Leadership and Management are Different but Mutually Inter-dependent. It is important to distinguish leadership from management since leadership is particularly crucial during times of change and innovation, according to Kotter.[3] Kotter makes the distinction as follows. Management is mainly focused on the effective and efficient execution of day to day operations and how to resolve issues using established procedures. Successful managers are capable of bringing stability and consistency to the operational side of a company. Leadership, on the other hand, is mainly focused on guiding people through processes of change, the kinds of change we currently see in technology and innovation management. Kotter proposes that good leaders have the ability to adapt to changing circumstances, conceive initiatives to deal with new challenges and motivate others to also be flexible and constructively contribute to initiatives intended to deal with change. Table 1 summarizes some of the differences between management and leadership. They are complementary and mutually dependent upon each other. Effective management requires good leadership and effective leadership requires good management.

Table 1: Comparison of Leadership and Management

Management	Leadership
Planning and budgeting	Setting a direction
Organizing and staffing	Aligning people
Controlling and problem solving	Motivating and inspiring

Source: Kotter[4]

7.1.2 Primary Team and Expeditionary Leadership

Primary Team and Expeditionary Leadership. Another important consideration for leadership in technology management has to do with explicit and implicit understandings of the scope of leadership activities. The traditional view is that leaders are only responsible for leading their assigned departments, teams or other organizationally defined groupings.[5] This model of leadership may work well for traditional hierarchical organizations but has serious limitations for innovative organizations which create change in the marketplace and must respond to rapid change created by others. Such organizations, in order to be successful, usually adopt more horizontal structures that involve cross-functional teams and other methods that bring diverse talents to bear on organizational challenges.[6] They also organize in ways that permit rapid response to change. In such organizations leaders are expected to be active outside their home departments as well as inside. They are expected to be generally active in the broader organization as part of their contribution to organizational success. In these organizations it is helpful to distinguish between primary team leadership and expeditionary leadership[7]. **Primary team leadership** is exercised through interactions with people in the home unit whereas **expeditionary leadership** is exercised through interactions with people outside that unit. For example, expeditionary leadership might be exercised through leading a team of fellow managers assembled on an *ad hoc* basis to develop a response to proposed government legislation. Expeditionary leadership might involve people above, below and the same level as oneself. It might involve leading an informal team of alliance partners, government representatives and people from one's own organization. Figure 1 is a representation of leadership of both kinds, expeditionary and primary team.

Figure 1: Expeditionary and Primary Team Leadership

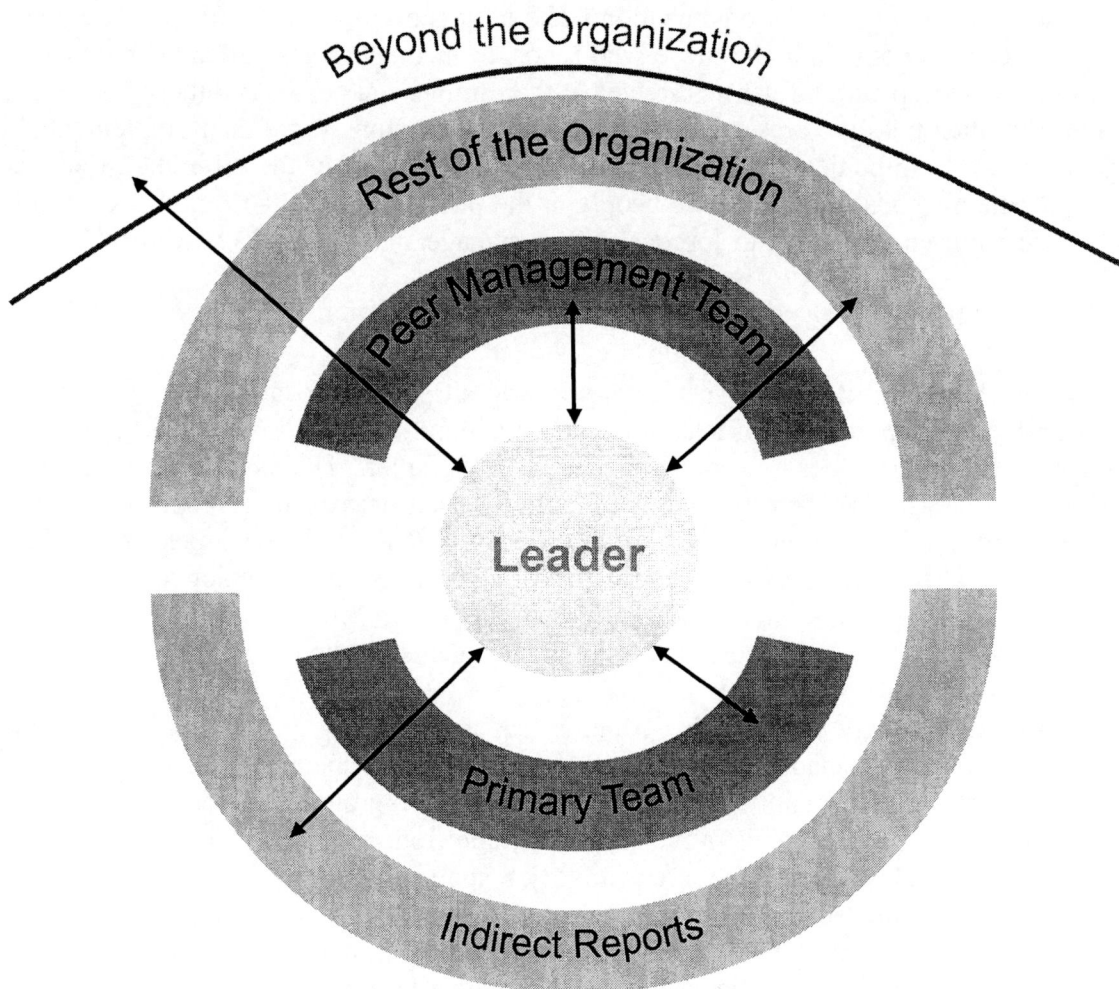

Source: Medcof[8]

The Growing Importance of Expeditionary Leadership. Research suggests that leadership outside the primary team and outside the home organization has become more important than it formally was. For example, the move to more inter-firm networking and alliances[9] suggests the need for more leaders who can effectively lead multi-organization and cross-functional teams. The literature on the increasing dynamism of organizational environments, and the associated need for more flexible organizations,[10] is also supportive. The importance of expeditionary leadership at all levels of the organization is suggested by the work of Mintzberg and Floyd and Wooldridge and the work on demand-side and supply-side leadership of Broadbent and Kitzis.[11] Expeditionary leadership tends to appear in organizations facing "undepartmented" challenges, i.e. challenges that are not clearly the responsibility of any particular department. Effective leaders at all levels of the organization should engage in both primary team and expeditionary leadership and the higher a leadership position in an organization, the more important expeditionary leadership will be for its effective execution[12]

Upward and Downward Influence. Expeditionary and primary team leadership are related to upward and downward influence. Leaders exercise downward influence when they influence those below them in the organization. The targets of downward influence are usually people in the leader's home unit and those who report to them. It is less often appreciated that leaders can also have upward influence, directed at their immediate bosses and those above them. Such influence often involves presenting new ideas and attempting to get them implemented by the organization. Communication styles may need to be different for the different directions[13]. For example, the methods used to inspire people in the primary team to accomplish operational tasks are different from those used to approach upper management to "sell" a new idea.[14]

7.1.3 Leadership and Levels of Management in the Organization

Junior, Middle and Senior Technology Leadership. Leaders at different levels in the organization have different kinds of tasks to accomplish and different kinds of people to lead. Consequently, their approaches to leadership need to be different. This is as true in technology management as it is elsewhere. Three commonly used terms to distinguish levels of leadership/management are; junior, middle and senior; and these will be adopted here. Junior leaders are also called first line-supervisors or first-line management. Senior leaders are also called executives or top management. Recently they have been referred to as those in the "C-suite". Senior leaders collectively constitute the top management team (TMT).

Junior Technology Leadership. Junior leaders are usually distinguished by direct reports who do not hold management positions. In technology management this usually means that their direct reports are mainly people with technical backgrounds in science, engineering and/or related fields. Some administrative support people from non-technical backgrounds may also be included. Leaders at this level are primarily responsible for the day-to-day activities of their units. Those units are typically functional departments or small project teams. For example, functional first-line technology leaders may head departments for different engineering disciplines such as mechanical or electrical. Junior project leaders might head teams assigned the development of multi-technology devices and/or processes for manufacturing them. Such projects are typically narrow in scope so they do not include much participation from non-technical people. Junior technical leaders typically report to middle managers in the technology function. The time horizons for decisions by junior leaders are measured in days, weeks or months and only occasionally extend out as far as a year or two.[15]

Middle Technology Leadership. This level of leadership is the bridge between junior and senior leadership. In a large organization several levels of middle leadership may exist. Some middle leaders report directly to senior leadership while others report to more senior middle leaders. The direct reports of some middle leaders are junior leaders while for others they are middle leaders at a more junior level. Collectively, middle leaders are charged with harmonizing day-to-day operations with the vision and strategic goals of senior leaders. This involves making sure that strategy is effectively implemented through downward influence. It also includes making sure that senior leaders develop strategies that reflect the realities of the day-to-day operations and the external environment, through upward influence. The decision horizons of middle leaders tend to be longer than those of junior leaders and are usually thought of as extending out into the region of five years.[16]

Senior Technology Leadership: The CTO. The most senior leader responsible for technology in the firm is often called the Chief Technology Officer (CTO). Other titles are also used such as Vice-President, Technology; or Chief Innovation Officer. In this chapter we will refer to them generically as CTOs for simplicity of discussion. The CTO is usually a member of the TMT (sits in the C-suite) so the peer management team of the CTO includes the CEO, the Chief Operating Officer (COO), Chief Information Officer (CIO), Chief Financial Officer (CFO) and the like. The broad mandate of the CTO is threefold. First is to ensure the effective operation of the technology function and its relationships with other functions. Second is to ensure the harmonization of firm and technology strategy. Third is to make an appropriate contribution as a member of the top management team to the overall success of the organization through contributions that go beyond the immediate mandate of the technology function. Senior middle leaders report to the CTO and the CTO reports to the CEO. Senior technology leadership is involved in decisions that tend to extend for a time horizon of 10 to 20 years or even longer.[17]

Skills Required at Different Levels of Leadership. The importance of different leadership skills varies with the level of leadership in the organization. Badawy[18] has proposed that three categories of skills are necessary for effective leadership at all levels: (1) technical, (2) interpersonal, and (3) and administrative/conceptual; and at different levels these skills have different levels of importance, as indicated in Figure 2. Note that Badawy uses slightly different terms for the three levels of leadership than those used here. **Technical skills** are specific to the technical field in which the individual has training or work experience. Junior leaders make many day-to-day decisions about issues involving technology and must lead people whose professional focus is technical so technical expertise is critical for making good decisions and for establishing credibility with the technical people being led. Technical skills are less important moving up to middle and senior levels where leaders do not focus on technical details. They must be more concerned with broader issues of leadership, strategy, management and good working relationships with a wide variety of people. **Interpersonal skills** are those that enable one to manage people effectively. Of the three skills in the mix, interpersonal skills are the most nearly equal in importance across all three levels of management, according to Badawy. Whether they are junior leaders of teams of scientists or CTOs leading teams of middle leaders, successful execution is highly contingent on good interpersonal skills. **Administrative/Conceptual skills**

have to do with the ability to understand how the organizational system works, what it is capable of doing, planning, and managing execution. These are most critical for senior leadership who carry out these functions at the highest level.

Figure 2: Skill Mix for Technology Leaders

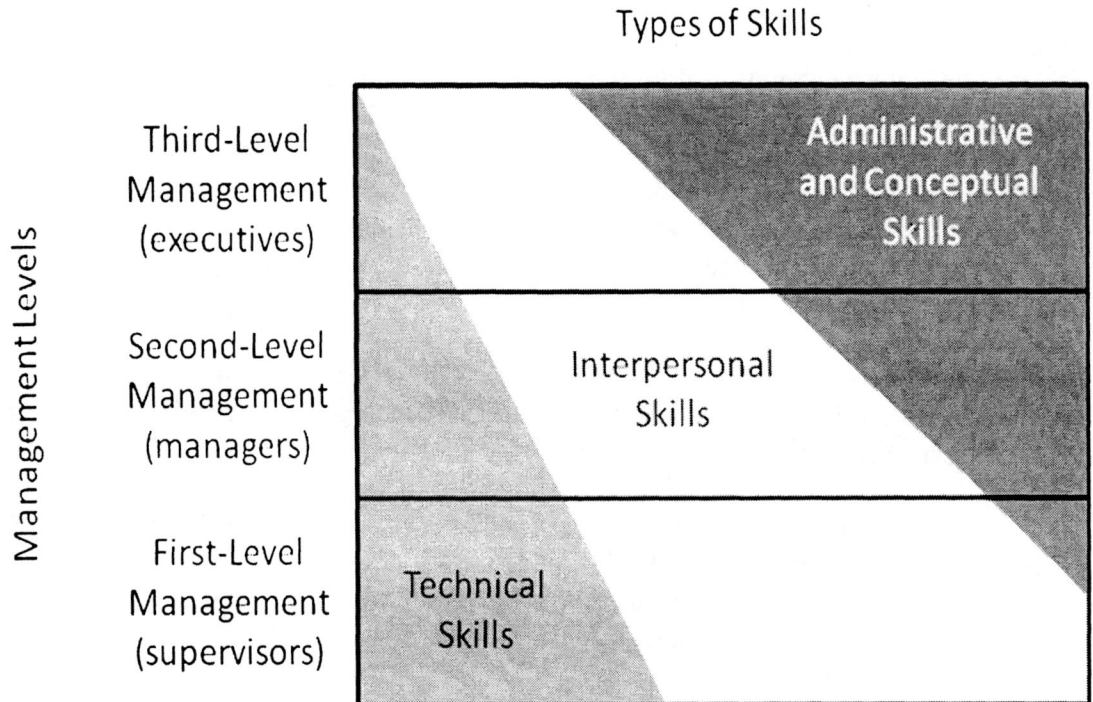

Source: Badawy[19]

Differences in Managing Individuals and Groups at Different Levels. Kraut, Pedigo, McKenna and Dunnette[20] did an empirical study of leadership skills at three levels of management. They found that managing individual subordinates became less important with higher management level. Managing groups, coordinating multiple groups and monitoring the environment became more important with increasing management level. Representing one's work group to outsiders was of similar importance across all levels.

7.2 JUNIOR LEVEL TECHNOLOGY LEADERSHIP

The Position of the Junior Leader. Junior leaders head primary teams consisting of people with no significant managerial responsibilities. In technology settings, junior leaders are usually project leaders, team leaders or the heads of technical departments. They are responsible for the ongoing operations of their departments/projects and for ensuring that the activities of their units are consistent with broader organizational goals. For the most part they lead technical professionals, technical support workers and some non-technical support staff. Because of their closeness to the technology, junior leaders must have a firm grasp of it but must also have leadership and managerial skills. Junior leaders must practice both primary team and expeditionary leadership although the former tends to dominate their role. In discussions of technology the terms "department" and "team" are not well differentiated in meaning. Some

6

authors distinguish clearly between project teams and functional departments. Others consider both project teams and functional departments to be forms of teams and do not distinguish strongly between them. The discussion here will use the term "team" to refer to people in both project teams and in functional departments, unless otherwise indicated.

7.2.1 Primary Team Leadership for Junior Technology Leaders

Three areas of junior primary team leadership that have had considerable attention from management practitioners and researchers are: human resource management, stimulating creativity and leading teams.

Human Resource Management

As part of the leadership of their teams, junior leaders need to provide a sound regime for human resource management. There are well established practices for this and Farris & Cordero[21] have reviewed research on them and identified the following key aspects of practice.

Hire for Broad Skills. Maintaining successful work teams requires that junior leaders hire people for more than just their technical skills. Other qualities to consider include leadership potential, commercial awareness, marketing and manufacturing skills, and communication skills. When junior leaders plan for and hire staff for both technical and non-technical skills it can help technical work become more effectively integrated with the other functions of the firm, helping reduce the amount of cross-functional friction in technical projects.

Career Management. Effective leaders are sensitive to the career aspirations of their team members. They work to provide opportunities for advancement inside the company that make use of company strengths. This helps to maintain employee motivation through on-going career advancement. In technical firms career paths can move in a variety of directions depending on the behavioural orientation and competencies of the technical professional and the opportunities in the firm. Technical professionals may progress on a purely technical ladder with increasing levels of technical responsibility, expertise and pay. Others may switch to the management track leaving technology behind, for the most part. Some may progress in line with their interest in the commercialization of a particular technology, following that new technology as it transitions through different stages and even different business units. Other technical professionals may have an entrepreneurial orientation and want to successively pursue new ideas for the company, taking up new ones as older ones reach maturity. For some professionals career preferences may change over time and these options may not be mutually exclusive.

Performance Appraisal. With the adoption of more cross-functional teams technical professionals increasingly work on projects headed by people from multiple different units in the firm and it is now common to have more than one person assesses the performance of a technical professional. This increases accountability across the organization and brings a wider perspective on performance appraisal and issue resolution. Technical merit is often measured with quantitative metrics such as number of patents or number of scientific publications. More qualitative measures are typically used for the non-technical aspects of the work and assessments may be provided by multiple peers, subordinates, superiors and other project stakeholders. Some technical professionals resist this more broadly based performance appraisal wanting their performance to be evaluated solely on technical merit and only with objective indicators.

Rewarding. Leaders need to ensure that technical professionals are suitably rewarded for their work in order to maintain motivation. Technical professionals are noted for the importance they give to intrinsic rewards such as the opportunity to take on difficult new technical challenges and to discover new ideas. Extrinsic rewards such as bonuses and pay increases are also important. Junior leaders need to be aware of the reward preferences of their professionals and take advantage of the work opportunities and monetary compensation the firm offers to provide as much as possible an optimal mix for each worker.[22]

Emerging Trends. Farris and Cordero[23] also identified a number of emerging human resource issues that increasingly present leadership challenges. As globalization and information technology advancements create information overload it is important that tools of **knowledge management** be embraced and promoted. This is accomplished by encouraging knowledge sharing among staff and providing supportive technical infrastructure. Junior leaders should create a culture that is conducive to sharing knowledge and maintain the system by recognizing those who participate. More companies are now employing knowledge management software; and such tools need to be endorsed by leaders. Another emerging trend is increased **demographic diversity**. The primary team needs to be led to an appreciation of diversity and the use of a variety of perspectives in solving problems. The alternative can be workgroup conflict and inappropriate insensitivity to different cultures.

Stimulating Creativity

The Challenge of Creativity in Organizations. Technology firms have the constant challenge of balancing the creativity needed to foster innovation with the efficiencies gained by following well established, standardized procedures that save money. Any firm that fails to provide both of these essentials will soon founder. The junior leader has the task of ensuring that this balance is maintained at the operational level where there is so much pressure for efficiency. In terms of the ICE model, stimulating creativity is important at all stages but it is particularly important at the create stage where imagination and inventiveness bring new ideas.

A Four Stage Process for Creativity. Junior leaders need to engage their teams in creative activity by providing motivation and inspiration. Shapero has proposed a four-stage process leaders can use to support and encourage creative activity: (1) preparation, (2) incubation, (3) illumination, and (4) verification.[24] **Preparation** involves an analysis of the problem and the collection of information. Creativity begins here although brainstorming and pondering at this stage often seem to be unproductive. Leaders need to appreciate that this stage is actually productive although often in an unstructured and unconscious way. Next is the **incubation** stage at which unconscious work seems to be done even when people are working on unrelated projects. Incubation hopefully leads to the **illumination** stage in which the "eureka" moment occurs and the essence of the solution is found. It can be productive for people to be concurrently assigned to more than one project so incubation and illumination can occur for one project while working on another. Finally, the creative process is concluded with **verification**, in which the creative ideas are proven using validity testing and/or a consensus from coworkers.

Leaders should be aware of these four stages and allow time for each to happen, even if nothing appears to be happening. Different teams and different projects may require different durations for the stages depending on their idiosyncrasies.

Threats to Team Creativity. Thompson[25] has identified four threats to team creativity: social loafing, conformity, production blocking, and downward norm setting. **Social loafing** occurs when an individual working in a team works less hard than s/he would if working alone. It appears to happen because the team responsibility for the outcome makes it difficult to notice if particular individuals are not making a contribution. Vigilance must be maintained to ensure that the individual tasks and contributions of group member are recognizable and that individuals are participating meaningfully in the process. Trained facilitators can help identify loafers and introduce motivation interventions. Introducing new group members can also reintroduce accountability and motivation to a team. **Conformity** prevails in teams where people are fearful of criticisms, or creativity is stifled by a short term results orientation. Conformity threatens creativity because it eliminates the quantity and variety of ideas. A strategy to deal with conformity is to diversify teams with members of different workgroups. This prevents the tendency for group norms to impede creativity. **Production blocking** occurs when an idea is not presented because there is no opportunity to speak or when there is self-criticism of an idea before it is spoken. Production blocking is common in brainstorming as people wait for their turn to speak which may never come, and/or they decide against speaking as they criticize their own idea while they wait. A strategy for combating production blocking is brainwriting. In this technique the team pauses the brainstorming session and, in silence, writes down their ideas, to be considered later. The fourth barrier to team creativity is **downward norm setting** in which team members gravitate towards the production levels of the lowest performers on the team. This can occur when people do not see their efforts differentially rewarded above those of low producers. It can be curbed by setting and articulating high standards for group performance and clearly and publically recognizing individuals for their contributions. Introducing new members to the team who are top performers can remind the team of high performance benchmarks.

Brainstorming. Brainstorming is an often used and often effective technique for generating creative ideas that is often recommended for technical professionals. It involves having a group of people collectively generate ideas for some specified purpose, be it the solution of a problem or an attempt to determine what the problem is. In brainstorming the emphasis is on the generation of ideas with no evaluation of them. Evaluation comes later. During the session a sense of energy is created by the ready acceptance of new ideas bubbling up from the subconscious. Thompson has provided a set of four rules that leaders should bear in mind in order for brainstorming sessions to be successful.[26] He suggests that technical education trains the critical mind and it is often difficult for technical professionals to set this aside while participating in brainstorming. Leaders have to be especially vigilant in overcoming this.

Thompson's Four Rules of Brainstorming:

> 1. **No criticism**
> 2. **Freewheeling welcome**
> 3. **Quantity desired**
> 4. **Combining/improving ideas is encouraged**

9

Brainstorming sessions should be free of criticisms. The quantity of ideas is what matters and the ideas can be evaluated later. Thompson uses the term freewheeling to suggest that all ideas are welcome, even those that seem unconventional and strange. Often the most creative solutions are a product of outrageous ideas. Leaders need to create a brainstorming environment in which participants do not feel intimidated nor that their ideas will be ridiculed. Finally, combining ideas or improving upon each other's ideas is welcome. In workgroups where peoples' capabilities are complementary, combining ideas can lead to full, creative solutions.

Creativity and the Junior Leader. In addition to understanding the technical operations of the unit and the desired strategy of middle/senior management, junior leaders need to create an environment conducive to creativity. This requires effective management to maintain order around the creativity process and also leadership to inspire technical professionals and motivate them for an agenda of constant change.[27]

Leading Teams

Teams in Technology Management. Teams are pervasive in technology driven firms and their presence is ever increasing. Practice has shown that they are an effective way to meet the ever-changing challenges faced by innovative firms in dynamic environments. They can be formed and disbanded as work challenges change. In recent years technical issues have become more complex and more multi-disciplinary and engineers and scientists are increasingly expected to be communicators across different work functions, technical and non-technical. The team environment often creates ambiguity of authority and responsibility. These trends have increased the challenges of team leadership that junior leaders have been facing in recent years. In addition to being aware of guidelines for effective team leadership and management, junior technical leaders must be prepared to meet the challenges of cross-functional teams, global teams and the unique characteristics of project management, as described below.

Guidelines for Technical Team Leadership. On the basis of their studies and experience, Thamhain and Wilemon have offered the following guidelines for technical team leadership and management.[28]

1. Clearly state team objectives so everyone has a good appreciation of end goal.
2. Effective planning of tasks and projects from the onset reduces frustration.
3. Team structure and responsibilities should be well defined at the team formation phase; this reduces role uncertainty and clearly assigns expectations.
4. Leadership positions should be well defined to ensure that credibility is maintained.
5. Build a strong team image to generate team pride and appreciation from other employees.
6. Foster commitment through frequent meetings and updates.
7. Conduct team-building sessions regularly to support healthy working relationships.
8. Where possible, use organizational development specialists to aid in addressing team conflicts and performance levels. This tactic is particularly useful in emotionally charged situations where mediation from an external party may be necessary.
9. Prevent conflicts from escalating by being proactive in the identification and resolution of interpersonal and or technical issues.

10. Understand the barriers to creativity and productivity and provide a work environment for team motivation.
11. Involve team members in decision making to establish ownership and accountability in work results.
12. Team leaders should be involved in staffing. This provides ownership and personal contribution to the team dynamics.
13. Carefully monitor and address team commitment and performance levels. This helps prevent downward norm setting.
14. Divide work into reportable segments that allow managers to quantitatively monitor progress for reporting purposes.
15. Seek support from senior leaders for resources, and endorsement at meetings and in company communications.

Cross-Functional Teams. Cross-functional teams consist of members from different parts of the organization. For example, a team involved in developing a new product may include technical people from more than one technical discipline if more than one kind of technology is included in the product. Even more diverse would be the addition of marketing and finance people if they are needed to deal with important issues. If representatives of alliance partners are added even greater diversity is introduced. Diverse, cross-functional teams are generally acknowledged to be more difficult to manage than homogenous teams because the diversity increases the likelihood of conflict within the team. People from diverse backgrounds are more likely to have differing unspoken assumptions about the work and its objectives and this can lead to conflict. People from diverse backgrounds are more likely to have differing communication styles and this can lead to misunderstandings, errors and the resultant conflict.

Engineering and Marketing in Cross-Functional Teams. The challenges posed by engineering and marketing people being together on the same teams have been of particular interest to technology leaders. This is because although this combination is often essential for quick and effective execution of strategy, the combination often causes conflict which hampers effectiveness. Workman[29] studied the differing perceptions of engineers and marketers and clarified some of the origins of cross-functional conflict. He found that engineers perceive that customers do not really know what they want, that marketers lack the expertise to properly communicate to customers, and that marketers provide product and competitive intelligence to engineers too late. In contrast, the perception of marketers is that engineers do not have perspective on customer wants and are too detail-oriented. Whereas marketing considers relationship management with the customer important, they feel that engineers do not appreciate earlier investments made in time commitments to and by customers. Engineers have a lack of appreciation for diverse markets and the need for diverse product features. Engineers create products that are technology-driven with subsequent input from marketing; too late for meaningful input from marketing.[30] The origins of the marketing/engineering divide are clear.

Guidelines for Effectively Leading Cross-Functional Teams. Souder has provided a set of guidelines for effectively leading cross-functional teams.[31] He noted that it is important to involve the various functions at the onset of a project or task. If a particular functional group joins later it may create conflicts as a result of lack of deep understanding of the objectives and lack of a sense of ownership for the outcome. Another tactic is to exploit specific cross-

11

functional relationships. For example, if an engineer and marketing employee work well together the leader might ensure that these two people are assigned to the same projects. This good working dynamic sets an example for the rest of the team and can spread to other team members. It is often advantageous to keep a cross-functional team small so that subgroups based on functions do not form and become antagonistic with each other. Smaller teams are also more conducive to personal meetings and better coordination.

Global Teams. As information technology advances and cross cultural understanding improves, the communication challenges arising from geographic distance have been diminishing and firms are finding increasing value in globally dispersed work teams. Barczak and McDonough,[32] in their study of global product development teams, found that firms use global teams for a variety of reasons. Sometimes it is useful to draw on geographically dispersed areas of expertise, or "centers of excellence." In other situations, a company may locate some of their own operations or ally with another company to improve proximity to markets. In such cases it may be advantageous to immerse some team members in the new market to improve understanding of them. The result is people in diverse locations who must work collaboratively on firm objectives. Global teams can also be useful in bringing together the distinctive resources of separate local teams. Barczak and McDonough found that the challenges of leading global teams can be both interpersonal and programmatic. Interpersonal reasons stem mainly from the distances involved which reduce the opportunities for face-to-face communication. Without face-to-face communication trust issues arise and uncertainties about team member roles and responsibilities. Programmatic reasons also involve distance complications related to scheduling, budgets, resources, and team communication tools due to differences in language and culture. Barczak and McDonough made recommendations for addressing the challenges of leading global teams. Meeting face-to-face at the beginning of a team initiative can establish trust among team members, help build comfortable interpersonal dynamics, and allow a clarification of team goals, roles, procedures and other fundamentals. A minimum of two or three days is recommended for such meetings. As the initiative moves forward it is important to optimize the frequency of team communication and monitor the quality of communication so that all team members are receiving the correct information. Face-to-face project progress meetings are important to keep the team tasks moving, maintain accountabilities and to maintain trust and team identity.

Leading Projects. Junior technical leaders often lead technical projects. Project management requires all the skills needed for management in general but also has some requirements specific to this particular challenge because of the unique nature of projects. Technical project management presents a dilemma. In many respects project leadership is business oriented in its planning, scheduling and monitoring. However, technical projects also require leaders with professional technical expertise. As a consequence, technical professionals are usually assigned to these leadership roles. They become project managers by default of their technical expertise. In a sense, these technical professionals become project leaders accidentally, not because they were actively seeking the role, as pointed out by Pinto and Kharbanda.[33] Pinto and Kharbanda call project leadership "the accidental profession". They also provide advice for technical professionals who find themselves in project leadership roles, as follows:
(1) Project work addresses a broader perspective than functional work. Project work is different from the work of functional departments. Work in functional department focused on a particular technology. Typically, the organizational structure of companies configures

departments to specialize in particular technical functions such as fluid engineering or polymer chemistry. In contrast, the work of projects tends to be unique, cross-functional, temporary and driven by project timelines. This means that projects are more unstructured and usually do not have the standard procedures in place that are found in functional units. Technical professionals moving into project work outside their home functional departments often take some time to get used to it. For example, resources for projects are often on a contingency basis and getting the right resources may take more persistence in the project than in the home department. Project work usually requires more interpersonal interaction and work with outsiders such as customers of alliance partners. In contrast, in the home department technical work can often be done more or less alone. Project work is more oriented to external stakeholders and their demands have to be more prominently considered.

(2) Project work is more uncertain than functional work. Team dynamics are more complex in project work. Technical managers need to use their interpersonal skills to guide project staff through work tasks, and understand that project team conflict can be a sign of progress. The recommendation is not to panic, but to address issues early on so that project work can continue and little time is wasted. Given the unstructured nature of project work, it is considered to be leadership intensive. Technology managers need to recognize the importance of addressing uncertainties in a proactive manner.

(3) Strict time management. Projects inevitably have time constraints and require strict time management. Technology leaders used to the more lenient schedules of research work may find this a significant challenge requiring special attention. Pinto and Kharbanda recommend the development of a solid, time-based implementation plan, extra care not to go off on "interesting" tangents, strong focus on the intended results, and good time management.

7.2.2 Expeditionary Leadership for Junior Technology Leaders

Expeditionary Leadership. As shown in Figure 1 and explained in the accompanying text, expeditionary leadership is exercised through interaction with people outside the primary team. It can be exercised through peers and superiors within one's own organization and through people outside, such as representatives of alliance partners or government agencies. It is of increasing importance in the current business environment. Expeditionary leadership can be exercised through a number of roles which will be described below. It is usually based on an effective set of networking activities which prepare the way for playing expeditionary roles.

Expeditionary Leadership Roles

Ancona and Caldwell[34] researched the expeditionary leadership activities of leaders of technical projects. They organized those activities into a number of roles which summarized the essential expeditionary activities of those managers. Ancona and Caldwell found that some project team members also took on these roles but not nearly as often as their project leaders. The expeditionary role activities identified by Ancona and Caldwell are as follow.

13

Expeditionary Leadership Roles

Scanning. Finding and collecting information from outside the project (about the firm, industry, customers, etc.), not directly related to any immediate task, that allows the leader and the team to be more attuned to the project environment.

Modeling. Forming of an organized understanding of the project environment including stakeholders, competitors, and where useful information may be retrieved. The resulting model of the environment is communicated to team members to improve their understanding of the project's situation.

Scouting. Searching for, identifying and retrieving external information for immediate use.

Feedback Seeking. Soliciting feedback from outsiders. For example, a product development project team might present its ideas to another group for evaluation of ideas and suggestions for improvement.

Ambassador. Representing the team in a positive way to external groups to establish and maintain goodwill and good working relationships with them.

Informing. Generally informing external individuals and groups of the progress of the team, its frustrations and requirements. This contributes to awareness and support.

Coordinating, Negotiating. Liaising with external stakeholders to ensure that coordination occurs and negotiating changes to keep the project on target.

Sentry. Receiving and monitoring information sent to the team by outsiders. The leader censors information and reduces distraction by only **allowing entry** to data that is considered useful to the group. Some information may require **translation** to the terminology of the team or interpretation to highlight its relevance. It may involve **filtering** large amounts of information into manageable data packages that take less time for group members to review and apply.

Guard. This involves monitoring the information sent to external sources. **Classifying**, or assessing external requests for information ensures that the request is reasonable and evaluates what effort is required to fulfill a request. **Delivering** includes the packaging of information and sending it to the external group. If a request if not reasonable, the leader manager is responsible for **protecting** the interests of the group and explaining to the external source that the request cannot be fulfilled.[35]

These expeditionary leadership activities are carried out to some extent by middle and senior leaders as well as junior. At the upper levels they can assume even more importance than at the junior. They are introduced here at the first level at which they are relevant but do apply to the discussion of expeditionary leadership at more senior levels.

Networking for Expeditionary Leadership

Networking in Technology Management. Networking is introduced here because it is essential for effective junior technology leadership. A number of the roles identified by Ancona and Caldwell and described in the previous section involve networking. But networking is a universal tool. It is also useful for technical specialists with no leadership role who wish to stay abreast of their technical fields and to ensure that their technical work is of maximum value to the firm. Networking may be even more important to middle and senior technical leaders whose work is often less structured than that of junior leaders and who therefore are more dependent upon informal communication channels for information important to their work. Networking is a developed skill that all can acquire to some degree. Ransley[36] has provided some advice for technical professionals at all levels to enhance their networking skills.

Attitude. For networking to be developed and effective it must be integrated into everyday activities. Assuming a "helpful" attitude is one way to develop it even if one initially seems to have no natural talent for doing it. Being helpful does not require strong communication skills but does use technical expertise to gain recognition. For example, a junior manager might assist a colleague that is struggling with a new computer code. This offering of ideas and expertise is a form of networking as now the person helped will be more open to sharing their knowledge and network. A helpful attitude involves giving to others without expecting instant return. Helping others can also lead to an understanding of their perspective. Understanding many perspectives is a key skill that transfers to successfully working in cross-functional teams and being sensitive to many viewpoints.

Developing Networks. Creating a networking plan can be a very helpful early step in developing a network. This is more the case with those not inclined to be sociable who would not spontaneously attend events at which networks can be built. Planning can start with drawing a networking diagram that brainstorms all possible networking contacts from work, professional organizations and personal relationships and then working with those possibilities to develop the most promising. Planning can also involve researching who is going to be at events and preparing questions or gathering material that people may find useful. These can be used to facilitate discussions. It is important to develop a system for organizing contact names and information for easy retrieval to prevent networking from becoming overwhelming.

Interactions. There are many things to keep in mind in networking interactions. For those who are not natural conversationalists it is important to prepare in advance to make a good first impression. Even something as simple as being able to present clear succinct and easily remembered personal information such as name, work title, experience, and skills may require some careful thought. Being an active listener who is perceptive to the direction of a conversation and actively contributing to it is important, as is discerning an appropriate time to end it. It is important to develop skills for gracefully exiting a conversation. Following a successful networking interaction, best practice involves maintaining by following through on promised actions, thanking contacts for information, and finding ways to meet the contact again on future occasions.

15

7.2.3 Challenges in the Transition from Technical to Leadership Roles

The Transition from Technical to Leadership Roles. Openings in junior technology leadership positions are usually taken up by individuals who have been working for some time in technical roles and now appear ready for leadership. Such people have usually been trained in a technical discipline such as engineering or science and have spent most if not all of their professional lives in predominantly technical roles. The assumption of junior leadership roles usually provides technical professionals with their first opportunity to exercise leadership and management on more than just an occasional basis. This move from technical to leadership positions can present a considerable challenge to technical professionals no matter how good their intentions and no matter how well they have prepared. Many who have made the transition believe that technical professionals have a more difficult time with it than do people from other backgrounds. This is because of the nature of technical work, the nature of technical training, and the type of people who are attracted to technical fields. This section will describe some of the often noted challenges of the transition to management for technical professionals. This list is based on Medcof[37] and Badawy.[38]

Social Interaction. Many technical people report discomfort with the level of social interaction involved in leadership as compared to purely technical work. Leadership demands a great deal of interaction with people if it is to be done well while technical work often involves working independently. Most technical people are comfortable with a low level of social interaction and they have even become stereotyped as "introverts". Some find it difficult to adjust to higher levels of social interaction. Consequently, some newly promoted technical people retreat to doing technical work or administrative work in their offices when they should out interacting with other people in a leadership role.   .

Objective Measurement Bias. Technical professionals are trained in the hard sciences where objective measurement is mandatory. They are comfortable with such objective measurement and many become uneasy when having to deal with information that is more judgmental. Leadership and management are activities that depend heavily on non-objective data for decision making. No matter how desirable objective data may be, it is often just not available for management decisions but the decisions have to be made nonetheless. Some technical people never become accommodated to this new way of making decisions, let alone become comfortable and confidently at ease with it. Such comfort and ease is necessary for good leadership, particularly at higher levels. Writers on this topic have talked about leadership being an art, not a science and the difficulty of learning to deal with opinion rather than facts.

Paralysis by Analysis. Technical professionals are trained to make decisions on the basis of a complete set of facts because science is founded on this premise and in many areas of technical work it is possible to have virtually complete information. Leadership and management, in contrast, are activities that demand decisions with incomplete facts. Some newly promoted leaders delay decision making while they hope to find more facts. But often, none are forthcoming. Others seem unable to make any decision at all until large numbers of facts are assembled and analysed carefully. Meanwhile the window of opportunity for a necessary action passes. Such delays in decision making are called "paralysis by analysis".

Management Expertise. Many newly promoted technical people simply lack knowledge of basic management and leadership information and techniques. They may not know the basics of accounting and financial analysis. They may not know the basic vocabulary of marketing and manufacturing. They may not know the basic procedures for doing certain activities in their firms. They may not know who key people are for getting jobs done and may not even know that they need this information. This lack of even the most fundamental expertise in management can be corrected with experience, training and education.

Leadership/Management Values and Attitudes. There are some factors, which often operate at an implicit level, which create a fundamental discomfort with leadership for technical people. These have been noted by technical people moving into management. Many technical people feel a strong loyalty to their technical profession and to "Science" as a noble human enterprise that has advanced civilization. They find it difficult to switch loyalty to the business firm they work for whose fundamental purpose is to make money. Yet, a sense of the legitimacy of the commercial enterprise and of the immediate employer is necessary for a true commitment to leadership in accomplishing the firm's objectives. Many technology people have a strong sense of self-reliance, independence and find great satisfaction in individual recognition for work well done by them. In leadership and management one is highly dependent on other people to get things done and there must be delegation, often to people who cannot do the work as well as the delegator could. Many technical people find it difficult to "let go" and to effectively delegate work. The satisfaction of being in a more highly ranked organizational position is not always highly valued by technical people who would prefer to be recognized for excellent technical work. This can make leadership less intrinsically rewarding than technical work.

7.3 MIDDLE LEVEL TECHNOLOGY LEADERSHIP

The Middle Leadership Role. Middle leaders are the bridge between junior and senior leadership. They are charged with ensuring that the activities which they lead work synergistically with the activities of the organization as a whole. Large firms usually have more than one level of middle management so a middle leader might report to another middle leader and have reports who are also middle leaders. In the technology management context, middle leaders have such titles as Director of R&D, General Manager of Research, Lab Director, and Director of Technology Development.

The Evolving Role of the Middle Leader. Traditionally, the middle leader's role was mainly operational, focusing on implementing senior leadership's strategy through overseeing the performance of functional units. They were also the conduit for funneling information up to senior management about operations. Such data funneling was thought of as being the objective reporting of objective data with no interpretive activity by the middle leader. But this traditional view has been changing in recent years as organizations have had to contend with more undepartmented challenges and more rapidly changing environments. Senior leaders have been calling on middle leaders to play a more significant role in strategy formation and in evolving the dynamic capabilities of the firm necessary for success in a dynamic business environment[39] Middle leaders are now being called upon to take on cross-functional assignments and to lead in a more flexible, entrepreneurial way. Floyd and Wooldridge[40] have found that these changes require middle leaders to exercise both upward and downward influence.

Downward Influence. The cornerstone of middle leaders' downward influence is their authority to allocate budgets, manage human resources, and define projects and teams. This formal authority can be augmented and leveraged with their personal leadership qualities. Middle leaders also have downward influence by communicating the firm's strategy to, and defining a model of the environment for, the primary team. Whether or not operations are aligned with corporate strategy depends heavily on middle leaders' ability to communicate to their teams. This downward influence is exercised mainly in the primary team.

Upward Influence. Middle leaders can have upward influence on more senior levels as well.[41] Senior leaders depend on middle leaders to provide summaries of information about the operations of the firm and information relevant to proposed strategic directions. Some of this information is presented in standardized report formats which leave little room for data selection or interpretation. Such reports often come through established information technology channels. Other reports, particularly those evaluating or proposing future strategic directions or other initiatives, do not come in standardized formats. In these, middle leaders must make judgment calls about what information to present and how it will be presented. Very often those reports contain recommendations for courses of action. Since senior leaders have limited time they often receive those recommendations more or less at face value, with some critical probing. It is in these judgment calls that middle leaders have some leeway to influence firm strategy. They can select the data and the mode of presentation to support some options and not others. They can engage in informal discussions with more senior leaders about such issues and proposals.

7.3.1 Primary Team Leadership for Middle Level Technology Leaders

Primary Team Leadership Challenges. Middle leaders head their primary teams and deal with the associated challenges. These include some of the issues reviewed above for junior leaders including; stimulating creativity, team leadership, cross-functionality, virtual teams and project management issues. Although these challenges are broadly the same across the two levels of leadership there are significant differences between the levels given that in the technology setting most of the junior leader's direct reports are technical specialists while most of the middle leader's are other leaders. There are also usually differences in the numbers of people who are to be led and the kinds of challenges that will be encountered at the different levels of the organization. Two challenges that are usually more significant for middle leaders than for junior are the designing of teams to carry out the organization's work and the management of multiple teams whose leaders constitute the primary team of the middle leader.

Designing Teams

Designing Team Structure. This activity is likely to be more important and challenging for middle leadership than for junior. This is because although junior leaders may be delegated some team formation activities, they usually have to design only one team at a time and are not likely to involve teams that are as large or significant as those that must be designed by middle leaders. There are team design options.[42] Some teams are planned to be relatively short lived, to carry out relatively minor tasks, and not to draw heavily on the time of those assigned to them. In such cases a **lightweight team structure** may be most effective. In this structure the team leader is drawn from an existing department and given the management of the team on a part-time basis. Team members are also drawn from existing specialty departments and assigned part-time to the team. Typically, the team leader has little formal authority and team members still look to the mangers of their home departments for most leadership, their annual performance reviews, and other important human resource functions. Team leaders in these cases must depend heavily on their informal leadership skills. In other cases projects are planned to be long, perhaps lasting for years; to involve many people, perhaps hundreds; and require heavy time contributions from team members, even full-time. For such team projects a **heavyweight team structure** may be most effective. The team leader is full time and is drawn from the ranks of middle leaders, or even from among senior leaders. Many team members may be full time. A formal organizational structure is drawn up for the project and there may also be many less formally defined management roles. The team leader may be given formal authority over at least the key team members for the duration of the project. At the end, team members will be re-assigned back to their functional departments or reassigned to other teams. The lightweight and heavyweight team structures are extremes on a continuum with many variations and combinations of them possible in the intermediate range. Team design and the assignment of people to teams can be a long and challenging process involving consultation with a wide variety of people and the resolution of capability, political and organizational strategy issues.

Designing for People. Taguiri[43] has suggested a number of considerations for establishing teams and many have to do with people issues. It is important that teams operate with a common and clear mission. The mission should be understood in the context of well-defined team objectives that are measurable and can be arrived at using the input from all team members. Taguiri emphasized the need for mission clarification in the cross-functional context in which teams are comprised of members with diverse attributes such as technical expertise, manufacturing skills and business savvy. The size of teams will vary depending on the task, but optimally should not consist of more than ten members. Multiple teams can be preferable to one big team. If possible, it is advantageous to design teams in which members have volunteered to participate. This usually enhances motivation, commitment, and buy-in to the intended results.

Designing for Research versus Development. It is important to bear in mind that research and development usually require different kinds of teams. Because research work involves a high level of ambiguity, and creativity is not easily managed, it is difficult to tightly schedule and manage research projects without inhibiting the underlying creativity and spontaneity required. Development work, however, comes into play when research has resolved most of the fundamental uncertainties and the necessary feasibility points have been reached. Given this, development projects can be realistically mounted with scheduling and management protocols that are more rigorous than those that work for research. More autonomous team structures and fewer bureaucratic protocols are recommended for research projects.

Managing Multiple Teams

The Challenges of Leading Multiple Teams. Middle level leaders are often charged with the leadership of multiple teams and/or departments and this can present a set of challenges that go beyond those of junior leaders who are usually given charge of only a single department or team at a time. Junior leaders must coordinate and lead the actions of individuals within their teams while middle leaders must coordinate and lead the activities of multiple teams through the

19

coordination and leadership of their team leaders. Junior leaders help with the coordination of their teams' activities with those of other teams, primarily through work in their peer management teams. Middle leaders have the prime responsibility for that coordination.

Practices for Leading Multiple Teams. Harris and Lambert[44] identified practices for leading multiple teams. Teams often have related or overlapping responsibilities and it is for the middle leader to ensure that team roles and responsibilities are clarified and that work on areas of overlap is coordinated effectively. In the event that conflicts do arise between and among teams the middle leader is usually expected to lead the resolution, by fiat of authority if necessary. The middle leader must also monitor and assess inter-team communication and intervene if problems are not being resolved by the involved teams. As the overall leaders of the teams led by their reports, middle leaders must ensure that organizational goals and strategy reach all members of all teams and that the leaders of individual teams are appropriately transmitting those messages. Middle leaders also do resource allocations to teams and must monitor their expenditure. This work is complicated by the inter-team rivalries that normally arise over resources.

7.3.2 Middle Level Expeditionary Technology Leadership

Middle Level Expeditionary Technology Leadership. Middle level leaders are increasingly taking on expeditionary roles as their firms struggle to deal with undepartmented challenges and the fast moving and increasingly networked environment. Traditionally, senior management would deal with cross-department issues, handle all the liaisons with outside bodies, and do all the strategy development. In the new reality middle leaders have been taking on an increasing load of such responsibilities partly because these challenges are so laced with implementation issues and activities that middle leaders must be involved.

Champions of Innovation

Champions. Champions are members of the organization who rise above their peers to promote new ideas, gain company-wide support, effectively address any resistance, and persist until the ideas are realized.[45] Howell and her colleagues found that champions of innovation are most often middle managers with many years of experience in their firms. They have a good understanding of the company's vision and an appreciation for how the different functions within the firm interact. Junior leaders sometimes become champions but they usually lack the years of experience needed for a deep understanding of the organization and to build networks for influence. Championship is expeditionary leadership as it involves influencing broadly, in the organization and beyond, to engage people to support the project. Champions excel in the use of influence over those over whom they have no authority. Champions are usually self-appointed.

The Champion "Personality". Howell and her colleagues[46] identified the personality traits, leadership qualities, and common career experiences of champions. They tend to be self-confident individuals who are not afraid to be persistent or take risks when presenting an idea. They are also energetic, charismatic, and attract people to their ideas. Often surrounded by technically capable but socially reserved fellow employees, champions emerge as the spokesperson within their teams. Although champions appear in the spotlight, their leadership capabilities are such that fellow employees are motivated to support them.

How champions Lead. Champions present innovative ideas, but give recognition to the people who originated the ideas, and work to develop the potential they see in others. The extensive career experience of middle level champions allows them to utilize what Howell and her colleagues called the participative process. By having an extensive network within a company champions pose innovative ideas to many people well before the idea is formally proposed to senior leaders. Coupled with the effective leadership qualities of the champion, the early support received from a number of people helps carry the idea. Champions also align ideas with the company's vision so it is difficult for anyone to reasonably resist. Once the idea is accepted, the probability of successful implementation is high because participants were involved early and the champion's leadership has created the motivation to see the idea work.

Issue Selling

Issue Selling. As described above, middle leaders can play a role influencing the strategy of an organization. This can take the form of leading peers and senior management to the adoption of a particular strategic measure. Such cases usually involve selling the concept to senior management. Dutton and her colleagues[47] call this "issue selling" and have done a series of empirical studies on this particular facet of expeditionary leadership. Dutton and colleagues organized issue selling activities into three categories: packaging, involvement and process.

Packaging Moves. These have to do with how the issue is presented. Careful planning is needed to develop a strategy around who the issue will be presented to and how it will be packaged for each such audience. How often and when it will be raised is also a consideration. The issue may be bundled with other issues to give it credibility.

Involvement Moves. These have to do with deciding who to involve as allies in the selling activities, what their roles will be, and the degree of their involvement. Understanding who may have an interest in seeing an issue resolved in a particular way and who will benefit are important considerations.

Process Moves. These have to do with the delivery of the issue. For example, will it be at a formal meeting or informally? Being well prepared and learning the audience's priorities are part of process.

Outsourcing

Outsourcing. Although it has been practiced for many years, the outsourcing of technology work has escalated in recent years as firms have realized its value as part of their open innovation strategies.[48] Although major outsourcing decisions are usually taken by senior leaders, some can be made by middle managers. Regardless of who makes the decision, it is usually middle leaders who carry the burden of managing outsourcing relationships and providing the necessary leadership.[49]

Leading Outsourcing. Schick[50] proposes that outsourcing requires some leadership and management skills not found in traditional in-house management. Middle leaders must manage the transition from in-house operations to outsourcing for a particular task. After the operations have moved outside the company the "stay-back team" must be led and managed to ensure that effective relationships between that group and the external partner team are maintained. For outsourcing to work well it needs more than good management, it also requires expeditionary leadership. The stay-back team and the external partner team should share a common vision of how the outsourcing relationship contributes to both their firms and the role that both teams play in accomplishing that vision. A well led relationship is not beset by errors, misunderstandings, and emotional clashes because all of those involved see themselves as working together to accomplish a shared, meaningful task. The outsourcing leadership role is challenging because the people involved are not co-located, communication opportunities may be limited and the formal authority of the leader may be very tenuous. If the company cultures are not compatible there will be additional challenges. Middle leaders can find themselves in leadership roles in multiple outsourcing relationships and that presents further challenges.

Alliances

Alliances. Sometimes two or more firms find it useful to work cooperatively on short-term or long term initiatives. When such alliances are formed, a middle leader is often assigned to lead the alliance activities. Alliance management may involve multiple middle leaders.

Leading Alliances. MacAvoy[51] suggests that alliances place greater demands on leaders as the level of uncertainty is greater than it is when managing within a single company. Alliances usually have a broader mandate than simple outsourcing, may involve multiple partners, and involve more complex relationship issues. The leader must consistently consider the initial rationale for the alliance, and monitor and adjust the alliance activities according to the original goals. There is an increased requirement to effectively manage relationships and be sensitive to the diverse organizational cultures of the alliance participants. In addition to having technical and business skills there are other important success factors: credibility, respect, and the networks that have formed as a result of maintaining relationships. One of the most important qualities is diplomacy and the ability to steer an alliance back on track without jeopardizing relationships. The leader needs a firm understanding on how the alliance is aligned with the strategy of all the firms involved. They are able to consider many viewpoints simultaneously, and offer solutions that serve the best interests of all parties.

7.3.3 Managing Organizational Politics

Organizational Politics. Organizational politics involves pursuing individual goals through calculated interactions within an organization.[52] It occurs in all organizations and at all levels of the organization. It has a positive side, a negative side, and all the shades of positive and negative in between. On the negative side it can lead to the blatant exercise of self interest to the detriment of the organization and all its stakeholders. On the positive, side an individual intending to ensure the success of the organization may use political process to prevail against those who are acting in their own self-interest. To be successful, in almost any sense of the term, the leader must understand and use political processes. Although politics is seen in junior leadership, participation in it may sometimes be avoided. It is in middle leadership that politics for the good of the organization become unavoidable.

Leading and Politics. Pinto[53] provides advice about politics and leadership.

1. **Understand and acknowledge your organization's political nature.**
   Politics in the workplace is inevitable, so leaders must understand how to work within the political environment and to adjust their actions appropriately.

2. **Cultivate appropriate political tactics.**
   Leaders must deal with organizational politics effectively. But overusing politics can be harmful if employees perceive that the leader is being aggressive and insensitive.

3. **Understand and accept "What's in it for me?" (WIIFM).**
   Most people are motivated and inspired to perform in the workplace when they understand and appreciate how the outcome of the work will benefit them. Leaders should not assume that all employees understand the benefits to themselves of the work they are doing. Leaders should be sure their people do understand.

4. **Try to level the playing field.**
   In projects, leaders are usually given some responsibility to formally assess the performance of team members. Often there is resistance to sharing this responsibility from the managers of the team members' home departments. It is important for project leaders to establish the legitimacy of their input in the assessment process to support their credibility as leaders, managers and assigners of work.

5. **Learn the fine art of influencing.**
   Being successful at influencing involves a number of tactics. The leader needs to develop some of these so they can influence beyond their level of formal authority.

6. **Develop your negotiating skills.**
   Negotiating is important in organizational politics. Leaders must understand the underpinnings of the political environment and predict the tactics of their counterparts in the negotiating situation. The key to good negotiating is to envision a resolution in which both parties benefit and negotiate towards that alternative.

7. **Recognize conflict as a natural side effect of leadership and management.**
   Technical leaders need to recognize that conflict is a natural part of the work environment. It indicates that team members are passionate about their work. From this perspective, the role of the leader is to ensure that the conflict does not escalate, to facilitate discussion, and to draw out solutions that benefit all parties involved.

7.4   SENIOR LEVEL TECHNOLOGY LEADERSHIP

The CTO. Senior technology leadership is the responsibility of the CTO and takes place at the level of the executive committee. According to Adler and Ferdows the CTO is the highest ranking manger in the firm charged with responsibility for technology.[54] The CTO has broad responsibility for both product and process technologies and reports directly to the CEO. Some firms do not have a position called the CTO or its equivalent (e.g. Vice-President Technology) but instead put the *functions* of the CTO in the portfolio of a senior executive with another title. For example, the Vice-President of Manufacturing might have the functions of the CTO embedded in their responsibilities. In some firms the CEO is very much the technology driver of the firm and the CTO's functions are housed in that role by default. Bearing in mind these other possible ways of organizing the CTO's functions, for convenience and clarity this module will discuss these functions as those of the CTO.

23

Three Leadership Roles of the CTO. The leadership activities of the CTO can be divided into three roles: functional, strategic and supra-functional.[55] **Functional leadership** focuses on the technology function itself and ensures that it operates effectively. This includes ensuring that activities such as research, new product development and some aspects of manufacturing meet the budgetary, temporal and effectiveness requirements set for them. **Strategic leadership** ensures that a technology strategy is developed for the organization and that it is consistent with corporate strategy. Ideally, this involves the mutual adjustment of corporate and technology strategy so they influence each other and achieve a joint optimization. **Supra-functional leadership** involves the CTO in the formulation and execution of corporate strategy for the success of the firm as a whole and involves the CTO in leadership activities that are outside the realm of the technology function. For example, if a new green initiative were an important strategic matter for the firm someone from the executive committee would be needed to lead it. The CTO, as a member of the executive team, might be asked to take that role. The CTO would take it on as an extra, over and above his/her functional and strategic responsibilities. Typically, all members of the executive team take on such "extra" jobs as a part of their corporate level roles.

Primary Team and Expeditionary Leadership of the CTO. The functional, strategic, and supra-functional roles of the CTO involve different degrees of primary team and expeditionary leadership. The execution of the functional role involves mainly primary team leadership as the CTO interacts with people within the technology function (usually middle leaders, the CTO's primary team) to ensure it is operating effectively. However, the functional role can also involve some expeditionary leadership. For example, the CTO may lead/influence other members of the executive team to increase the R&D budget of the firm. The CTO might even persuade executives from another firm to enter a technology alliance with his own firm that provides cost savings to them both. Strategic leadership, in contrast, tends to involve a more balanced mix of primary team and expeditionary leadership. It is the CTO's role to lead the technology function in the development of a technology strategy. This will require considerable detailed work within the function which will involve primary team leadership. But the CTO is also expected to lead the integration of technology strategy with firm strategy. This involves selling the technology strategy to the executive team, persuading them to alter the firm strategy to accommodate the technology strategy, and to agree to adjustments to the technology strategy to fit it to firm strategy. In short it is the CTO's role to lead the harmonization of technology and firm strategy within the context of the executive committee. This is expeditionary leadership. So the CTO's strategic leadership role involves significant proportions of both primary team and expeditionary leadership. Take note that at this point in the explanation of CTO strategic leadership we are discussing only the development of technology strategy and its harmonization with firm strategy. As will be described below, the CTO also has other roles to play in organizational strategy formation. Turning to the CTO's supra-functional leadership role, it is predominantly an expeditionary task. Supra-functional leadership is concerned with the business of the firm as a whole and not the business of the technology function. For example, as a member in good standing of the executive team, the CTO might be asked to take leadership of the initiative to transform company culture to one that more strongly promotes innovation. This would be an organization-wide mandate and involve the leadership of senior managers and executives from across the organization. The technology function would fall within the mandate for change as would marketing, procurement, finance, manufacturing and other functions. The

CTO is asked to take on this expeditionary leadership role as an officer of the organization as a whole and in that sense it is supra-functional, not just technological. This is so notwithstanding that a CTO might be the most appropriate person for this job given his/her background in the technology function. As a member of the executive team the CTO might be called upon to discuss marketing strategy, how it synchronizes with firm strategy, and how firm strategy might be changed to better accommodate marketing issues. This is a discussion of strategy which is not directly focused on technology so it is supra-functional and not a functional one for the CTO. These supra-functional activities may involve leading individuals from the technical function from time-to-time but this constitutes a small proportion of primary team leadership compared to the expeditionary leadership which is the mainstay of the supra-functional role.

7.4.1 Primary Team Leadership in Senior Technology Management

As described above, the CTO's primary team leadership is of people in the technology function primarily for the effective operation of that function. A number of papers have reported research about this role[56] and they identify the following activities: meeting budgets and schedules, management of intellectual property, human resources planning, knowledge management, managing international R&D, utilizing new information technology, measuring and improving R&D effectiveness, building collaborative relationships across the technology function, building and maintaining core technical competencies, augmenting R&D capabilities, and managing the selection of research projects. Much of this work is delegated to middle managers but the CTO is responsible for overall leadership and may at times take on specific projects, such as managing a particularly large and strategically important development project.

7.4.2 Expeditionary Leadership in Senior Technology Management

As described above, the expeditionary leadership roles of CTOs are concerned with outcomes in three different realms; within the technology function, in strategic planning and in the work of the organization as a whole (supra-functional).

Functional Expeditionary Leadership by the CTO. Research has identified a number of activities of CTOs which constitute expeditionary leadership primarily intended to enhance the effectiveness of the technology function.[57] These include: coordination and leadership across business functions to ensure the progress of technology based innovations, driving commercialization across functions, solving business unit emergency problems that involve technology, scanning for and accessing external sources of technology, scanning for technological competitive intelligence, identifying and evaluating threats and opportunities contained in technological discontinuities, and leading technological alliances and collaborations with other organizations. As with the primary team leadership of the technology function, many of these aspects of leadership may be delegated to middle managers but the CTO retains overall responsibility for leadership. All these examples involve leading people outside the technology function in initiatives that enhance the operations and outcomes of the technology function.

Strategic Expeditionary Leadership by the CTO. The CTO has an important role to play in ensuring that technology strategy and corporate level strategy are aligned through interactions with people outside the technology function. Research has shown that CTOs engage in the following activities in this regard:[58] integrating commercial and technical strategies; consulting the CEO and top management team on strategically sensitive technology decisions; generally selling R&D to top management; developing the R&D business case; evaluating and interpreting technical information for the executive team; technology roadmapping; balancing long and short-term R&D objectives; and advising on strategically important and technology heavy mergers, acquisitions and alliances. Again, many of these activities may be delegated to middle managers but the CTO maintains overall leadership responsibility. Most of these activities are imbued with innovation and the development of new approaches for the organization.

Supra-Functional Expeditionary Leadership by the CTO. As a member of the top management team the CTO has an important leadership role to play in matters of concern at the corporate level, over and above ensuring the alignment of corporate and technology strategy. Although members of the top management team have responsibilities with respect to their particular functions, they also have a corporate level responsibility. They must rise above championship of their home functions and support decisions and lead initiatives for the overall prosperity of the organization. Research has found the following CTO activities in this leadership role:[59] leading strategic innovation, leading the introduction of knowledge management, building a company culture of innovation, building networks for gathering competitive intelligence on important organizational issues (not just technology), and making substantive contributions to strategy discussions not based upon technical expertise.

Common Challenges across Roles. Although these various leadership roles of the CTO have been differentiated, there can be commonalities among them. For example, in the supra-functional role the CTO can be involved in the review and discussion of important human resource issues in the executive team. For example, there might be succession issues in marketing at the middle management level which the executive team would discuss. A fully functioning CTO would join that discussion and effectively contribute in a way that does not draw heavily on the specifics of technology management. However, if the discussion were about middle management in the technology function, the CTO would probably be expected to play a larger role in the discussion and even take leadership. Direct technology management experience would probably have more relevance in this case. In the primary team leadership of the technology function human resource issues can also arise. The CTO might lead middle managers from the technology function in a discussion of human resource issues in that function. Human resource issues can arise almost anywhere in the organization and although they have common elements they will also have significant differences because of the varying contexts. Effective CTOs will be aware of those differences and will modulate their contributions accordingly. CTOs with narrow backgrounds in just the technology function may not appreciate the differences and may not have the background necessary to contribute effectively at the strategic or supra-functional level. The same applies to many other leadership issues such as building culture, advising on mergers and acquisitions and working with external stakeholders. CTOs who do not have a broad enough background or who for other reasons cannot contribute meaningfully to supra-functional discussions will find their credibility and influence within the executive team stunted.[60] This can limit their ability to promote an appropriate technology agenda at the senior level and negatively affect their career opportunities.

7.4.3   Organizational Influence in Senior Technology Management

CTO Influence. The CTO must wield influence in the primary team, in the rest of the organization, and beyond the organization, in order to carry out his/her assigned responsibilities. Within the primary team the CTO's high organizational position, with its prerogatives for hiring, promoting, performance appraisal and sanctions, provides a considerable basis for influence and motivating people to act. These position powers must be supplemented by personal charisma, interpersonal skills and informal leadership skills if CTOs are to be truly effective at primary team leadership. In expeditionary leadership, outside the primary team, position power carries much less weight than it does in the primary team. For this reason the development of other bases of influence is essential if CTOs are to wield the influence necessary to carry out their strategic and supra-functional roles. Medcof[61] has reviewed the research on CTO expeditionary influence and developed the model shown in Figure 2 to summarize the results of that research.

A General Model of CTO Influence. The underlying logic of Figure 2 is that CTO influence is founded on the CTO's personal power base which is rooted in the five sources of power shown across the bottom of the figure: ownership, expertise, relationships, structural position and prestige. But even if the CTO has built up a power base on those sources, influence may not result because four factors in the CTO's surrounding environment influence the degree to which that power base can be mobilized. Those four are shown in rectangles in the upper left side of the Figure: the firm's competitive environment, the firm's strategy, the CEO's management style and the CTO's leadership role. If these conditions are right then the CTO's power base can be turned into influence. That influence can then be used to further build up the power base and to modify the environmental factors to further enhance the CTO's influence. The parts of this influence model will now be described in more detail.

The CTO Personal Power Base

The CTO's personal power base is built upon the five sources shown in the rectangles across the bottom of Figure 2.

Ownership Power. This comes from owning a significant share of the firm so the CTO can prevail in making important decisions in the governance of the firm. The ability to prevail ensures that others will ultimately have to concede to the CTO or find themselves relegated to lesser roles or even forced to leave the firm. Knowing that the CTO ultimately has this power will cause many to be influenced.

Expert Power. Knowledge of technology, the organization and/or the environment is the source of expert power. That knowledge is a valuable asset for the firm and allows the CTO to have credible and correct opinions about strategic and other issues. People who believe the CTO has such knowledge and good judgment about it will be influenced by the CTO.

Relationship Power. This comes from good interpersonal relationships with people in many places in the organization and its environment. Those relationships can be professional and/or personal and they lay the groundwork for harmonious and trusting interactions. The credibility that results increases the CTO's influence.

Figure 2. The dynamics of CTO power and influence

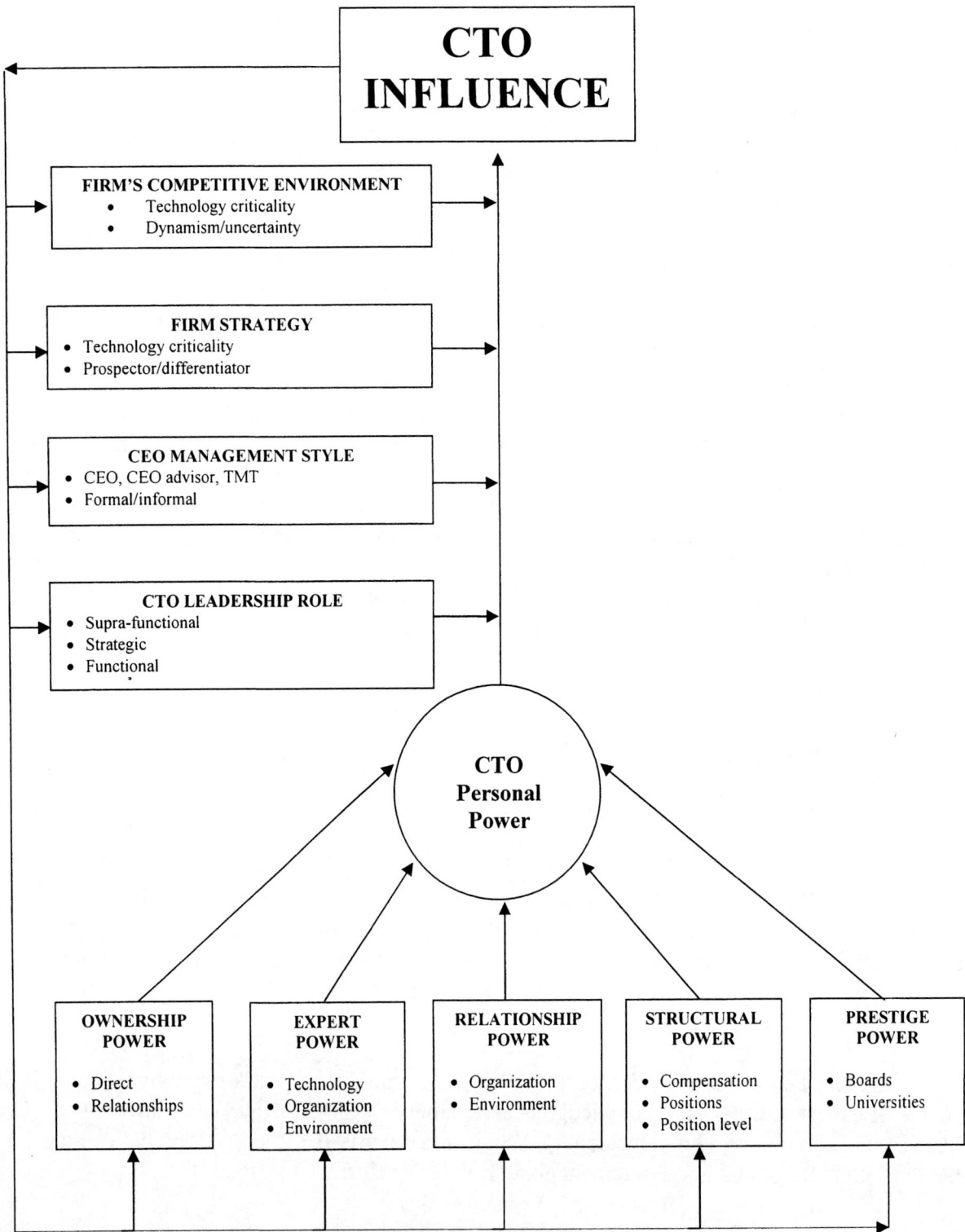

Source: Medcof[62]

Module 7 Leadership 2008 09 08 F

Structural Power. Position in the organizational hierarchy is the basis for this kind of power. The CTO's executive position gives powers that can be wielded to support influence and provides a credibility that also supports influence.

Prestige Power. This results from good positioning with prestigious members of the institutional environment of the firm, by such means as holding directorships on the boards of other firms, belonging to the right golf club, or having family relationships. This prestige, like the credibility that comes from high structural position enhances influence capability.

The Personal Power Base. Every CTO is different and every organization is different so there is no simple formula as to how to build an operative power base from the five sources just described. CTOs must look at their personal situations and their personal capabilities in order to decide how to most effectively build a power base. Different CTOs draw on these various bases to different degrees. Sometimes the best option is to move to another organization to find a more suitable situation.

Circumstantial Contingencies and Influence

Circumstantial Contingencies. The four circumstantial contingencies factors, shown in the rectangles in the upper left of Figure 2, are contingencies that determine whether a personal power base can actually be turned into personal influence for the CTO.

The Firm's Competitive Environment. First, the criticality of technology in the firm's industry affects the degree to which the CTO can use technical expertise as a basis for influence. Most CTOs come from a technical background and can use their technical knowledge as a basis for power. However, if technology is not very important in the industry, technical knowledge may not be valued by other executives. Marketing may be more important, in which case the Vice-President of marketing may be more influential. Second, the dynamism/uncertainty of the environment affects the relative effectiveness of informal and formal means of influence. In highly dynamic industries, executives tend to depend more on informal consultation processes. If that is the case, the value of position power as a source of influence for the CTO is diminished. In such cases CTOs may turn to relationships, expertise and other sources.

Firm Strategy. First, the more important technology is in the firm's strategy, the more effective technical expertise will be as a basis of influence. Second, if the firm pursues a prospector or differentiator strategy, as opposed to a defender or cost leadership strategy, as described by Miles and Snow,[63] the effectiveness of informal influence will be enhanced in comparison to formal. Prospector and differentiator strategies usually involve more flexible organizational processes thus diminishing the influence value of position power.

CEO Management Style. CEO's tend to have their individual management styles and these can influence the amount of influence the CTO and other executives have. If a CEO follows a "CEO Model" of management most decisions are made by the CEO alone after brief consultation with others. With such a CEO there is little opportunity for anyone else to have much influence, including the CTO, no matter how well built the personal power base. At the other extreme, a CEO operating on the "TMT Model" brings executives and other appropriate

29

people together to discuss all significant decisions until a consensus is arrived at. With such a CEO the scope for CTO influence is considerably increased. The level of informality of the CEO's style also makes a difference. Some CEOs operate formally, calling formal meetings of the executive team for most important decisions. The CTO can participate in these and have an influence. Other CEOs consult more informally with selected people regarding decisions. In such cases the CTO cannot depend upon formal position on the executive team as the route to decision inclusion. Other, more informal bases for being included will have to be sought, such as a good personal relationship with the CEO or ready availability for informal meetings.

CTO Leadership Role. Regardless of the leadership role to which a CTO aspires, the culture of the executive team and/or the biases of the CEO may hold the CTO to a more limited role than the CTO desires. For example, the CEO and executive team may believe for various reasons that the CTO should play a purely functional role. They may not open the door for CTO participation at the strategic or supra-functional levels. Whatever power base the CTO may have may have to be used to get the role expanded before higher levels of influence can be exercised. Until that time the CTO may have very little influence at the executive level.

CTO Options

Given the dynamics of power bases and contingency factors, CTOs have to strategize as to how to gain influence given their circumstances. For example, alert CTOs will give serious attention to relationship power if they have noted that the firm's environment is dynamic, the firm's strategy prospector, and the CEO's style informal. CTOs who note that technology is a very important critical contingency at both the environment and firm levels can build and promote technical expertise as a basis for influence. CTOs can also influence their circumstances, as represented by the boxes on the upper left. CTOs who have already built some expertise about the firm's environment might take every opportunity to demonstrate the value of that expertise when supra-functional issues are under discussion. Over time, if credibility is built, they may build a larger presence for themselves in supra-functional discussions and more influence in their organizations. By influencing other executives to understand how critical technology is to competitive success, and convincing them to give it a more central place in firm strategy, CTOs can enhance the influence value of their already present expertise in technology. These examples following the model indicate that CTOs' influence situations are very much negotiated and can be constantly evolving. If CTOs take a proactive approach and continually and skillfully influence the interpretation of the firm's environment, the firm's strategy, the CEO's management style, and his own expected role; organizational influence can increase. Astutely building power bases to be synergistic with these negotiated interpretations will also contribute to influence.

[1] Yukl, G. **Leadership in Organizations.** Pearson/Prentice Hall, 2006.

[2] Elenkov, D.S., Judge, W., & Wright, P. Strategic leadership and executive innovation influence: An international multi-cluster comparative study. *Strategic Management Journal*, 2005, 26: 665-682.

[3] Kotter, J.P. What leaders really do. *Harvard Business Revie,* December, 2001, 85-96.

[4] Kotter, J.P. What leaders really do. *Harvard Business Review: Breakthrough Leadership,* December 2001, p.85-96.

[5] House, R. J., & Aditya, R. N. The social scientific study of leadership: Quo Vadis? *Journal of Management*, 1997, 23(3): 409-473.

[6] Hitt, M., Keats, B. & DeMarie, S. Navigating in the new competitive landscape: Building strategic flexibility and competitive advantage in the 21st century. *Academy of Management Executive*, 1998, 12(4): 22-39.

[7] Medcof, J. W. **Expeditionary Leadership: Leaders Impacting their Contexts.** *Presented at the Annual Meeting of the Academy of Management*, August, 2008, Anaheim.

[8] Medcof, J. W. **Expeditionary Leadership: Leaders Impacting their Contexts.** *Presented at the Annual Meeting of the Academy of Management*, August, 2008, Anaheim.

[9] Lavie, D., Lechner, C. & Singh, H. The Performance implications of timing of entry and involvement in multi-partner alliances. *Academy of Management Journal*, 2007, 50(3), 578-604.

Sampson, R. R&D Alliances and Firm Performance: The impact of technological diversity and alliance organization on innovation. *Academy of Management Journal*, 2007, 50(2), 364-386.

[10] Teece, D., Pisano, G. & Shuen, A. Dynamic capabilities and strategic management. *Strategic Management Journal*, 1997, 18(7): 509-533.

Simon, D., Hitt, M. & Ireland, R. D. Managing firm resources in dynamic environments to create value: Looking inside the black box. *Academy of Management Journal*, 2007. 32(1), 273-292.

[11] Mintzberg, H. **The Nature of Managerial Work**. New York: Harper & Rowe 1973.

Floyd, S. W., & Wooldridge, B. Middle management involvement in strategy and its association with strategic type: a research note. *Strategic Management Journal,* 1992, 13: 153-167.

Floyd, S. W., & Wooldridge, B. Dinosaurs or dynamos? Recognizing middle management's strategic role. *Academy of Management Executive,* 1994, 8(4): 47-57.

Floyd, S. W., & Wooldridge, B. **Building Strategy from the Middle**. Thousand Oaks, CA: Sage Publications Inc., 2000.

Broadbent, M., & Kitzis, E. S. **The New CIO Leader**. Boston: Harvard Business School Press, 2005.

[12] Medcof, J. W. **Expeditionary Leadership: Leaders Impacting their Contexts.** *Presented at the Annual Meeting of the Academy of Management*, August, 2008, Anaheim.

[13] Floyd, S.W. & Wooldridge, B. Dinosaurs or dynamos? Recognizing middle management's strategic role. *The Academy of Management Executive;* 1994, 8(4), 47 – 57.

[14] Floyd, S.W. & Wooldridge, B. Dinosaurs or dynamos? Recognizing middle management's strategic role. *The Academy of Management Executive,* 1994, 8(4), 47 – 57.

[15] Yukl, G. **The Nature of Managerial Work**. Pearson/Prentice Hall, 2005.

[16] Yukl, G. **The Nature of Managerial Work**. Pearson/Prentice Hall, 2005.

[17] Yukl, G. **The Nature of Managerial Work**. Pearson/Prentice Hall, 2005.

[18] Badawy, M.K., **Developing managerial skills in engineers and scientists: succeeding as a technical manager.** *Van Nostrand Reinhold Co., Inc., 1982.*

[19] Badawy, M.K., **Developing managerial skills in engineers and scientists: succeeding as a technical manager.** *Van Nostrand Reinhold Co., Inc., 1982.*

[20] Kraut, A.I., Pedigo, P.R., McKenna, D.D., & Dunnette, M.D. The role of the manager: what's really important in different management jobs. *Engineering Management Review*, 2006, 34(2), 49 63.

[21] Farris, G.F. & Cordero, R. Leading your scientists and engineers. *Research Technology Management,* 2002, 45(6), 13-25.

[22] Medcof, J. W., & Rumpel, S. High technology workers and total rewards. *Journal of High Technology Management Research,* 2007, 18, 56 – 72.

[23] Farris, G.F. & Cordero, R. Leading your scientists and engineers. *Research Technology Management,* 2002, 45(6), 13-25.

[24] Shapero, A. Managing creative professionals. *Research Technology Management,* 1985, 12(2), 33 - 40.

[25] Thompson, L. Improving the creativity of organizational work groups. *Academy of Management Executive,* 2003, 17(1), 96-111.

[26] Thompson, L. Improving the creativity of organizational work groups. *Academy of Management Executive,* 2003, 17(1), 96-111.

[27] Thompson, L. Improving the creativity of organizational work groups. *Academy of Management Executive,* 2003, 17(1), 96-111.

[28] Thamhain, H.J. & Wilemon, D.L. Building high performance engineering project teams. *IEEE Transactions on Engineering Management,* 34(3), 130-137.

[29] Workman, J.P. Engineering's interactions with marketing groups in an engineering-driven organization. *IEEE Transactions on Engineering Management,* 1995, 42(2), 129-139.

[30] Workman, J.P. Engineering's interactions with marketing groups in an engineering-driven organization. *IEEE Transactions on Engineering Management, 1995, 42(2),* 129-139.

[31] Souder, W.E. Managing relations between R&D and marketing in new product development projects. *Journal of Product Innovation Management,* 1988, 5, 6-19.

[32] Barczak, G. & McDonough, E.F. Leading global product development teams. *Research Technology Management,* 2003, 46(6), 14-18.

[33] Pinto, J.K. & Kharbanda, O.P. Lessons for an accidental profession. *Business Horizons,* Mar/Apr, 1995, 41-50.

[34] Ancona, D.G. & Caldwell, D.F. Beyond task and maintenance: defining external functions in groups. *Group & Organization Studies,* 1988, 13(4), 468-494.

[35] Ancona, D.G. & Caldwell, D.F. Beyond task and maintenance: defining external functions in groups. *Group & Organization Studies,* 1988, 13(4), 468-494.

[36] Ransley, D.L. Network more effectively with this checklist. *Research Technology Management,* 1995, 38(6), 12-13.

[37] Medcof, J. W. Training technologists to become managers. *Research Management,* 1985, 12(1), 18-21.

[38] Badawy, M.K., **Developing managerial skills in engineers and scientists: succeeding as a technical manager.** *Van Nostrand Reinhold Co., Inc.,* 1982.

[39] Floyd, S.W. & Wooldridge, B. Dinosaurs or dynamos? Recognizing middle management's strategic role. *The Academy of Management Executive,* 1994, 8(4), 47 – 57.

[40] Floyd, S.W. & Wooldridge, B. Dinosaurs or dynamos? Recognizing middle management's strategic role. *The Academy of Management Executive,* 1994, 8(4), 47 – 57.

[41] Floyd, S.W. & Wooldridge, B. Dinosaurs or dynamos? Recognizing middle management's strategic role. *The Academy of Management Executive,* 1994, 8(4), 47 – 57.

[42] Clark, K. & Wheelwright, S.C. Organizing and Leading "Heavyweight" Development Teams. *California Management Review,* 1992, 34(3), 9-28.

[43] Taguiri, R. Using teams effectively. *Research Technology Management,* 1995, 38(1), 12-13.

[44] Harris, R.C. & Lambert, J.T. Building effective R&D teams: The senior manager's role. *Research Technology Management,* 1998, 41(5), 28-35.

[45] Howell, J.M. & Higgins, C.A. Champions of technological innovation. *Administrative Science Quarterly,* 1990, 35(2), 317-341.

[46] Howell, J.M. & Higgins, C.A. Champions of technological innovation. *Administrative Science Quarterly,* 1990, 35(2), 317-341.

[47] Dutton, J.E., O'Neill, R.M, & Lawrence, K.A. Moves that matter: issue selling and organizational change. *Academy of Management Journal,* 2001, 44(4) 716-736.

[48] Chesbrough, H. W. **Open Innovation**. Boston, MA: Harvard Business School Press, 2003.

[49] Schick, S. Outsourcing breeds it own middle management. *Globe and Mail Update,* December 14, 2006.

[50] Schick, S. Outsourcing breeds it own middle management. *Globe and Mail Update,* December 14, 2006.

[51] MacAvoy, T.C. Choosing an alliance manager. *Research Technology Management,* 1997, 40(5), 12-14.

[52] http://www.businessdictionary.com/definition/organizational-politics.html

[53] Pinto, J. K. Make politics work for you. *Research Technology Management,* 1997, 40(1), 9-10.

[54] Adler, P. S., & Ferdows, K., The Chief Technology Officer. *California Management Review,* 1990, 32(3), 55-62.

[55] Uttal, B., Kantrow, A., Linden, L. H., & Stock, S. Building R&D leadership and credibility. *Research Technology Management,* 1992, 35(3), 15-24.

[56] Adler, P. S., & Ferdows, K., The Chief Technology Officer. *California Management Review,* 1990, 32(3), 55-62.

Bridenbaugh, P. Credibility between CEO and CTO-a CTO's perspective. *Research Technology Management,* 1992, 35(6), 27-33.

Herstatt, C., Tietze, F., Nagahira, A., & Probert, D. The chief technology officer (CTO) in literature and practice – a review and results from field research in Japan. *International Journal of Innovation and Technology Management,* 2007, 4(3), 323-350.

Smith, R. The chief technology officer: Strategic responsibilities and relationships. *Research Technology Management,* 2003, 46(4), 28-36.

Uttal, B., Kantrow, A., Linden, L. H., & Stock, S. Building R&D leadership and credibility. *Research Technology Management,* 1992, 35 (3), 15-24.

[57] Adler, P. S., & Ferdows, K., The Chief Technology Officer. *California Management Review,* 1990, 32(3), 55-62.

Bridenbaugh, P. Credibility between CEO and CTO-a CTO's perspective. *Research Technology Management,* 1992, 35(6), 27-33.

Herstatt, C., Tietze, F., Nagahira, A., & Probert, D. The chief technology officer (CTO) in literature and practice – a review and results from field research in Japan. *International Journal of Innovation and Technology Management,* 2007, 4(3), 323-350.

Smith, R. The Chief Technology Officer: Strategic Responsibilities and Relationship. *Research Technology Management,* 2003, 46(4), 28-36.

Uttal, B., Kantrow, A., Linden, L. H., & Stock, S. Building R&D leadership and credibility. *Research Technology Management,* 1992, 35 (3), 15-24.

[58] Adler, P. S., & Ferdows, K., The Chief Technology Officer. *California Management Review,* 1990, 32(3), 55-62.

Bridenbaugh, P. Credibility between CEO and CTO-a CTO's perspective. *Research Technology Management,* 1992, 35(6), 27-33.

Herstatt, C., Tietze, F., Nagahira, A., & Probert, D. The chief technology officer (CTO) in literature and practice – a review and results from field research in Japan. *International Journal of Innovation and Technology Management,* 2007, 4(3), 323-350.

Smith, R. The Chief Technology Officer: Strategic Responsibilities and Relationship. *Research Technology Management,* 2003, 46(4), 28-36.

Uttal, B.; Kantrow, A., Linden, L. H., & Stock, S. Building R&D leadership and credibility. *Research Technology Management,* 1992, 35 (3), 15-24.

[59] Adler, P. S., & Ferdows, K., The Chief Technology Officer. *California Management Review,* 1990, 32(3), 55-62.

Bridenbaugh, P. Credibility between CEO and CTO-a CTO's perspective. *Research Technology Management,* 1992, 35(6), 27-33.

Herstatt, C., Tietze, F., Nagahira, A., & Probert, D. The chief technology officer (CTO) in literature and practice – a review and results from field research in Japan. *International Journal of Innovation and Technology Management,* 2007, 4(3), 323-350.

Smith, R. The Chief Technology Officer: Strategic Responsibilities and Relationship. *Research Technology Management,* 2003, 46(4), 28-36.

Uttal, B., Kantrow, A., Linden, L. H., & Stock, S. Building R&D leadership and credibility. *Research Technology Management,* 1992, 35 (3), 15-24.

[60] Uttal, B., Kantrow, A., Linden, L. H., & Stock, S. Building R&D leadership and credibility. *Research Technology Management,* 1992, 35(3), 15-24.

[61] Medcof, J. W. **Expeditionary Leadership: Leaders Impacting their Contexts.** *Presented at the Annual Meeting of the Academy of Management,* August, 2008, Anaheim.

[62] Medcof, J. W. **Expeditionary Leadership: Leaders Impacting their Contexts.** *Presented at the Annual Meeting of the Academy of Management,* August, 2008, Anaheim.

[63] Miles, R. E., & Snow, C. C. **Organizational Strategy, Structure and Process.** New York: McGraw-Hill, 1978.

The New Rules

THE GLOBAL 500 • GM: WHAT WOULD CARLOS DO?

FORTUNE

JULY 24, 2006 $4.99

Sorry, Jack!

Welch's Rules for Winning
Don't Work Anymore
(But We've Got 7 New Ones That Do)
BY BETSY MORRIS

Once upon a time, there was a route to success that corporate America agreed on. But in today's fast-changing landscape, that old formula is getting tired. And a search is on for . . .

THE NEW RULES

BY BETSY MORRIS • Even now, nearly five years after his retirement from General Electric, Jack Welch commands the spotlight. He is still power-lunching, still making the gossip columns, still the charismatic embodiment of the star CEO. His books are automatic bestsellers. More than any other single figure, he stands as a model not just for the can-do American executive but for a way of doing business that revived the U.S. corporation in the 1980s and dominated the world's economic landscape for a quarter-century. Just try to find an executive who hasn't been influenced by his teachings. What came to be known as Jack's Rules are by now the business equivalent of holy writ, bedrock wisdom that has been open to interpretation, perhaps, but not dispute.

But the time has come: Corporate America needs a new playbook. The challenge facing U.S. business leaders is greater than ever before, yet they have less control than ever—and less job security. The volatility of the markets is so unpredictable, the pressure from hedge funds and private-equity investors so relentless, the competition from China and India so intense, that the edicts of the past are starting to feel out of date. In executive suites

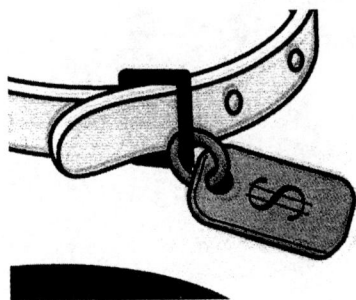

across the country, a dramatic rethinking is underway about funda-
mental assumptions that defined Welch and his era. Is an emphasis on
market share really the prime directive? Is a company's near-term stock
price—and the quarterly earnings per share that drive it—really the best

measure of a CEO's success? In what ways is managing a company to please Wall Street bad for competitiveness in the long run?

Jack Welch, needless to say, is having none of it. When FORTUNE caught up with him recently, he was as confident and outspoken as ever. "I'm perfectly prepared to change," says Welch (who co-writes a column in *Business Week* with his wife, Suzy). "Change is great." But, he asserts, he sees no reason to back away from the principles by which he and other star CEOs like Roberto Goizueta of Coca-Cola managed. If applied correctly, Welch contends, his rules can work forever.

Sorry, Jack, but we don't buy it. The practices that brought Welch, Goizueta, and others such success were developed to battle problems specific to a time and place in history. And they worked. No one questions today that bloated bureaucracy can kill a business. No one forgets the shareholder—far from it. Yet those threats have receded. And they have been replaced by new ones. The risk we now face is applying old solutions to new problems.

Early on, Welch argued that lagging businesses—those not No. 1 or No. 2 in their markets—should be fixed, sold, or closed. In a 1981 speech titled "Growing Fast in a Slow-Growth Economy," he announced that GE would no longer tolerate low-margin and low-growth units. GE, he told analysts at the Pierre Hotel in New York, "will be the locomotive pulling the GNP, not the caboose following it." As much as any other single event, Welch's words marked the dawn of the shareholder-value movement. And GE eventually became its star. No question who was Welch's boss. His report card: the stock price. His goal: consistent earnings growth.

As his ruthlessly efficient strategy wrenched GE into high performance, the company's stock took off. Soon virtually everything Welch said became gospel—often to the extreme. When Welch embraced Six Sigma, the program began to proliferate all over corporate America. He talked about being the leanest and meanest and lowest-cost, and corporate America got out its ax. Welch advocated ranking your players and weeding out your weakest, and HR departments turned Darwinian. As time went on, the mantra of shareholder value took on a life of its own. Cheered on by academics, consulting firms and investors, more and more companies tried to defy history (and their own reality) to sustain growth and dazzle Wall Street as Welch was doing. Accounting tricks, acquisition mania, outright thievery—executives went overboard. "It became all about 'real men make their numbers,' " says one CEO. "What were we thinking?"

This, says Harvard Business School's Rakesh Khurana, is the legacy of the Old Rules. Managing to create shareholder value became managed earnings became managing quarter to quarter to please the Street. "That meant a disinvestment in the future," says Khurana, author of *Searching for a Corporate Savior.* "It was a dramatic reversal of everything that made capitalism strong and the envy of the rest of the world: the willingness of a CEO to forgo dividends and make an investment that wouldn't be realized until one or two CEOs down the road." Now, he believes, "we're at a hinge point of American capitalism."

There is another model. In breathtakingly short order, the rock star of business is no longer the guy atop the FORTUNE 500 (today Rex Tillerson at ExxonMobil), but the very guy those

BIG CHANGE: Size matters less than agility.

WELCH FIRES BACK
Neutron Jack defends his turf.

JACK WELCH was about to head to a television studio for what he calls "the best job I've ever had"—on-air analyst for the Boston Red Sox pre-game cable show—when we caught up with him. As usual, he had no shortage of opinions.

▶ **On the power of size.** It's great to be big. Being big doesn't mean you have to be slow. It doesn't mean you have to have tons of layers. It doesn't mean you can't have highly entrepreneurial people. ... You can get fat. Monopolies are often guilty of not moving. If GE had stayed pat and we didn't grow in financial services and we stayed No. 1 in light bulbs, we'd have been in deep yogurt. But that doesn't mean you don't want to be big and strong.

▶ **On leadership.** You want to be No. 1. There's nothing wrong with that. You don't want to be a loser. Nos. 3, 4, and 5 don't have the same flexibility. You don't have the same level of resources. You can't do R&D at the same level. I agree being No. 1 in a static environment is not by itself sufficient. No. 4 might have smarter management that uses money more wisely. What you do with the resources that come from being a leader—that's what determines your future.

▶ **On keeping lean.** I was all for de-layering and flattening organizations. Today I'd flatten them even more. Some companies are still too hierarchical. Some are right out of Bethlehem Steel.

▶ **On exploiting niches.** It's not inconsistent at all with wanting to be No. 1, No. 2. In a big company you'd better be out exploring new niches. Today's niches, tomorrow's big things. Those aren't inconsistent.

▶ **On customers.** When has there ever been a divergence between shareholders and customers? No one is out saying, "Let's screw this customer today, and if we do, our share price might go up 20 cents." They're just not doing it.

▶ **On looking outward.** GE in the 1990s was all about looking outward. We traveled to other companies constantly to bring back best practices. It is one of the great ways to multiply the intellect in your organization.

▶ **On ranking employees.** That was very controversial. Weed out the weakest. The Red Sox and the Mets are playing tonight. Guess what? They're not putting on the field guys in the minors. It's all about fielding the best team. It's been portrayed as a cruel system. It isn't. The cruel system is the one that doesn't tell anybody where they stand.

Welch: Still confident

FORTUNE 500 types used to love to ridicule: Steve Jobs at Apple. The biggest feat of the decade is not making the elephant dance, as Lou Gerstner famously did at IBM, but inventing the iPod and transforming an industry. Dell spectacularly upended Compaq and Hewlett-Packard, yet few big companies paid close enough attention to see that new technologies and business models were negating the power of economies of scale in myriad ways. Nobody has proved that more than Google.

Yet in the corridors of corporate power, the old rules continue to cast an outsized shadow. Many CEOs are following a playbook that has, at best, been distorted by time. "How do you think about building shareholder value when a lot of people are really just going to hold the share for the moment?" says Jim Collins, a former Stanford Business School professor and the author of *Good to Great* and *Built to Last*. "The idea of maximizing shareholder value is a strange idea when [many shareholders] are really share flippers. That's a real change. That does make the notion of building a great company more difficult."

That doesn't mean everything about Welch's era is wrong. Indeed, we named him "manager of the century" in 1999. Were he at GE today, he might well be in the forefront of the current wave of rethinking, as his successor, Jeffrey Immelt, surely is. Still, in the way of all good analogies, we must begin by tearing down the old so that we can really open ourselves to something different. In that spirit, then, here are seven old rules whose shortcomings have become apparent and seven replacements that point toward a new model for success. Some of the old rules are inspired directly by Welch's teachings; others are not. You may not agree with all of our conclusions (Welch certainly didn't—see box at left). We welcome the debate. What's most important is to get the discussion started.

> "It became all about 'real men make their numbers.' What were we thinking?"

OLD RULE: BIG DOGS OWN THE STREET.
NEW RULE: AGILE IS BEST; BEING BIG CAN BITE YOU.

UNTIL THE VERY END of the last century, big meant good in the business world. B-schools taught the benefits of economies of scale. The greater your revenue, the more you could spread fixed costs across units sold. With size came dominance—of airwaves, store shelves, supply chains, distribution channels. Until the mid-1990s, a company's market value usually tracked its revenue.

Then strange things started to happen. Microsoft's market cap passed IBM's in 1993, even though Bill Gates' $3 billion in revenue was one-twenty-second that of IBM. Scale didn't insulate GM from near-catastrophic decline. The big dogs seemed to hit a wall. (The median FORTUNE 500 company is now three times the size it was in 1980, in real terms, and thus much harder to manage.) Citigroup, built through acquisitions by Sandy Weill to deliver consistent earnings, suddenly found the market focused on whatever bad news emerged in Citi's far-flung units instead of

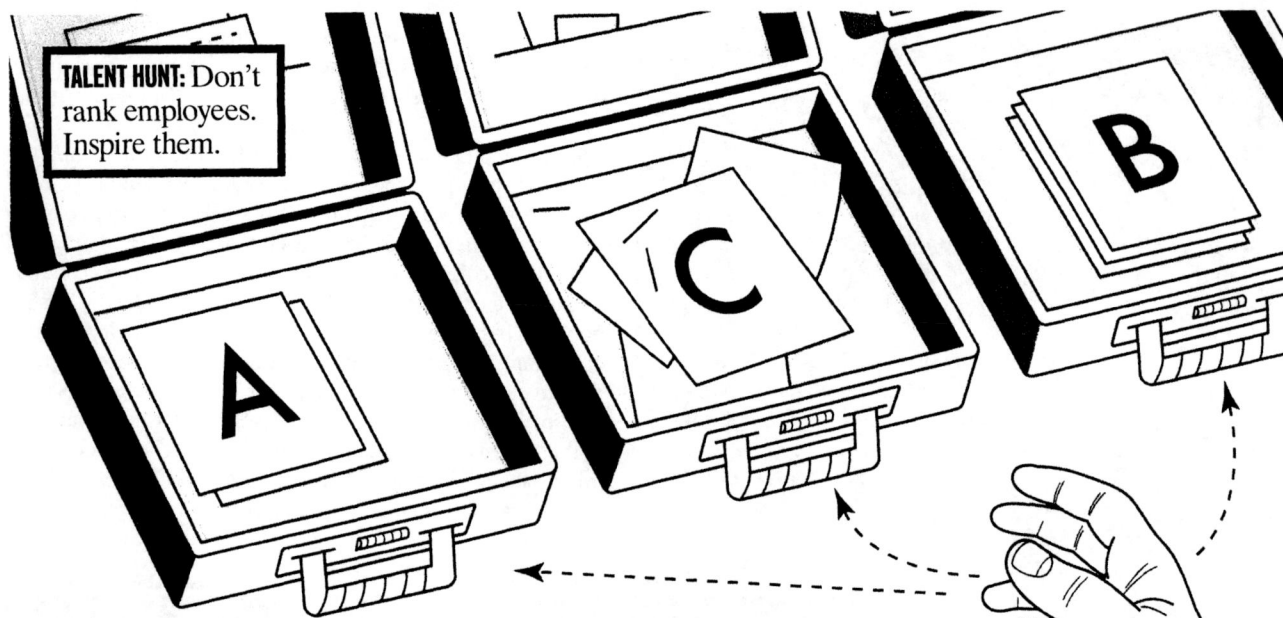

TALENT HUNT: Don't rank employees. Inspire them.

on the smoothness of its overall performance. Big Pharma used to be prized for its unmatched R&D spending; now it is the smaller biotech firms that generate the cutting-edge drugs—and drugmakers Merck, Bristol-Myers, and Eli Lilly all have smaller market caps than biotech Genentech, despite significantly higher revenue and profits.

Technological advances and changing business models have diminished the importance of scale, as outsourcing, partnering, and other alliances with specialty firms (with their own economies of scale) have made it possible to convert fixed costs into variable ones. Dell, it turned out, was not an anomaly, it was just the beginning—a pioneer at all this, keeping its costs down by outsourcing disk drives, memory chips, monitors, and more, freeing itself to focus on (and clean up in) direct selling and just-in-time assembly.

> With size came dominance—of airwaves, store shelves, supply chains. But risks arose.

OLD RULE: BE NO. 1 OR NO. 2 IN YOUR MARKET.
NEW RULE: FIND A NICHE, CREATE SOMETHING NEW.

NOBODY WANTS TO BE a laggard, of course, and there is much to be said for being the market leader. Nike, Wal-Mart and Exxon certainly don't wish they were anything else. But more and more, market domination is no safety net. Disney's stranglehold on animated films meant nothing once Pixar's digital innovation hit the scene. AOL's established user base couldn't slow down Google.

Look at Coca-Cola, whose still-strong No. 1 position in cola turned out to be not an insurance policy but proof of what consulting firm McKinsey calls the "incumbent's curse." Coke's archrivalry with Pepsi was always about market share—capturing it or defending it by tenths of a percentage point in grocery stores, restaurants, and faraway lands. Coke executives defined their industry as "share of stomach"—that is, the total ounces of liquid an average person consumes in a day and what per-

centage of it can be filled with Coke. CEO Roberto Goizueta told Jack Welch in a conversation in FORTUNE a decade ago that the soft drink industry wouldn't run out of growth until "that faucet in your kitchen sink is used for what God intended"—dispensing Coke from the tap.

But eventually Coke's monomaniacal focus backfired. When bottled waters like Evian and Poland Spring began to gain traction, Coke didn't pay sufficient attention. Its board vetoed management's proposal to buy Gatorade in 2000 (sending the sports drink into the arms of Pepsi). Such niche products were viewed as low-volume distractions. Yet last year, in a turnabout that would have been inconceivable a decade ago, soda sales fell, and water, sports drinks, and energy drinks all soared. The jaw dropper: Energy drinks—which boast a profit margin of 85%, according to Bernstein Research—are now expected to outearn every other category of soft drink within three years.

Not everyone missed the opportunity. Out in Corona, Calif., tiny Hansen Natural Corp. didn't care about being No. 1 or No. 2. CEO Rodney Sacks was instead noticing how consumers were migrating from carbonated soft drinks to juices, iced teas, and "functional drinks." So in the '90s he began moving Hansen beyond its base as a maker of natural sodas (Mandarin Lime, Orange Mango) toward vitamin and energy drinks. Never mind that the energy-drink market was tiny then. "We look for niches and see how they grow," he says. Since launching an energy drink called Monster four years ago (deftly packaged in a dramatic-looking 16-ounce can adorned with a clawmark), Hansen's sales have quadrupled to $348 million, vaulting its shares to $79 from a split-adjusted $2.

Coke has gotten religion. CEO Neville Isdell's team is pushing an array of new drinks, including a half dozen of its own energy entries that have earned the company a significant stake in the U.S. market. "We believe there is value in those niches,"

Isdell told FORTUNE this spring. "It will not drive the volume number, but volume is something we've often chased to the detriment of the long-term business."

Starbucks, on the other hand, is a drink-seller that has avoided the incumbent's trap. "We've never said we wanted to be No. 1 or No. 2," says CEO Jim Donald. Starbucks isn't a brand per se; it's more an identity that's morphed from a product (a latte) to a place to get wireless, to a place with music to meet friends. "If we said we wanted to be the No. 1 coffee company, that's what would be on our mind," Donald says. Instead, the company has kept moving, evolving, trying new things. "It doesn't matter where you end up," says Donald. "It matters that you're the company of choice."

OLD RULE: SHAREHOLDERS RULE. NEW RULE: THE CUSTOMER IS KING.

WHENEVER YOU ASK A CEO about the importance of customers, you hear the requisite platitudes. But in fact, customers have often lost out in the relentless push to maximize shareholder value (as represented by the stock price) and to maximize it immediately. One Bain & Co. study found a huge gap between the perceptions of executives—80% of whom think they are doing an excellent job of serving customers—and the perceptions of customers themselves: Only 8% of them agree. Every four years, according to Bain, the average company loses more than half its customers. Aggressive pricing (on hotel phone bills, rental-car gas charges, and credit card fees, to name a few examples) has increased as the profit pressure on companies has mounted, says Bain's Fred Reichheld. Abusing customers this way, says Reichheld, "destroys the future of a business." He believes that such behavior—and not scandals like Enron and Tyco—is why fewer than half of all Americans have a favorable opinion of business today.

This is shareholder-value theory taken to the extreme: the tail wagging the dog. One CEO, who asked not to be named, describes the pressures this way: Businesses became disconnected from their fundamentals, producing "perceived value" instead of real value, because that's what the stock market rewards. When investor-driven capitalism took over from managerial-driven capitalism, as Harvard's Khurana puts it, CEOs began managing the company by earnings per share instead of focusing on details like new products, service calls, customer-satisfaction scores—all those things that are sup-

TRENDSETTERS
Plain-talking execs

"We've never said we wanted to be No. 1 or No. 2."
Jim Donald, CEO, Starbucks

"If you're not nimble, there's no advantage to size. It's like a rock."
Anne Mulcahy, CEO, Xerox

"If we see opportunity at a short-term cost, we'll do [it] every time."
Art Levinson, CEO, Genentech

posed to produce the earnings per share.

Yet some renegades thumbed their noses at Wall Street and truly kept the consumer experience front and center. Think Apple, which has from inception been predicated on dreaming up what customers want before they know it. Or look at Genentech, whose employees are greeted each day by billboards of the cancer patients who take its drugs, to remind everyone of the importance of their work. At GE, CEO Immelt has instigated what he calls "dreaming sessions" to brainstorm with key customers. He also requires all businesses to be judged using a metric called Net Promoter Score, developed by Reichheld and his colleagues at Bain, that measures how likely a customer is to have you back. "When everything is focused on delivering for customers, that makes employees proud," Reichheld says. "They become the powerful engine."

OLD RULE: BE LEAN AND MEAN. NEW RULE: LOOK OUT, NOT IN.

IN 1995 JACK WELCH "went nuts," as he later put it, over Six Sigma, a set of methods for improving quality—plus a powerful way to reduce costs—that had been developed by Motorola in the '80s. At GE's annual managers' meeting in Boca Raton the following January, he told his troops that embracing Six Sigma would be the company's most ambitious undertaking ever. GE's "best and the brightest" were redeployed to put the methods into action. And it worked. Welch would later write that Six Sigma helped drive operating margins to 18.9% in 2000 from 14.8% four years earlier.

No wonder that after Welch adopted Six Sigma (to which he devotes a chapter of his book *Winning*), more than a quarter of the FORTUNE 200 followed suit. Yet not all firms were able to find the same magic. In fact, of 58 large companies that have announced Six Sigma programs, 91% have trailed the S&P 500 since, according to an analysis by Charles Holland of consulting firm Qualpro (which espouses a competing quality-improvement process).

One of the chief problems of Six Sigma, say Holland and other critics, is that it is narrowly designed to fix an existing process, allowing little room for new ideas or an entirely different approach. All that talent—all those best and brightest—were devoted to, say, driving defects down to 3.4 per million and not on coming up with new products or disruptive technologies. Innovation is "a meta-stable entity," says Vishva Dixit, vice president for research of

Genentech, who oversees 800 scientists at a company that has created some of the most revolutionary anticancer drugs on the market. "Nothing will kill it faster than trying to manage it, predict it, and put it on a timeline."

An inward-looking culture can leave firms vulnerable in a business world that is changing at a breakneck pace—whether it's Craigslist stealing classified ads from local newspapers or VoIP threatening to make phone calls virtually free. "The availability of information and the opening of key markets is exploding," says Clay Christensen, a Harvard Business School professor and the author of *The Innovator's Dilemma*, "and now you put a few million Chinese and Indian engineers to the test of disrupting us too." No business can afford to focus its energies on its own navel in that environment. "Getting outside is everything," says GE's Immelt (who still deploys Six Sigma). From the day he took over as CEO, he says, he knew the company would need to be "much more forward-facing in the future than we ever were in the past." He explains: "It's not about change. It's about sudden and abrupt and uncontrollable change. If you're not externally focused in this world, you can really lose your edge."

OLD RULE: RANK YOUR PLAYERS; GO WITH THE A'S.
NEW RULE: HIRE PASSIONATE PEOPLE.

AT GE UNDER WELCH, employees were ranked as A, B, or C players, and the bottom group was relentlessly culled. "We're an A-plus company," Welch told his executives in 1997, according to Robert Slater's book, *Jack Welch and the GE Way*. "We want only A players. Don't spend time trying to get C's to be B's. Move them out early."

Pretty soon places as diverse as Charles Schwab and Ford began ranking employees. But as with Six Sigma, the practice became overdone. Welch's "vitality curve," in the hands of less deft managers, became the "dead man's curve," or "rank and yank." Everybody, it seemed, was expendable. There was a price to pay. According to a Rutgers and University of Connecticut poll in 2002, 58% of workers believed most top executives put their own self-interest ahead of the company's, while only 33% trusted that their bosses have the firm's best interests at heart. "All of a sudden, when big companies had to change and respond to the marketplace and move quickly, they found out they couldn't, because they didn't have people engaged and aligned around the corporate mission," says Xerox CEO Anne Mulcahy. "Then being big is a disadvantage. If you're not nimble, there's no advantage to size. It's like a rock."

While studying companies trying to transform themselves, Christopher Bartlett of Harvard Business School and a colleague found the major obstacle was inefficient use of increasingly disenfranchised employees. "People don't come to work to be No. 1 or No. 2 or to get a 20% net return on assets," Bartlett says. "They want a sense of purpose. They come to work to get meaning from their lives."

Steve Jobs has emphasized that Apple hires only people who

are passionate about what they do (something that, to be fair, Welch also talked about). At Genentech, CEO Art Levinson says he actually screens out job applicants who ask too many questions about titles and options, because he wants only people who are driven to make drugs that help patients fight cancer. GE still ranks employees, but Immelt has also added a new system of rating—red, yellow, or green—on five leadership traits (including creativity and external focus). Employees are rated against themselves, not one another. Immelt doesn't talk about jettisoning the bottom 10%. He talks about building a team. "When you're 18 years old, you say, 'The iPod is neat,' " Immelt explains, "but people don't dream about making a gas turbine. If we can recruit the best 22-year-olds, we can double and triple in size. If not, then we're already way too big. You've got to be pragmatic about what turns people on."

OLD RULE: HIRE A CHARISMATIC CEO.
NEW RULE: HIRE A COURAGEOUS CEO.

AS BIG SHAREHOLDERS began to throw their weight around in the 1980s, boards sacked their CEOs and named dazzling replacements. And the celebrity CEO was born. The stars of that era were a varied crew: Jacques Nasser, Lou Gerstner, George Fisher, Michael Armstrong, Jack Welch, Ken Lay, Al Dunlap, Sandy Weill, Carly Fiorina. Some got more credit than they deserved, others more blame. A voracious business press helped burnish (or break) reputations. The bull market fueled the myth that a truly superior CEO could hit earnings targets quarter after quarter and propel the stock price unrelentingly higher.

But the tactics used by this generation of leaders—squeezing costs, deftly managing financial and accounting decisions, using acquisitions to grow—did not always provide long-term solutions. (A McKinsey study of 157 companies that bulked up through acquisition in the '90s found that only 12% grew significantly faster than their peers, and only seven firms generated returns that were above industry-average.) Today many of those methods have fallen out of favor. Tellingly, one top management tool du jour is the stock buyback, which can buoy share prices and pacify investors—but also indicates that the CEO has no better ideas for deploying capital.

If the celebrity CEO needed a spotlight, then today's leaders need internal fortitude. Of 940 executives surveyed by Boston Consulting Group last year, 90% said organic growth was "essential" to their success. But less than half were happy with the return on their R&D spending. And therein lies the rub: Organic growth is not a quick fix.

Real growth requires placing big bets that probably won't pay off until far into the future—and today's impatient culture offers little incentive. What practically killed Xerox was its leaders' resistance to making the technological leap from analog copying to digital, which was almost guaranteed (as most such changes are) to cut margins. By the time they were finally forced to, their business was in free

REPORTER ASSOCIATE *Patricia Neering*

> "Nothing will kill innovation faster than trying to put it on a timeline."

GOOD WORKS: Defy short-termism. Stress the future.

fall. The company was eventually charged with improperly accelerating revenues and overstating earnings. (It settled without admitting wrongdoing and paid a $10 million fine.)

"You have to change when you're at the top of your game in terms of profit," says Mulcahy, who cleaned up the mess, made the changes to digital and color, and is now trying to jump-start revenue. "It's hard to do. Your business looks its best. Your margins are at their best. All that makes your job easier. Then you're like, 'Oh, shit, here we go again.' You've got to jump into that risk pool, and once again you're in this mode of 'You know, this could fail.' "

Never before has a CEO more needed to take risks, but rarely has Wall Street been less receptive. A recent Booz Allen study found that a CEO is vulnerable to ouster if his stock price has lagged behind the S&P 500 by an average of 2% since he took the top job. Cisco Systems CEO John Chambers says he knows a number of colleagues who are planning to step down because of the difficulty of balancing the short-term pressures of the Street with what's in the long-term best interest of the company.

But standing tall is precisely what all those corner-office pros get paid the big bucks for, isn't it? "You have to have the courage of your convictions," says Chambers. Immelt agrees that you must be willing to spend time "in the wilderness with no love." And directors need some courage too: to resist pressure to judge a CEO by the company's stock price today and get back to harder measures like return on invested capital. Hark back again to that seminal Jack Welch speech in 1981. It hardly took the world by storm—in fact, Welch has talked about how little it seemed to impress analysts that day, barely moving the stock. But leadership is not about following the rules of the past. It is about standing up for what you believe is best, regardless of the consequences.

FEEDBACK bmorris@fortunemail.com

> **Real growth requires big bets that probably won't pay out until years later.**

OLD RULE: ADMIRE MY MIGHT.
NEW RULE: ADMIRE MY SOUL.

TODAY BRAVADO IS DANGEROUS. Soft-drink companies became bad guys when they were slow to leave the school lunchroom. Nike got smacked by sweatshop allegations. Try surfing wakeupwalmart.com to see how powerful a critical community of Internet activists can be. That old notion that has served Goldman Sachs so well is creeping back into vogue: It's okay to be greedy as long as it's "long-term greedy." Says Isdell at Coke: "I do not [agree with] Milton Friedman—that the role of the corporation is solely to make money. Our legitimization in society is a very important part of what we do."

Having a "soul" as a corporation is more than contributing to causes or being transparent about executive compensation or adhering to environmental regulation (though it is certainly all of those things). It is defining a company's vision in a sustainable, long-term way—and to hell with what the hedge funds or other pay-me-now investors say. CEOs must get better at courting long-term investors—explaining their strategies, saying exactly what they intend to do, avoiding the temptation to sugarcoat. "There is so much pressure to hit your numbers," says Genentech's Levinson. "I've been very clear with Wall Street since 1995 that if we see an opportunity to make better drugs and more money down the road at a short-term cost, we will do that every time. And you need to know that's the kind of company we are."

That's easier to do, of course, when you're a glamorous, fast-growing little biotech. So it raises the question: Does the rest of corporate America have the moral fiber to defy the present, when needed, and focus on the future? And do shareholders have patience enough to support them? In other words, are they willing to be long-term greedy—or are they just greedy? **F**

THE EDUCATION OF ANDY GROVE

A Harvard historian explains how Intel's legendary chief became **the best model we have for leading a business** in the 21st century. **AN ESSAY BY RICHARD S. TEDLOW**

———————◆———————

In 1991, an instructor at Stanford's Graduate School of Business presented his class with a case study. It went like this: A CEO was scheduled to address a major industry gathering, and he could give one of three speeches. The first would publicly commit his company to incorporating a sexy, sophisticated new technology in its products. The second speech would reaffirm the company's commitment to developing its existing technology. The third speech would do neither, leaving the decision to "the market." The stakes were enormous: A wrong decision could well ruin the business. What should the CEO do? The question was more than academic, because the CEO described in the case was also the man at the front of the classroom. Dr. Andrew S. Grove, like professor Indiana Jones, was better known for his exploits as "Andy," the famous leader of Intel Corp. But unlike Indy, Grove wasn't simply biding time here between ad-

PHOTOGRAPH BY BEN BAKER—REDUX

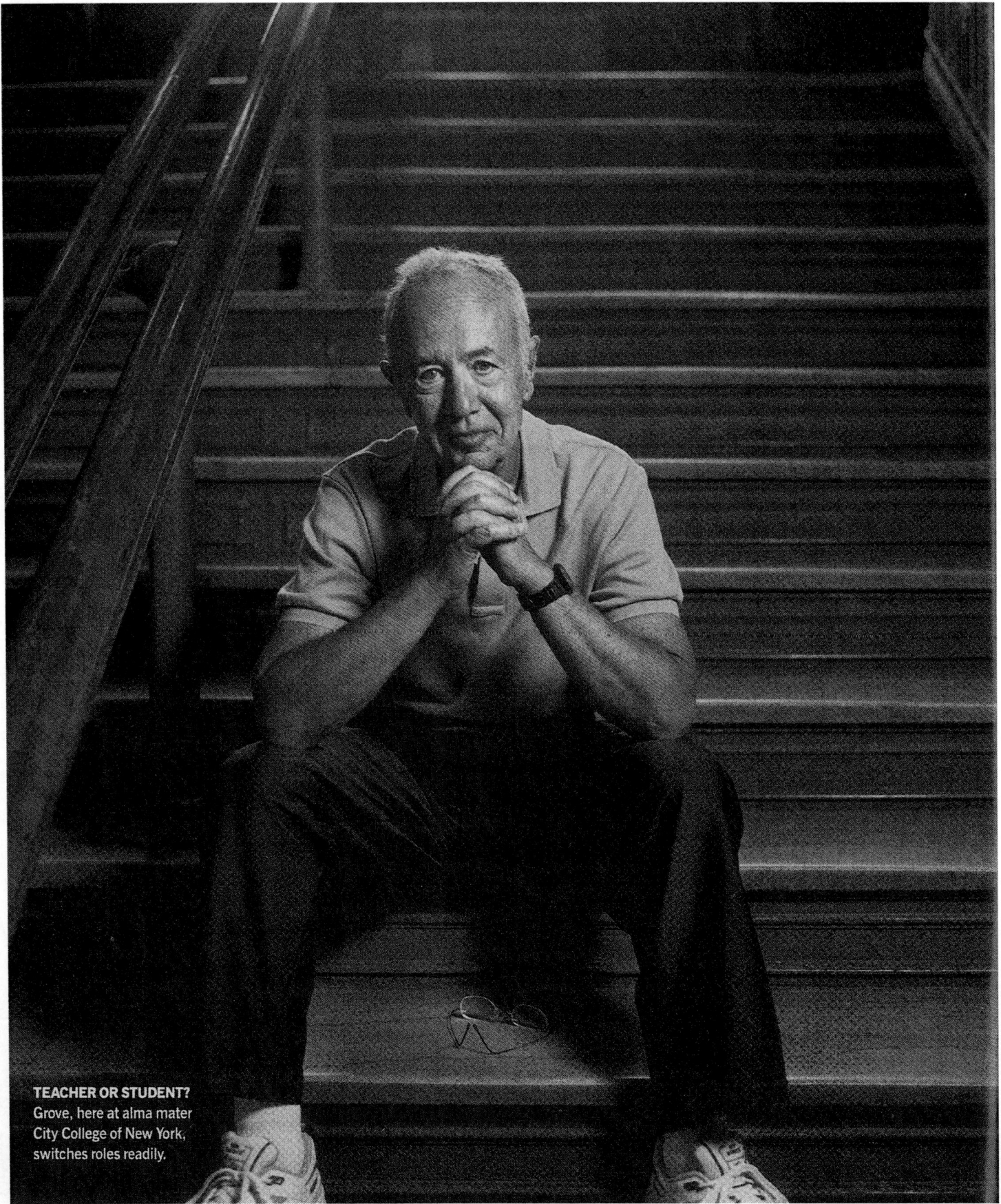

TEACHER OR STUDENT?
Grove, here at alma mater
City College of New York,
switches roles readily.

ventures. His question was meant not just to challenge students' thinking but to advance his own. That big speech was three weeks away, and Grove had yet to make up his mind. He didn't know the answer.

It's not common for any CEO to stand before an audience and say, "I don't know what to do. What do you think?" It's even less common for that CEO to listen to the responses and take them seriously. But Grove, 69, has never lost track of the truth: that Intel has always been one wrong answer away from disaster—and that a closed mind is a trap door to the abyss.

Grove and Intel are now embedded so deeply Inside our minds, our computers, and our culture—the man has been on 77 magazine covers, by one count—that with hindsight, their success seems foreordained. But the opposite is the case: By all odds, Intel should have failed. It should have been destroyed by the same brutal international competition that has killed apparel companies, tire companies, and television companies, or fallen into obscurity like Zilog and other successful chipmakers. Intel, too, should have stumbled on the terrifying treadmill of Moore's Law, which requires betting billions upon billions of dollars on ever more costly factories to make chips you're still developing for customers who've yet to demand them. It should have been eclipsed by an upstart competitor with a better mousetrap. Intel's success should never have happened—it was an anomaly, an outlier, a freak.

That's why Grove had chosen himself as the day's case study in the class he was teaching with professor Robert Burgelman, his longtime collaborator and the author of *Strategy Is Destiny*. In business you often don't see the cliff until you've already walked over it. Visibility on the ground is bad, and the roadmap—well, that can't be trusted either. To spot the next cliff, Andy Grove was willing to let go of his instincts—since they could be wrong—and view himself as a student might: from outside, peering down with the wide-angle, disinterested perspective of the observer. Did the man below seem aware of his surroundings? Was he choosing the correct path? Was there a 1,000-foot drop ahead?

Normally, our society observes a division of labor. Musicians don't critique, and critics don't compose. Quarterbacks decide on Sunday, and fans deride on Monday. It is the singular ability to inhabit both roles at once—subject and object, actor and audience, master and student—that sets Grove apart. And it's why, for everything that has been written by and about him, we have yet to appreciate his biggest legacy. Andy Grove is America's greatest student and teacher of business.

By analyzing the decisions he made on the road to becoming a great leader, you can learn to hone your own leadership skills. Because there's no gain in being able to recruit great employees, handle a board, dazzle Wall Street, or rally your cavalry for a glorious charge at dawn's early light if you haven't figured out which way to point the horses.

Grove's output as a teacher of management has been prodi-

"That is not the right question," Grove will say— and push you to dig for the truth.

gious. He has taught from the lectern, in the op-ed pages, in his famous (sometimes feared) one-on-one sessions, and with his books, including 1983's *High Output Management* and 1996's *Only the Paranoid Survive*, whose title entered the lexicon along with its phrase "strategic inflection point," which Grove defines as "a time in the life of a business when its fundamentals are about to change." His teaching would have been an impressive career in itself. Yet it is one thing to search for truth in the ivory tower and quite another to take those lessons, however wrenching, and apply them to a living, breathing business like Intel. Grove's most powerful lessons have been in the doing.

What can others learn from Grove's odyssey? As we face a future where change is not only constant but accelerating, reality will transform itself more swiftly than most humans—or most companies—are hard-wired to handle. Even startups that overturn one reality are easily overturned by the next big change. Grove has escaped natural selection by doing the evolving himself. Forcibly adapting himself to a succession of new realities, he has left a trail of discarded assumptions in his wake. When reality has changed, he has found the will to let go and embrace the new.

It's a performance as remarkable as his life story. There will not be another CEO who survived both the Nazis and the communists before becoming a naturalized capitalist. And yet Grove is the best model we've got for doing business in the 21st century. If you hope to thrive in an environment of rapid change, it is this outlier—his strengths forged in a distant and vanished world—that you should follow. Begin your lesson in leadership the same way Andy Grove attacks a problem: by setting aside everything you know.

As a historian whose subjects have been, until now, no longer living, I found it a jolt to face a very alive Andy Grove. When he gets to a particularly intense point in a conversation, Grove leans forward and fixes you directly with his eyes, which are a startling blue. "That is not the right question," he will say, briefly taking over the duties of the interviewer. It's not personal. It's about an invisible third party: the truth. The truth is so precious and so hard to coax into view—surrounded by its bodyguard of politics and half-truths—that there is simply no time for fuzzy thinking. There are moments when you can almost ex-

FEEDBACK *fortunemail_letters@fortunemail.com*

perience firsthand the flow of self that went into Intel. And Grove's state-of-the-art memory can transport you from the deck of his home—where a commanding view of Silicon Valley spreads out at his feet—to vivid places in time. Like the day not long after the Stanford case study when Intel executives Craig Kinnie and Dennis Carter arrived in his cubicle to confront him.

In the run-up to the speech about technology choices, Grove had uncharacteristically wavered. He'd told Stanford's Burgelman that he was inclined to stick with Intel's mainstay chip technology known as CISC (for complex instruction set computing—don't ask). But when Intel published its annual report, the cover included a new, fashion-forward RISC chip (for reduced instruction set computing). Engineers across the industry were enamored of RISC because of its elegance: It required fewer transistors to accomplish most computing tasks. Grove had even appeared in an Intel rap video to promote RISC.

But Kinnie and Carter had trained at the Grove school of management—Grove's MO as a leader has always been to depend on "helpful Cassandras" to make sure that he doesn't win an argument he ought to lose. The two were blunt. "Andy, you can't do this," Carter said. Abandoning CISC for RISC, they argued, would truncate one of the most profitable franchises in business history for … what? Leveling the playing field for Intel's competition? When the discussion ended, Kinnie and Carter had achieved a feat of monumental difficulty. They'd won an argument with Andy Grove.

Grove has been grateful to them ever since. He looks back at this episode with anger—at himself. "We almost wrecked the company," he told me. "We had established our technology as the industry standard. This franchise was worth millions, billions. We … I … almost walked away from it because the elegance of a new product seduced me into taking my eye off the market." The sun is shining, the view is stunning, and Andy Grove is berating himself for a mistake he didn't make a decade and a half ago. It's a measure of the demanding life he has lived—a life that, at critical junctures, has hung on Grove's ability to transform himself, to move from role to role as the moment required.

The Early Adapter
To be born a Hungarian Jew in 1936 was to be born on the wrong side of history. Grove was forced to adapt to a succession of threatening realities from the very beginning.

FLUID DYNAMICS is easier than the human kind, grad student Grove (in a Berkeley lab in the 1960s) would ultimately learn.

> ## "I almost wrecked the company because a new product seduced me."

Transformations were the story of Grove's young life. When the Nazis invaded Hungary in 1944, his mother changed his name from Andras Grof to the Slavic Andras Malesevics. When the communists arrived the following year, he once again became Andras Grof. As a young man, he switched from journalism to chemistry after publishers started rejecting his articles for political reasons.

Communism nauseated him. One of his most vivid recollections is the May Day parade of 1950. Cheering was broadcast from loudspeakers around Budapest. But when Andy and his schoolmates arrived at Heroes' Square, they discovered there was no crowd at all: The cheering was recorded. Six years later, when the Hungarian Revolution caused the border with Austria to be open for a brief period, Grove faced an immediate and unanticipated decision. He had never been outside Hungary. An only child, he would be leaving parents he might never see again. He had little idea of what he'd be running to. If ever there was a plunge into the unknown, that was it.

He arrived in the U.S. on Jan. 7, 1957—the same day that *Time*'s "Man of the Year" issue featured THE HUNGARIAN FREEDOM FIGHTER on its cover. Soon he would change his name for a third and final time. At the City College of New York, where he enrolled, Andras Istvan Grof was struck from the transcript and above it was written Andrew Stephen Grove. He had left behind his home, and he needed a name people could pronounce.

The Self-Made Manager
By the late 1960s Grove had earned a Ph.D. in chemical engineering at the University of California at Berkeley and joined Fairchild Semiconductor, birthplace of the integrated circuit. When colleagues Robert Noyce and Gordon Moore quit to start Intel, Grove declared he was coming too. In 1968 they put their 32-year-old protégé in charge of operations. That forced Grove into an unfamiliar role: having to lead people.

Quite suddenly Grove found himself on the shop floor of a manufacturing startup. There the human dynamics proved far more complex than the fluid dynamics he'd studied at Berkeley. The job, he quickly recognized, required something he knew nothing about: It required management. What was that, anyway? Grove decided he had to figure it out.

On July 4, 1969, he opened a school notebook and pasted in a clipping from a story in *Time* magazine about movie directors. "Vision to Inspire," it read. "Any director must master formidable complexity. He must be adept at sound and camera work, a soother of egos, a cajoler of the artistic talent. A great director has something more: the vision and force to make all these disparate elements fuse into an inspired whole." Above the clipping, Grove wrote with a red pen: "My job description?"

So began the self-education of Andy Grove, manager. It was a quest in which he immersed himself. His classroom would be a remarkable set of journals that he kept for years —and that have never, until now, been revealed. They're a window into the mind of an engineer grappling with the challenge of managing people. How did a company's growth rate, for instance, relate to its employees' ability to grow? In an entry from the early 1970s, Grove noted, "Three groups of people can be identified: (A) don't belong in their jobs in the first place. These are "defective choices," nothing to do with growth. (B) These are the previously discussed cases, people who can't grow with their jobs. (C) This is everybody else, including those that have demonstrated all kinds of growth capability before.

"The point is, there is a growth rate at which *everybody* fails and the whole situation results in a chaos. I feel it is my most important function (as being the highest-level manager who still has a way to judge the impending failure) to identify the maximum growth rate at which this wholesale failure phenomenon begins."

Grove succeeded where others didn't, in part, by approaching management as a discipline unto itself. There's real urgency in his efforts to school himself: He never lost his Hungarian refugee's apprehension of the risk of imminent failure.

The Change Agent

By 1983, when Grove distilled much of his thinking in his book High Output Management *(still a worthwhile read), he was president of a fast-growing $1.1-billion-a-year corporation, a leading maker of memory chips, whose CEO was Gordon Moore. Could Grove and Moore save the company from an industry that was filled with ferocious competitors?*

In many ways change was in Intel's DNA. It was Moore who had famously observed that the number of transistors you could cram onto a chip tended to double every couple of years (later refined to 18 months). What Moore's Law did not and could not predict was that Japanese firms, too, might master this process and turn memory chips into a commodity. That was change of a different order, and not even Intel was prepared for it.

The company's top executives simply could not believe the growing evidence that they were being outcompeted in a mar-

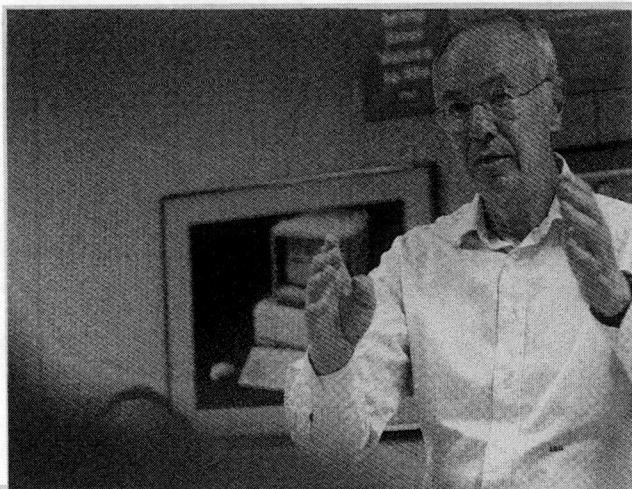

SENIOR ADVISOR GROVE brainstormed at headquarters in August with Intel teams bent on expanding into "digital health."

> ## "There is a growth rate at which *everybody* fails, [resulting] in a chaos."

ket they had created. Intel was the memory company, period. Its chips were in many of the best minicomputers and also in the new breed of machine that was then taking off, the personal computer. In the early 1980s profits from other products helped to sustain the delusion that memories were a viable future.

Intel kept denying the cliff ahead until its profits went over the edge, plummeting from $198 million in 1984 to less than $2 million in 1985. It was in the middle of this crisis, when many managers would have obsessed about specifics, that Grove stepped outside himself. He and Moore had been agonizing over their dilemma for weeks, he recounts in *Only the Paranoid Survive*, when something happened: "I looked out the window at the Ferris wheel of the Great America amusement park revolving in the distance when I turned back to Gordon, and I asked, 'If we got kicked out and the board brought in a new CEO, what do you think he would do?' Gordon answered without hesitation, 'He would get us out of memories.' I stared at him, numb, then said, 'Why shouldn't you and I walk out the door, come back, and do it ourselves?'"

The words "I stared at him, numb" suggest that in the crucial moment, Andy ceased to be Andy. Instead he was Dr. Grove the engineer, the teacher, looking down at his own case study. And from this realm of pure reason he could see that Intel's present course had an obvious ending: disaster. It was a cognitive *tour de force*, yet within moments Andy Grove the executive returned—and was dismayed by what Andy Grove the teacher had concluded. Professors overturn ideas, but they don't upend lives. "To be completely honest about it," Grove wrote, "as I started to discuss the possibility of getting out of the memory chip business, I had a hard time getting the words out of my mouth without equivocation." One of his managers even persuaded him "to continue R&D for a product that he and I both knew we had no plans to sell." Grove's devotion to reason did not mean that he was a machine. Far from it. What he found in the end was the will to do what was painful, the will to let go.

"Welcome to the new Intel," Grove said in a speech not long afterward, to rally the troops behind the decision to exit memories. Intel the memory company was dead, he explained, but there was another product on which it could stake its future: the microprocessor. Invented at Intel in 1971, it had spent the 1970s timing traffic lights and helping bacon packers slice their bacon into even strips. Not all that exciting. *continued*

205

But once IBM chose Intel's microprocessor to be the chip at the heart of its PCs, demand began to explode. Even so, the shift from memory chips was brutally hard—in 1986, Intel fired some 8,000 people and lost more than $180 million on $1.3 billion in sales—the only loss the company has ever posted since its early days as a startup.

The Reality Shifter

Grove and Moore had no way of knowing that Intel was on the verge of a remarkable ten-year run. They did know they were betting the company—and that to make the shift they had to risk angering IBM. The $60-billion-a-year giant was not only Intel's biggest customer but also its biggest shareholder—it had bought a large stake in the company to shore up its shaky supplier.

Intel did not set out to dominate the computer industry any more than humans set out to dominate the planet. In both cases the main concern was survival. Humans were so vulnerable to being eaten by larger, faster creatures that their only hope of survival was to control their environment. The "new Intel," too, was subject to forces beyond its control. Grove would later use a graphic that depicted Intel as a castle with the 386 chip in the center. The castle was under siege by rival chipmakers Sun Microsystems, Harris, Motorola, and NEC, not to mention RISC. But in the mid-1980s, before the graphic was ever made, Intel faced a more basic challenge: It was not so much a kingdom as a vassal state. Its dominant customer, IBM, had long insisted that Intel license its microprocessor designs to other chipmakers so that Big Blue could always be certain of a ready supply of chips at a pleasant price.

Grove decided that had to change. "Finally, we had a real winner of a device," Grove says of the 386 chip. But if Intel wanted a more secure future, "we not only had to win; we had to win our way." The 386 marked a genuine milestone of computer engineering. As Microsoft and other software developers figured out how to make full use of the new chip, Grove knew, the PC market would probably grow even hotter. Yet as long as Intel had to share its designs with other chipmakers, it would always face the anonymous and uncertain life of a parts supplier, subject to the whim of a customer 60 times its size.

To become its own kingdom, Grove realized, Intel had to

GROVE OF ACADEME

A photo shoot and a chance encounter spark **a $26 million gift** to his alma mater.

Grove graduated from the City College of New York with a degree in engineering in 1960. He returned to campus for FORTUNE's photo shoot in August. Though no longer tuition-free, CCNY still offers an excellent low-cost education that draws many first- and second-generation Americans. Inspired by the visit, Grove gave the school $26 million—the largest gift in its history. The bulk will go to the undergraduate engineering school, which will be named after him. He spoke with reporter Kate Bonamici.

ON BEING ON CAMPUS AGAIN

We shot in a number of locations, and there was a lot of hurry up and wait. My daughter was with me, so I went around and showed her where my lab used to be, and as I was doing that, I was kind of warming up on the inside. It was like visiting the village where you were born or something. Somebody dragged up [freshman] David Bauer, the Intel Science Talent Search winner. So my heartstrings are pinging more and more. Other than the fact that he has no accent, it's me. He's from the Bronx; he

BACK TO SCHOOL At CCNY he's pumping money into undergraduate engineering.

takes the same subway I used to take to class. He's studying chemistry. It just struck me—the machinery of the American dream machine is turning. Almost 50 years later it's starting again, and David Bauer is there.

ON WHY HE DECIDED TO GIVE SUCH A BIG GIFT

They had asked that I make a substantial gift to the school.... I don't like giving money to an unspecified cause; I prefer to be more hands-on, so I never considered it. But the day of the shoot, I started to think, "Oh, maybe I should do it. Where else would I do it? Mumble, mumble, mumble." I repeated the visit—I poked my nose into labs and got lost and got directions from students. The students are different, and some of the buildings didn't exist when I was there. But the place is the same, which is what I needed to discern for myself.

ON HOW HE ENTERED CCNY IN 1957

I asked for the admissions office, and somebody sits me down, and I tell them my story. I was wondering what shoe was going to hit me in the head this time, but they accepted me with respect, without condescension. They gave me a start, and they gave it in a classy way. It's an institution that is crucial to the workings of America, and America should be proud of it. I am.

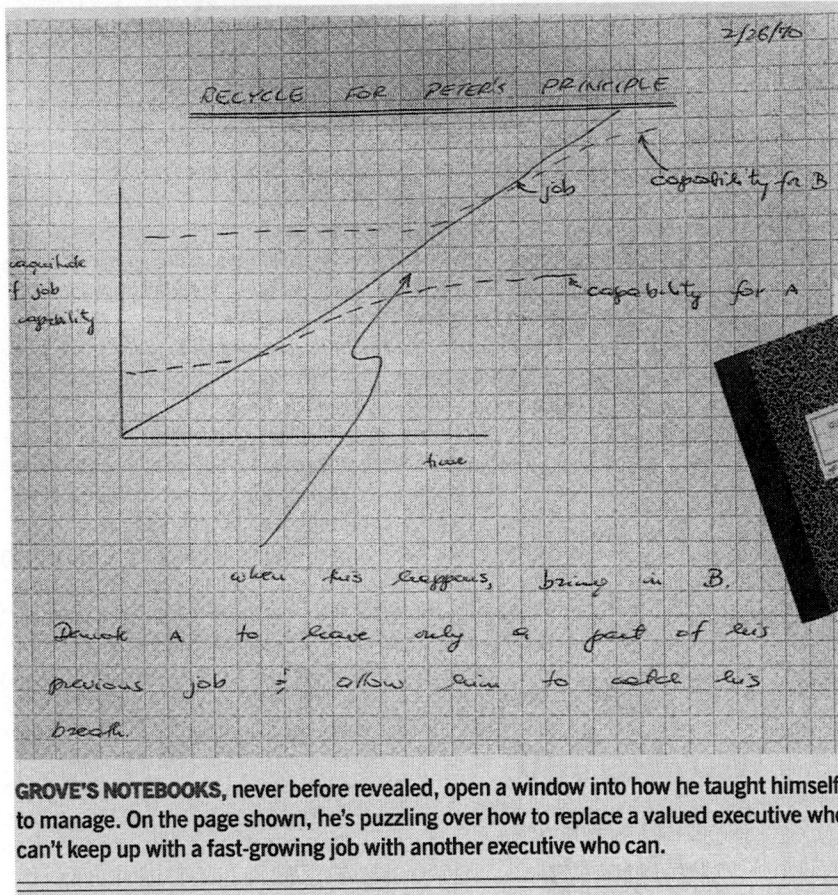

GROVE'S NOTEBOOKS, never before revealed, open a window into how he taught himself to manage. On the page shown, he's puzzling over how to replace a valued executive who can't keep up with a fast-growing job with another executive who can.

make itself effectively the sole source of microprocessors. Getting IBM to buy the idea posed a challenge—he had no way of knowing how his giant partner would react—but he knew the status quo did not give Intel the freedom it needed to grow. So Intel moved unilaterally: In 1985, when it launched the 386, it declared the technology would not be licensed to other producers. IBM at first did not build 386s into its machines. But as archrival Compaq picked up the chip, IBM came around, cutting a deal with Intel to make some of the 386s it expected to use in its own chip factories. The gamble had paid off. "To insist on our way meant we might lose," Grove says. "But to me, that is better than losing by compromising your advantages away."

The Fallible Human

During Grove's 11-year tenure as CEO, Intel grew at a compound annual growth rate of nearly 30%. Together with Microsoft, Intel supplanted IBM as the dominant standard in computing. In 1992, Intel's profits topped $1 billion for the first time—on $5.8 billion of sales. What made such extraordinary growth possible under Grove's leadership was his continuing ability to adapt to shifting realities—but even Mr. Strategic Inflection Point could stumble.

The 386 caught on, and sure enough, Microsoft used it to transform computing—its smash-hit Windows 3.0 operating system, which debuted in 1990, was designed to work on 386-based machines. Grove's breakthrough about changing the rules of the game opened the door to an epiphany about brand-ing and marketing. In 1990 marketing chief Dennis Carter—the same Dennis Carter who had badgered Grove on RISC—came to him with a scheme to launch a large-scale consumer marketing campaign around the slogan "Intel Inside." It is hard to recapture how foreign the concept of branding was at an engineering company like Intel. According to Carter, when he pitched the idea to a roomful of Intel senior executives, "most of them thought it was nuts. But not Andy. He said, 'It's brilliant. Go make it happen.'" Improbably, it turned an internal component into one of the most recognized brands in the world. Grove so loved the idea of marketing to consumers that he selected the name Pentium himself.

There's a rate of growth, though, at which *everybody* fails, including Andy Grove. His biggest tumble from the learning curve began in 1994. That fall Thomas Nicely, a mathematician at Lynchburg College in Virginia, spotted "inconsistencies" in the way Intel's latest Pentium chip performed a rare, complex scientific calculation.

Intel engineers knew about the bug but deemed it too insignificant to report. By their calculations, a spreadsheet user would encounter it once every 27,000 years of spreadsheet use. But when Nicely's findings were posted on an Internet newsgroup, the discussion became a tempest, then burst into public view. Soon IBM announced it was suspending shipments of its Pentium-based computers.

It was a moment when Grove should have switched into observer mode and asked, "What has changed here?" Instead, he kept thinking like an engineer and waded into the online mob himself, as though it were purely a technical debate. The uproar grew, though, until Grove was forced to adopt a no-questions-asked replacement policy and to apologize to customers. The apology was not very gracious. "What we view as a minor technical problem has taken on a life of its own," he declared. "We apologize. We were motivated by a belief that replacement is simply unnecessary for most people. We still feel that way." In effect he was telling consumers that they wanted something they did not need, but Intel had decided to indulge their irrationality.

A customer replied on the Internet with a poem:

When in the future we wish to deride
A CEO whose disastrous pride
Causes spokesmen to lie
and sales streams to dry
We'll say he's got Intel Inside™.

For a man who strives to grasp objective reality, Grove had missed a fundamental shift in the nature of his business. Intel had become a marketing company. And while a chip is built in a factory, a brand is co-created with the customer. This required a rethinking of the meaning of "objectivity." In branding, a customer's subjective reality, even if confused, becomes your objective reality. The learning experience was more expensive than most: The Pentium recall required a $475 million writedown that marred Intel's year.

The Data-Driven Patient

A few months later Grove faced crisis again: He was diagnosed with prostate cancer. In the intense period that followed, he remained on the job for all but two-and-a-half days. He handled the decision about his treatment the same way he handled decision-making at Intel: as if life depended on it.

Grove had never been one to rely on others' interpretations of reality. Hungary, in this regard, served as How-Not-To-Do-It University. Reality there was shaped by one's position in the system. At Intel he fostered a culture in which "knowledge power" would trump "position power." Anyone could challenge anyone else's idea, so long as it was about the idea and not the person—and so long as you were ready for the demand "Prove it." That required data. Without data, an idea was only a story—a representation of reality and thus subject to distortion. Hungary had been a grotesque funhouse mirror. The slim man looked fat, and the fat man slim. But when he was diagnosed with prostate cancer in 1995, Grove found himself in the position of most patients: frightened, disoriented, and entirely reliant on the advice of doctors. Their advice was straightforward: Surgery was the best option, and that was pretty much all there was to it.

Was it, though? It took very little to discover that there was much, much more to it. There were alternatives to surgery. No surgeon advised him to take them seriously. But the expert opinions, Grove soon determined, were just that—opinions, based on little if any hard data. Data did exist. What Grove found most shocking is that no one had done the hard work of pulling it together. Plainly, Grove would have to do it himself.

The patient, in effect, became his own doctor. It was a massive research undertaking whose details Grove chronicled in a 1996 story for FORTUNE. One is left with the image of Grove, awake late at night, plotting and cross-plotting the data in his own methodically constructed charts. What did the data tell him? That he would be better off with an alternative procedure known as radiation seeding. That was the treatment he selected.

What Grove found most appalling, in the end, was the utter fixity of belief among doctors who failed to separate knowledge from conventional wisdom. Even the doctor who carried out Grove's procedure was captive to it. "If you had what I have, what would you do?" Grove asked him at one point. The doctor said he'd probably have surgery. Confounded, Grove later asked why. The doctor thought about it. "You know," Grove remembers him saying, "all through medical training, they

> **Grove's hard lesson about selling to consumers cost Intel $475 million.**

drummed into us that the gold standard for prostate cancer is surgery. I guess that still shapes my thinking."

"Let's Think for Ourselves"

Grove stepped down as CEO in spring 1998 to become Intel's chairman. The betting at Intel was that he'd never really let go of the reins, but Andy surprised everyone. He dug into his new assignment as he has every other—setting out to examine and improve the way the board governed Intel and thereby to set an example for corporate boards everywhere (see "Inside Andy Grove's Latest Crusade" on fortune.com).

Last May, when Paul Otellini succeeded Craig Barrett as CEO, Grove officially became "senior advisor" to the company. The title didn't matter. Grove was still teaching.

On a Monday last month, Grove stood before 400 or so Intel employees, the advance troops of the company's health-care initiative. (Intel wants to make its chips the basic building blocks of 21st-century health-care and medical technology.)

Many had never seen Grove in person before, and he got a standing ovation before he said a word. His speech was a strong statement about strategy. Understanding comes from action. So "be quick and dirty," he said. "Engage and then plan. And get it better. Revolutions in our industry in our lifetime have taken place using exactly this formula. The best example is the IBM PC"—created on the fly by a team in Boca Raton.

Then he took questions. A European software engineer stood up with microphone in hand. He asked about handling health-care information. "How can we address the problem of privacy protection and data protection?"

"Stay with me for a minute," Grove said quickly. "Can I ask you a question? Why do you care?"

"Because health-care information might find its way to insurance companies and might result in higher insurance rates," the engineer replied.

"Explain to me why," said Grove, almost before the engineer could finish speaking.

"Many people have said it would be a bad thing if insurers knew all about the health history of everyone in the population," he replied.

Intel's senior advisor sized up the engineer's comments this way: "I think we have a tendency toward adding imaginary complexities to a problem which is already unimaginably complicated." He added, "Let's think for ourselves. Let's not repeat mindlessly ... excuse me, automatically ... suppositions that are true merely because somebody else says they are."

Did the engineer care about having been cross-examined and momentarily called mindless in the presence of 400 co-workers by his legendarily blunt leader? He smiled at Grove's choice of words. "Go ahead," he told Grove. "I was prepared." **F**

RICHARD S. TEDLOW *is a historian at the Harvard Business School. His book,* The American: The Life and Times of Andy Grove, *will be published next fall. For this essay he has drawn on his research, which includes interviews with Grove and many other executives, unpublished documents, and published reports.*

FIRST

BLACKBERRY HELD HOSTAGE

PAY UP—OR YOU'RE DONE FOR

Patent cases have always been costly. Could they now be fatal too?

By Roger Parloff

WHAT WOULD OSAMA BIN LADEN GIVE to be able to knock out every BlackBerry in America and achieve an instant, sweeping disruption of commerce? The good news is he can't do it. The weird and disconcerting news is that a company called NTP can and, unless it's paid off, probably will sometime before Christmas.

NTP has this remarkable power because it is nearing victory in its four-year-old patent litigation with Research in Motion, the maker of the BlackBerry. As FORTUNE went to press, RIM faced the real likelihood of a court-ordered BlackBerry blackout (government devices would be exempted) unless it agrees to pay essentially whatever sum NTP names, which some analysts think will approach ten figures.

However the endgame plays out, it vividly illustrates a recurring lightning-rod

FEEDBACK *first@fortunemail.com*

issue in patent debates—one that pits the information technology industry, which favors reform, against many others, such as the pharmaceutical industry, which don't. Should plaintiffs like NTP—which does not market a competing product, never has, and never will—be entitled to an automatic injunction shutting down a productive infringer such as RIM?

NTP was founded in 1991 by the late inventor Thomas Campana and his patent attorney, Donald Stout, of Arlington, Va. It has no employees and makes no products. Its main assets, Campana's patents, have spent most of the past decade in Stout's file drawer. But in 2002 a federal jury found that RIM had infringed five NTP patents that relate to integrating e-mail systems with wireless networks. An appellate court largely agreed in August 2005, and in late October the U.S. Supreme Court declined to issue a stay while it ponders whether to hear the case.

No one has claimed that RIM ever copied NTP's patents. But under the law—and this isn't even the controversial part—that doesn't matter. As long as NTP staked its claim first, if RIM later independently wandered into the same intellectual territory and managed, unlike NTP, to invent

Who should you fear: the patent troll or the foreign infringer?

and produce a wildly popular product, it is an infringer.

Here's the controversial part: Should plaintiffs in NTP's position be entitled not merely to a reasonable royalty but also to an injunction shutting down the infringer? To elevate an already troubling situation to a surreal one, the U.S. Patent and Trademark Office began reexamining NTP's patents in 2003 and as of September 2005 had preliminarily invalidated all 1,921 claims in the eight pertinent NTP patents, including all those that form the basis for NTP's suit. But U.S. District Court Judge James Spencer of Richmond said at a Nov. 9 hearing that he probably won't wait for a final decision—thought to be two or three months off—explaining, "I don't run their business, and they don't run mine." (RIM co-CEO James Balsillie has claimed that his company has a technical "work-around" that will enable it to continue its service legally even if an injunction is entered; NTP has promised to challenge any work-around in court.)

In nonpatent cases, courts grant permanent injunctions only when a plaintiff faces "irreparable harm" beyond what can be remedied by money damages. But the Court of Appeals for the Federal Circuit, which handles all patent appeals, has consistently held that almost any victorious patent plaintiff meets this standard, since a patent grants "exclusivity" over the invention, not just the right to a royalty. At presstime, the Supreme Court was deciding whether to hear a case in which a tiny patent holder has been given the theoretical power to shut down portions of eBay. (If the Supreme Court declines to take the case, eBay would have to use a work-around or settle.)

The Business Software Alliance, led by companies like Apple, Intel, and IBM, has argued before Congress that there is often no "irreparable harm" when the plaintiff isn't making any product, since a reasonable royalty will give that plaintiff everything to which it is entitled. "The patent troll"—the derogatory term for such plaintiffs—"has zero interest in killing the goose laying golden eggs," says Matt Powers, a patent litigator at Weil Gotshal & Manges who represents Intel and Microsoft. Though the troll wants to negotiate a license, he adds, his potential power to shut down the defendant's product line gives him an unfair advantage. The situation is exacerbated, he notes, when the product—a Pentium processor, for example—contains thousands of inventions.

But others see exclusivity as the core of the patent right and vehemently oppose trimming the ability to impose an injunction. "That's the seeds of disaster for the patent system," says Stout of NTP. Though that sounds self-serving, most industries agree with him. "It's like owning a piece of land," says Philip Johnson, the chief patent counsel of Johnson & Johnson, "and having somebody on your land." If you win your trespass case, he says, "the person on the land is supposed to get off it." Pharma companies, for example, fear—legitimately—that weakening exclusivity might be a step toward compulsory licensing. That could harm their bargaining stance with foreign nations that would love to infringe on pharma patents in exchange for whatever royalties they deem reasonable. Because of this opposition, a House subcommittee has removed language about injunctions from the latest version of a patent reform bill.

That leaves it up to the Supreme Court, which could wipe away the patent injunction problem with a simple step. The court would merely have to construe "irreparable injury" in a commonsense manner, rather than allowing the Federal Circuit to effectively define all injuries as irreparable. Such a reform wouldn't automatically deny an injunction to inventors who don't make products. There are many such inventors: universities, for instance; technology designers like QualComm; or independent inventors like Dean Kamen or, for that matter, Ben Franklin. Courts are good at weighing all the circumstances, and all they need here is the opportunity to do that—rather than being forced to issue an injunction automatically.

Defining a "patent troll" can be difficult, but courts are up to the task. As the late Justice Potter Stewart once said in another context, "I know it when I see it."

TO MANAGE INNOVATION, LEARN THE ARCHITECTURE

R&D managers need to understand the different rules and dynamics of the games they compete in. These seven are a place to start.

Roger Miller and Xavier Olleros

OVERVIEW: *Innovation is often perceived as an unmanageable process. At best, sophisticated selection procedures can impose discipline and guidance so as to contain costly errors. The research reported here, conducted with 923 chief technical officers and senior R&D managers, yields a more nuanced view. Innovation becomes manageable when managers move away from prescriptions that view the process as uniform and recognize that different rules and practices apply in different contexts. The main argument presented here is that product architecture has become a key element of innovation strategy. Innovation focuses not only on stand-alone items but increasingly on systemic as well as modular products and services. Product architecture interacts with market dynamics, which leads to distinct "games of innovation," seven of which have been identified empirically. These games are not predetermined but leave ample room for creative actions.*

KEY CONCEPTS: *product architecture, innovation strategy, competition, market creation.*

Roger Miller is the Jarislowsky Professor of Innovation and Project Management at the École Polytechnique, Montréal, Québec, Canada, and a founding partner of SECOR, a strategy-consulting firm with offices in Montréal, Toronto and Paris. Professor Miller holds a doctorate from the University of Louvain (Belgium), a master in science from Stanford, and an M.B.A. from Columbia University. He has been a research fellow at Harvard University's Center for International Affairs, as well as in MIT's International Motor Vehicle Program. His work has focused on strategy and industry dynamics, public policies in science and technology, and the management of large engineering projects. He is a Fellow of the Canadian Academy of Engineering.
roger.miller@polymtl.ca

Xavier Olleros is a professor of innovation management at the Université du Québec in Montreal. He holds a major in economics and an M.B.A. from McGill University, Montreal, and a Ph.D. in business administration from l'École des Hautes Études Commerciales, Montreal. He has published in Research in Marketing, Industrial and Corporate Change, The International Journal of Innovation Management, Technovation, *and* The Journal of Product Innovation Management. *He is currently investigating the design and evolutionary dynamics of communities of creation in the digital commons.* **olleros.xavier@uqam.ca**

Theorizing about innovation often devolves into universal and reductionist claims. We believe the time has come to emphasize instead the rich variety of innovation patterns in the real world. This article reports on our findings and attempts to enlarge the scope of analysis and the strategic concern of R&D managers.

Commonly accepted theories view innovation as science-based searches followed by patent-based races for market domination. By contrast, the study that we have conducted identified multiple patterns (see "How the Study Was Conducted," next page). Each pattern has its own distinct logic of innovation, requiring different strategies and practices. We call these patterns "games of innovation" to signify that they are coherent scenarios of value creation and capture involving activities of collaboration and rivalry.

R&D managers need to become aware of the various pathways for creating and capturing commercial value beyond the conventional scenario. More specifically, the central claims based upon our empirical findings are:

1. R&D managers should worry less about imitating best practices and more about correctly identifying the innovation game in which they are involved, the collective opportunity windows, and the emerging turning points.

2. R&D managers need to develop an architectural understanding of business strategy and product design.

0895-6308/08/$5.00 © 2008 Industrial Research Institute, Inc.

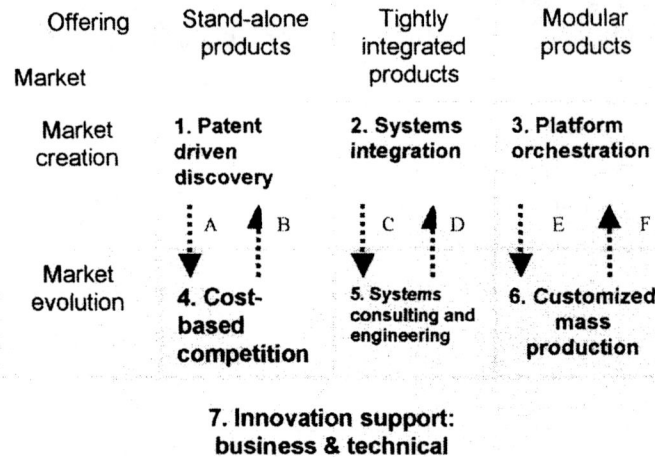

Offering / Market	Stand-alone products	Tightly integrated products	Modular products
Market creation	1. Patent driven discovery	2. Systems integration	3. Platform orchestration
	A ↓ ↑ B	C ↓ ↑ D	E ↓ ↑ F
Market evolution	4. Cost-based competition	5. Systems consulting and engineering	6. Customized mass production

7. Innovation support: business & technical

Games of innovation are distinct patterns of value creation and capture.

Systems and platforms are as prevalent as stand-alone products; services are intertwined with products and platforms.

3. R&D managers also need to develop a holistic and enlightened view of what constitutes a new technology's success—a view that encompasses suppliers, rivals and complementors (by which we mean collaborators who provide complementary products or services). Both competition and collaboration are required to expand markets and turn potentially negative-sum games into positive-sum ones.

There are six sections in this paper. In the first, we outline the limitations of universal models of innovation. In the second, we discuss the importance of product architecture for managing innovation. We discuss games of innovation in the third section and follow this with an empirical taxonomy of seven different games. We then sketch the persistence of games over time and the migrations of sectors, industries and firms across games in the

How the Study Was Conducted

The idea of multiple games of innovation emerged from two Industrial Research Institute Research-on-Research subcommittees. In 2000, building on discussions with 75 CTOs and VPs of R&D, the subcommittee on Managing R&D for Growth observed that there were no best practices for innovation management across sectors and suggested that best practices vary according to context. Firms in biotechnology, telecommunications, software, aerospace, aluminum, pulp and paper, engineering and construction, and multimedia were covered. Further, the subcommittee on R&D Structures and Globalization noted in 2006 that the organization of R&D depends on games of innovation as well as on the distribution of sales and centers of expertise around the world.

The Managing Innovation in the New Economy (MINE) research program at École Polytechnique in Montreal, Canada, conducted qualitative and quantitative studies to gain an understanding of the diversity of games of innovation. Almost 925 CTOs and senior managers of R&D from Asia, North and South America and Europe, across all industrial sectors, responded to a global survey. The survey tool is available at *www.minesurvey.polymtl.ca*. Respondents came from such firms as Intel, Synopsys, Motorola, IBM Global Services, Novartis, and Boeing. Executives were asked which competitive forces impact innovation, which value-creation- and -capture activities are pursued in innovating, and which strategies and practices are used.

Clustering analyses led to the identification of seven distinct and stable groups, each containing at least 100 firms that create and capture value in similar ways. Three games focus on market creation: patent-driven discovery, systems integration, and platform orchestration. Three other games focus on market maintenance: cost-based competition, systems consulting and engineering, and customizing mass production. Innovation support forms the seventh distinct game of enabling innovation. Each game is characterized by statistically different value-creation and -capture activities.—**R.M. and X.O.**

fifth section. We conclude by summarizing the key lessons of our approach for executives.

Innovation Approaches: Conventions and Realities

The conventional view of innovation builds on Joseph Schumpeter's theory of internalized R&D management (1). Large incumbent firms, such as Industrial Research Institute (IRI) members, tend to invest in R&D, develop steering processes and build competencies for launching new products (2). Several assumptions underpin this model:

• Innovation is primarily based on in-house R&D.

• New products need to be fully developed before they are launched.

• Markets are exogenous spaces waiting to be filled with new products that meet preexisting and discernible customer needs.

• Demand results from the simple addition of individual clients' choices, each of which is independent of all others.

• The complexity of products and processes is largely hidden from users.

• The market selects winning products strictly on the basis of relative merits, according to an established set of buyer utility and preferences.

• The capture of value relies on strong intellectual property protection, often resulting in temporary monopolistic positions.

The real world of innovation does not always fit this model, however. Table 1 compares the assumptions with the realities observed in recent studies on innovation. In the conventional approach, products are self-contained, while in reality many are systemic and bundled with services (3). Markets do not always preexist, but become actualized in response to the launch, redesign and coevolution of systemic products and their complements (4). R&D management takes place within complex ecosystems and clusters of complementary organizations (5). Value capture in the conventional model relies on strong patents, while in contests involving systemic products, patents are used simply for cross-licensing agreements that tend to level the playing field. Rather, market success depends on bold strategies for building brands, reputation and dominant architectures.

Preeminence of Architecture

In recent years, product design has become a richer and more complex art. In the past, a good product design was simply one that suited the needs of users. Nowadays, fitting a product to users' needs is almost taken for granted, while the leading edge of product design has moved to a set of more strategic considerations. Unless a

Table 1.—Comparison of Assumptions: Conventional Model and Recent Studies on Innovation

Subject	Assumption of Conventional Model	Findings from Recent Research
Management of R&D and innovation	Innovation is primarily done in-house. Best practices increase effectiveness.	Firms are embedded in ecosystems of complementary players (17, 19). Effective innovation requires a collective approach, well-orchestrated efforts, and access to resources.
Market growth	Markets are exogenous spaces waiting to be filled with products meeting preexisting, discernible needs.	Markets become actualized in response to the launching of new systemic products and their complements (4). Markets, customer needs and technical capabilities co-evolve through several generations of platforms and modules.
Product development	Products are fully developed before launch. Safety requires approvals and certifications.	First generations of systemic products are barely functional, incomplete prototypes. Complementors furnish missing elements to expand markets. Performance ceilings are reached well after the initial product hits the market, if ever.
Nature of demand	Demand is the aggregation of the various independent individuals' preferences.	Demand grows with social interactions. Decisions to adopt products are dependent on other users' choices. Winners often take all because of network externalities (20).
Product complexity	Users buy self-contained appliances. Complexity of processes and products is hidden from consumers.	Product complexity is apparent to users. User learning is costly. Interactions between producers, complementors and users are essential to producing new generations of systems (16). Early players may end up with orphan products.
Selection by markets	Selection is strictly on the basis of merits and utility. Prior success carries no market guarantee.	With open systemic products, network effects produce skewed results; selection is not always responsive to technical merits.
Value capture	The capture of value relies on strong patent protection and product superiority, often resulting in temporary monopoly.	Product superiority and patents do not guarantee lasting success in markets built around open platforms. Value will be captured on the basis of economies of scale and scope, dominant market positions resulting from reputation, learning and network effects, and effective orchestration of platforms and ecosystems (5).

215

product is simple and self-contained, architectural considerations will be preeminent (6).

Value is created or captured in different ways, depending on product architecture. "Platform" is a key element of the new thinking. Unlike a product, a platform is primarily a locus of new business opportunity. Whereas a product offers immediate market value, a platform offers option value (7). Whereas new products are expected to be profitable, new platforms are supposed to be flexible, scalable and evolving. Products may or may not be built to last; platforms are built to evolve.

A critical dimension of a platform is its degree of openness. A closed platform is restricted to a firm and its network of certified subcontractors. Innovation in closed platforms thus tends to be highly controlled and directed by technology roadmaps An open platform, on the other hand, allows independent third parties to create and capture value around its common core, without the need for prior contractual agreements. Thus, peripheral players self-select their tasks and terms of work, and rely directly on the market for their rewards. Open approaches not only tap a wide array of knowledge at the source but also greatly increase the design freedom of peripheral players while freeing core players from a host of burdensome tasks (8). An open platform thus becomes an ideal vehicle for decentralized innovation.

Not all platforms should be open, certainly not at all times. Similarly, not all open platforms need be decentralized. The degree and timing of the opening and decentralization of a platform are the main concerns of a platform orchestrator.

Games of Innovation Defined

Product architecture interacts with market dynamics to form distinct games of innovation. In spite of the many parallels, these games are neither sports plays nor game-theoretical problems. Game theory is a set of analytical tools for understanding simple strategic interactions among a limited number of players and options (9). Games of innovation, as we have observed, involve many interdependent players, persist over time and are strategically complex. They are distinct, coherent scenarios of value creation and capture involving activities of collaboration and rivalry. More precisely:

1. Each game involves a distinct logic of innovative activities that is largely contingent on product architectures and the stage of the market life cycle. Firms in different industries facing similar contexts tend to follow similar rules for innovation.

2. Games are not fully determined by their contexts but afford degrees of strategic freedom to interact with members of relevant ecosystems and to adopt collaborative and competitive moves that expand markets.

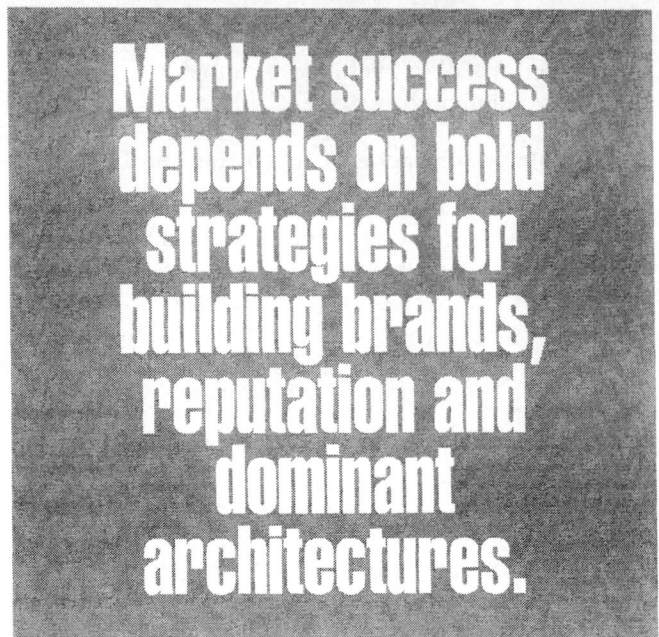

Market success depends on bold strategies for building brands, reputation and dominant architectures.

3. Games follow persistent trajectories. Despite their open-endedness, games are bound by basic economic and technical forces, and thus tend to fall into a small number of *natural trajectories* (10). In this paper, we identify seven of the trajectories that persist over time.

4. Games result in differing levels of performance. Market-creation games involve radical innovations, grow fast and display high variations in profitability. By contrast, market-evolution games are characterized by process innovations and a slower pace of growth, but good profitability. Depending on the strategies pursued by players, games may lead to healthy growth, just as they may fall into competitive traps or negative-sum results (11).

A given game type may cut across sectors and industries. Similar patterns of value creation and capture can be found in many sectors that face comparable technical, competitive and regulatory contexts. By contrast, some sectors and even industries involve many games.

A Taxonomy of Innovation Games

The illustration on page 18 presents a taxonomy of seven games of innovation that best correspond to patterns observed from our survey. The taxonomy is depicted in a two-by-three matrix embedded in the wider innovation support game. The main axes are the following:

1. *Product architecture (offering).*—Along the horizontal axis, we consider three distinct categories of exchanges between buyers and producers: simple stand-alone products, marketable to all kinds of buyers; closed integrated systems, designed for expert clients; and open modular systems, in which a platform leader coordinates the complementary offers of independent component suppliers into evolving products and services.

216

2. *Market dynamics.*—Two stages in the evolution of games were considered: a market-creation stage in which new technologies are brought to the point of market launch, and a market-evolution stage that ranges from growth to maturity and eventual rejuvenation or decline. We shall now discuss the dynamics prevailing in each game. Table 2 summarizes our discussion for each game by comparing value exchanges between clients and sellers, the dominant logic and levers of innovation, and investments in innovation efforts, capabilities and eco-systems. "Games of Innovation," next page, provides examples of games 1–6.

Patent-driven discovery

Patent-driven discovery games fit well with the conventional model of innovation. Buyers of pharmaceutical drugs, orthopedic devices, electric batteries, anti-virus software, and similar products have well-known needs. Market research can help specify the attributes that best meet user needs (*12*). Buyers can select products by rapidly assessing product performance or relying on expert advice (e.g., from physicians) or on the experience of other users.

The dominant levers for innovation are: recruiting the best possible scientists and engineers; building a balanced portfolio of research projects in search of patentable solutions; developing superior products and, if needed, gaining regulatory approval before launch. In the cluster of firms playing this game, R&D

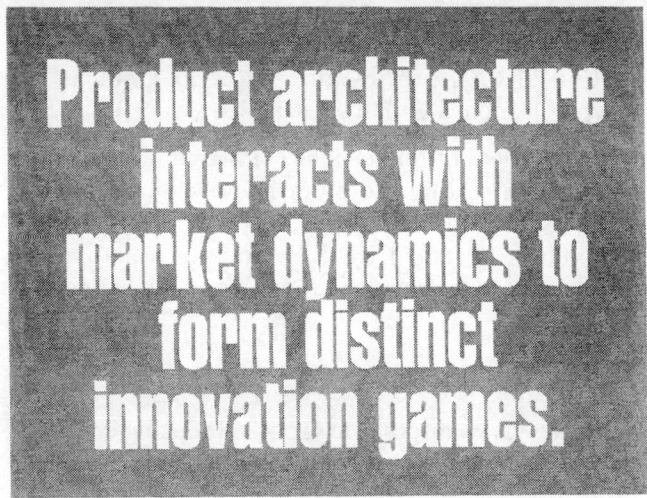

Product architecture interacts with market dynamics to form distinct innovation games.

expenditures average 13.3 percent of sales, with an additional 5.5 percent of sales to build capabilities. Staff time allocated to innovation averages 20 percent. Innovation activities are largely in-house, with approximately 60 percent of relevant ideas emerging internally.

Winning products eventually lose their edge as their legal protection disappears and superior options challenge them. Firms need to relentlessly invest in R&D or migrate toward less innovative (and less profitable) products. Value capture is generally achieved by a combination of patents, regulatory approvals and demonstrable product superiority. Sales growth averages 20 percent per year of sales; return on investment (ROI) averages 17.5 percent, while 35 percent of profitability

Table 2.—Dynamics of Value Creation and Capture in Each Game

Name → ↓ Dimension	Patent-driven Discovery	Cost-based Competition	Systems Integration	Systems Consulting and Engineering	Platform Orchestration	Customized Mass Production	Innovation Support
Value creating exchanges	Value is in IP-based products: Buyers have clear merit criteria.	Buyers select commodities on price. Substitutes loom.	Integrated solutions selected on merits and performance.	Buyers invest in mission-critical systems. Integrated platform tailored and implemented through services.	Buyers select open platforms vying for dominance. High learning.	Buyers want unique customized products.	Buyers stick to core. Buy specialized data and tools to innovate.
Examples of products	Pharma & biotech products.	Generic drugs, petrochemical, aluminum	PLM, ERP, CRM	Aircraft, e-commerce network	VoIP, info mediation services.	Cell phones, cars, high-end watches.	Decision-making tools.
Dominant levers for innovation	Relentless search for patents. Scouting in ecosystem. Portfolio of projects.	Hunting for scale and process efficiency. Fighting substitutes. Spillover gains.	Integrated solutions. Complex problems of lead users. Systems engineering capabilities.	Capital projects to improve productivity and product development. Customizing packages. Superior project management skills.	Shaping open platform. Leveraging decentralized creativity and ecosystem. Orchestration of co-evolution.	Brand and variety management. Global design and assembly. Control of critical components.	Focused, specialized learning and expertise. Offering of advice.

stems from innovations (a subjective estimate of the proportion of total profits attributable to products and services launched within the past five years).

The ecosystem of the game is composed of a few large competitors surrounded by many specialized complementary firms (usually small). The relentless process of innovation is fueled by the symbiotic relationships between small science-based "explorers" and large mass marketers

Cost-based competition

This game is widespread in sectors producing commodities no longer protected by patents. As imitators enter the fray, profits erode. In the absence of switching costs, buyer loyalty is minimal. Buyers constantly reconsider their selection of generic drugs, metals, industrial gases, aluminum, oil and gas, petrochemicals, electrical power, and other commodities on the basis of price.

The dominant levers for innovation are: pursuing process efficiency relentlessly, seeking and targeting specialized market niches to avoid or contain commoditization, and developing new applications to fight potential substitutes. Incremental improvements, rather than radical innovations, are emphasized. Investments in innovation average 3.5 percent of sales for R&D, with an additional 1.3 percent of sales for capability building. Staff time devoted to innovation averages 4.3 percent; sales grow at 15.9 percent per year on average; ROI averages 9.9 percent, and 24 percent of profitability is attributable to innovations.

The innovation ecosystem is composed of networks of suppliers and consultants to complement in-house innovation capabilities. Competitors capture value by focusing on scale efficiency, streamlined processes and industrial secrets. Late entrants can compete effectively if they have the marketing clout and financial resources to rapidly reach optimal scale.

Systems integration

The game of systems integration provides demanding, usually large, buyers with high-performance, tightly

Games of Innovation in the Real World

Patent-driven Discovery

Pharmaceutical firms look for successful products based on internally developed therapeutic drugs and intellectual property. With the difficulties encountered by the blockbuster model in funding portfolios of large projects costing hundreds of millions of dollars, new approaches are tried. For instance, Johnson & Johnson has 204 operating companies selling medicines, nutritional supplements, medical devices, diagnostics, and consumer products. Overall, 11 percent of sales is invested in R&D, but the bulk of product innovation efforts take place through venture investments in partnerships, internal development and spin-offs. Operating companies focus on existing markets, leaving to corporate ventures the tasks of developing promising scientific ideas and exploring new markets. The firm's growth model not only builds on internal discovery but also on leveraging externally developed technologies, licensing and acquisition activities, and a portfolio of venture bets made at an early stage.

Cost-based Competition

Aluminum producers have traditionally focused much of their R&D effort on cost reduction, optimization, and developing environmentally acceptable production methods. To expand markets and fight the threat of substitutes, Norsk Hydro, a Norwegian aluminum producer, has set up a number of partnerships with leading customers. For instance, a partnership has been formed with BMW to cover all aspects of marketing, production and joint research activities. Similarly, Pechiney Packaging (now part of Alcan) does most research projects with customers and packaging-equipment suppliers to solve customers' problems.

Systems Integration

Early computers were tightly integrated systems assembled by expert firms for leading customers. Today, tightly integrated systems include product life-cycle management (PLM), enterprise resource planning (ERP), and customer relationship management (CRM). In the electronic design automation field, for instance, Cadence Design Systems, with sales of US$1.6 billion, has the goal of helping chip designers and manufacturers meet the need for increasingly powerful semiconductors. R&D expenditures at Cadence reach 32 percent of sales, with a further 15 percent for innovation efforts in building marketing, engineering, and training capabilities. New versions are developed every 2 to 3 years for markets such as computers, telecommunications, biomedical devices, and automotive electronics. R&D partnerships with customers help to provide an understanding of their specific problems.

integrated, equipment and tools. Examples of tightly integrated systems are drug-design software for pharmaceutical firms, electronic design-automation tools sold to semiconductor manufacturers, and design engineering systems used by aircraft or car builders.

Buyers undertake complex tasks, such as testing product design hypotheses or accelerating product development, that often require coordinating hundreds of engineers around the world. While well aware of the costs and risks of such tools, buyers demand high performance. Market selection is highly meritocratic. Sales grow at 28 percent per year on average; ROI averages 10.7 percent, while 54 percent of profitability can be ascribed to innovations.

The dominant levers for innovation are: interacting with lead customers to try and solve their toughest problems; entering early and building proprietary closed systems; and raising expectations for new versions. System integrators do most of their R&D work in-house; highly specialized work is subcontracted to complementary ecosystem firms. Heavy investments in innovation are required; R&D expenditures average 28 percent of sales, with an additional 9.8 percent of sales to build capabilities in strategy, marketing and production. Almost 30 percent of staff time is devoted to innovative activities.

Value is captured not so much by patents as by product superiority and reputation. This often results in competing non-interoperable integrated systems sharing the market; even marginal market positions become sustainable. Buyers face high switching costs as engineers learn and build knowledge around the chosen systems.

Systems consulting and engineering

Operators of large financial, retailing or industrial networks want to streamline cost structures, improve delivery of new products or build e-commerce transaction systems. The major capital projects that are undertaken to build or tailor integrated systems to their contexts often put operators at risk because of the

Systems Consulting and Engineering

Hydro-Québec, a North American power utility, wanted to improve engineering design efficiency by moving toward three-dimensional modeling and data sharing with its consulting engineers. After Hydro-Québec contacted a number of suppliers, one of them, IBM Global Services, in collaboration with Dassault Systèmes, proposed PLM (Product Lifecycle Management) and CATIA (Computer-Aided Tridimensional Interactive Application) tools. IBM Global Services invested substantial R&D efforts to test how car-design methodologies could be adapted to hydroelectric dams. A pilot project involving Hydro-Québec, IBM Global Services, Dassault Systèmes, and SNC (consulting engineers) was put in place to conceptualize strategies and prove the workability of conceptual solutions, convince and train engineers, and develop architectural solutions and implement tools. Although limited to conceptual and detailed engineering for the moment, the project led to a multi-million-dollar R&D partnership involving not only tools but training, knowledge transfers and the building of databases. Relationships between the parties in this project will expand over the next 15 years.

Platform Orchestration

Telecommunications (telecom) systems used to be closed, tightly integrated networks of landlines and cables for transmitting voice and data. Public regulators acknowledged the economies of scale arising from monopolies and issued rules to achieve the social goals of universal access, optimal efficiency and reasonable prices. This situation lasted for over half a century. However, during the last 20 years, the combined effects of technical changes and deregulation have thrust the telecom sector into platform-orchestration mode. New entrants, such as Vonage and Skype, offer voice-over-Internet protocol (VoIP) services competing with fixed lines or cellular phones. Information mediators like Yahoo, Google, MySpace, and YouTube, build communities of users around specific services. Advertising, rather than communication charges, is the main source of revenues. Platforms are continually recombining and shifting. For instance, Internet mobile communications moved from being primarily tools for business communications to entertainment services targeted at young customers. Winning architectures keep changing and new services continuously emerge from technology-based recombination. Will operators survive or will they be dwarfed by info-mediators, Internet service providers, or cable distributors? Only the competitive process will tell.

Customized Mass Production

Like stand-alone products, systems eventually become commodities. The Fihta Group in Shenzen, China, assembles luxury watches targeted at young, upwardly mobile business executives. Brand management and product design are at the core of Fihta's business model. Investments in R&D and product-design activities represent about 9 percent of sales. Teams of fashion designers form virtual networks that supervise each model. Extensive tests of prototypes are made with focus groups. Assembly then combines standardized components imported from Japan and Switzerland, where automated factories produce dozens of millions of watch movements per year. In the same vein, Samsung of Korea is developing cell line assembly to achieve very short runs, produce high levels of variety, and meet expectations in heterogeneous market segments.—**R.M. and X.O.**

financial commitments, the impact of cost overruns and the functional risks involved.

The dominant levers of innovation are: selecting experienced consultants by clients to jointly conceptualize bold new solutions; structuring governance processes for problem-solving projects between clients and specialized consulting and engineering firms; and developing project management competencies to cope with critical changes.

Consultants in this game invest on average 4.7 percent of sales in R&D, with an additional 1 percent of sales to build capabilities; 10.6 percent of staff time is devoted to innovation. Knowledge accumulation takes place through: networks of experts, university professors or vendors; formalization of knowledge into decision methodologies; and codification of past learning and experience. Many consulting firms also fund separate research institutes to visualize the future evolution of sectors. Sales grow at 15.8 percent per year on average; ROI averages 14.2 percent, while 27 percent of profitability is attributable to innovations.

Specialized consultants comprise the ecosystem around projects. Strategy consultants help to define problems and visualize solutions; they capture value by building reputation and experience, thus gaining further assignments. Engineering consultants tailor software packages or build new solutions; they capture value by accumulating knowledge through partnerships with operators, strategy consultants and vendors.

Platform orchestration

Platform-orchestration games are market-creation contests in which sponsors promote open platforms that can integrate modules, components and services. Only a few platforms survive the disputatious process (*13*). Platform orchestration exists principally in information-related sectors such as Internet, telecommunications and personal computer/personal digital assistant (PC/PDA) devices.

Demand does not preexist, but is the result of a three-way coevolution among buyers' learning, the strategies of platform orchestrators, and those of their complementors. Early open platforms are often baffling since buyers are ill-informed about relative performance and survival prospects of alternatives (*14*). As a result, early buyers risk finding themselves holding orphan products that end up being abandoned by the market.

The dominant levers for innovation are based less on scientific prowess and unassailable patents than on enabling the emergence of promising new platforms by dint of daring commitments; by leveraging and orchestrating the inventive power of the market by a timely and judicious opening of the platform to third-party developers; and by promoting open standards and coalitions. Par-

ticipants in this game spend on average 18.4 percent of sales on R&D, with an additional 6.7 percent of sales to build capabilities; 35.8 percent of staff time is devoted to innovation; sales grow at 30 percent per year on average; ROI averages 18.8 percent, and 40 percent of profitability stems from innovations.

Characteristics of open-platform orchestration include:

• The first generation of an open platform is a barely functional prototype, launched not with the intent of conquering a large market but with the hope of attracting the attention of potential entrepreneurs capable of furnishing the crucial complementary infrastructures and peripherals.

• Regardless of the promise and potential of the core, a platform leader will often have to stimulate growth by subsidizing early adopters and/or early complementors. Platform leaders will have to invest for as long as it takes for the platform to reach the stage of self-sustained growth.

• Generous licenses and transparent interfaces serve to open up the platform. Standards are proposed and suppliers and customers are invited to rally around them. To get there, however, a competitive process of the alignment of core architectures, peripheral components and standards takes place.

• Because of systemic interdependencies, market growth is subject to strong threshold effects. Beyond a critical threshold, network externalities accelerate growth, but below such a threshold they act as brakes on growth. Few firms have the resources to persist through the long and profitless stage of initial platform development.

• Platform orchestration becomes all the riskier and more complex when an emerging open platform faces direct competition not only from established alternatives but from comparable promising platforms. In this case, network externalities will likely cause the ensuing inter-platform competition to turn into a high-stakes contest for survival and a frantic race to enlist the most powerful set of complementors. Because success is self-reinforcing, advantages gained by fast movers will likely prove decisive.

The ecosystem is critical to successful platform orchestration. The new system is not designed solely by a focal firm but by a coalition of interdependent firms. Platform leaders develop alliances with complementary producers to increase technical options and develop market applications.

Product superiority and patents do not guarantee value capture in markets built around open architectures (*15*). Instead, strong network effects result in winner-take-most platform battles where fast-mover solutions are

.
likely to leave little room for incompatible products and services (*16*).

Customized mass production

When a platform competition is finally settled in favor of a particular set of coherent architectural choices, interface standards stabilize and mass production becomes possible. Customized mass production becomes a battle of brands catering to heterogeneous market niches within the technical parameters specified by the dominant design platform.

Product commoditization is avoided, or at least postponed, through market segmentation and product differentiation. Assemblers cater to the diverse needs of customers by combining highly flexible assembly with the mass production of components. By targeting different market segments, not only will competitors stay away from each other's turf, but they will also increase the size of the overall market. Sales grow at 11.2 percent per year on average; ROI averages 12.6 percent; and 31 percent of profitability is attributable to innovations.

The levers of innovation basically combine the design, styling and branding capabilities of assemblers with peripheral innovation in the mass production of components and global coordination of supply networks. R&D investments average 6.2 percent of sales, with an additional 1.7 percent of sales to build capabilities, and 6.8 percent of staff time devoted to innovative activities. Assemblers tend to perform product design R&D activities in-house, as designs are strategic to branding. Outsourced product design is on the rise, however.

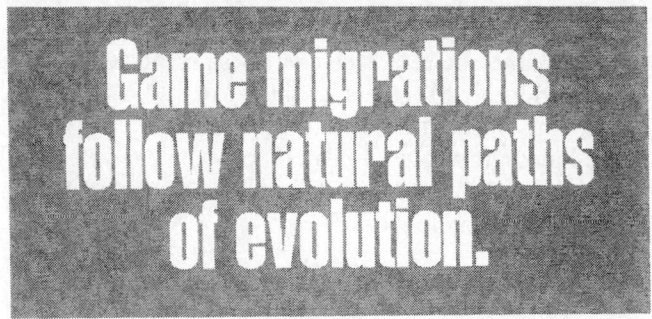

Game migrations follow natural paths of evolution.

Value capture will be favorable to the platform leader if it succeeds in developing some difficult-to-imitate advantage at the platform core. As an open platform matures and becomes entrenched, barriers to entry rise at the core but fall at the periphery. It becomes increasingly difficult to dislodge the platform but increasingly easy to extend it and add value to it. Quite often, the highest profits will migrate to suppliers of critical and strongly patented components and subsystems (e.g., Intel).

Innovation support

A substantial group of organizations, such as Battelle, Forrester Research and the Frauenhofer Institutes, provide services, information and tools to help other firms innovate. Contract R&D organizations are repositories of specialized knowledge, capabilities and services. They provide advice about technologies and markets, find partners and knowledgeable individuals, and facilitate access to publicly funded programs.

The dominant rules of this innovation game are: develop specialized technologies; accumulate knowledge and expertise through projects across many organizations;

Applying the Games of Innovation Approach

In a consulting assignment, we helped the senior management of a company we shall call "XT Telecommunications" make sense of its new competitive situation. Over the previous two years, XT had lost 30 percent of its fixed-line customers to new entrants from the Internet and the cable sector offering flat-fee bundles of VoIP, video and data communications. Furthermore, many research firms were informing the company that by 2010, 50 percent of fixed-line telephones would disappear.

Most theories used to frame XT's strategic issues were compounding the problem. For example, Schumpeterian theories stressing creative destruction suggested that disruptive entrants should eventually displace incumbent telephone operators. Life-cycle theories pointed out that industries go through emergence, growth, maturity, and, eventually, decline. With such deterministic views of the future, anxiety was on the rise!

The games of innovation approach provided a more open-ended way of framing strategies and helping executives understand that they were operating in three distinct games that called for different innovation strategies.

First, XT's main business—voice communications—was no longer one of optimizing established networks but had moved to a game of platform orchestration. By learning to become providers of value-added communications as well as being information mediators, operators could fight new entrants with new services and hope to retain some markets.

Second, they could build on their consulting experience with large networks to help large corporations and public organizations develop their own communications network.

Third, in their own infrastructure networks, the game continued to be one of optimizing to achieve higher quality at reduced costs.

From fixed lines, XT's networks are now moving toward new-generation networks (NGNs) based on Internet protocols in order to handle voice, data, video, movies, and any other digital content for delivery to all kinds of customers. Thus, by using these three games, different scenarios could be built to develop both reactive and proactive strategies.—**R.M. and X.O.**

and develop methodologies for solving problems. Firms in this game spend 5.8 percent of sales on R&D, with an additional 1.8 percent of sales to build capabilities; 8 percent of staff time is allocated to innovation activities. Sales grow on average 17 percent per year; ROI averages 16.2 percent, and 26 percent of profitability is attributable to innovations.

Value capture is difficult in this game. Contract research and consulting are highly competitive, low-margin activities. Unless they are very innovative, firms in this game will not be very profitable.

Persistence of Games and Migrations

Innovation games do not follow rigid scripts. Rather, they evolve along their trajectories according to the opportunities opened up by technical and market changes, as well as by the vision and resources the various players bring to bear. However, when the contextual conditions and the strategies pursued by firms become misaligned, an entire industry or sector has reached a turning point and is ready for a game change. Watershed events, such as the rapid expansion of a mass market, the loss of intellectual property protection, or the emergence of a dominant design, modify contextual forces to such an extent that firms are forced to either change games rapidly or disappear.

Game migrations generally follow natural paths of evolution. Unexpected discoveries and radical innovations often thrust mature sectors, industries and firms back into market-creation games. There is a bandwagon element to all of these trajectories. Thus, for example, if in a closed-platform regime one competitor moves decisively toward an open-platform regime, other system integrators will be under pressure to follow suit, lest they be marginalized into a precarious niche.

Migrations to commodities and back

Markets for self-contained products tend to evolve from a game of patent-driven discovery to one of cost-based competition and back again, through alternating rounds of breakthroughs, displacement, monopoly, and commoditization. Migrations, as indicated by arrow *A* in the illustration on page 18, take place when the key underlying patents come to the end of their valid life. Products then become commodities and customers buy primarily on the basis of price. A reverse migration occurs when unexpected discoveries open up new opportunities (arrow *B*). When this happens, the game returns to the relentless search for patentable discoveries. This dynamic fits well with the classic account of entrepreneurial innovation offered by Schumpeter.

From systems integration to extension and back

System integrators also face commoditization. Arrow *C* refers to the transition from closed, proprietary and inte-

> ## R&D managers need an architectural understanding of business strategy and products.

grated systems, designed initially for leading customers, to affordable versions that can cater to a larger market. Arrow *D* refers to the rarer migration that occurs when best-of-breed firms develop applications that thrust them back into market-creation games.

To customized mass production and back

When platform choices have crystallized around one or a few dominant open architectures, migrations from platform orchestration to customized mass production occur (arrow *E*). By contrast, strong command structures are needed to move an industry from a decentralized status quo back toward a stage of market emergence or transformation (arrow *F*).

From closed to open systems and back

Chesbrough (*17*) and Christensen and Raynor (*18*) have proposed a cyclical model in which systemic innovations start in a tightly integrated mode and eventually move toward an open platform as uncertainty about optimal product configurations decreases, complementary markets develop, and critical product attributes move from functionality and reliability toward variety and low cost. Later, as radically new technologies loom on the horizon, innovators must revert to closed platforms and centralized governance regimes in order to offer functional and reliable systems on the basis of the new technologies.

Major Themes

Three major themes emerge from our analyses. First, multiple patterns of innovation exist largely as a function of distinct competitive and technical forces. Games of innovation are distinct value-creating exchanges between clients buying products and service providers and producers delivering innovative solutions. We have built a taxonomy of seven patterns of innovation, each of which calls for different strategies and practices.

Managers of innovative firms need to understand the different rules and dynamics of the game(s) they compete in. If managers misread their current game or the one they are moving toward, they stand no reasonable chance of thriving in either. Moreover, in most cases, firms need to surround themselves with complementary firms that also understand the game. A clueless player can easily spoil the game for all.

Second, we have stressed that R&D managers need an architectural understanding of business strategy and products. Systemic products and services and their markets evolve in ways very different from those of stand-alone products. We have also argued that closed and open systems exhibit very different, though sometimes complementary, dynamics.

Third, R&D managers also need to become adept in the art of recognizing and managing a constant flow of sometimes interacting multiple games and plays. Firms playing only one game of innovation can develop processes to routinize activities. The problem gets a bit more complex when a firm must play multiple games; it can decide to build many strategic business units (SBUs) or become polydextrous. In any case, multiple games require versatile human resources, managers making trade-offs, and systematic processes to manage different patterns. ⊛

References

1. Schumpeter, J. 1934. *The Theory of Economic Development.* Cambridge, MA: Harvard University Press. (New York: Oxford University Press, 1961.) First published in German, 1912.
2. Chandler, A. 1977. *The Visible Hand: The Managerial Revolution in American Business.* Cambridge, MA: Harvard Belknap.
3. Baldwin, C. Y. and Clark, K. B. 2000. *Design Rules.* Cambridge, MA: MIT Press.
4. Day, G., Schoemaker, P. J. H. and Gunther, R. E. 2000. *Wharton on Managing Emerging Technologies.* New York: John Wiley & Sons.
5. Iansiti, M. and Levien, R. 2004. *The Keystone Advantage: What the New Dynamics of Business Ecosystems Mean for Strategy, Innovation, and Sustainability.* Boston, MA: Harvard Business School Press.
6. Morris, C. and Ferguson, C. 1993. How Architecture Wins Wars. *Harvard Business Review,* March–April, pp. 86–96.
7. Kogut, B. and Kulatilaka, N. 1994. Options Thinking and Platform Investments: Investing in Opportunity. *California Management Review,* Summer, 36(2), pp. 52–71.
8. Olleros, X. 2007. The Power of Non-contractual Innovation. *International Journal of Innovation Management* 11(1), pp. 93–113.
9. Osborne, M. J. and Rubenstein, A. 1994. *A Course in Game Theory.* Cambridge, MA: MIT Press.
10. Nelson, R. and Winter, S. 1982. *An Evolutionary Theory of the Firm.* Cambridge, MA: Harvard Belknap.
11. Chakravorty, B. 2003. *Slow Pace of Fast Change.* Boston, MA: Harvard Business School Press.
12. Kim, W. C. and Mauborgne, R. 2005. *Blue Ocean Strategy: How to Create Uncontested Market Space and Make Competition Irrelevant.* Boston, MA: Harvard Business School Press.
13. Cusumano, M. and Gawer, A. 2003. The Elements of Platform Leadership. *MIT Sloan Management Review* 31(1), pp. 51–58.
14. Langlois, R. and Robertson, P. L. 1992. Networks and Innovation in a Modular System: Lessons from the Microcomputer and Stereo Component Industries. *Research Policy* 21(4), pp. 297–313.
15. Teece, D. 1998. *Economic Performance and the Theory of the Firm: The Selected Papers of David Teece.* 2 vols. London: Edward Elgar Publishing.
16. Arthur, W. B. 1989. Competing Technologies, Increasing Returns, and Lock-in by Historical Events. *Economic Journal* 99, pp. 116–131.
17. Chesbrough, H. W. 2003. *Open Innovation: The New Imperative for Creating and Profiting from Technology.* Boston, MA: Harvard Business School Press.
18. Christensen, C. and Raynor, M. 2003. *The Innovator's Solution: Creating and Sustaining Successful Growth.* Boston, MA: Harvard Business School Press.
19. Porter M., Schwab, K. and Lopez-Claros, A. 2006. *The Global Competitiveness Report, 2005–2006.* New York: Palgrave Macmillan.
20. Pavitt, K. and Steinmuller, E. 2002. Technology and Corporate Strategy. In *Strategy and Management,* A. Pettigrew, H. Thomas and R. Whittengton (eds.). London: Sage.

'Startups are wonderful. But they don't create employment.'

How to Make an American Job. By Andy Grove

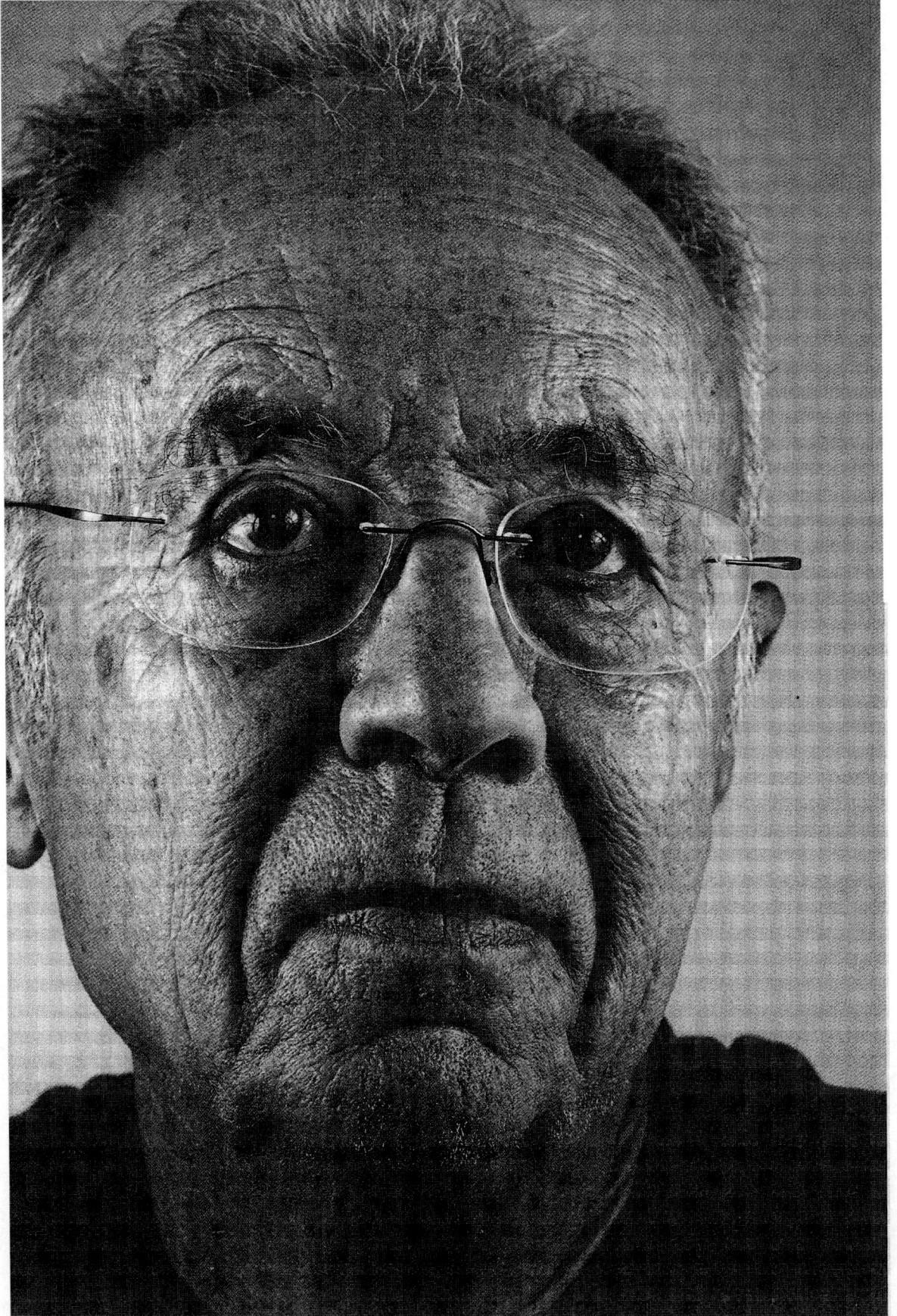

Recently an acquaintance at the next table in a Palo Alto (Calif.) restaurant introduced me to his companions, three young venture capitalists from China. They explained, with visible excitement, that they were touring promising companies in Silicon Valley. I've lived in the Valley a long time, and usually when I see how the region has become such a draw for global investments, I feel a little proud.

Not this time. I left the restaurant unsettled. Something did not add up. Bay Area unemployment is even higher than the 9.7 percent national average. Clearly, the great Silicon Valley innovation machine hasn't been creating many jobs of late—unless you're counting Asia, where American tech companies have been adding jobs like mad for years.

The underlying problem isn't simply lower Asian costs. It's our own misplaced faith in the power of startups to create U.S. jobs. Americans love the idea of the guys in the garage inventing something that changes the world. *New York Times* columnist Thomas L. Friedman recently encapsulated this view in a piece called "Start-Ups, Not Bailouts." His argument: Let tired old companies that do commodity manufacturing die if they have to. If Washington really wants to create jobs, he wrote, it should back startups.

Friedman is wrong. Startups are a wonderful thing, but they cannot by themselves increase tech employment. Equally important is what comes after that mythical moment of creation in the garage, as technology goes from prototype to mass production. This is the phase where companies scale up. They work out design details, figure out how to make things affordably, build factories, and hire people by the thousands. Scaling is hard work but necessary to make innovation matter.

The scaling process is no longer happening in the U.S. And as long as that's the case, plowing capital into young companies that build their factories elsewhere will continue to yield a bad return in terms of American jobs.

What Went Wrong?

Scaling used to work well in Silicon Valley. Entrepreneurs came up with an invention. Investors gave them money to build their business. If the founders and their investors were lucky, the company grew and had an initial public offering, which brought in money that financed further growth.

I am fortunate to have lived through one such example. In 1968 two well-known technologists and their investor friends anted up $3 million to start Intel, making memory chips for the computer industry. From the beginning we had to figure out how to make our chips in volume. We had to build factories, hire, train, and retain employees, establish relationships with suppliers, and sort out a million other things before Intel could become a billion-dollar company. Three years later the company went public and grew to be one of the biggest technology companies in the world. By 1980, 10 years after

Andy Grove, senior adviser to Intel, was the company's chief executive officer or chairman from 1987 until 2005.

our IPO, about 13,000 people worked for Intel in the U.S.

Not far from Intel's headquarters in Santa Clara, Calif., other companies developed. Tandem Computers went through a similar process, then Sun Microsystems, Cisco, Netscape, and on and on. Some companies died along the way or were absorbed by others, but each survivor added to the complex technological ecosystem that came to be called Silicon Valley.

As time passed, wages and health-care costs rose in the U.S. China opened up. American companies discovered that they could have their manufacturing and even their engineering done more cheaply overseas. When they did so, margins improved. Management was happy, and so were stockholders. Growth continued, even more profitably. But the job machine began sputtering.

The 10X Factor

Today, manufacturing employment in the U.S. computer industry is about 166,000, lower than it was before the first PC, the MITS Altair 2800, was assembled in 1975 (*figure* **B**). Meanwhile, a very effective computer manufacturing industry has emerged in Asia, employing about 1.5 million workers—factory employees, engineers, and managers. The largest of these companies is Hon Hai Precision Industry, also known as Foxconn. The company has grown at an astounding rate, first in Taiwan and later in China. Its revenues last year were $62 billion, larger than Apple, Microsoft, Dell, or Intel. Foxconn employs over 800,000 people, more than the combined worldwide head count of Apple, Dell, Microsoft, Hewlett-Packard, Intel, and Sony (*figure* **C**).

Until a recent spate of suicides at Foxconn's giant factory complex in Shenzhen, China, few Americans had heard of the company. But most know the products it makes: computers for Dell and HP, Nokia cell phones, Microsoft Xbox 360 consoles, Intel motherboards, and countless other familiar gadgets. Some 250,000 Foxconn employees in southern China produce Apple's products. Apple, meanwhile, has about 25,000 employees in the U.S. That means for every Apple worker in the U.S. there are 10 people in China working on iMacs, iPods, and iPhones. The same roughly 10-to-1 relationship holds for Dell, disk-drive maker Seagate Technology, and other U.S. tech companies.

You could say, as many do, that shipping jobs overseas is no big deal because the high-value work—and much of the profits—remain in the U.S. That may well be so. But what kind of a society are we going to have if it consists of highly paid people doing high-value-added work—and masses of unemployed?

Since the early days of Silicon Valley, the money invested in companies has increased dramatically, only to produce fewer jobs. Simply put, the U.S. has become wildly inefficient at creating American tech jobs. We may be less aware of this growing inefficiency, however, because our history of creating jobs over the past few decades has been spectacular—masking our greater and greater spending to create each position. Should we wait and not act on the basis of early indicators? I think that would be a tragic mistake, because the only chance we have to reverse the deterioration is if we act early and decisively.

Already the decline has been marked. It may be measured by way of a simple calculation—an estimate of the employment cost-effectiveness of a company. First, take the initial investment plus the investment during a company's IPO. Then divide that

'The cost of creating jobs grew from a few thousand dollars per position to a hundred thousand today'

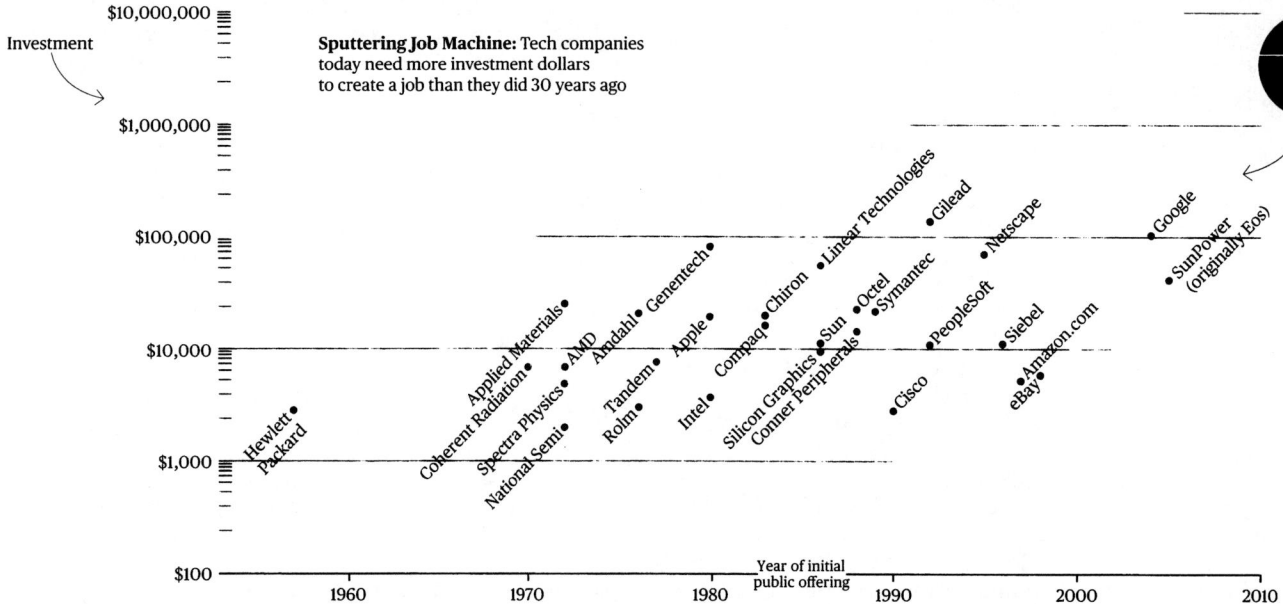

Investment

Sputtering Job Machine: Tech companies today need more investment dollars to create a job than they did 30 years ago

Figure **A**

$10,000,000

$1,000,000

$100,000

$10,000

$1,000

$100

| Company markers (by IPO year) |
Hewlett Packard · Coherent Radiation · Applied Materials · Spectra Physics · National Semi · AMD · Amdahl · Genentech · Tandem · Rolm · Apple · Intel · Compaq · Chiron · Silicon Graphics · Conner Peripherals · Sun · Octel · Linear Technologies · Symantec · Gilead · Cisco · PeopleSoft · Netscape · Siebel · eBay · Amazon.com · Google · SunPower (originally Eos)

Year of initial public offering

1960   1970   1980   1990   2000   2010

*Investment restated in 2010 dollars. Dollars invested before and in the IPO, divided by worldwide employment 10 years after the IPO. Data: Andy Grove

by the number of employees working in that company 10 years later. For Intel this worked out to be about $650 per job–$3,600 adjusted for inflation. National Semiconductor, another chip company, was even more efficient at $2,000 per job. Making the same calculations for a number of Silicon Valley companies shows that the cost of creating U.S. jobs grew from a few thousand dollars per position in the early years to a hundred thousand dollars today (*figure* **A**). The obvious reason: Companies simply hire fewer employees as more work is done by outside contractors, usually in Asia.

The job machine breakdown isn't just in computers. Consider alternative energy, an emerging industry where there's plenty of innovation. Photovoltaics, for example, are a U.S. invention. Their use in home energy applications was also pioneered by the U.S. Last year, I decided to do my bit for energy conservation and set out to equip my house with solar power. My wife and I talked with four local solar firms. As part of our due diligence, I checked where they get their photovoltaic panels–the key part of the system. All the panels they use come from China. A Silicon Valley company sells equipment used to manufacture photo-active films. They ship close to 10 times more machines to China than to manufacturers in the U.S., and this gap is growing (*figure* **D**). Not surprisingly, U.S. employment in the making of photovoltaic films and panels is perhaps 10,000–just a few percent of estimated worldwide employment.

There's more at stake than exported jobs. With some technologies, both scaling and innovation take place overseas.

Such is the case with advanced batteries. It has taken years and many false starts, but finally we are about to witness mass-produced electric cars and trucks. They all rely on lithium-ion batteries. What microprocessors are to computing, batteries are to electric vehicles. Unlike with microprocessors, the U.S. share of lithium-ion battery production is tiny (*figure* **E**).

That's a problem. A new industry needs an effective ecosystem in which technology knowhow accumulates, experience builds on experience, and close relationships develop between supplier and customer. The U.S. lost its lead in batteries 30 years ago when it stopped making consumer electronics devices. Whoever made batteries then gained the exposure and relationships needed to learn to supply batteries for the more demanding laptop PC market, and after that, for the even more demanding automobile market. U.S. companies did not participate in the first phase and consequently were not in the running for all that followed. I doubt they will ever catch up.

The Key to Job Creation

Scaling isn't easy. The investments required are much higher than in the invention phase. And funds need to be committed early, when not much is known about the potential market. Another example from Intel: The investment to build a silicon manufacturing plant in the '70s was a few million dollars. By the early '90s the cost of the factories that would be able to produce the new Pentium chips in volume rose to several billion dollars. The decision to build these plants needed to be made years before we knew whether the Pentium chip would work or whether the market would be interested in it.

Lessons we learned from previous missteps helped us. Some years earlier, when Intel's business consisted of making memory chips, we hesitated to add manufacturing capacity, not being all that sure about the market demand in years to come. Our Japanese competitors didn't hesitate: They built the plants. When the demand for memory chips exploded, the Japanese roared into the U.S. market and Intel began its descent as a memory chip supplier. Despite being steeled by that experience, I still remember how afraid I was as I asked the Intel directors for authorization to spend billions of dollars for factories to produce a product that did not exist at the time for a market we could not size. Fortunately, they gave their O.K. even as they gulped. The bet paid off.

My point isn't that Intel was brilliant. The company was founded at a time when it was easier to scale domestically. For one thing, China wasn't yet open for business. More importantly, the U.S. had not yet forgotten that scaling was crucial to its economic future.

How could the U.S. have forgotten? I believe the answer has to do with a general undervaluing of manufacturing—the idea that as long as "knowledge work" stays in the U.S., it doesn't matter what happens to factory jobs. It's not just newspaper commentators who spread this idea. Consider this passage by Princeton University economist Alan S. Blinder: "The TV manufacturing industry really started here, and at one point employed many workers. But as TV sets became 'just a commodity,' their production moved offshore to locations with much lower wages. And nowadays the number of television sets manufactured in the U.S. is zero. A failure? No, a success."

I disagree. Not only did we lose an untold number of jobs,

we broke the chain of experience that is so important in technological evolution. As happened with batteries, abandoning today's "commodity" manufacturing can lock you out of tomorrow's emerging industry.

Wanted: Job-Centric Economics

Our fundamental economic beliefs, which we have elevated from a conviction based on observation to an unquestioned truism, is that the free market is the best of all economic systems—the freer the better. Our generation has seen the decisive victory of free-market principles over planned economies. So we stick with this belief, largely oblivious to emerging evidence that while free markets beat planned economies, there may be room for a modification that is even better.

Such evidence stares at us from the performance of several Asian countries in the past few decades. These countries seem to understand that job creation must be the No. 1 objective of state economic policy. The government plays a strategic role in setting the priorities and arraying the forces and organization necessary to achieve this goal. The rapid development of the Asian economies provides numerous illustrations. In a thorough study of the industrial development of East Asia, Robert Wade of the London School of Economics found that these economies turned in precedent-shattering economic performances over the '70s and '80s in large part because of the effective involvement of the government in targeting the growth of manufacturing industries.

Consider the "Golden Projects," a series of digital initiatives driven by the Chinese government in the late 1980s and 1990s. Beijing was convinced of the importance of electronic networks—used for transactions, communications, and coordination—in enabling job creation, particularly in the less developed parts of the country. Consequently, the Golden Proj-

52

'Foxconn employs more than ... Apple, Dell, Microsoft, HP, Intel, and Sony combined'

Figure
B

Computer manufacturing jobs in the U.S. have been on the decline since 1984*

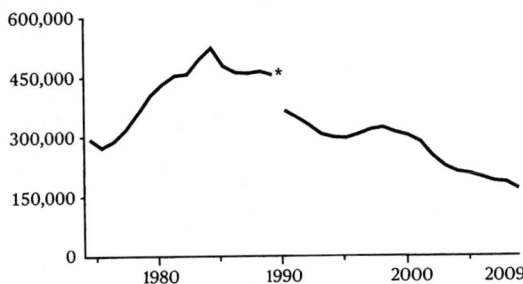

* Before 1990; includes office equipment Data: Bureau of Labor Statistics

Figure
C

Hon Hai (Foxconn) head count

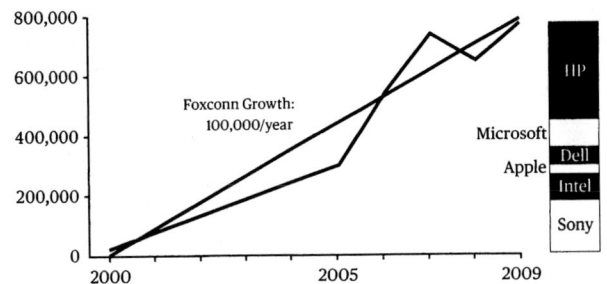

Data: Thompson Financial Extel Company Reports

229

'What chips are to computing, batteries are to electric vehicles. The U.S. share of the battery market is tiny'

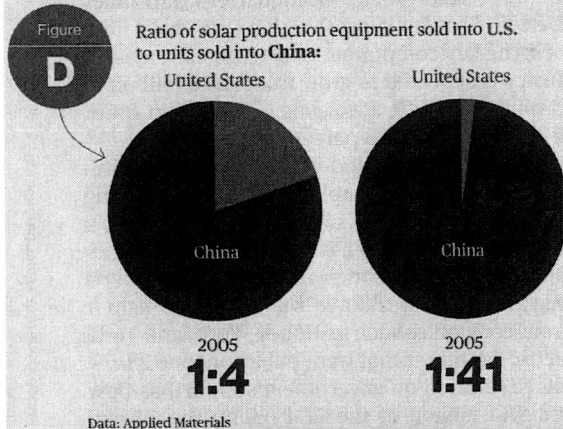

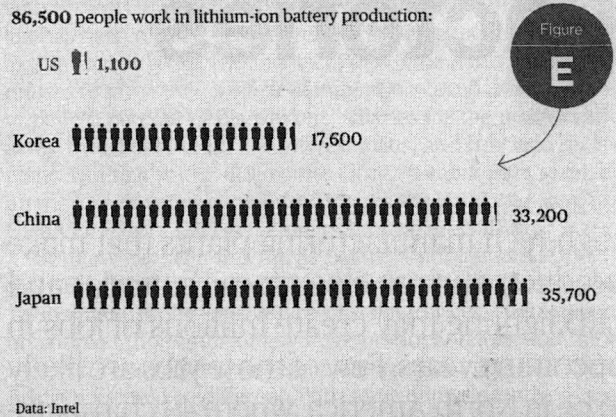

Figure D

Ratio of solar production equipment sold into U.S. to units sold into **China**:

United States / China — 2005 — **1:4**

United States / China — 2005 — **1:41**

Data: Applied Materials

Figure E

86,500 people work in lithium-ion battery production:

US 1,100

Korea 17,600

China 33,200

Japan 35,700

Data: Intel

---

ects enjoyed priority funding. In time they contributed to the rapid development of China's information infrastructure and the country's economic growth.

How do we turn such Asian experience into intelligent action here and now? Long term, we need a job-centric economic theory–and job-centric political leadership–to guide our plans and actions. In the meantime, consider some basic thoughts from a onetime factory guy.

Silicon Valley is a community with a strong tradition of engineering, and engineers are a peculiar breed. They are eager to solve whatever problems they encounter. If profit margins are the problem, we go to work on margins, with exquisite focus. Each company, ruggedly individualistic, does its best to expand efficiently and improve its own profitability. However, our pursuit of our individual businesses, which often involves transferring manufacturing and a great deal of engineering out of the country, has hindered our ability to bring innovations to scale at home. Without scaling, we don't just lose jobs–we lose our hold on new technologies. Losing the ability to scale will ultimately damage our capacity to innovate.

The story comes to mind of an engineer who was to be executed by guillotine. The guillotine was stuck, and custom required that if the blade didn't drop, the condemned man was set free. Before this could happen, the engineer pointed with excitement to a rusty pulley, and told the executioner to apply some oil there. Off went his head.

We got to our current state as a consequence of many of us taking actions focused on our own companies' next milestones. An example: Five years ago a friend joined a large VC firm as a partner. His responsibility was to make sure that all the startups they funded had a "China strategy," meaning a plan to move what jobs they could to China. He was going around with an oil can, applying drops to the guillotine in case it was stuck. We should put away our oil cans. VCs should have a partner in charge of every startup's "U.S. strategy."

The first task is to rebuild our industrial commons. We should develop a system of financial incentives: Levy an extra tax on the product of offshored labor. (If the result is a trade war, treat it like other wars–fight to win.) Keep that money separate. Deposit it in the coffers of what we might call the Scaling Bank of the U.S. and make these sums available to companies that will scale their American operations. Such a system would be a daily reminder that while pursuing our company goals, all of us in business have a responsibility to maintain the industrial base on which we depend and the society whose adaptability–and stability–we may have taken for granted.

I fled Hungary as a young man in 1956 to come to the U.S. Growing up in the Soviet bloc, I witnessed first-hand the perils of both government overreach and a stratified population. Most Americans probably aren't aware that there was a time in this country when tanks and cavalry were massed on Pennsylvania Avenue to chase away the unemployed. It was 1932; thousands of jobless veterans were demonstrating outside the White House. Soldiers with fixed bayonets and live ammunition moved in on them, and herded them away from the White House. In America! Unemployment is corrosive. If what I'm suggesting sounds protectionist, so be it.

Every day, that Palo Alto restaurant where I met the Chinese venture capitalists is full of technology executives and entrepreneurs. Many of them are my friends. I understand the technological challenges they face, along with the financial pressure they're under from directors and shareholders. Can we expect them to take on yet another assignment, to work on behalf of a loosely defined community of companies, employees, and employees yet to be hired? To do so is undoubtedly naïve. Yet the imperative for change is real and the choice is simple. If we want to remain a leading economy, we change on our own, or change will continue to be forced upon us. **B**

53

Churning Out Factories

High-tech manufacturing plants that make products such as electric-car batteries and LED lighting may create millions of jobs in upcoming years. Few of those jobs are likely to be in North America, where 49 chip factories have shut down since 2000. In the same period, Taiwan and China have built dozens. Many technology executives say the only antidote is government assistance, which has been far greater in other parts of the world. Now some U.S. officials are responding with subsidies and tax breaks, in an effort to combat high unemployment. Here's a look at three companies that are seeking to take advantage and create high-tech manufacturing jobs at home.

Detroit Power Play

As the U.S. economy unraveled in October 2008, Andrew Liveris, chief executive officer of Dow Chemical, asked his director of business development, Ravi Shanker, how they could create jobs near Dow's Midland (Mich.) headquarters, 130 miles northwest of Detroit. Shanker suggested that Dow make lithium ion batteries, the key component of electric-car engines. The Li-ion industry is expected to grow from $200 million to more than $25 billion by 2015, according to Needham & Co. In 2008, Asian companies had 98 percent of the market.

On June 21, Liveris broke ground on an 800,000-square-foot plant in Midland that will employ 800 people making 60,000 Li-ion batteries a year. It's owned by Dow Kokam, a joint venture created in 2009 with a U.S. partner that licenses technology from South Korean battery maker Kokam. Liveris is hoping Michigan's skilled workforce will be able to help it win business from companies such as Honda, Ford, and Tesla Motors, the electric-car maker that went public on June 28.

The deal was predicated on government support, as Dow Kokam received $161 million of the $2.4 billion the Obama Administration has earmarked for the electric-car industry. That covered half the cost of the 400,000-square-foot first-phase plant. An additional $180 million in Michigan tax incentives will help fund the second phase. "We would never have built it in Michigan, or the U.S., without that aid," Liveris says. "It takes some of the risk away from the investment."

Dow is using federal and state grants for a facility in town to make solar roofing shingles, employing an estimated 1,200 people. In addition to the 2,000 permanent workers at the two factories, Liveris believes the projects will create 14,000 jobs in local industries and services.

To make real progress, Liveris says the U.S. needs to cut corporate taxes and adopt an energy policy that promotes American-made alternative technologies. As a member of Thailand's Board of Investment, he advises the Thai government on how to craft the sorts of financial incentives he wishes were available in the U.S. "It's not a level playing field," he says. —*Jack Kaskey*

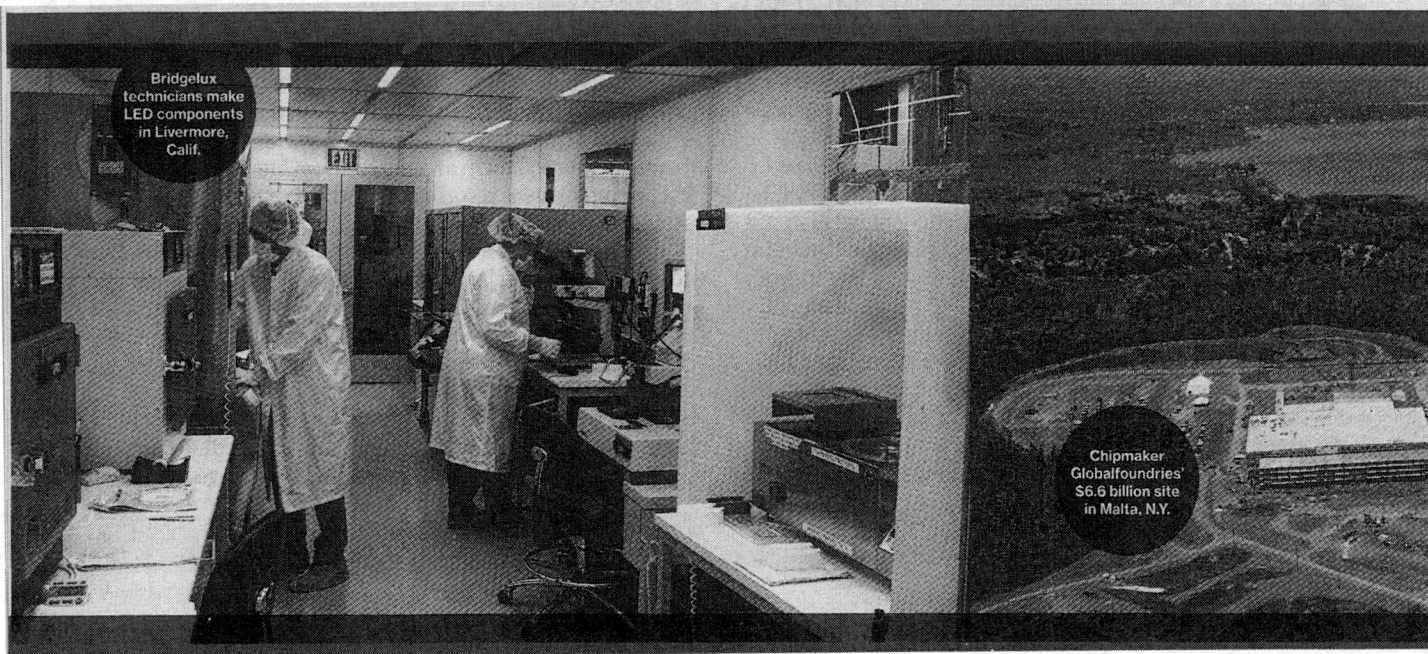

Bridgelux technicians make LED components in Livermore, Calif.

Chipmaker Globalfoundries' $6.6 billion site in Malta, N.Y.

54

Funded by Abu Dhabi

When chipmaker Advanced Micro Devices announced it was getting out of the manufacturing business in 2007, people in Malta, N.Y.–a town of 13,000 that is 20 miles from Albany–worried about the fate of the massive plant AMD was planning to build there. Help came from an unexpected source: the government of Abu Dhabi.

The $6.6 billion, 300,000-square-foot factory project has been taken over by Globalfoundries, the company created when Abu Dhabi's Advanced Technology Investment bought AMD's plants in Dresden, Germany, and took over the Malta project. As in Michigan, subsidies were essential. New York State committed up to $1.2 billion in tax breaks and other incentives, depending on how many jobs the Malta facility creates. According to the Semiconductor Industry Assn., building a chip plant in the U.S. adds $1 billion in costs over its lifetime.

With both a state-funded nanotechnology research center and IBM's headquarters nearby, Malta has a healthy population of top engineers who are suited to this highly skilled work–which is part of the appeal for the company. (You try depositing a layer of chemicals that is one atom thick on a chip.) The jobs will pay well for the 1,300 people who will work there when the Malta factory opens in 2012. Dennis Mullen, chairman of the Empire State Development Corp., says his agency expects the project to create three or four times as many jobs outside the plant. —*Ian King*

The Costs Don't Work

When Bill Watkins took over Bridgelux in January, he hoped it would bring hundreds of jobs to the chip factory the company had just bought in Livermore, Calif., 40 minutes east of Silicon Valley. Bridgelux makes electronic lights based on the same light-emitting diodes that illuminate laptops and some flat-panel TVs–a technology that is expected to displace Edison's incandescent bulb as the core of the $100 billion-a-year lighting industry. All Watkins needed, he said, were some big customers, such as state or local govern-

ments, to commit to buying enough Bridgelux LEDs to get the business off the ground.

So far, Watkins has made "zero progress" on getting help for his Made in the U.S.A. plan. While senators, state officials, and utility executives talk about job creation, none has offered contracts that would allow him to add to the small crew of workers at his Livermore factory. Instead, he plans to move ahead with projects in China, India, Malaysia, and other places Bridgelux has been offered deals to retrofit streetlights or office buildings in exchange for creating local jobs. One Asian country–he refuses to say which, for fear of imperiling negotiations–offered to pay 80 percent of his workers' salaries for the next decade, along with a tax break, low-interest loans, and free land for the plant. Nothing in the U.S. comes close. "I think Bill's given up on the idea of volume manufacturing in the U.S.," says longtime friend Eli Harari, CEO of memory-chip maker SanDisk.

Watkins has seen this movie before. Until January 2009, he was CEO of Seagate Technology, the world's largest drive maker. To maintain profits in the face of falling prices, the company outsourced thousands of low-wage production jobs and, more recently, research and development positions. He had hoped Bridgelux would be different. With some minor incentives–such as a 10% premium over rock-bottom prices in a few big municipal contracts–he thinks Bridgelux could gain enough volume to compete with anyone. He would like to invest $150 million in the Livermore factory, in addition to $50 million already invested, and nearly triple its staff, to more than 350. The obstacle, he believes, is politics. While Americans want jobs, they want their low, low prices even more: "I'm going to spend the next year trying to find someone that is willing to pay to have something made in the U.S." When Watkins tells foreign government officials about his plans to boost American manufacturing, he says, "They laugh. Everyone knows the costs don't work."

Of course, Watkins isn't willing to mortgage his company's future for pure patriotism. He expects sales to double, to more than $60 million in 2011. "I want to create jobs here for my own personal reasons, but at the end of the day it doesn't matter," he says. "I can make Bridgelux successful wherever the jobs are." **Ⓑ**—*Peter Burrows*

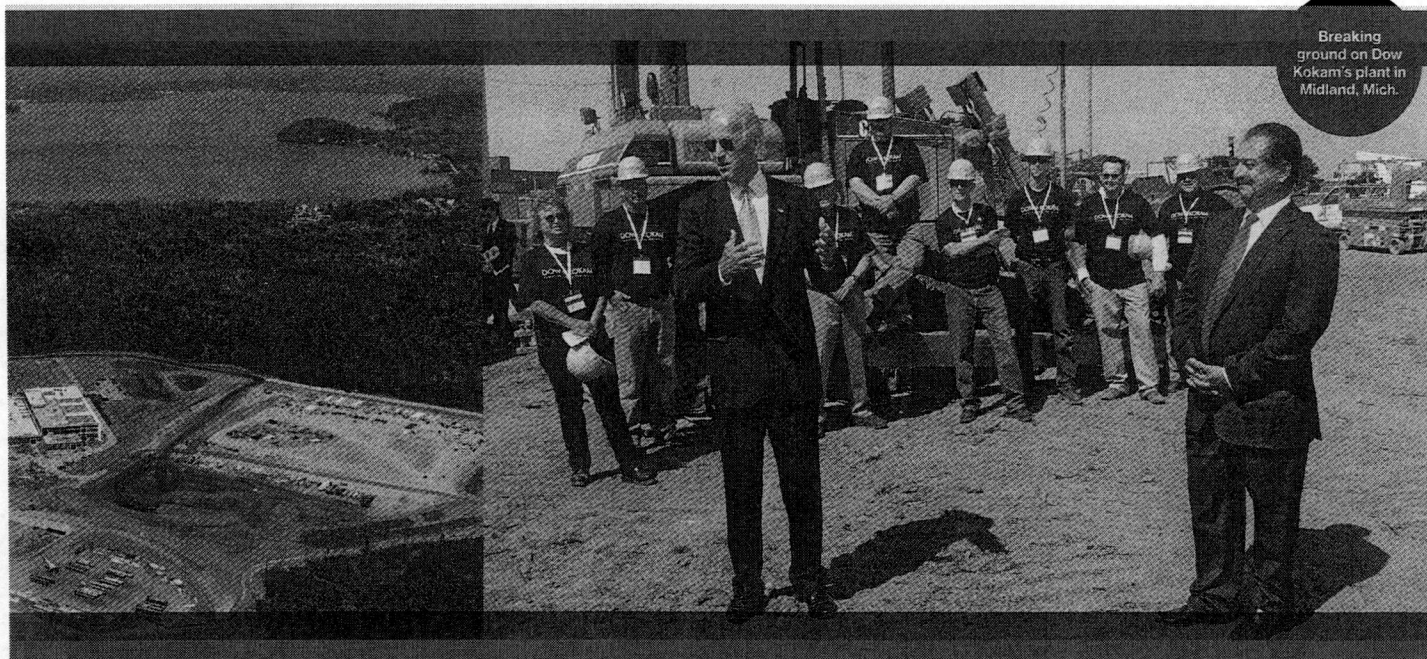

Breaking ground on Dow Kokam's plant in Midland, Mich.

▶▶THOUSANDS OF PEOPLE MIGHT CONTRIBUTE TO THE CURE OF ONE PERSON◀◀

←EXTRA-LARGE 3D PRINTOUT OF A VIRUS

ANDREW HESSEL

PRINTING MEDICINE

BY CAROLINE WINTER   **PHOTOGRAPH BY ETHAN SCOTT**

AT AUTODESK, HESSEL'S TEAM IS DESIGNING SOFTWARE THAT MAY HELP CROWDSOURCE A CANCER CURE

Six months ago, Autodesk opened a skunk works on Pier 9 in San Francisco. The two-story waterfront space–a TechShop on steroids–houses top-of-the-line 3D printers, a precision water jet cutter, wood and metal shops, an industrial kitchen, and pretty much any other tool an inventor could possibly want. Tucked away in a corner, there's also a skunk works within the skunk works. Here, Andrew Hessel and a team of designers, programmers, and scientists are working on what is perhaps Autodesk's most ambitious project: building software and hardware that will simplify the task of designing and fabricating living things, including viruses, bacteria, and even human organs. "What's beautiful about software is that it makes complex jobs easy," he says.

Hessel is an evangelist for synthetic biology, a radical cousin of genetic engineering done with digital tools. He's also a distinguished research scientist at Autodesk, the $11.4 billion software company best known for AutoCAD, which engineers use to design everything from sunglasses to skyscrapers. It is not yet clear when Autodesk will commercialize its newest design tools, but democratizing access to synthetic biology may hasten growth in a field that could, according to Hessel, revolutionize energy production and water purification, to name two areas.

Oh, and maybe cure cancer. Each tumor has its own DNA. Hessel's mission is to create straightforward, accessible tools to synthesize viruses that will attack only cells carrying specific genetic markers. And because each medicine would be unique to one patient, there would be no need to wait for U.S. Food and Drug Administration approval. "Oncolytic viruses are really well studied," he says. "The only thing I'm bringing to this [idea] is, well, now you don't have to be a drug company or even a biologist to go make a virus."

At a bistro not far from Autodesk's offices, Hessel pours himself cup after cup of coffee. "If not for my wife, this is all I'd ever consume," he says. Lanky with close-cropped salt-and-pepper hair and stubble, he's wearing red-framed Marc Jacobs glasses, jeans, a black sports coat, and black boots. A small circle is tattooed on his left ring finger, his version of a wedding band. Naturally, he met his wife at a TED conference.

Hessel, a 50-year-old Canadian, worked from 1995 to 2002 in genomics and bioanalysis at Amgen, the pharmaceutical company. The race to sequence the human genome was going strong, and he spent his days surrounded by computer monitors. "You had to drag me away from work to sleep," he says. At one point, he sold his house and moved into the office, though he also bought a 38-foot sailboat where he slept some nights. "My workplace was the address on my driver's license," he says. "I even installed one of those compact European washer-dryers in our conference room."

Eventually, Hessel grew frustrated by slow results. "In seven years we never made another drug, despite spending $1 billion on research," he says. "Everything we'd done hadn't changed drug development, hadn't made it faster or cheaper."

In 1999, Hessel heard about a group that had modified an inkjet printer, replacing the ink with a chemical needed to synthesize DNA. "When I saw that you could print short segments of DNA in really high density, I knew that synthetic biology would be possible," he says. Floored by what seemed like the next logical step in medicine and life sciences, he went to his bosses. "I said, 'Let's start building tools to write DNA'–and they weren't interested." In 2002, Hessel sold his boat and divested from Amgen. He spent the next 10 years crisscrossing North America, visiting academics and biohackers to learn everything possible about his future field, which had not yet been given a name.

These days, the system for delivering better cancer drugs still needs a jolt. President Nixon declared a war on cancer during his 1971 State of the Union address, but progress in fighting the disease remains dismal. In 2012, 8.2 million people died of cancer, according to the World Health Organization, up from 6.4 million in 2000, a per capita increase from 105 per 100,000 to 116. Drug companies can take 15 years and spend more than $1 billion to develop new treatments. Once on the market, the drug may be used on thousands of patients broadly, although each patient suffers from a genetically unique cancer. That means any two patients with prostate cancer, for example, may have drastically different reactions to the same drug. Companies such as Genentech are working to improve the pharmaceutical industry's trial system through such methods as identifying patients likely to benefit from a particular drug and enrolling only those with appropriate genetic or molecular signatures.

Hessel is impatient for bigger disruptions and says synthetic biology could deliver them. Over the past decades, scientists have learned how to translate the four letters of the genetic alphabet–A (adenine), C (cytosine), G (guanine), and T (thymine)–into the ones and zeros of binary code. Synthetic biology is the reverse process. "Cells are like tiny computers," says Hessel. "And DNA is like software." Today, dozens of DNA print shops can turn digital designs into

63

➔P.64

biology, essentially by what Hessel calls "3D printing DNA." Biohackers and academics at prestigious institutions are using these tools to do all sorts of things, both freakish and useful. They've grown glow-in-the-dark plants and managed to add unnatural base pairs, such as X and Y, to the DNA alphabet. Groups at several universities have engineered bacterial cells that selectively target and invade cancer cells before releasing toxic enzymes.

Meanwhile, young people are flooding the field. Even Bill Gates told *Wired* that if he were a kid today, he'd go into hacking biology. Hessel is certain that we're on the cusp of a revolution that will surpass information technology as a driver of economic growth and societal change. "There's only a few things I'm absolutely sure about in life," he says. "One of them is computers get faster, better, cheaper. And the other one is that reading and writing DNA also gets faster, better, cheaper."

There remain significant dangers. In 2002 a Stony Brook University professor synthesized the polio virus using mail-order DNA. Three years later influenza researchers re-created the 1918-19 Spanish flu virus, which at the time killed more than 20 million people. Hessel warns it may eventually become possible to create personalized bioweapons targeting only people with a specific genetic makeup. And genomic information is easy to acquire: "If Brad Pitt goes for coffee, the spoon [he uses] has his DNA," says Hessel. "You can sequence it and learn more about Brad Pitt's medical background than Brad knows."

Some safeguards are already in place. Reputable DNA synthesis shops scan every order for dangerous sequences to ensure they don't unwittingly produce the Ebola virus, smallpox, or other known pathogens. Hessel says global bioterrorism and biosecurity establishments are still far behind the curve and that more safety measures need to be put in place, but he's convinced synthetic biology will do more good than harm.

Autodesk has already created tools for scientists, such as CADnano, used to design 3D DNA origami nanostructures. It has also released a rolling beta of Project Cyborg, a cloud-based platform for programming matter that offers a range of services, including molecular modeling and simulation. Users can look at viruses in 3D, "like you're looking at the design of a building," says Hessel. "It becomes real;

it's really fantastic—and underneath that 3D model is the genetic code."

The software giant has several research partners, including Organovo, a startup that uses bioprinting technology to manufacture human tissues, and Harvard's Wyss Institute, which develops biologically inspired materials and devices. George Church, a professor at Harvard and the Massachusetts Institute of Technology and a leading researcher in synthetic biology and genomic science, says Autodesk's tools "have been quite relevant to our efforts." Skylar Tibbits, who directs MIT's Self-Assembly Lab, says he's excited about Project Cyborg's cross-disciplinary potential. "I could use it, a biologist could use it, an engineer could use it, and we could all work on similar phenomenon," he says. "That's a huge paradigm shift."

Tools, of course, aren't everything. "Biology is hard, and design tools really aren't the rate-limiting thing," says Neil Gershenfeld, director of MIT's Center for Bits and Atoms. "What's rate-limiting is getting control of the biological mechanisms." Still, he says, we will likely see a co-evolution of tools and scientific progress: "I view what Autodesk is doing as a great indication of the acceptance and beginning of maturation of the field," he says. As for Hessel, Gershenfeld doesn't know him but says he is likely oversimplifying the challenges of synthetic biology, though that's not necessarily a bad thing. "Futurists can have a poor reputation among the scientists, but they serve a useful role," he says. "They help articulate implications that people aren't recognizing." Gershenfeld adds, "They have a pretty good record of doing it."

Hessel has already started building a community of would-be users. In 2009, before joining Autodesk, he founded Pink Army Cooperative, a nonprofit, member-owned biotech startup that aims to one day use open-source development to produce cheap cures for breast cancer. "Can you imagine a cancer treatment made just for you, in a day, for free? And with almost no side effects," Hessel wrote on Pink Army's website. "It sounds like science fiction, but I believe it's within reach if we work together."

The idea is that doctors would take samples of a patient's tumor and sequence their DNA. Next, Pink Army members and anyone interested would analyze the genomic information online and design a virus strain to track down and kill cells bearing the cancer's specific biological traits. The virus particles would then be produced and purified. Before injecting the resulting medication into a patient's tumor or bloodstream, doctors would test it on samples of both the patient's normal and diseased tissues.

Because tumors can have a mixed population of cancer cells and these cells can have hundreds of DNA mutations, patients would likely need to be treated with several custom-made viruses, but Hessel points out that his open-sourced model could create an essentially bottomless pharmacy. "If it costs me next to nothing to make the design and I'm testing it on your cells in a dish anyway, I can test a thousand designs," he says. "Thousands of people might contribute to the cure of one person."

Hessel sold almost 600 Pink Army memberships for $20 each before putting the fundraising on hold. He recognizes that the organization is still more of an idea than reality. "The reason I'm working with Autodesk is so we have the capabilities for a group like Pink Army to actually work," he says.

Hessel freely admits that his visions are far off. "I like to say I live five years in the future," he says. "I know it's going to come together; all I'm trying to do is grease the wheels a little." As for Pink Army, he says doctors will be skeptical and that the hardest part will be getting the idea to work at all, let alone work well. But that doesn't damp Hessel's optimism. "We've been fighting cancer for so long," he says, "we actually forget that we might win."

CODE CUSTOM VIRUSES TO FIGHT CANCER

❶ SEQUENCE CANCER CELLS, FIND BEST WAY TO TARGET THEM

ATGCGCGC

❷ DRAW UP BLUEPRINT FOR A CANCER-KILLING VIRUS

❸ BESPOKE VIRUSES INFECT AND DESTROY CANCER CELLS, LEAVING HEALTHY ONES

GOTCHA!

BUILD TINY DRUG DELIVERY SYSTEMS TO FIGHT CANCER

❶ PRINT DNA THAT SELF-ASSEMBLES INTO DRUG DELIVERY PODS

❷ LOAD PODS WITH CANCER THERAPIES, LOCK THEM SO THEY ONLY RELEASE THEIR PAYLOADS WHEN THEY TOUCH A CANCER CELL

❸ PODS DUMP DRUGS ONLY ON CANCER CELLS, KILLING THEM

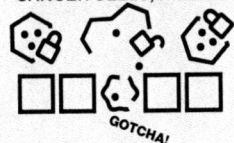

GOTCHA!

GRAPHIC BY BLOOMBERG BUSINESSWEEK. DATA: ANDREW HESSEL, SHAWN DOUGLAS, IDO BACHELET, AND GEORGE CHURCH, "A LOGIC-GATED NANOROBOT FOR TARGETED TRANSPORT OF MOLECULAR PAYLOADS," 2012

64

YOU'RE BEING FOLLOWED
WE ARE ALL BEING TRACKED AS WE GO ABOUT OUR EVERYDAY ROUTINES

Rap star Jay Z last came to Toronto in January and his concert at Air Canada Centre was packed, drawing thousands of fans to the arena in the downtown core. To gauge the success of this concert by the hip-hop mogul of "Empire State of Mind" and Beyonce-spouse fame, promoters in the past would have typically relied on the estimated attendance, while nearby businesses could look at how flush their cash registers were by night's end.

Now, thanks to the ubiquitous cellphone, Toronto-based company Viasense Inc. can figure out that roughly 13,000 people filled the stands, but they also know how much time concertgoers spent at the show, where they went before and after, and where they ultimately spent the night. Viasense doesn't know the concertgoers' names or what they look like, but the marketing and analytics company can recognize the unique identifier linked to the cellphones people carry and trace their paths. "We were able to see exactly the makeup of the audience," says Mossab Basir, founder and CEO of Viasense.

Location data silently emitted by the cellphones, smartphones and other electronic devices most of us carry throughout the day has triggered a new gold rush for marketers who want to harness it and for companies that covet the insights it can provide. The patterns of places a person, even if nameless, frequents can reveal plenty. Their pathways can paint a picture of a yogi with a penchant for gambling or a busy parent ferrying children to school, hockey and ballet. It can also shed light on traffic patterns through a mall, or inside a store or airport to help improve services.

Privacy and consumer advocates say we're moving into uncharted territory, and it's possible that in the future we will know where everyone is, and was, at all times. This may have far-reaching implications that we and the law are not yet prepared to deal with. And the practice is only going to intensify as companies rush to capitalize on consumers' "data exhaust," says Geoff White, counsel for the Public Interest Advocacy Centre (PIAC). "There is no defence for this level of surveillance," he says, pointing out companies are profiting off the information while consumers either don't know it is happening or have little control over it. "You wouldn't sanction the ability to walk up and put a GPS tracking device in your purse or back pocket."

But on the surface, this data collection seems relatively benign. For example, Viasense analyzes bulk cellphone data, as well as data from sensors that detect Wi-Fi- or Bluetooth-enabled smartphones and other devices, to collect location information. The insights they generate, Basir and his business partner Kerry Morrison say, are meant to be "micro-generalizations" about groups to help clients, and are not linked to an individual. Plus, they encrypt and protect the data they gather, and are working with privacy groups to put in the right checks and balances. "It's entirely anonymous," Basir says. "We have absolutely no idea who that person is, or even what their phone number is."

Of course, lots of firms already know a lot about any given consumer. In exchange for, say, a bank account or a mortgage, people willingly and knowingly give up personal information from their income levels and credit histories to home addresses and other contact info. Companies have also long benefited from the advent of Internet cookies, the ability to log what a person surfing the web is clicking on, and for how long, over time. That information is used to decide what ads pop up on screen and how to target customers. But that ability to track online behavioural patterns, on a massive scale, is now possible in the real world.

It began with apps such as Foursquare, where users "check in" to let their social network know where they are, and sometimes get a discount or special deal from a merchant in return. People also willingly share their daily activities and whereabouts via social media such as Twitter, Facebook and Instagram. But in the next phase, consumers will no longer have to do anything at all for businesses and marketers to learn information about them, except have a cellphone or turn on the Wi-Fi or Bluetooth capabilities on their smartphone, tablet or laptop.

In Canada, about 80% of residents own a cellphone. Smartphones are also becoming more common, with 62% of Canadian residents using the devices in 2012, up from 45% a year earlier, according to comScore. The passive pings constantly emitted by these devices are being compiled and collected by Viasense, Toronto-based Turnstyle Solutions Inc., Winnipeg-based Mexia Interactive Inc. and dozens of others around the world.

The Location-Based Marketing Association, based in Toronto, estimates the global market is worth roughly US$9 billion currently, and will grow to as much as US$16 billion by 2016. "We're familiar with cookies in the online world, tracking when people are going to the website, where they've been, and when they come back," says Asif Khan, the association's executive director. "But I think that location is the new cookie going forward." Khan estimates there are roughly 80 to 100 companies focused on location-based marketing around the world.

"It's one of the technologies that almost every retailer is using, testing or looking to use in 2014," Jules Polonetsky, executive director of the Future of Privacy Forum, based in Washington, D.C., told the *Financial Post* in January. The goal of using these technologies is to assess where a person is, and use that information to better entice that consumer, but there are a variety of ways to track whereabouts.

Location data garnered from cellphone signals is one method. Viasense buys bulk, raw anonymous data from a Canadian carrier, and crunches the aggregate data to figure out where those cellphone signals are being emitted from. Once a device hits the network, Viasense attaches its own unique ID to it and captures where it is travelling throughout the city, Basir says.

Since the company officially launched last year, it has been building a database of this information stretching as far back as July 2013. Viasense processes 600 location pings per second, or 50 million pings per day, and has compiled anonymous profiles of roughly four million devices. The company can even determine if a device-holder is an avid runner by the speed at which the signal is travelling across, say, Toronto's Trinity-Bellwoods park. Viasense can also match a profile's home location — defined as where the device spends the hours between midnight and 7 a.m. — with census data for that postal code to get demographic information, Basir says.

"We call it persistently profiling... which just means that as you

VIASENSE PROCESSES 600 LOCATION PINGS PER SECOND AND COMPILED ANONYMOUS PROFILES OF FOUR MILLION DEVICES

move throughout the city throughout the day, you go from home to your office to maybe a yoga studio later, or whatever, we can see that these movements are happening in the city," says Basir. "And we start to profile the totally anonymous user based on that."

Viasense will not name the Canadian carrier that it purchases the aggregate phone data from due to confidentiality agreements, but it has a 40% share of the market, says Kerry Morrison, founder of Norm, an umbrella company of marketing and analytics services that Viasense is a part of. Telus Corp. and BCE Inc. say they don't sell this type of customer data. Rogers Communications Inc. says it provides anonymous data to third-party providers that it has service agreements with, such as vehicle traffic information to determine the flow on roadways. But this data is anonymous and cannot identify an individual's location. "We have been approached by Viasense, but do not have a direct business relationship with the company," says a Rogers spokesperson.

Wireless carriers in the U.S., such as Verizon Wireless, have reportedly already begun selling aggregate data. Verizon in 2012 announced the launch of its Precision Market Insights division, which draws data from its 86-million-plus subscriber base, anonymizes it, and "advanced analytics engines then provide a deeper perspective to help you reach and engage with your target audiences," says Verizon's website. Its customers who choose not to participate are exempted, it adds. Telecom companies already have this data at their fingertips, and many are trying to figure out what to do with it, Morrison says. No Canadian carriers have announced such programs. But Viasense is in discussions with the other two of the Big 3, he says. "We have one carrier now, we will shortly have the other[s]," Morrison says. All three carriers say they were not in discussions with Morrison and Basir's company.

Norm also has two other analytics methods: using algorithms to comb through social media for mentions and references of brands, and in-store sensors that detect Wi-Fi- or Bluetooth-enabled devices. The long-term aim is to combine all three, though that's not possible yet, Morrison says.

Perhaps the most popular, or easiest to implement, method of gathering location data is to use small sensors that detect Wi-Fi- or Bluetooth-enabled devices. When a laptop, smartphone or tablet has

The most obvious way location-based marketers gather data is by detecting cellphones and other devices that can emit pings. But there are other ways companies use location data that are off the beaten path.

For example, many retailers have cameras throughout their store, largely for security purposes so the footage is little looked at outside of an incident. But U.S. company Prism Sky-

labs Inc. can take that real-time video from merchants' existing network of cameras and analyze the movement of customers within each store to determine where people tend to walk, what merchandise most often catches their eye, and what placement actually results in a purchase. To protect consumers' privacy, images of individual consumers are blurred.

Placemeter, a New York-based startup,

uses algorithms to analyze live video feeds and calculate pedestrian and vehicular traffic flow at various public places in the city. If, say, you wanted to know what the line was like outside a particular movie theatre, you could click on one of their cameras to get a live look. Their network consists of live video cameras as well as video feeds from old iPhones and Androids placed in people's windows (people get paid a

those capabilities turned on, it is automatically trying to connect with the nearest Wi-Fi router or Bluetooth device. These sensors, which have a radius of as much as 45 metres, can detect a device's signals and log its unique 12-character alphanumeric identifier called a MAC address, without ever actually connecting to it. These sensors or beacons will recognize the MAC address whenever that device comes near it, how long it stays, and what areas of the store it lingers in based on the strength of the signal. Turnstyle Solutions can develop an anonymous portrait of these users based on the pattern of locations it sees from its network of sensors.

Turnstyle's network has grown to more than 200 sensors across Toronto since it launched as a pilot program in January 2013, and 400 globally. These can also function as Wi-Fi routers, allowing retailers to provide Internet to their customers. If a consumer agrees to opt in using a social-media account, that merchant will know his or her name and other personal data as well. But Turnstyle doesn't ask consumers for consent before tracking a device's Wi-Fi signal, because it's not linked to a person's identity, CEO Devon Wright says. Turnstyle now has about 3.5 million unique customer profiles in Canada and close to seven million worldwide. Mexia Interactive, whose clients include airports, shopping malls and large retailers, has sensors in about 3,000 locations worldwide, says founder Glenn Tinley. And one of the biggest players doing in-store analytics is U.S. company Euclid Analytics, whose clients include high-end retail chain Nordstrom and Home Depot, according to *The New York Times*.

But data gathering for location-based marketing is not just limited to detecting cellphones. As surfing on screens moves to the Internet of things, location data can be collected from Internet-enabled cars, shirts and other wearable technologies, Khan said at a January meeting of the LBMA in Toronto. Location data is already being used for digital advertisements that can detect the profiles of people around it, and display relevant ad content, just like in the sci-fi Tom Cruise movie *Minority Report*.

Consumers, of course, are more willing to share their information when they are getting an appropriate benefit from the use of their data, Khan says. "Everybody has a price for their data, and the onus is on the market or the brand to deliver that value proposition in an effective way that convinces the consumer to say, 'I

THERE'S A GROWING SENSE AMONG CANADIANS THAT THEIR ABILITY TO PROTECT THEIR PERSONAL INFORMATION IS DIMINISHING

want that and, therefore, I'm going to give up my data in exchange for that.'"

People use Facebook and Gmail when its clear those services are free in exchange for user data. However, there's a growing sense among Canadians that their ability to protect their personal information is diminishing, according to a survey conducted in 2012 by Canada's Privacy Commissioner. More than half (56%) say they are not confident that they have enough information to know how new technologies affect their personal privacy — the highest level since the survey began in 2000. Plus, 53% say they would adjust the settings of their mobile phones or apps to limit the amount of personal information they share with others. About 38% of those surveyed say they would turn off the location-tracking feature on their mobile devices because they are concerned about others accessing that information.

Canada's Personal Information Protection and Electronic Documents Act (PIPEDA) does not address location-data gathering specifically, but it does require that organizations explain the purpose for collecting personal information and obtain consent for its use. A spokesperson for the privacy commissioner says it wouldn't be in a position to determine the legality of location-data gathering practices without investigating in response to a complaint. The commissioner's office hasn't received any complaints and doesn't have any ongoing investigations specifically related to such gathering.

Technologies involving location data are evolving rapidly, and while they can be "extremely useful," some can raise privacy concerns, the commissioner's spokesperson says. "Information about where a person has been could be very sensitive," she says in an email. "Some of the privacy issues raised with respect to tracking a person's location can include: Who has access to that information? How is it protected? How long is it kept? How easily could a specific person be identified based on the data?"

BCE has already come under fire for its collection and use of wireless customer data, including location information. The Public Interest Advocacy Centre and the Consumers' Association of Canada in January filed an application with the Canadian Radio-television and Telecommunications Commission complaining that BCE's program for marketing purposes is "counter to Canadians' reasonable expectations of privacy."

monthly fee in return). Placemeter is also looking to sell this data, according to its website.

Another technique involves using digital screens to personalize content as people walk by, à la the Tom Cruise sci-fi thriller *Minority Report*. Asif Khan, executive director of the Location-Based Marketing Association, cites a project he was involved in two years ago in New York where they outfitted a bus with a

digital screen that would tailor its content to those around it, based on demographic data garnered via social media and location data. "While the bus was still stationary, we served an ad on the side of the bus to reflect the people who were actually at the intersection," he says. "And when the bus moved to the next intersection, we did it all over again."

Marketing and technology company +re-

habstudio has also developed a prototype where a digital storefront can recognize a shopper using Bluetooth, and instantly react to a set of personal data stored on that person's mobile device, such as shopping habits and preferences. "Shoppers can swipe through personalised content, place items in a virtual shopping cart, and purchase straight from the display," the company says on its website.

The argument that the data collected is anonymous, and therefore doesn't infringe on a person's privacy rights, doesn't hold weight, says PIAC's White, as it is not impossible to connect the dots from a person's device to a name. PIAC is also looking into whether the reception of these signals is in contravention of the Radiocommunications Act. "There are challenges with the current privacy legislation, and this type of marketing activity is highlighting some weaknesses in the privacy legislation, and the enforcement of it as well," he says.

In early April, Industry Minister James Moore unveiled the Digital Privacy Act to amend PIPEDA, perhaps a sign of Canadians' growing concern about how their personal data are used. The amendments include requiring organizations to clearly communicate with their target audience when obtaining consent and to consider whether their target audience is able to understand the consequences of sharing their personal information. However, the act did not touch on the issue of location data. "[It] doesn't bring needed express recognition of location-based information as potentially very sensitive and something for which full disclosure and express consent should, naturally, be sought," White says.

Turnstyle, Viasense and Mexia say they are very cognizant about privacy concerns. Turnstyle and Mexia are working with the Future of Privacy Forum, a think tank that seeks to advance responsible data practices, and are two of the 11 firms that have signed on to its Mobile Location Analytics code of conduct. Viasense says it's in the process of signing the code as well. With this code, companies pledge to take "reasonable steps" to ensure their clients put up signage in a conspicuous location telling people mobile location analytics data are being gathered there. The Forum also has a central portal, where people can submit their MAC addresses and opt out from tracking by the 11 signatories. Still, that requires people to know it's even happening to opt out, White says.

Without clear government regulation in the mobile location analytics sphere, industry and privacy groups are still trying to figure out the best way to handle the gathering of location data. "We, and anyone in this space, need to stay on top of things, keep communicating with the commissioner and concerned groups," Norm's Morrison says.

But even the players in this space don't always see eye to eye. Mexia founder Tinley says his company does not combine the analytics of multiple clients to draw bigger demographic conclusions about their consumers, nor does it package the info and sell it in any other way. "We may not sell our company for $3 billion or some crazy valuation," he says. "But I have children. I'm going to wake up every morning not feeling that we're doing anything wrong... and my shareholders and board of directors and my clients appreciate that." Nor does he want to profile Mexia's consumers, so it limits the way the data it compiles are given to clients, and shared between them. "Call me the black sheep of the industry, [but] I don't think consumers should be profiled, Tinley says. "I don't want to be profiled." **FP**

241

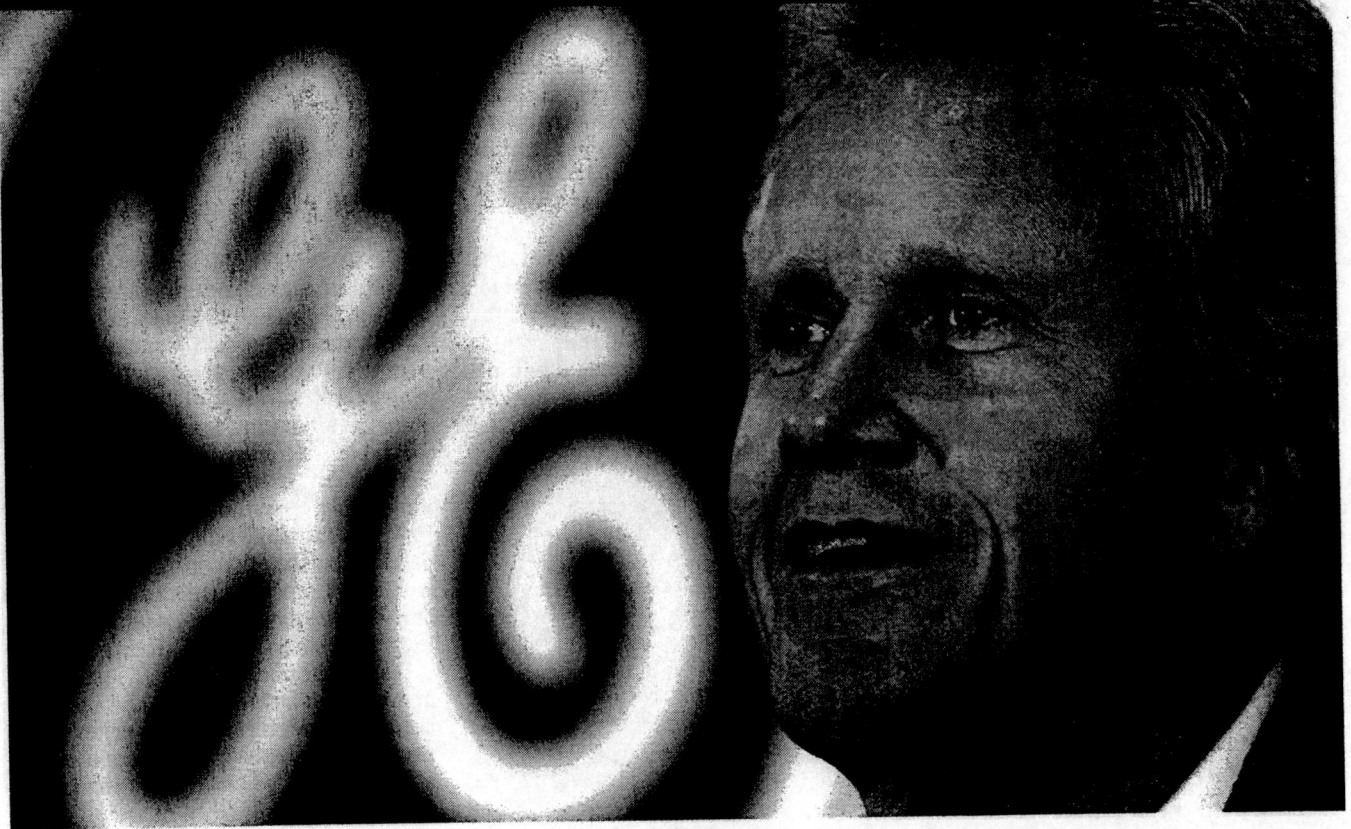

A lean, clean electric machine

Jeffrey Immelt is betting the future of his company on environmental technologies

NEXT month General Electric's corporate bosses will drop a bombshell on the hard-charging managers of its global businesses. In future they will be judged not only by all the usual measures, such as return on capital, that investors typically care about: they will also be held accountable for helping to save the planet.

Every GE business unit will have to cut its emissions of carbon dioxide (CO_2), the main greenhouse gas (GHG) behind global warming, by a different target. Energy-intensive divisions such as plastics and loco-motive manufacturing will need to make big cuts in emissions, while the paper-pushers at the group's financial-services divisions will be told to aim at smaller, but still ambitious, cuts.

GE's new goal is to cut its overall GHG emissions by 2012 to 1% below their level in 2004. That might not sound ambitious, but if no climate policies are enacted, the company's projected revenue growth would increase its GHG emissions by 40% above 2004 levels. The firm also vows to cut the intensity of its GHG emissions (that is, the amount of GHG emitted in terms of

its economic activity) by 30% by 2008. By comparison, the UN's Kyoto Protocol calls for Europe to reduce its GHG emissions by 2012 to 8% below the 1990 level and George Bush's voluntary climate scheme calls for an 18% cut in America's GHG intensity from the level in 2002 by 2012.

This is a dramatic U-turn by any measure, but will be especially startling to environmentalists, who have long pilloried GE for boosting coal and nuclear power and for dumping chemicals in New York's Hudson River. It will also come as a surprise to many of GE's industrial customers, who have long thought it a staunch ally against environmental campaigners. Many in both camps may be tempted to dismiss GE's latest rhetoric as "greenwash", little more than a public-relations ploy to confuse the public about the true nature of its businesses.

But that would be a mistake. GE's new-found embrace of greenery appears both genuine and substantive. Jeffrey Immelt, GE's boss, is leading the effort himself, campaigning for it both inside and outside the company, as well as backing it with

large amounts of new investment. In fact, it is not an exaggeration to say that Mr Immelt is embarking on the most ambitious and risky strategy for GE since the 1980s, when the combative Jack Welch, then its boss, reshaped the company by slashing costs and selling business units.

Mr Immelt is so convinced that clean technologies will be the future of GE that, invoking the colour of American money, he has made his new mantra: "green is green". If he is right, then not only will GE benefit, but businesses everywhere will have to follow in its tracks in one form or another. If he is wrong, Mr Immelt will have led one of the world's biggest and most powerful companies down a dead-end, and the cost to its reputation, if not its financial performance, is likely to be huge.

Until Mr Immelt's change of direction, green technologies have not played much of a part in GE's growth. For decades the company's energy business has been focused on fossil-fuel power plants or nuclear energy. Nuclear power may now be garnering support from some environmentalists, but GE's past interest in the atom had little to do with the environment. In the 1960s defence contracting helped fuel the company's growth. In the 1990s financial services took on that role.

Look at GE today and greenery has moved front and centre. Mr Immelt has embraced a sweeping new strategy—dubbed "Ecomagination"—that he hopes will persuade Wall Street that clean energy can be a lucrative business. The firm has ▶▶

rolled out a flashy advertising campaign to promote its new "clean coal" technologies. GE is targeting politicians too. Mr Immelt himself launched the new campaign in Washington, DC, Brussels and Tokyo, repeating his "green is green" slogan.

The new campaign makes some extravagant promises. The company vows to double its revenues from 17 clean-technology businesses, ranging from renewable energy and hydrogen fuel cells, to water filtration and purification systems, to cleaner aircraft and locomotive engines. This would take such products from $10 billion in sales in 2004 to $20 billion by 2010, with more ambitious targets thereafter. To get there, Mr Immelt has promised to double research spending on clean products, from $700m per year to $1.5 billion, by 2010. (GE's total research expenditure was $3.1 billion in 2004 and its revenues were $152.4 billion.)

Most striking, however, is GE's new position on climate change, an issue that divides corporate America. Some large industrial groups have long argued that the climate problem is real. Three dozen such big firms—including DuPont, United Technologies and Whirlpool—have been united by the Pew Centre on Global Climate, a non-partisan charity, to lobby for action by America's federal government to curb CO_2 emissions. Many others, notably Exxon-Mobil, but also much of America's coal-burning utility sector, have remained deeply opposed to any such efforts—as has President Bush. Awkwardly, many of those utility firms are GE's customers.

It is therefore remarkable that Mr Immelt and other senior GE officials now publicly proclaim that global warming is real, and also call for American government regulations to deal with it. GE is sticking its neck out and, among the most influential big American businesses, it has taken something of a lead.

Two big questions will determine whether GE's green initiative pays off. First, is Mr Immelt right to believe that greenery can be handsomely profitable, as well as socially responsible? Second, can he really transform GE's recent approach to innovation, which has concentrated mostly on incremental improvements of well understood technologies, to one pursuing riskier and less-proven technologies such as fuel cells, solar energy, hydrogen storage and nanotechnology?

Given GE's history, many environmental campaigners have been understandably sceptical about Mr Immelt's Ecomagination initiative. After all, Jack Welch turned GE into a target of green ire with his arrogant defence of the company's refusal to excavate noxious chemicals it had dumped into the Hudson River (which was legal at the time). Mr Immelt has wisely accepted defeat on the matter in order to move on, and GE is now removing

the offending chemicals from the Hudson's riverbed.

GE otherwise has a good record on purely local environmental standards and this may yet prove an unexpected bonus as it tries to reshape itself to exploit opportunities created by national and global efforts to control GHG. Daniel Esty, who heads Yale University's Centre for Environmental Law and Policy, applauds GE for its high standards, detailed use of data and holding its managers accountable for local green goals. The public may not be aware of this, but other companies seem to be. In Mr Esty's polls of bosses at big firms, GE comes out top for the most "underrated" environmental performance.

There is good reason to think Mr Im-

Rich pickings
US environmental industry revenues, $bn

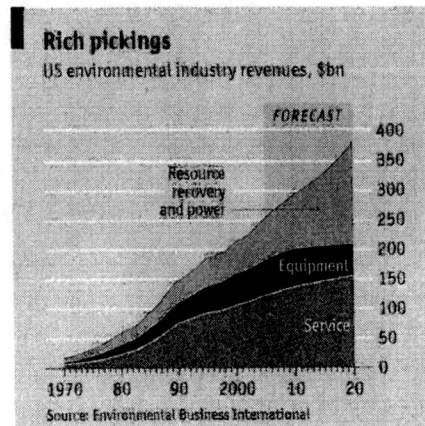

Source: Environmental Business International

melt is sincere about his green strategy. GE does not need to make a bally-hoo about greenery to defend its existing businesses. As an industrial firm that deals primarily with other industrial companies and governments (and rarely direct with consumers), GE is in a better position than many to ignore criticism from environmental groups or the threat of green boycotts. Furthermore, the company is involved in such a range of energy technologies (including dirty coal plants, nuclear generators, natural-gas turbines and wind) that it does not need carbon regulations in the way, say, a narrowly focused fuel-cell or solar-cell maker might. Despite all this, Mr Immelt is pushing for action by America's government on carbon emissions. And he wants to turn GE a deep shade of green.

To understand why, turn to the first question hanging over Mr Immelt's plan: is he right that green is green? Although scepticism towards such claims is generally warranted, Deane Dray of Goldman Sachs, an investment bank, endorses Mr Immelt's judgment: "Every one of the Ecomagination initiatives looks commercially viable, even without the green angle."

One reason to think GE's chief may be right is the potential for dramatic growth for infrastructure technologies in developing markets. David Calhoun, a GE vice-chairman, identifies China and India as

the key to rapid growth in demand. In both countries water and sewerage systems need to be vastly expanded, and governments in both countries are also coming under intense public pressure to curb what are often appalling levels of local pollution from factories and power plants. They say they want both to maintain rapid economic growth and to do it more cleanly than in the past. Mr Dray expects 60% of GE's overall revenue growth to come from such markets over the next decade. Sales of greener technologies, if they can be priced correctly, should be a big part of that.

GE's hopes are not limited to poor countries. Even in America, overall sales related to environmental technology have been growing rapidly and, if anything, look as if they will accelerate (see chart). Not content to rely on this trend, the company will also seek to build new markets, says Beth Comstock, GE's head of marketing. "Environmental technologies must have a business model around them to succeed," she declares.

Ms Comstock points to the ways GE markets its greenery. One is a sales "scorecard" that explains to customers in dollars and cents exactly how the lower emissions and higher fuel efficiency of a new GE product (for example, its cleaner locomotive engines) convert into money saved on fuel. Another pushes service contracts for maintaining water-filtration systems or maintaining windmills. These can be five or more times as lucrative for GE as the initial sale of capital equipment. Ms Comstock also points to entirely new lines of business: the company wants to become an "energy services" consultancy and to enter the green construction field.

Listen to the customer
Ultimately, green will turn green only if GE's customers actually want greener products. Before launching the new strategy, the firm spent 18 months discussing it with customers. GE invited bosses from various industries to two-day "dreaming sessions" where they were asked to imagine life in 2015—and the products they would need from GE. The company says it took away a clear message: rising fuel costs, ever tighter environmental regulations and growing consumer expectations will translate into demand for cleaner technologies, especially in the energy industry.

Pointing to those customer sessions, Mr Calhoun says, "This is not just GE jamming environment down their throats. We decided that if this is what our customers want, let's stop putting our heads in the sand, dodging environmental interests, and go from defence to offence."

Another reason to think that Mr Immelt is not wasting shareholders' money is one that he perhaps might not advertise openly. He is asking for government intervention on carbon emissions not just to ▶▶

help the planet, but also because he believes it will create opportunities that his company may be better placed to exploit than rivals stuck with older, dirtier technologies. Indeed, GE's effort, argues Myron Ebell of the Competitive Enterprise Institute, an industry-friendly think-tank in Washington, DC, is a form of rent-seeking that should raise eyebrows.

Even so, it is a noble endeavour, argues Jim Rogers, head of Cinergy, a coal-fired American utility and GE customer. The most interesting of GE's dreaming sessions were those with electric utilities—which are at the heart of the global-warming controversy. Mr Rogers was at one such event. As he puts it, "in private, 80-85% of my peers think carbon regulation is coming within ten years, but most sure don't want it now." After trotting in renowned experts to talk about energy poverty and climate change, Mr Immelt himself made the case for low-carbon technologies, including clean coal. "Jeff was clearly pushing for his economic advantage, but he was masterful," says Mr Rogers. He thinks that GE's "visionary leadership, just a little ahead of my industry" may soon help push the American energy business "from denial to pragmatic acceptance" of mandatory caps on carbon emissions.

If so, it would spell still more sales for GE. American Electric Power (AEP), the utility that burns more coal than any other in the western hemisphere, bitterly opposes mandatory action on carbon. However, after Mr Immelt began arguing for Ecomagination, the firm agreed to a joint-venture to test new clean-coal technology that GE is pioneering. One AEP official explains the apparent contradiction: it now expects carbon regulations to come "sometime over the next 30 years". It wants to encourage low-carbon technologies that will give coal a new lease on life. If carbon caps are enacted by America earlier than that, GE's already fast-growing wind-turbine business, as well as its long-established nuclear-reactor business, would also benefit enormously.

Not enough green?
If Ecomagination is not greenwash—and might even make GE some money—that still leaves the final, and hardest, question: can the company pull it off? The answer is not yet clear. Two big obstacles could stand in the way of Mr Immelt's scheme.

First of all, the environmental markets that the pundits forecast and GE is betting on may not materialise. Grant Ferrier of Environmental Business, an industry publishing outfit, observes wryly that this is not the first boom the sector has seen. Back in the 1980s and 1990s, many blue-chip firms, ranging from DuPont and Dow to big French and British water companies such as Suez, forged into environmental services. Many were confidently predict-

ing long-term double-digit growth and some invested heavily in developing-country markets.

Alas, by the late 1990s many of these firms had scaled back their investments. The market continued growing, but not at the sizzling pace they had originally expected. GE may be better positioned than those earlier entrants, argues Mr Ferrier, given its deep pockets and top-level commitment to the approach. Even so, forecasts of endlessly fast growth should be treated with caution.

That lesson has already been learned by BP, which ran into a similar problem with its "Beyond Petroleum" campaign. The company generated much enthusiasm early on with its lofty talk of a clean-energy revolution, but now appears to be back-pedalling on when it thinks renewables and fuel cells will take off. To be fair, BP did invest large amounts of money in those areas. And the company has just unveiled plans to invest some $8 billion more over the next decade in its newly created low-carbon energy division, which it hopes will earn $6 billion a year in sales by 2015. And yet change comes slowly in the energy business, because refineries and coal plants last for 40 or 50 years. Branding aside, BP will remain a mostly oil-and-gas business for a long time. Lord Browne, BP's chief executive, observes that it is dangerous to promise too much on green issues—a lesson GE would be wise to heed. "Be very careful to separate aspirations from actual promised actions," warns Lord Browne, "Business is about doing business, it's not a surrogate for government or public service."

Even if the green markets that Mr Immelt dreams of do arrive as soon as he hopes, they may not prove as profitable as his shareholders would like them to be.

Another profit opportunity

China and India are booming. They may crave the latest and cleanest technologies, but do they really want to pay rich-world prices for them? Push Mr Calhoun hard and he concedes that margins in China are, in fact, tight—especially in the energy business. He has just sold no fewer than 300 locomotives there, he says. But at what margin? He suggests obliquely that margins will eventually improve, as the last 100 of the locomotives will be built with Chinese labour and parts.

Taking a big swing
The other big risk to Ecomagination comes from GE's own culture. Some experts argue that GE does not have a record of successful product breakthroughs, unlike such famously innovative firms as 3M or DuPont. Gina Colarelli O'Connor of the Rensselaer Polytechnic Institute, a respected engineering university, has studied innovation at big firms for years. She points out that the company is famous for its relentless pursuit of "Six Sigma", which was championed by Mr Welch. The axioms of this statistics-based approach to quality control have permeated every aspect of the company's operations, and are credited with making GE managers extraordinarily good at delivering exactly what they promise. That is fine for a company focused on incremental improvements and fiercely disciplined execution. But that culture may not be ideally suited to creating the innovations and nimble new businesses the green strategy requires. Even if the firm's laboratories produce the technological breakthroughs, she says, marketing and sales teams may be reluctant to embrace them.

Lorraine Bolsinger, the head of Ecomagination, agrees that Six Sigma emphasised "execution and frowned on deviations from the plan", and that the new project departs from this way of thinking. It is also different from Six Sigma, she says, in that it starts with the customer and "it is vastly about technology". During the years when GE's profits at its finance arms stole the limelight from the industrial and research parts of the firm, she concedes that "techies like me were lonely and overshadowed". When Mr Immelt announced he would double the research budget for clean technologies, officials at the firm's Global Research Centre in upstate New York started "doing the Snoopy dance out in the parking lot".

Mr Immelt has set out a vision for growth and is backing it up with hard targets and lots of money. But he is asking his managers to depart from a well-known and successful path. Can GE rise to the challenge? It remains an open question. "Jeff is asking us to take a really big swing. Fail early, fail fast," says Ms Bolsinger, a 25-year GE veteran—before adding, with endearing honesty: "this is hard for us." ∎

068 | GREEN BIZ

Spinmeisters: A technician tends one of an array of windmills in Germany's north

The Wind At Germany's Back

Cutting-edge tech and government incentives have made it a world-beater in renewable energy

By Jack Ewing

To see Germany's latest cash crop, take a train across the flat plains between Hannover and Berlin or cruise the waters off the gusty North Sea coast. In both places, you can't miss the rows of windmills marching to the horizon, quietly generating some 7% of the nation's electricity needs—and powering an important new industry.

Thanks to smart regulation, Germany has become a global powerhouse in green energy, producing more electricity from wind than any other country. While the industry owes some of its success to German expertise in fields such as aerodynamics, the biggest boost has come from the government. The nation's energy law guarantees operators of windmills and solar generators an above-market price for power for as long as 20 years. Other countries have similar policies, but few have applied them as consistently as Germany. "The crucial point," says Paul Buchwitz, a Deutsche Bank fund manager who focuses on renewable energy, is "you know how much you will get in advance."

JOB GENERATOR

Now, as oil prices surge and global warming concerns fuel demand for green energy, Germany is seeing the payoff. The sector—both energy suppliers and equipment manufacturers—employs more than 235,000 people and generates annual sales upwards of $33 billion, government figures show. Nearly 60 companies in Germany specialize in wind systems. Enercon, based near the North Sea, is in a dead heat with General Electric's wind-power unit and Spain's Gamesa for the No. 2 slot in the global market for wind generators. The leader, Denmark's Vestas, produces key components such as windmill blades in Germany. Winergy, a unit of Siemens, says half the world's windmills use its parts.

Despite Germany's reputation for gray skies, the energy law has also helped build up a solar industry. Nearly 100 companies manufacture solar cells or supply the sector, with more than half of those in the old East Germany, which has earned the nickname Solar Valley. One of the stars, 9-year-old Q-Cells, is second only to Japan's Sharp in producing solar cells. And last year, Phoenix-based First Solar opened a $170 million solar-module plant near the border with Poland.

First Solar is just one of a slew of foreign outfits investing in renewables in Germany. GE makes turbines near the Dutch border and is expanding production. Solar wafer maker EverQ, backed by Massachusetts' Evergreen Solar, has opened two factories in eastern Germany since 2006 and now employs 800 people there. And India's Suzlon last year acquired a majority stake in REpower, a Hamburg wind-equipment supplier.

The challenge for Germany will be staying ahead. While the country leads in wind-generation capacity, the U.S. market is growing faster. As sales shift to other regions, so, inevitably, will manufacturing. To hold on to its lead, Germany will have to keep its edge in innovation. Siemens, which has 7% of the global wind-turbine market, aims to gain share via its expertise in conventional power and its strong relationships with utilities. And Germany's network of research institutes continues to work on renewables. One group hopes to cheaply produce silicon impregnated with hydrogen, creating a fuel that's easy to transport and can be used to power fuel cells, solving the problem of getting energy from remote wind and solar farms to cities. Another outfit is working to commercialize a generator that combines elements of sun and wind power, in which solar collectors at ground level produce hot air that rises through a chimney and turns a power-generating turbine. Says Q-Cells CEO Anton Milner: "This industry is still in the warm-up phase." |BW|

Sustainability, but for Managers

There's a big — and getting bigger — public discussion about sustainability, but it's not the one managers need. Here are some early findings from a different kind of inquiry.

BY MICHAEL S. HOPKINS

ABOUT HALFWAY THROUGH the *Wall Street Journal*'s recent ECO:nomics conference — a confab of several hundred A-list corporate executives and several dozen green-strategy headliners — there was A Moment.

On stage was Al Gore — Nobel laureate, Oscar winner, global warming frontman and, before all that, a high elected official. He was being interviewed, and he's good at it. Equal parts zeal and data, he touted his plan to get utilities off carbon fuels within a decade. He described the end of polar ice. He talked about how the systems engineers in NASA's Houston control room when Neil Armstrong stepped onto the moon were an average age of 26 — "which means," he said, "that when they heard [John F. Kennedy's go-to-the-moon] challenge, their average age was 18." Which means, he was implying, that if you think his climate goals are too high, it's only because your notion of what's possible is underdeveloped. There's help coming, Gore was telling us, and the people bringing it will be more capable — or at least less daunted — than we are.

Gore on this day was resplendent, and most of the crowd loved him. But now it was

Former Vice President Al Gore continues to wield the bully pulpit in the climate change discussion. But is his kind of discussion the one business chiefs should be having?

? THE LEADING QUESTION

What's the publicly pursued sustainability discussion all about? And if it's not the kind of discussion that managers need to have, then what is?

FINDINGS

Issues central to most sustainability debates: carbon emissions, alternative energy, regulatory policy, global politics.

In the press, the focus is on policy making, not on management or wider sustainability concerns.

Executives define sustainability much more broadly, and have begun acting on opportunities.

question time, and first there was a (self-identified) scientist who questioned all Gore's science; Gore effortlessly backhanded him by citing "3,000 scientists" of his own. And then came Bjorn Lomborg, the self-styled "skeptical environmentalist" and head of the Copenhagen Consensus Center, a think tank that analyzes how governments and philanthropists can get the most bang for their world betterment buck.

Lomborg, standing genially at his seat, began, "Hi, Mr. Vice President. I'm Bjorn Lomborg. It seems to me you're probably the most well-known person arguing that we should be spending a large sum of our money, and we should be spending most of our concern, on cutting carbon emissions, and cutting very very soon."

To several of us looking on, this analogy seemed a little hard on Lomborg, but maybe Gore wouldn't agree — and in any case Lomborg wouldn't be getting any chance for rebuttal. (Gore's answer to Lomborg's request was plenty clear enough. Lomborg: Wanna debate this? Gore: Um, no.)

"We have long since passed the time when we as a civilization," Gore said, "let alone we as the United States of America, should pretend that this is an on-the-one-hand, on-the-other-hand kind of situation...."

(Now building momentum for his close...) "It's really kind of silly, for those of us in this generation, to look at those coming after us, and figure out what we're going to say to them if the North

No one could agree on anything. No facts ever held still. It sometimes felt like screenwriter William Goldman's Hollywood, where "nobody knows anything." Uncertainty, indeed.

He continued, "I would argue that the Copenhagen Consensus, and a lot of well-esteemed Nobel laureates, tell us that scientifically and economically it's not a very good way to spend our money. So my point is to say, should we have that debate? I know you've sort of dodged that bullet before, and I don't mean to corner you. Well, maybe I do mean to corner you. Do you want to have a debate on that? Would you be willing to have a debate with me on that point?"

Eyes swung from Lomborg to Gore — for whom this could hardly qualify as being cornered. Still, the room went silent for a few more beats than were comfortable. Then Gore, in a tone somewhere between hesitant and exasperated, said, "Look, I think I want to be polite to you.

"But, you know, the scientific community has dealt with this. The approach [comparing the worldwide economic and social return-on-investment for various public initiatives] is extremely misleading.... It's not an either/or proposition."

Gore then proceeded to liken questioners of Lomborg's ilk to the tobacco industry rejecting the surgeon general's report and claiming that cigarettes weren't all that bad for you, after all — "and millions and millions of people died as a result."

Pole ice cap goes away.... I mean, it's not a matter of theory or conjecture, for goodness' sake, it's going on right now."

Then the setup: "For every one meter of sea level rise there are 100 million climate refugees. It's already started. The Maldives had a new line item in their budget this year...."

And the punchline: "It was listed as 'fund to buy a new country.'"

Exit to applause.

Uncertainty, Bewilderment and the Question of What to Do

At least two things are interesting about the Gore-Lomborg exchange — not to mention the ECO:nomics exploration as a whole, which was at every turn both smart and serious, if often puzzling.

One is that while the audience seemed squarely behind Gore and his anti-carbon-emissions message during his appearance (and during most other sessions, too), only hours earlier it had voted squarely against him. Which was not the only time at the conference when all the ambiguous forecasts, authoritative but contradictory policy plans and certain predictions of uncertainty bred bewilderment.

No one could agree on anything. No facts ever held still. It sometimes felt like screenwriter William Goldman's Hollywood, where "nobody knows anything" but everybody would have to go back home and run a business anyway. Uncertainty, indeed.

The second thing is how Gore-Lomborg epitomized another characteristic of not just ECO:nomics but most of the public discussion about sustainability and business: It's nearly always a policy maker's debate, with managers left to fend for themselves. If you're a government official, this is good news. If you're a business executive, it's probably not.

The contradictory carbon-emissions vote came in the morning before Gore's talk, during a session when Lomborg himself took the stage and conducted a "priority setting exercise" that asked the audience to weigh the cost vs. benefit facts about six programs designed to do good in the world, at least the facts as Lomborg sees them. Then they were asked to vote — ranking the six as public policy priorities. The initiatives variously addressed problems in health care, education and global warming, and for each one Lomborg and his Copenhagen Consensus had assessed a likely return per dollar invested. According to Lomborg, the highest return of the six would come from a program to eradicate tuberculosis ($30 of "good" done for each dollar spent). The lowest return: efforts to immediately cut carbon emissions ($0.90 of "good" for $1 spent).

Given those specs, it's no surprise that the 300 or so executives in the banquet room found it tough to get behind CO_2 reduction. Only 11% prioritized it first.

The top-voted priority of the six was, instead, "lowering the cost of schooling" worldwide — which the Copenhagen Consensus has determined would yield $20 of benefit for every dollar invested. It was chosen by 32% of voters. A global warming strategy was ranked second, garnering a nearly identical 30% of votes, but it wasn't the emissions-reduction approach that Gore and so many others advocate. Rather, it was what Lomborg called "energy R&D," or investment in all sorts of potential technological solutions for cutting carbon or remediating its effects. The projected return on each dollar spent: $11.

Maybe Lomborg's little exercise in democratic instant policy making should be dismissed on account of bad methodology (the audience had been led by the sleeve; no researcher would have respected

FROM THE EDITOR

Concerning history's instructive value, there are two edges to the blade. We've all been told since high school that we should learn from the past or we'll be doomed to repeat it. Of course, we've also been told that if we draw the wrong lessons from the past, we'll end up fighting the last war instead of the one we actually face.

Upshot: Learn, but get it right. Cast an eye rearward, but with fingers constantly feeling for the new contours of the present. (Better still, turn an ear to listening at the same time for soundings from the future, if you can manage to put yet another sense to simultaneous work.)

That's what we've tried to do in this issue's downturn series. As every journal in the land inevitably takes up the subject of the economic crisis, we decided to contribute by re-examining classic management wisdom about how to survive — or even thrive — in a downturn, and then asking, what wisdom still applies? (As well as asking: What wisdom doesn't? What wisdom still does apply but only in freshly modified form?) What do the lessons extracted from past downturns have to offer us today?

We talked with scholars, thinkers and authors, from all domains of management expertise, who've done some of the world's best work on learning from downturns past — and this issue's lineup is the first result. (You can find more right now in our Downturn Manifesto special report online at sloanreview.mit.edu. And there'll be additional insights in future issues of the *Review*.) You'll discover advice about:

■ how to rethink resource investment (pg. 31);
■ planning through a downturn (pg. 45);
■ unique opportunities for organizational reinvention (pg. 25);
■ how to nurture morale amidst downsizing (pg. 39); and
■ strategies that the natural world has developed for handling adversity, and that businesses can learn from.

There's even an exploration of the downturn's causes and potential unseen consequences (pg. 53) — including some possibly groundshifting changes to the business landscape that dangle opportunity. (Will "risk accounting" finally be realized? Will effective organizational transparency become the next great source of competitive advantage?)

"Disruption" always feels too bloodlessly technical a term for what many businesses and individuals are grappling with in these bracingly novel days; nevertheless, disruption is what's here. And along with it comes the opportunity for leaders — in organizations, in communities — to make a difference that's profound. We at the *MIT Sloan Management Review* hope that our work here helps you seize that chance.

Please let us know what you think.

— **Michael S. Hopkins, Editor-in-Chief**
mhopkins@mit.edu

the outcome). To be sure, for the rest of the conference, it more or less was. The discussions centered on carbon tax vs. cap-and-trade, or how high to push the price of gasoline or whether to substitute natural gas for oil and build an auto transportation system that could run on it (the widely publicized pitch by executive T. Boone Pickens). Almost always the theme was energy — how to change its source (can renewables succeed?) or how to use it more efficiently.

And as policy making goes, these are seminal questions. There may be few more important to

THRIVING IN THE SUSTAINABILITY ECONOMY: CAPABILITIES REQUIRED

More than 75 global organization leaders and sustainability thinkers were interviewed in phase I of a three-phase project to explore how the growing imperative for sustainable business practices will transform managerial decision making and strategy. A survey and targeted research are to come, with findings appearing in a special issue of the *Review* in the Fall. Below are preliminary observations from one of the interview questions: "What will organizations need to be good at in order to thrive in the emerging sustainability economy?"

CAPABILITIES	HEARD IN THE INTERVIEWS…	QUESTIONS/CHALLENGES RAISED
Integrating activities, not siloing • All parts of organization collaborate • Sust.* strategy embedded throughout	"Making sust. part of strategy and not an add-on" "New organizational structure needed" "Hardwiring into the corporate structure, inclusion in core strategy, setting regular guidance…" "Integrationist thinking is needed — understanding systems of operation and integrating sust. within"	■ What organization structure and processes promote lateral strategic and tactical collaboration across the business? ■ How can sust. business case be built for all units/activities?
Systems thinking • Understanding integrated systems • Building them • Role of design	"A systems mental model is required" "Systems = design" "Understanding systems in which we operate" "Understanding of product life cycle; short-term savings vs. long-term costs" "Need to get people to look at world as a design problem"	■ What can nature teach us? What sust. design principles and strategies follow? ■ How to map systems in full, beyond company boundaries?
High-collaboration partnering • Based on trust/interest alignment • Collaborative innovation with every kind of stakeholder	"Need to promote corporate partnerships — thinking through the whole value chain" "It's going to require different patterns of interaction — not traditional, formal ones" "I'll often open an initial meeting with a supply chain partner by asking, What's your view on sustainability?" "Developing constructive dialogue with government"	■ How to engage supply chain partners to identify and realize sust. opportunities? ■ How to change model from legalistic/ adversarial partnering to non-zero-sum, collaborative?
Learning; knowledge sharing • Capacity to see, absorb, share signals of all kinds • Processes to ensure it	"Build sust. learning organization — with knowledge and skills distributed" "Decentralized, collective, open intelligence models will trump conventional hierarchal ones" "Ability to allow fresh thinking and new ideas to enter company — people at every level are internally focused to point of myopia"	■ How to overcome existing cultural barriers to open company to new ideas and initiatives — especially from external sources? ■ How to utilize open source networks or other methods?
Communication; under- standing information's new currency • Managing unprecedented in- formation flow and demand • Capitalizing on new age of transparency	"Sust. requires effective communication — with policy makers, stakeholders, consumers, suppliers, investors, etc." "Corporations will face a major change in the degree of openness and management of stakeholders required" "What consumers know about inner workings of a company is so much more transparent now"	■ How has the value of information changed, and how should it be managed to mitigate risk and capture opportunity? ■ Can credible transparency be turned to competitive advantage?
Valuing the long term • Scenario planning • Enlisting stakeholders in long term • Trend sensing	"Sust. can be achieved by understanding long-term trends — need capabilities to anticipate" "As the CEO, if 98% of your attention is just fire fighting around today's products and processes, you're in big trouble" "No incentive for CEO to take a long-term view of the world"	■ How to drive cultural change that focuses organization on long-term goals? ■ How to develop a robust trend-spotting and scenario planning capability?
Measurement and reporting • Metrics, methods for self-assessment • Credible for sharing	"Quantification and monitoring of sust. — review performance on new sust.-based metrics" "Can't manage what can't measure … so you have to try" "We don't yet have a grip on what we're doing — much less how to measure it. That has to change."	■ How to develop robust measurement and reporting systems — e.g., sust. scorecard?
Experimenting, not planning • Manage portfolio of experiments • Enable organizational adaptation	"Experiments create 'optionality,' enable company to be adaptive in future unforseen conditions" "Mini innovation projects on sust. can be implemented to build credibility of concept and confidence" "Means creating some real options"	■ How to incubate and seed small-scale innovation experiments?

*"Sustainability" consistently abbreviated as "sust."

SOURCE: THE MIT SLOAN MANAGEMENT REVIEW, IN COLLABORATION WITH THE BOSTON CONSULTING GROUP

address. (And the focus on them wasn't entirely un-expected. ECO:nomics, after all, was clearly advertised as aiming "to assess the risks and opportunities in the massive new market of environmental capital.")

But it was hard to escape the notion, during coffee-break chats and in the taxi rank with our rollaways packed to leave, that from a manager's perspective there might have been a utility problem here. Not to discount the scenario planning benefits of all that speculation about the future fuel of choice, but people were confused. They were going home. They were far better informed than they had been. But Monday they'd be back at their desks, faced with choices that sustainability-related forces would affect.

And they still wouldn't know what to do.

An Invitation

Of course, that's a gross oversimplification; no one expects to return from a conference with definitive operating instructions in hand. In many ways, we'd all better get used to being confused. Strategy thinkers everywhere will tell you (high in the conversation, even) that profound uncertainty is going to remain a defining condition of the economic landscape. What's more, skill at managing in those conditions — coping with uncertainty — is often touted as a fundamental new leadership requirement.

Neither is the point here to undervalue the kinds of essential policy discussions being held in the press and at official meetings all over (and that were conducted especially well at ECO:nomics). It's to offer an invitation to a differently hopeful exploration of sustainability, which we've already pushed into deeply (see "Thriving in the Sustainability Economy: Capabilities Required"), and with which we now especially need your help.

What we're interested in at the *MIT Sloan Management Review* is not sustainability policy alone but its deceptively widespread management implications. Our inquiry: Define and explore how the growing imperative for sustainable business practices will transform managerial decision making and strategy, how that imperative will require new organizational structures and ways of working, how it will reshape the organizations of the future — and how it will present leaders with new kinds of choices,

whether they want to confront them or not. Our job here is to figure out those choices. To figure out, from a manager's perspective, what to *do*.

The invitation: As this issue goes to press, we're launching a global survey about sustainability and its strategic management implications, and we hope you'll join us by taking it and sharing your views (if you haven't done so already). Just go to sloanreview.mit.edu/links/ and you'll find a link to the survey along with other links related to this article.

The survey has been shaped by more than 75 personal interviews with global organization leaders, scholars and sustainability thinkers. Those interviews and now the survey itself aim to explore everything from how executives define sustainability to which sustainability-related issues will be drivers of competitive strategy to what sustainability-related opportunities and threats managers foresee (as well as what impediments they encounter when trying to address them). In other words, what will the new, sustainability-altered competitive landscape look like? And finally, what will businesses have to become in order to succeed in it? What new capabilities and characteristics will leaders have to cultivate in their organizations? In the emerging sustainability economy, what will businesses have to be good at in order to thrive?

In "Thriving in the Sustainability Economy" on page 14, you can see some preliminary answers to that last question, along with snippets of comment from the interviewees and follow-on questions that the preliminary answers prompted.

The findings from all of the interviews, along with the results of the current survey, will be explored and interpreted in depth in the months to come — in the *Review*, at sloanreview.mit.edu and ultimately in a special report on Sustainability & Strategy in the Fall (produced in collaboration with the Boston Consulting Group, our partners in the sustainability initiative).

We hope you'll return to learn what we're discovering.

But first, please take the survey to help us discover it.

Reprint 50301.

Copyright © *Massachusetts Institute of Technology, 2009.*
All rights reserved.

Google has spent an estimated $3 million to $4 million to install 395 fast chargers for electric cars on its corporate campus.

GOOGLE'S ZERO-CARBON QUEST

THE SEARCH GIANT HAS AN AMBITIOUS PLAN TO ACHIEVE ITS GOAL: BECOMING THE WORLD'S MOST ENERGY-EFFICIENT COMPANY. by Brian Dumaine

A

S THE DOUBLE-DECKER BUS turns onto Charleston Road and starts winding through Google's Mountain View, Calif., campus, I stretch out in the business-class-size seat, admiring the smoothness of the black leather and the plush gray carpeting at my feet. A spacious table expands to hold a laptop, which can connect to the vehicle's Wi-Fi system. This $800,000 luxury double-decker is one of 73 buses that Google owns and operates. (It leases 26 others.) Each day the fleet transports about 4,500 employees, or about a third of those working at the Googleplex, as the company's headquarters is known.

It turns out that Google isn't offering a free ride simply as an employee perk—the buses actually save the company money. Yes, there's the added productivity of 4,500 employees working an extra couple of hours each day while riding to and from work. But Google's bus service is about much more than that. Real estate in Mountain View is expensive. Underground parking spaces cost as much as $85,000 to construct. (Really!) If Google had to build a parking space for each of the bus riders, the price tag would run to almost $400 million. And that's not counting the lost opportunity cost of not using that land for new office buildings.

Google has made other investments in transportation too. If, during the day, a Google-ite needs to run an errand or pick up a sick kid at school, he or she can hop into one of 52 electric and hybrid cars parked on campus. The company also encourages employees to drive electrics. It has spent an estimated $3 million to $4 million to install 395 chargers—the largest corporate electric-vehicle infrastructure in the country.

Finding creative solutions to energy issues has become a major priority for Google co-founder and CEO Larry Page in recent years. For the obvious reasons—a growing population, increasingly scarce resources, and climate change—he believes that the corporate world needs to operate more sustainably, and he is determined to build the nation's first zero-carbon company. This means a business that ultimately is so energy efficient and uses so much clean power that it emits no greenhouse gas—a very tall order indeed. Experts aren't sure whether it's even possible for a company to emit no carbon, but Google is trying to come as close to that goal as possible. "As we became a bigger user of energy, we wanted to make sure we were not just part of the problem, but part of the solution," says Urs Hölzle, Google's employee No. 8 and a senior vice president who oversees the company's green initiatives.

To reach its audacious zero-carbon goal, Google is taking a three-pronged approach. First, it's making its server farms, office buildings, and commuting habits more energy efficient. (Apparently Page's Boeing 767, which he owns with co-founder Sergey Brin, doesn't get counted in the equation.) Then the company is investing heavily—$915 million to date—in solar and wind producers to make clean energy more available. And finally it is buying enough carbon offsets to make the company carbon neutral—at least on paper—until it can meet its overall goal.

If the plan works, Page will have created a blueprint that other companies can use to reduce their own energy use and—as important—save money at the same time. But Google has already learned some hard lessons.

IN JUNE 2007, Page and his top execs issued a staff memo declaring that the company would become carbon neutral. The catch? The existing power infrastructure is so dependent on fossil fuels that no major company in the world has yet achieved this goal without buying carbon credits. Page began buying carbon credits from organizations that, say, capture methane from landfills to offset the greenhouse gas Google emits. Then he set the company on a long march to reduce the amount of energy it

consumes while increasing its use of carbon-free wind and solar power.

Later that year Page, to the amazement of many in the IT industry, also announced that Google was getting into the clean-energy business. In a Nov. 27, 2007, press release, the company introduced an additional initiative based on the formula RE < C, which translates as "renewable energy is cheaper than coal." Page believed Google could become carbon neutral faster by applying the formidable brainpower of its engineers to the problem. He wanted to help produce one gigawatt of renewable power—about the equivalent produced by a nuclear power plant—that was cheaper than coal within a few years. This goal, however, turned out to be more devilish than anyone thought.

Page asked his managers to focus on a basic question: How much carbon are we emitting? Google's executives started asking themselves how they could use less power in their data centers, how they could make their office buildings more efficient, and where they could buy clean energy for their operations.

Becoming a zero-carbon company is no easy task. In 2011—some four years after Page's memo—Google reported that it still had emitted 1.5 million tons of carbon in the previous year. It was the first time Google had publicly revealed its carbon footprint. To put that in perspective, Google's 30,000 employees and its fleet of data centers last year emitted the same amount of CO_2 as a city the size of Fargo, N.D. (pop. 202,000). The good news: If the company hadn't embarked on Page's quest to become carbon neutral, the numbers would have been much worse. That 1.5 million tons of carbon is more than Google emitted in 2007, but much less than would have been expected considering that the company's annual revenue since then has more than doubled, to $38 billion.

Google's largest source of greenhouse gas emissions is its data centers—those buildings stuffed with computers that handle each of the 3 billion searches its customers perform every day. According to Jonathan Koomey, a Stanford professor, server farms account for about 2% of America's total electricity use. (That's roughly the same greenhouse gas impact as the airline industry's.) However, they are one of the fastest-growing sources of CO_2 emissions.

Server farms also account for Google's biggest use of energy. One thing the company realized early on is that the managers in charge of building data centers were not the same people who operated them. "It's incredible how much people waste in a company," says Google executive Hölzle. "The facility department pays construction costs and utility bills, but the IT people buy the servers, so they don't care about how much electricity they use." To eliminate that conflict, Google made sure that the person paying the utility bills and the one buying the computers was the same.

Now the economic incentive exists to cut energy use. Typically a server farm consumes as much energy for lighting and cooling as for the computers themselves. By using customized hardware and applying innovative cooling techniques, the need for air conditioning is reduced. Joe Kava, Google's director of data center operations, cites as an example the search giant's new server farm in Finland—on the site of a former paper mill—that sits on the Gulf of Finland and uses seawater in its cooling system.

N O MATTER how efficient Google makes its server farms, it will still need clean power to meet its zero-carbon goals. Soon after Page launched the RE < C program in 2007, he set up a handful of green skunkworks projects and created a team to make venture investments in green energy. Google put money into promising companies like BrightSource Energy, which is building a cutting-edge, solar thermal plant in the Mojave Desert. The search giant even had an internal engineering team working to improve a type of concentrating solar power technology called the solar power tower. It invested in AltaRock to foster innovations in geothermal energy. It also sponsored research to develop the first geothermal map of the U.S. to better understand the potential for geothermal energy.

Driving the price of renewables below that of fossil fuels is an ambi-

Google decided that the best way to create carbon offsets was to pay for reductions in methane emissions from landfills and swine farms.

tious goal, especially for a company that has no background in power generation. The energy field, as Google eventually learned, is much more capital-intensive and has a far longer time horizon than is typical in Silicon Valley—where a new company with a garage full of software geeks can scale to billions in revenue seemingly overnight. After four years of effort, Google quietly dropped its RE < C program in late 2011.

Google execs explain that relatively speaking, not much money was invested—perhaps $50 million. (Google has kept its equity investments in BrightSource and AltaRock but has disbanded its green-tech engineering efforts.) It couldn't have helped that the company had been taking flak from a group of shareholders who didn't understand why Google was spending money on clean tech. In 2011, Justin Danhof, the general counsel of a conservative think tank, the National Center for Public Policy Research, filed a shareholder proposal criticizing Google's lack of transparency about its green investments. (It didn't pass.)

WHILE GOOGLE has abandoned its quest to be an innovator in clean-energy technology, it hasn't stopped investing in green power. Today Google has signed contracts to buy about 12% of its total energy from wind and solar farms, up from 4% just two years ago. (Add in existing sources of clean energy on the grid, and that number rises to 27%.) "As a company we are looking at ways we can support the renewables industry," says Rick Needham, Google's director of energy and sustainability. "We have a long vision of being a company powered by renewable energy, but how do we get from here to there?" Google pays more for clean energy than it would for power off the grid. However, it has locked into long-term pricing contracts for renewables and expects those contracts to eventually make money as conventional power becomes more expensive over time.

Google has also been investing directly in wind and solar projects to the tune of $915 million. It began in 2008 by financing a couple of wind farms—in North Dakota and Oregon—in need of funding after the financial meltdown had frozen the capital markets. A key to Google's strategy is that it wants the money it invests to expand utilities' solar and wind operations; otherwise it won't be adding capacity to the system. As the wind projects become operational and begin selling electricity to big utilities, Google gets a piece of the cash flow. This type of deal—a form of tax equity investment—gets sweetened by federal tax credits.

Google was one of the first companies—if not the first—outside the banking, energy, and utility sectors to start investing in these tax deals. Instead of keeping its cash in the corporate treasury and earning only 1% or 2% on it, it can earn as much as 15% to 20% through the tax credit investments, says Google.

The company may be increasingly cleaning up its act, but it is still a polluter. In the meantime, it continues to buy carbon offsets. Carbon offsets, however, are controversial. One common way is to, say, pay an organization to plant a tree to offset the carbon you emit when you fly cross-country. But how do you know if the tree ever gets planted or if someday a drought kills it? Some criticize offsets as just a guilt-free way to indulge in polluting habits.

Well aware of the problems posed by offsets, Google searched for ones that were verifiable and additional—meaning that the reduction in carbon is real and wouldn't have happened without Google's buying the offset. It decided the best way to create carbon offsets was to pay for reductions in methane emissions from landfills and swine farms. Says Jolanka Nickerman, Google's program manager for carbon offsets: "The gold standard for offsets is methane gas, which is 20 to 25 times more potent than carbon dioxide." These methane-capture projects can cost anywhere from $500,000 to $1 million. In Yadkinville, N.C., Google, in partnership with Duke Energy and Duke University, helps the Loyd Ray Farms, home to 9,000 hogs, capture methane from manure to power its operations.

So far the company has spent upwards of $15 million investing in or purchasing carbon credits for dozens of such projects. That will offset about 5 million tons of CO_2—more than enough to make Google a carbon-neutral company on paper.

When asked how long it will take to become a truly zero-carbon company, Google execs say they don't really know. What they do know is that the green program has made the company stand for something more than just making money. That's a message that Google's bus riders are reminded of each day. ∎

THE DEATH

Tech giants—and startups like **Square**—want you to use your phone to pay for everything from gum to train rides. Here's how they plan to achieve cash-free nirvana.

BY MIGUEL HELFT

$1.5 BILLION

1.0

0.5

0

2011   **2017**

Money Goes Mobile
Purchase payments made via mobile-phone wallets are projected to soar to $1.4 billion by 2017.

SOURCE: JAVELIN STRATEGY & RESEARCH

OF CASH

CAFÉ GRUMPY IS the kind of hipster hangout that wouldn't deign to trumpet itself. Tucked away on a quiet street in New York's Chelsea neighborhood, it's easy to miss. There's no sign out front, just a frowning face stenciled on a large shop window. And yet when I walked in for the first time, I immediately felt like one of the regulars. "Charge it to Miguel," I told the barista after ordering a cappuccino, and charge it he did—to my phone. Not that I ever pulled my iPhone from my pocket. Seconds after the barista tapped my order on Grumpy's minimalist register—an iPad mounted on a stylish countertop stand—my phone vibrated in my coat pocket, signaling that our transaction was complete. I couldn't wait to check that everything had worked as promised. (It had.) For the first time ever I was tickled by the act of paying for something.

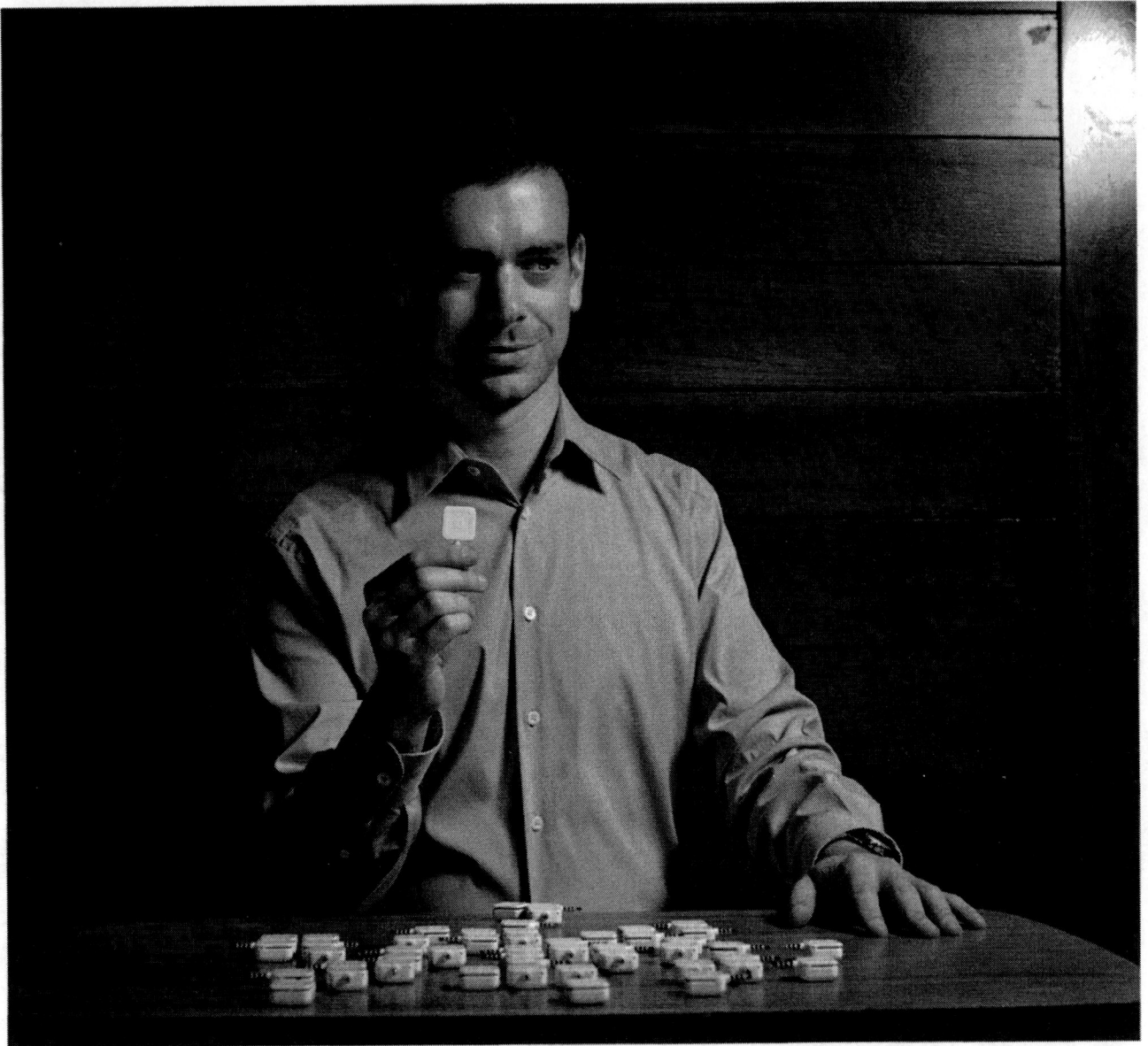

Square founder Dorsey, with his Card Readers that unleashed the mobile-payment movement in the U.S.

Perhaps you, too, have experienced a gee-whiz moment at the checkout counter when you used your phone to pay for a Starbucks latte, a blouse at Macy's, or a box of screws at Home Depot. Perhaps you've read how smartphone payments, already popular in parts of Asia and Europe, are coming to the U.S. in a big way. Or you may have read about Jack Dorsey, the Twitter co-founder, who is now disrupting the byzantine world of payments with his new company, Square. The white-hot San Francisco startup is already responsible for many breakthrough products, including the so-called digital wallet app I used for my touchless, cashless cappuccino purchase at Grumpy. (The café is a Dorsey favorite, and he steered me there. The coffee's good too.)

These are telltale signs that the mobile-payments revolution has arrived. But what the glowing profiles of Dorsey—he's often compared to Steve Jobs—and the breathless predictions about your phone replacing your wallet don't tell you is this: Changing the way Americans pay for stuff is going to be really hard work. For starters, retailers and their partners will have to offer mainstream shoppers some pretty sweet perks to get them to replace a swipe of a plastic card

Photographs by WINNI WINTERMEYER

261

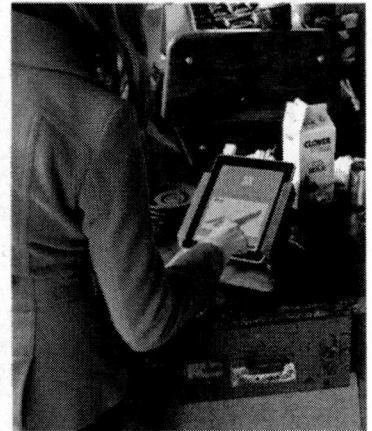

with a tap of a phone. Then there's the chicken-and-egg problem: Merchants don't want to upgrade pricey point-of-sale terminals so that they can work wirelessly with smartphones unless e-wallets become mainstream, and e-wallets won't become mainstream until consumers can use them just about everywhere.

And it's not just innovative startups like Square that hope to reinvent payments for the mobile era, but also everyone from mega-technology companies to financial institutions, giant telecoms, and national retailers. Until those companies agree on common technology standards and platforms, mobile payments won't work across devices, wireless networks, credit card types, and retailers. (Imagine if Target took only an American Express card that had to be triangular, Wal-Mart took only a round US Bank Visa and a square Citibank MasterCard, and Starbucks would let you pay only with a prepaid Starbucks card. It's that absurd.)

Yet once these issues are sorted out—and with so many billions at stake, they will be—cash will find itself on the endangered-species list. Paying by phone will be as transformative as the advent of the credit card in the 1950s. It will change the way we shop and bank. With powerful smart-phones and tablets taking center stage on both sides of the checkout counter, it will reshape the relationship between buyer and seller. Not only will the phone or the tablet become a wallet for consumers, but it will also turn into a credit card reader and a register for merchants. Shoppers will use their mobile device as a coupon book, a comparison-shopping tool, and a repository of those unwieldy loyalty cards they carry from everyone from giant retail chains to the corner bakery. And your smartphones will serve as beacons that will alert a retailer when you walk into its store so that it can recommend products, show you reviews, or direct you to aisle five, where that beanbag chair you didn't buy last week still beckons—and you can now have it for

10% off. You won't even need a few singles to tip the valet or pay the dog walker, because they'll take mobile payments too.

What's in play: millions of merchants, billions of transactions, and trillions of dollars in commerce. Which is why the burgeoning revolution has already turned into a free-for-all. Everyone wants in, from big phone companies like AT&T and Verizon to the credit card networks like Visa and MasterCard to tech giants like Google, Microsoft, and eBay's PayPal unit. Scores of startups have joined the fray; so have traditional banks, retailers, and makers of point-of-sale hardware like VeriFone. All those contenders are eager to know whether Apple, which has 400 million credit cards on file, or perhaps Facebook or Amazon, will enter the game soon. Indeed, Apple seemed to tiptoe into the space in June when it announced that the iPhone will soon hold boarding passes, movie tickets, and prepaid store cards (see chart).

While this revolution will be powered by complex technology, its ultimate effect will be to greatly simplify things for consumers. Think about my experience at Grumpy. While I had to fiddle with my phone ahead of time—to upload my credit card to the Square app and to authorize it to talk to the Grumpy register—once there, the phone never left my pocket. All I had to do was order my cappuccino. That's just the kind of experience that Dorsey was after when he built Pay With Square, the app that powered

> TO ME THAT IS THE PINNACLE OF TECHNOLOGY— WHEN THE TECHNOLOGY DISAPPEARS COMPLETELY."
> —Jack Dorsey, CEO, Square

the transaction. He tells me it is his company's proudest creation to date. "To me that is the pinnacle of technology—when the technology disappears completely," he says. And with technology out of the way, he adds, there's room for a more personal interaction between buyer and seller, one that harks back to a quainter time, when our great-grandparents walked into the general store, picked up a shovel, and walked out after telling the owner to write the purchase on his ledger. "You just have to focus on what you want and how much it is," Dorsey says. "All the mechanics of payments fade away."

T'S 9:15 A.M., and the bugle call "Reveille" begins to play at Square's San Francisco headquarters. Never mind the dissonance between the martial tune and the eclectic group of young urbanites who toil in Square's post-industrial office space. As they do every morning, engineers and product managers across the floor heed the call to get up from their desks for their daily "standups." They huddle in small groups, where, one by one, they explain what they did the day before and what they plan to do today.

Square, founded in 2009, offers a window into the promise and complexities of the mobile-payments future—and not necessarily because it will lead us there. In fact, as a pioneer, Square has a big bull's-eye on its back. But because Dorsey is hugely ambitious, building out products for nearly every part of the transaction chain, Square's journey helps show why the business is so ripe for disruption—and why it will be so hard for any company to single-handedly upend the system.

Most people still know Square for its first product, its hugely successful white plastic credit card reader that plugs into a smartphone. The invention has allowed some 2 million small, cash-based merchants—hairdressers, piano teachers, cabbies, and even babysitters—to ac-

cept credit cards, and it's growing at warp speed. Merchants are now processing transactions with Square's Card Reader at a rate of $6 billion a year, up from just $2 billion a year in October, making Square one of the fastest-growing young companies ever by revenue and one of the buzziest in Silicon Valley's hot startup scene. It has raised plenty of money from A-list investors, including Visa, which sees Square as a way to boost the use of credit cards. Today the company is attracting talented engineers and executives from Apple and Google. It helps that Square may eventually go public or be acquired for a nice premium, making its stakeholders fabulously wealthy. Valued at $1.6 billion after a $100 million cash infusion last year, it was seeking additional financing at twice that valuation in June.

Dorsey hatched the company in his 400-square-foot San Francisco apartment, after the Twitter board asked him to step down as CEO. (Dorsey returned to Twitter triumphantly in 2011 and is now its chairman and chief product guru.) Every morning Dorsey would flip up his Murphy bed to make room for Jim McKelvey, a glassblower, entrepreneur, and Square's co-founder, and Tristan O'Tierney, an engineer specializing in mobile apps. Within a month the trio had built a system that could swipe a card and complete a transaction.

It's not hard to see why Card Reader became a hit almost overnight. Retailers no longer had to fill out a lengthy application form, submit to a credit check, and wait—sometimes several days—for an answer, which could often be a denial. After asking for a few pieces of information to verify a person's identity, Square approves more than 90% of new applicants in a matter of seconds. Square's Card Reader is free, so there's no need to buy pricey, and often unsightly, hardware. And Square set transaction fees at 2.75%, bringing simplicity and transparency to what can be a thicket of pricing options, including teaser fees that rise over time. With no sales force and minimal marketing, the Square reader spread largely by word of mouth. The credit card industry, which had been struggling to expand its

Who's Who in Mobile Payments

Square faces stiff competition from Google and eBay's PayPal—and Apple and Amazon are circling. Here is a sampling of the players (and a few would-be operators)—and the different parts of the transaction chain they touch.

Photograph by THOMAS HANNICH

COMPANY	CARD READER?	WALLET?	HOW WALLET WORKS	WHAT'S IN THE WALLET	WHO TAKES IT?	LAUNCH DATE
Square	●	●	Touchless	All credit/debit	75,000 mostly small merchants in metropolitan areas	10/2010
PayPal	●	●	Mobile number and PIN, touchless	All credit/debit cards, bank accounts, PayPal	16 national retailers (J.C. Penney, Jamba Juice, Abercombie) starting this summer	3/2012
Google		●	Near field communication (NFC)	Citibank MasterCard, Google prepaid card	25 national retailers (Peet's, Gap, Duane Reade, Foot Locker, Macy's) and MasterCard PayPass merchants	9/2011
Microsoft		●	NFC	Not announced	Not announced	Fall 2012
NCR	●		Not applicable (N.A.)	N.A.	N.A.	7/2012
VeriFone	●		N.A.	N.A.	N.A.	5/2012
ISIS (AT&T, T-Mobile, Verizon)		●	NFC	AmEx, Visa, MasterCard, and Discover from select banks	More than 50 merchants in Salt Lake City and Austin	Summer 2012
Visa V.me*		●	NFC	Any payment card	Online only but plans to expand offline	11/2011
MasterCard*		●	NFC	Any credit/debit card	Some 200,000 MasterCard PayPass merchants in the U.S.	By end of 2012
Intuit	●		N.A.	N.A.	N.A.	5/2009
Starbucks		●	Barcode	All credit/debit and PayPal	Starbucks	1/2011

LURKERS	ASSETS	NOTES
Apple	Has 400 million accounts with payment credentials in iTunes store; is introducing PassBook, an e-wallet for boarding passes, movie tickets, and store cards, such as Starbucks'.	* VISA'S PAYWAVE AND MASTERCARD'S PAYPASS TECHNOLOGIES ALLOW NFC-BASED PHONES AND APPS, INCLUDING THOSE FROM GOOGLE AND ISIS, TO BE USED. VISA IS ALSO AN INVESTOR IN SQUARE.
Facebook	Fifteen million members have paid via Facebook for virtual and digital goods in apps.	
Amazon	Has payment credentials for more than 173 million active customers.	

base of merchants for years, welcomed the new additions. And many merchants say the ability to accept cards boosted sales by as much as 20%. Early this year Chris Timbrell, who co-owns Grumpy with his wife, used Square to replace a $2,000 point-of-sale system that was slow and buggy. "We love it," Timbrell says.

But on its own, Square's sugar-cube-shaped reader, which has spawned a string of copycats, was never going to help Dorsey fulfill his ultimate ambition. "We want to carry every transaction in the world," Dorsey says without a hint of self-doubt. And so the company has expanded beyond the reader with Pay With Square and Square Register, an app that allows merchants to run stores from an Apple iOS device.

A walk through the daily "standups," when employees discuss the intricacies of Square's products, is an eye-opening lesson about Square's aspirations. With Register, Square is going after point-of-sale terminals used in retailers small and large, a business now dominated by hardware makers such as VeriFone and NCR. Register also allows retailers to keep track of their customers and inventory (think lightweight enterprise software) and to offer loyalty deals and discounts (think Groupon but better targeted). Register also delivers analytics that tell merchants what their customers buy and when they buy it—the kind of data that, until now, only large offline retailers could afford to track.

Pay With Square not only stores your payment credentials but also includes a directory of merchants. It gives merchants a way to have a simple app on mobile devices that displays their menus or merchandise, hours, and other features. And it recently became a repository for loyalty cards from select merchants.

Now Square is planning to expand aggressively into yet another area: hardware. Earlier this year it hired Jesse Dorogusker, an Apple refugee who led the team that built headphones, docking stations, and other peripherals for iOS devices, as its vice president of hardware. "We are going to be doing a lot of hardware," says Keith Rabois, chief operating officer of Square

Cash, Charge, or Digital?

As transaction volumes have grown, so have all forms of payments. But the share of dollars spent using cash and checks has declined from 85% to 39% in the last 20 years.

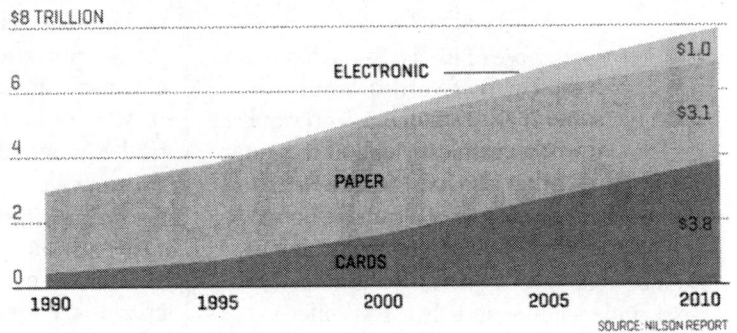

SOURCE: NILSON REPORT

and a former executive at PayPal and LinkedIn. Rabois cagily declines to elaborate, but consider this: In a pilot program the company recently began installing a software and hardware bundle that includes Square-powered iPads and iPhones in New York City taxicabs. It serves as a payment mechanism and replacement for those annoying TV screens that are common in the backseats of cabs. People with knowledge of Square's plans say that in the future the company hopes to develop similar bundles for other vertical markets. It also plans to build different versions of its reader as it expands overseas. (Did we mention that Dorsey is ambitious?)

Taken together, Square's products begin to offer a glimpse of what a utopia for buyers and sellers could look like: You're in a new city and feel like sushi, so you fire up your phone and Square's software offers you a series of suggestions that reflect your tastes; a nearby eatery offering you 20% off your bill catches your eye. Once you're at the sushi bar, your phone talks wirelessly to the restaurant's register and settles your bill, including the discount. And the restaurant collects a slew of information about you, which it can use to market to you in the future. "We are reinventing payments from the ground up, based on the principle that everyone is carrying a general-purpose computer in their pocket," Rabois says.

47%
OF ALL N.Y.C. TAXI RIDES ARE PAID BY CREDIT CARD

50 to 66%
OF THE VALUE OF U.S. CURRENCY IS HELD ABROAD

SOURCES: N.Y.C. TAXI AND LIMOUSINE COMMISSION (TAXI), FEDERAL RESERVE (CURRENCY)

THE PROBLEM WITH Square's utopia—and those of its rivals—is that it is a bit of a walled garden, for now at least. Pay With Square works only at some 75,000 small merchants (and it works seamlessly only at the much smaller number that also have Square Register). Say you are in search of a caffeine boost. You'll be able to use Square at a smattering of mostly independent, mostly urban coffee shops. You can pay with your phone for coffee at Peet's, as long as you have Google's competing Wallet app, which connects to registers via a gentle bump of your phone. Oh, but it only works with MasterCard, on a handful of phones running on Sprint. You prefer Starbucks? No problem: You can use your smartphone there too, as long as you have the Starbucks app. It has great features, but don't expect to use it anywhere other than Starbucks.

And that's just coffee. "You have a potential situation where consumers are confused into doing nothing," says Drew Sievers, CEO of mFoundry, the company that helped Starbucks develop its mobile app. For all the investment in mobile wallets and readers, the marketplace is at a bit of a standstill: Until mobile wallets are more mainstream, retailers won't rush to accept them, and until wallets work in more places, consumers won't embrace them. "There is no ubiquity, so a mobile wallet is a complement to your wallet, not a replacement," says James Slavet, a venture capitalist at Greylock Partners, who has invested in payment startups.

And the landscape is only becoming more crowded and potentially more confusing for consumers and retailers alike. Every month seems to come with an announcement of another giant—say, Microsoft or MasterCard—going after e-wallets. Many are powered by a wireless technology called NFC (for "near field communications") that is endorsed by several phonemakers but not by Apple. Square and some of its competitors have pooh-poohed NFC, and many retailers are taking a wait-and-see attitude. Meanwhile mobile card readers are proliferating. In March eBay's PayPal unit introduced a card reader for mobile phones and added capabilities to its mobile app that mirror those of Pay With Square. "We can help small businesses wherever they do business," says David Marcus, president of PayPal. (Soon after, PayPal expanded a program that gives customers access to their PayPal account with their mobile-phone number and a PIN for purchases at 16 major national retailers.) Less than two months after PayPal, VeriFone also introduced a card reader and a point-of-sale system that can work with products from other companies, like digital wallets from Google or ISIS, a joint venture of AT&T, Verizon, and T-Mobile. And both PayPal and VeriFone set their processing fees at 2.7%, undercutting Square by five hundredths of a percentage point. NCR's own reader is launching in July.

None of that is good news for Square unless it's going after a prize for most imitated company. Just about every Square rival has something the hot startup lacks: scale. Most also have far more financial resources, deep ties to the mobile phone or the financial services industries, and a global footprint, whereas Square has yet to expand outside the U.S. "I'm not quite sure what all the hype is about," says Doug Bergeron, the chief executive of VeriFone, whose terminals process trillions of dollars in transactions every year. "It is common knowledge that Square is now being surrounded by many competitors with real business models, and that they continue to bleed mountains of cash." Dorsey and his team brush off such remarks. "It's the same tech story all the time," says Rabois. "There are always large, entrenched players that have lots of assets that are trying to compete with a focused startup with a compelling vision and a lot of talent." His point: Focus, vision, and talent will leave incumbents in the dust.

Indeed, there are no indications that Square's core business is slowing at this point. "We had pretty heroic growth expectations for the business, and they have consistently met or exceeded those expectations," says Mary Meeker, a partner at Kleiner Perkins Caufield & Byers and a Square board member.

Still, Square is starting to show some signs of strain. Some employees have griped, both privately and on Quora, a question-and-answer website, that Square is being mismanaged and has become a challenging place to work. Some people who work with Square say that Dorsey has been too focused on the design of Square's products and not enough on engineering. And they complain that his divided attention—every day he spends eight hours at Twitter and eight hours at Square—robs Square of the focus it needs from its CEO. (Dorsey dismisses such critics. "I am going to do whatever it takes in my life to make sure that both succeed massively," he says.) For all its success, the company remains relatively small. Square won't disclose its finances; however, its 2.75% commission on a reported $6 billion in annualized transactions translates to about $165 million in revenue. Square pockets only a small fraction of that, as the majority goes to the payment processors and credit card networks.

WHILE SQUARE REMAINS a work in progress, the Starbucks experience suggests that consumers will warm to digital wallets. By all accounts the coffee retailer may have built the No. 1 mobile payments system in the U.S., through a relatively simple mobile app that allows users to upload their Starbucks loyalty cards to their phone and then use their phone to pay. The company won't give precise dollar figures for mobile transactions, though it says in the last nine weeks of 2011 alone, it processed more than 6 million mobile transactions. While the pay-by-phone feature is convenient for customers and has sped up checkouts, payments were not the primary focus of the app. "We look at the app as a way to tell the Starbucks story," says Adam Brotman, chief digital officer for Starbucks. Brotman says the biggest benefit of the mobile app is that it has increased customer participation in its loyalty program, which drives multiple billions in revenue for Starbucks each year.

Indeed, a cashless future is more real than many suspect. In *The End of Money*, author David Wolman set out to live an entire year without using cash, and he largely succeeded. For the rest of us, the departure from cash is more likely to proceed in fits and starts. Credit card networks like MasterCard and merchants have certainly helped with the first wave by allowing small transactions to go through without a signature, and by installing credit card readers in taxicabs. We may embrace one app first, like Starbucks' or PayPal's or Square's, and slowly grow more comfortable using our phones to pay for more and more things. And the credit card companies and retailers may lead the way to uniform standards and registers that can accept all forms of payment, just as they have with plastic. "Financial institutions are going to have a big role to play," says Bill Gajda, the global head of mobile at Visa. No proprietor wants to turn away a customer because he has the wrong kind of phone.

Dorsey, for his part, seems confident that the change is proceeding apace. On a recent trip to St. Louis, where he grew up, Dorsey managed to use Square to pay for lunch, dinner, and coffee. Adoption of the technology, he says, is happening faster than he expected because people are yearning for a more high-touch experience in all aspects of their lives, including at the checkout counter. "I think there is a general desire in American culture right now to find something that is more crafted, that is more personal," he says. And as anyone who has ever received money as a gift will tell you, there's nothing more impersonal than cash. ∎

> "THERE IS NO UBIQUITY, SO A MOBILE WALLET IS A COMPLEMENT TO YOUR WALLET, NOT A REPLACEMENT."
> —James Slavet, Greylock Partner

43%
· OF ALL ADULT AMERICANS SAY THEY'VE GONE A WEEK WITHOUT PAYING CASH

SOURCE: RASMUSSEN REPORTS

NOAH BERGER—BLOOMBERG

267

Why Venture Capitalists Are Right to Be Crazy About Bitcoin

INSIGHTS

Value of one Bitcoin (Mt.Gox)

$1,000
750
500
250
0

$8962

$13

|2013   2014|

BITCOIN MANIA. While much of the focus on Bitcoin has been around its skyrocketing value, venture capitalists are more excited about its potential outside of currencies.

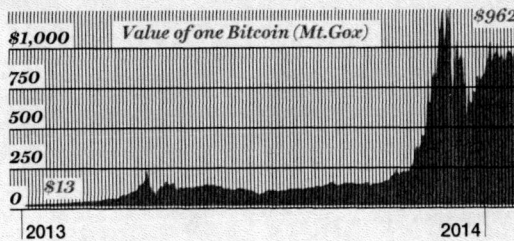

By
Dan Primack

dan_primack@fortune.com

BITCOIN IS CONTROVERSIAL. Some people believe that it's the future of money, destined to relegate dollars, euros, and yen to the dustbin of history (along with German marks and shiny pebbles). Others argue that it's nerd delusion, carelessly elevating new software over time-tested economics. It's sliced bread vs. New Coke.

Unfortunately, this debate is focused on the wrong thing. Bitcoin's primary significance is not about whether it supplants cash. It's about a revolutionary computer-science breakthrough that has the potential to upend all sorts of established industries.

Here's an analogy: Email was the Internet's original application, but 40 years later we all recognize that the Internet has countless more uses than just the electronic exchange of text. Likewise, currency is Bitcoin's original application, but Bitcoin will not ultimately be defined by currency.

The key to Bitcoin is that it enables verified transactions without requiring a centralized third party to do the verifications. Kind of like the difference between handing a merchant a $10 bill and handing him a Visa card. It does so via what computer scientists call a distributed ledger, in which users are entering (or exiting) a fixed number of ledger slots (i.e., the "coins").

This system could obviously present a major challenge to the existing payment industry, which includes all sorts of intermediaries like banks, credit card companies, and wire-transfer services. Not only does Bitcoin dramatically lower the fees for making and receiving payments, but it also eliminates both consumer fraud (from the merchant's side) and the possibility of information theft (from the consumer's side, as we recently saw at Target). For context, the Boston Consulting Group reports that the global payment and transaction-banking business generated $524 billion in revenue last year—a figure that it expects will rise to $1.1 trillion over the next decade. Just imagine all the new businesses that could eat into that.

What's really fascinating, however, is that the distributed-ledger concept has all sorts of theoretical applications that don't specifically concern payments. Take identity, for example. What if you no longer needed a phone company to create phone numbers? Or what if your web searches no longer needed to go through Google's servers? It sounds crazy, but few predicted that the technology behind email would eventually destroy record stores.

"There are so many things that currently exist only in the confines of centralized, larger institutions that could become targets of this," says Anders Brownsworth, a Boston-area Bitcoin technologist.

Not surprisingly, a number of well-known venture capitalists are paying close attention to Bitcoin and Bitcoin-related startups (most of which, so far, focus on payments). Andreessen Horowitz, for example, has already invested nearly $50 million in the sector. Early Facebook investor Accel Partners recently helped lead a $9 million investment into a Bitcoin startup from serial entrepreneur Jeremy Allaire, while original Twitter backer Union Square Ventures is deep into a well-funded Bitcoin "wallet" company called Coinbase.

All these investors obviously hope to make money on their early Bitcoin deals. But it reminds me a bit of what Howard Anderson, founder of both the Yankee Group and Battery Ventures, said in 2006 about American venture capitalists investing in Chinese startups: "Most of the VCs I see going to China will get clobbered ... They say, 'Yes, we know all that. It's the cost of joining the club.'" In other words, take an educational beating today so that you can succeed in the future.

VCs are playing a similar long game on Bitcoin because they recognize its ability to exponentially increase Internet functionality, both in payments and beyond. And in the end, they won't care what currency they are paid in. **◧**

China Bites Into Bitcoin

A speculative frenzy turned Bobby Lee's BTC China into the world's biggest Bitcoin exchange. Then Beijing dropped the boom. Easy come, easy go.

BY KASHMIR HILL

Bitcoins were worth nothing in 2009, when the digital cryptocurrency was first minted on the computer of its mysterious creator, Satoshi Nakamoto, who claimed to live in Japan.

Four years later the value of one Bitcoin surpassed $1,100, thanks in large part to a surge in speculative interest from China. A little-known Shanghai company called BTC China met the demand and quickly became the world's largest Bitcoin exchange, with more than 100,000 of the virtual coins, or $100 million, traded on a single day, nearly double the market share of its closest competitor, Japan's Mt. Gox.

BTC China attracted headlines and a $5 million investment in the fall from Silicon Valley's Lightspeed Venture Partners as well as its China arm. But its rapid growth, and that of Bitcoin, also attracted the attention of the Chinese government.

Unwanted attention, as it turned out. In December the People's Bank of China decreed that merchants may not accept Bitcoin and forbade banks and payment processors from converting Bitcoin into yuan. The price of Bitcoin fell below $500 in response.

Bitcoin is still widely embraced by technophiles and libertarians (and porn and pot-dealing websites) because the currency is all digital, easily transported across borders and resistant to state controls. A Bitcoin is "mined" on privately owned, specialized computing equipment and passed around by a global, peer-to-peer network of computers. Transactions are trackable, but the parties to each transaction are not. Bitcoin has attracted entrepreneurs and investors excited about its legitimate use: cutting out the middlemen in online payments. In December venture capital firm Andreessen Horowitz placed the biggest Bitcoin bet so far with a $25 million investment in San Francisco's Coinbase, a platform for buying, selling and storing Bitcoins in the U.S. "As the world becomes more digital, paying physically with bills, gold or credit cards will seem archaic. Everyone will have Bitcoins," says BTC China CEO Bobby Lee.

But China's actions over the past weeks have put BTC China's future in doubt. After Chinese regulators held a closed-door meeting to warn financial companies against working with exchanges, BTC China was swiftly abandoned by two payment processors. "There are 300 payment processors in China. We're going to go down the list and find one that will work with us," says an optimistic Lee. He doesn't think the government is trying to put him out of business but rather put the screws on Bitcoin to cut down on the rampant speculation. "They haven't declared exchanges illegal. That gives us room to ma-

His investors hope BTC China CEO Bobby Lee has the gravitas to make the case for Bitcoin to Beijing regulators.

neuver, so there's still hope."

Lightspeed's Jeremy Liew is keeping a distant focus. "Anyone investing in Bitcoin companies and Bitcoin specifically should be doing so with the expectation that there will be a lot of volatility driven by regulatory announcements. We invest over 5- to 10-year horizons, not over two-week horizons," says Liew. "For Bitcoin to be credible, we need executives who have the gravitas to make its case to regulators. That's Bobby."

Lee, 38, was born in the Ivory Coast to parents who had moved there from China to set up a flip-flop factory. He was sent to an elite boarding school in the States, graduated from Stanford and spent eight years as an engineer at Yahoo in California. He moved to China in 2006 to work as an engineer at EMC. In 2011 he became Wal-Mart's chief technology officer in China, charged with helping to build its commerce site.

Lee first heard about Bitcoin in the spring of 2011 while visiting his family in California. Lee's brother, Charles, was using some of his computer equipment to mine Bitcoin at home. Lee thought he would do the same back in China and bought a bunch of graphics cards from his brother. He started mining in July, the same month he started at Wal-Mart. Neither lasted long.

"It was a hot summer, and the computers created a lot of heat," says Lee. "My wife said it was too noisy and hot, and so I turned it off in October." He mined 25 coins, which struck him as a "waste" because they were worth just $300 total at the time and he had spent $1,000 on mining gear.

When Wal-Mart decided to partner with an existing e-commerce site in 2012 rather than build its own, Lee found himself jobless. His mind returned to those Bitcoins gathering digital dust on his computer. His brother had founded a competing cryptocurrency called Litecoin, but Lee wanted to focus on bringing Bitcoin to China. BTC China had popped up two years earlier as the country's first site for Bitcoin trading. "It was just two guys working part-time on it," says Lee. They were charging a 0.3% trading fee, but seeing just a few hundred trades per day. Lee sought out its cofounders to convince them it could be bigger. Lee became CEO in April.

They relaunched the site in June and went out looking for venture capital. When they landed the round from Lightspeed in September, they eliminated their fee. That kicked off a bidding frenzy fueled also by the free Bitcoin p.r. that came when the FBI took down Bitcoin-only drug site Silk Road and Baidu announced it would accept Bitcoin for security services, plus the positive buzz around U.S. Senate hearings on the digital currency.

But then the People's Bank of China, responding to what it says was a wave of consumer concerns, declared in December that Bitcoin wasn't a recognized currency and shouldn't be used in the market, prompting Baidu and other Chinese firms to stop taking it as payment. As the extent of the real-world ban became clear, the price of a Bitcoin dropped to $345 on BTC China.

Lee initially saw the declaration as just a speed bump. Chinese citizens were still free to trade Bitcoin. BTC China stayed on the good side of the government's concerns about money-laundering by asking customers for official identification. BTC also reinstated trading fees to cut down on the frenzy. But days later the government crushed hopes of a thriving trading business when it unofficially barred payment processors from working with Bitcoin exchanges. Suddenly BTC China and others would no longer be able to move their customers' funds from yuan to Bitcoin and back—which is what exchanges exist to do. "We're reading the tea leaves," says Shanghai Bitcoin entrepreneur Jack Wang. "But it looks like they're going to squeeze the exchanges until they're not able to operate."

China's move is not without precedent. Eleven years ago Chinese Web service Tencent created a virtual currency called Q Coin for use in games. It became increasingly valuable offline and started trading on exchanges along with renminbi and gold. The government declared such use illegal in 2007, sending its real world value crashing to nothing.

China is still letting people play with Bitcoin in its country, but by cutting off ways to convert it to real money, it is turning it into the digital Monopoly money that skeptics have always dismissed it as being. "If necessary, we'll go into other Bitcoin services," says Lee. The company plans to launch a secure online Bitcoin wallet called Picasso at the end of December. "This is not the end. It may be the end of a chapter, but it's not the end of our company." **F**

Markets&Finance

Individual Investors Duped by Derivatives

▸ **Wall Street peddles complex securities to a yield-hungry public**

▸ **Such a complicated product "raises questions about suitability"**

YOUR INVESTMENT

David Parkins 2010

Leona Miller, an 84-year-old retired beautician, says she was seeking safe and steady income from bonds two years ago when she bought securities recommended by her **Wachovia** broker, Robert Baldacci, paying 9 percent interest. Within six months, Miller lost about 30 percent of her $20,000 investment, and the bonds were converted into shares of **Merck** in a falling stock market. "I just wanted him to make some money for me, like anybody else," says Miller, who lives in San Diego. "I still don't understand too much about it."

Miller had bought a structured note—a bond combined with a derivative. In her case, it was a reverse-convertible note with a knock-in put option tied to Merck stock. The option meant the security could offer a relatively high

interest rate. It also added risk, as Miller learned too late. A decline in the drugmaker's shares, to below 32 from 40 when Miller bought the notes, triggered the put option. That allowed the note's issuer, the Oslo-based export-credit agency **Eksportfinans**, to pay Miller off with Merck shares, then trading at 26. Kathryn Ellis, a spokeswoman for San Francisco-based **Wells Fargo**, which acquired Wachovia in 2008, and Baldacci, who no longer works for the bank, declined to comment.

While customized derivatives have been criticized for their role in the credit crunch, securities laws allow them to be sold to individuals as long as they're bundled with bonds into structured notes, and the financial sector reforms enacted since the crisis have not ad-

dressed the issue. The Securities and Exchange Commission's enforcement division started a group this year to investigate structured products, including those marketed to individual investors. "We're concerned about the sale of complex structured notes to retail customers because people don't always understand the risks they're exposed to," says Kenneth R. Lench, head of the SEC's Structured and New Products unit.

With interest rates near 0 percent, investors are ignoring potential risks and snapping up bonds that promise higher yields, even if they carry obscure names such as Leveraged CMS Curve and S&P 500 Index Linked Callable notes. Reverse-convertible notes paid 13 percent interest, on average, this year, according to Bloomberg data. That's more than 10 times the average 1.2 percent rate on one-year certificates of deposit and more than three times the average U.S. investment-grade bond yield of 3.73 percent.

Sales of structured notes rose to $31.9 billion through August, up 58 percent over the same period last year, according to data compiled by Bloomberg and StructuredRetailProducts.com. "People develop a product which makes a modicum of sense, then they extend it to the point of ludicrousness," says Satyajit Das, a former Citigroup derivatives banker. Das, the author of *Traders, Guns & Money*, says investors are often "seduced" into purchases without understanding the risks.

The notes are targeted at individual investors to boost banks' profit margins, Das says. **Morgan Stanley**, for example, charged a 3.5 percent fee on the Leveraged CMS Curve notes that it sold on Aug. 20, according to a prospectus. Underwriting commissions for U.S. investment-grade bonds this year average 0.5 percent, Bloomberg data show.

Individual investors are incapable of valuing structured notes and their underlying derivatives, says Kevin Kelly, manager of Scottsdale (Ariz.)-based hedge fund **Tontine Capital**.

43

273

Markets&Finance

Most structured notes are more complex than those Miller bought, he adds. Morgan Stanley's CMS Curve securities offer a fixed 10 percent rate for two years. The yield for the next 13 years is five times the difference between long- and short-term constant maturity swap rates, not to exceed 18 percent annually, earned when the Standard & Poor's 500-stock index doesn't dip below 875, according to a regulatory filing.

"It raises questions about suitability for the investor when you have products that are that complicated," says Daniel Bergstresser, a Harvard Business School professor. "Is that complexity a response to a legitimate desire the investor has or is it a smokescreen?" Mark Lake, a spokesman for Morgan Stanley, declined to comment.

Buyers are compensated fairly for the risk they take on and don't need to know the details of how derivatives work to evaluate the securities, says Keith Styrcula, chairman of the Structured Products Assn., a trade group. Issuers disclose potential pitfalls of the investments in documentation provided to buyers. Many of the products are less risky than stocks because sellers guarantee investors won't take losses even if the market falls, says Styrcula, a former JPMorgan Chase structured-notes banker. "There's a reason the market is booming," he says. "Investors are having successful experiences with structured investments, and they're coming back as repeat buyers."

Miller and Wells Fargo are in arbitration, according to her San Diego lawyer, Ronald Marron. In a February 2009 letter, the bank's legal department told Miller that the broker "explained very thoroughly his recommendation." The letter, which was provided by Marron, also said that "Mr. Baldacci recalled that you were familiar with Merck & Co. as they manufacture one of your medications." —*Zeke Faux*

The bottom line Wall Street is selling complex securities to yield-hungry investors who may have no idea how they work—or how risky they are.

Slow Cop, Fast Beat

▶ The SEC is taking its time studying the market before issuing rules to curb speed traders

▶ "I think you really do want to do a soup-to-nuts review"

ILLUSTRATION BY 731

When Mary Jo White appeared before the Senate in March 2013 seeking confirmation as chair of the Securities and Exchange Commission, she told lawmakers that understanding high-frequency trading's impact on the stock market would be a "very, very high priority." She spoke about the "sense of urgency" the SEC needed to bring to the issue so that "appropriate regulatory responses can be made." More than a year later, lawmakers, investors, and SEC commissioners are still waiting to see what that response will be.

The controversy over high-frequency trading (HFT) kicked into high gear with the publication of Michael Lewis's *Flash Boys* on March 31. Lewis argues that the $23 trillion U.S. stock market is rigged in favor of speed traders, who he says prey on slower investors by getting early access to nonpublic information. The book and the media attention it has received have revived and magnified concerns that have circulated for years. The FBI had already been probing potential criminal activity associated with HFT. On April 4, U.S. Attorney General Eric Holder said the Justice Department is investigating whether HFT violates insider trading laws. So is New York Attorney General Eric Schneiderman. In a March 31 interview on Bloomberg TV, Schneiderman urged the SEC to speed up its review of HFT and quickly issue new regulations.

Yet White is in no rush. The SEC chief says her agency will make sure any rule changes are supported by data as it conducts a survey of the entire market, rather than focusing specifically on speed traders. "I think you really do want to do a soup-to-nuts review," says White, who stresses that any study will begin with the presumption that "the markets are not rigged."

White's go-slow approach has the backing of some market participants who fear that premature attempts at reform may do more harm than good. Included in that camp are some of the investors that HFT's critics say are being taken advantage of the most. One criticism of speed traders is that they use sophisticated trading algorithms to detect the moves of big institutional investors and then jump in front of their large orders. Speed traders can then profit from buying and then quickly selling a stock for a slightly higher price to the bigger, slower investor. Yet Joe Brennan, global head of equity investing at Vanguard Group, the world's largest mutual fund company, says the majority of high-frequency traders "play within the rules" and even "knit together" the fragmented market by ensuring that prices stay in line with each other across different trading venues. That makes the markets more efficient and lowers trading costs for many participants, he says. This is not to say there aren't bad actors, he adds, who "unfairly tax the system."

The trick for regulators is finding ways to prevent abuses without blocking high-speed firms that actually benefit investors. And that will take more time, according to White. "If there are changes that should be made, we will make them," she says. "We are taking a very data-driven, disciplined approach."

The problem is that the SEC doesn't have all the data it needs. In 2012 the agency spent $2.5 million on a surveillance system named Midas (Market Information Data Analytics System) that collects information from all 13 public exchanges in the U.S. This essentially gives the SEC the same view of ▶

◀ the market that many speed traders have. It doesn't, however, give it a picture of the whole market. Only about 70 percent of trades happen on public exchanges; the rest take place offline, either inside large wholesale brokerages that match buy and sell orders internally or in private trading venues called dark pools. To see that activity, the SEC needs a much more powerful system that can track the life of every stock quote, order, and trade, including when the transactions occur, the brokers involved, and the customers on whose behalf they are acting.

In 2010, White's predecessor, Mary Schapiro, approved a project to build such a system to funnel terabytes of information every day into one massive feed that regulators could monitor. Called the consolidated audit trail (CAT), the system would allow the SEC to conduct detailed forensic analysis and weed out abuses. The contract for the huge project, which will cost more than $1 billion, still hasn't been awarded. The SEC estimates that CAT won't be finished until 2016.

The SEC took its first deep dive into HFT in January 2010, before many other enforcement agencies had waded into the debate. As part of a broad review of market structure, it examined how brokers route the electronic orders of speed traders and questioned whether that put other investors at a disadvantage. The report elicited more than 400 comment letters from banks, exchanges, retail brokerages, and large institutional investment firms.

Critics of HFT were encouraged. "We were very hopeful that something substantative was going to get done," says Jeff Connaughton, then chief of staff to Ted Kaufman, a Delaware Democrat who, within months of joining the Senate in 2009, began railing about how speed traders were threatening the stability of the stock market. Then, on May 6, 2010, the flash crash sent the Dow Jones industrial average down 600 points in five minutes. The SEC, along with the Commodity Futures Trading Commission, the main U.S. derivatives regulator, spent the next four months trying to figure out what had caused the crash. By the time they issued a report in September, the regulators had a bigger task on their desks: the 848-page Dodd-Frank financial reform law that needed to be implemented. Speed traders could wait.

The SEC still hasn't introduced many rules aimed specifically at high-frequency traders. Some commissioners are getting restless. "The perception for many is that the markets aren't fair for the average investor," says Republican Commissioner Daniel Gallagher, who has repeatedly called for the agency to review its trading rules since 2012. "Even if that's not supported by the facts, that perception is a reality that we need to address as soon as possible." Speaking to reporters on April 8, Democratic Commissioner Kara Stein said the SEC needs new rules to keep pace with the changing market: "A lot of our rules were written for people and not necessarily for computers."

Such calls are unlikely to sway White from her deliberate approach. "I think she's proceeding exactly as she should," says Republican Harvey Pitt, who served as chairman of the SEC from 2001 to 2003. "The mere existence of high-frequency trading does not by itself indicate a violation of the law. One of the things that gets drilled into people at the SEC is that the power to investigate is the power to destroy." —*Dave Michaels, Matthew Philips, and Silla Brush*

The bottom line The SEC needs a multibillion-dollar data system to determine if speed traders are doing more harm than good.